FEAR OF ENEMIES AND COLLECTIVE ACTION

What makes individuals with divergent and often conflicting interests join together and act in unison? *Fear of Enemies and Collective Action* explores how the fear of external threats shapes political groups at their founding and helps preserve them by consolidating them in times of crisis. It develops a theory of "negative association" that examines the dynamics captured by the maxim "The enemy of my enemy is my friend" and then traces its role from Greek and Roman political thought, through Machiavelli and the reason of state thinkers, and Hobbes and his emulators and critics, to the realists of the twentieth century. By focusing on the role of fear and enmity in the formation of individual and group identity, this book reveals an important tradition in the history of political thought and offers new insights into texts that are considered familiar. This book demonstrates that the fear of external threats is an essential element of the formation and preservation of political groups and that its absence renders political association unsustainable.

Ioannis D. Evrigenis is Assistant Professor of Political Science and Bernstein Faculty Fellow at Tufts University. He undertook his graduate studies at the London School of Economics and Harvard University, where his dissertation was awarded the Herrnstein Prize. He is coeditor of Johann Gottfried Herder's *Another Philosophy of History and Selected Political Writings* (2004) and the author of chapters and articles on Thucydides, Plato, Aristotle, Machiavelli, Hobbes, Jefferson, and Koraes.

FEAR OF ENEMIES AND COLLECTIVE ACTION

IOANNIS D. EVRIGENIS
Tufts University

CAMBRIDGE
UNIVERSITY PRESS

CAMBRIDGE UNIVERSITY PRESS
Cambridge, New York, Melbourne, Madrid, Cape Town, Singapore, São Paulo, Delhi

Cambridge University Press
32 Avenue of the Americas, New York, NY 10013-2473, USA

www.cambridge.org
Information on this title: www.cambridge.org/9780521886208

First published 2008
Reprinted 2008

Printed in the United States of America

A catalog record for this publication is available from the British Library.

Library of Congress Cataloging in Publication Data

Evrigenis, Ioannis D., 1971–
Fear of enemies and collective action / Ioannis D. Evrigenis.
p.   cm.
Includes bibliographical references.
ISBN 978-0-521-88620-8 (hardback)
1. Political science–Philosophy.   2. Political sociology.   3. Political psychology.
4. Group identity–Political aspects.   5. Fear–Political aspects.   I. Title.
JA71.E94   2008
306.2 – dc22   2007023626

ISBN   978-0-521-88620-8 hardback

To Tra

But it is not possible, Theodorus, that evil be destroyed – for it is necessary that something always be opposed to the good.

– Socrates

CONTENTS

ACKNOWLEDGMENTS

Many individuals and institutions have honored me with their support during the writing of this book. I am indebted to my teachers at Harvard, whose readiness to read and discuss my writing made me feel more a colleague than a student, and I am profoundly grateful for their interest in my work and their contributions to its improvement. Collectively, they provided the necessary support for this project whilst allowing me to map and pursue my own course. Individually, each of them contributed something essential to the experience of researching and writing it. Stanley Hoffmann's sound judgment and authoritative grasp of history and politics helped put things in perspective. With his incisive questions at the right junctures, Harvey Mansfield prompted me to consider important implications of my argument. Russ Muirhead's enthusiasm and good advice encouraged me to keep moving forward. Finally, Nancy Rosenblum's extraordinary ability to identify the heart of the matter helped me maintain focus and confront the most difficult challenges. My colleagues at Tufts University have picked up where they left off. I am especially grateful to David Art, Jeff Berry, Consuelo Cruz, Rob Devigne, Kevin Dunn, Jim Glaser, Yannis Ioannides, Andrew McClellan, Malik Mufti, Vickie Sullivan, and Jeff Taliaferro for providing a supportive and encouraging environment in which I could complete the book.

During the research and writing stages, I received generous financial support from Harvard University's Graduate School of Arts and Sciences, Minda de Gunzburg Center for European Studies, and Program on Constitutional Government, as well as from the Alexander S. Onassis Public Benefit Foundation, the Harry Frank Guggenheim Foundation, the Earhart Foundation, and Tufts University's Faculty Research Awards Committee.

With exemplary patience and good humor, Daniele Archibugi, David Art, the late Seth Benardete, Janet Coleman, Kevin Dunn, Bryan Garsten, Daniel Gilbert, Victor Gourevitch, Russell Hardin, Andreas Kalyvas, Stathis Kalyvas, Mark Kishlansky, Paschalis Kitromilides, Gerald V. Lalonde, Mathilda

Liberman, Mark Lilla, Bruno Macaes, Christie McDonald, Haris Mylonas, Isaac Nakhimovsky, Daniel Pellerin, Edward Philips, Peter Rajsingh, Vickie Sullivan, Richard Tuck, Dana Villa, Jan Waszink, and the late Robert Wokler discussed aspects of the project with me, answered my questions about matters in their areas of expertise, and pointed me to useful sources. Ariel Hopkins provided first-rate research assistance in the final stages. My editors, Lew Bateman and Eric Crahan, offered valuable help and guidance as I turned the manuscript into a book.

Mark Somos discussed the project with me from beginning to end. His insightful comments throughout have improved the argument considerably, and I am grateful to him for his assistance and friendship. Theodoros N. Ikonomou read the entire manuscript and discussed with me the issues examined herein on numerous occasions. Our conversations have shaped my views in more ways than I can point to and remain a rare source of pleasure and inspiration. Aristotle lists good friends among the chief possessions of the εὐδαίμων man, and in Vangelis Himonides and Yianos Kontopoulos I have been blessed with the best.

Demetrios Evrigenis's earliest questions awakened my interest in political thought, and his integrity and memory continue to inspire me. Chryssoula Evrigenis's unconditional support and encouragement allowed me the freedom to pursue that interest. In their own ways, Konstantinos Protopapas, Maria Evrigenis, Mikis Pavlidis, Socrates Antsos, Alex Vratskides, Steryios Yannoulis, Jan Inman, Richard Jones, Kurt and Mikala Rahn, and Mark and Kerri Abernathy made the process a little easier and more enjoyable. Georgia Danae, who arrived near the end of the project, lit everything up.

My greatest debt is to my wife and best friend, Tra. She read and commented on the entire project, and her suggestions and influence have improved it beyond measure. Her patience, kindness, and love made this book and much else possible. I dedicate it to her as a small token of my affection.

PROLOGUE

During the rivalry between Rome and Carthage, Marcus Porcius Cato was famous for concluding every speech in the Senate – regardless of the subject matter – with the call that Carthage be destroyed. On the other side, Publius Scipio Nasica would counter that Carthage ought to be saved, because fear of the threat that it posed to Rome was the only thing that prevented the nobles and the plebs from descending into civil war. Nasica's advice, immortalized by Sallust and cited by Saint Augustine in *City of God*, became paradigmatic of the realization that human beings form and sharpen their identities as much by positive means as by reference to how they differ from others.

The history of political thought is filled with accounts of the mechanism captured by the old dictum "The enemy of my enemy is my friend," and yet studies of group formation and collective action pay little explicit attention to this negative mechanism. In the only work of its kind, Wood identifies as "Sallust's Theorem" the realization that *metus hostilis*, the fear of enemies, "promotes internal social unity," and proclaims it "a founding axiom of modern political thought."[1] Wood anticipates that modern readers may find Sallust's Theorem platitudinous. What is more, students of social movements may be tempted to ascribe the observation to Simmel, or to Sumner, who bequeathed to us the concepts of "in-group" and "out-group." Yet their accounts, influential though they have been, are merely parts of a very long tradition that recognizes the social utility of contradistinction from and conflict with, others, outsiders, and enemies. In this tradition, thinkers who are otherwise quite different see outsiders as essential signposts that enable human beings to form a better understanding of who they are both as individuals and as members of political groups.

[1] Wood, "Sallust's Theorem," 181, 175. Unless otherwise indicated, all translations are the author's.

xi

The world around us is complex and puzzling, and it is often hard to understand and even harder to manage. Psychological and philosophical theories of perception and cognition often note that the human mind develops mechanisms in order to make this complexity manageable. Thus, for example, we set arbitrary starting points, ignore information that we lack, lump invisible factors into broad and often meaningless categories, and use analogies and metaphors that are limited in their application. These heuristic devices are necessary if we are to be able to function in the midst of such complexity. One such device is the use of outside entities for comparison and contrast. We often supplement our understanding of something in useful ways by contrasting it with something else. This method is constantly at work on a more or less conscious level and is an integral part of the most lengthy and demanding process of understanding, our attempt to understand ourselves.

From a biological perspective, these mental devices may be seen as defense mechanisms that enable us to continue to exist. Fear is a very different device, but with a similar function. Too much fear is paralyzing, but too little fear may prove deadly. The right amount of fear, however, enables us to sense danger and take measures to thwart it. The fear of enemies is in some sense, then, the point at which these two mechanisms meet. Outside entities tell us something about who we are not, and the emergence of one can transform our view of another. Thus, a new threat on the horizon may lead to the formation of alliances between previously unrelated and uncooperative individuals or groups. The process through which these new groups come into being and the resulting identification with and membership in them transform the identities of their members. Through contradistinction, individuals often discover new boundaries. Questions that might never have arisen find their answer in the way one feels about the practices of others. Exposure to their ways and customs helps us hone our understanding of ourselves. For example, someone who is otherwise indifferent to animals might become fond of them as a result of witnessing a dog being mistreated.

Metus hostilis of Carthage was a central theme of Roman historiography and political discourse, and an important lesson learned by those who were educated by Sallust, Plutarch, and Polybius. Beyond history books and political treatises, however, unlikely alliances, marriages of convenience, and strange bedfellows of all kinds confirm its prescience and render the truth captured by Nasica's advice familiar. This book develops a theory of "negative association," which begins with the observation that differentiation from outsiders shapes the identities of political groups and their members in fundamental ways and thus forms their bottom line. In times of crisis, when the identities of these groups are challenged and the individual interests of their members interfere with their ability to act in unison, appeals to this bottom line may be the only means of forestalling their dissolution. Among motives for negative association, fear provides the strongest link because it speaks to another bottom line, the fundamental concern with self-preservation. When this concern is heightened, and threats to survival and security loom large, individuals and small social groups find a bond in their common fear that enables them to set their differences aside and unite in the pursuit of goals that are otherwise unattainable.

This study of negative association in political thought begins with Thucydides, who considers fear to be the cause of the Peloponnesian War, and whose account is filled with descriptions of pleas for the formation of alliances appealing to the need to deal with common enemies. The centrality of fear and security may not be surprising in Thucydides, but it is not what one associates with Aristotle, whose declaration of man as a ζῷον πολιτικόν in the opening lines of the *Politics* is usually taken to mean that man is by nature sociable. Nevertheless, Aristotle proceeds to explain that what distinguishes the *political* association (the polis) from other, subordinate forms is that it is self-sufficient. Before goods and services, however, self-sufficiency involves defense and security. Those who can provide these for themselves are either Gods or beasts. Man, on the other hand, needs allies if he and they are to be secure. That Aristotle is keenly aware of the primacy of security is apparent later on in the *Politics*, when he counsels those who govern to keep some dangers near, so as to keep the citizens on their guard.

The lesson of Thucydides and Aristotle regarding the fear of external threats acquired a particular urgency in Rome during the Punic Wars. At the outskirts, Rome ruled over an ever-expanding territory and a multiplicity of peoples. At the center, it was characterized by constant tension between the nobles and the plebs. Roman historians from Posidonius to Sallust, and beyond, saw the fear of the threat posed by Carthage as the force that kept Rome from descending into civil war. This specter became so entrenched in Roman life that nurses would threaten "fractious children that Hannibal was coming to fetch them."[2] Sallust's paradigmatic account broke new ground because it placed descriptions of negative association in the broader context of his assessment of Rome's decay. Whereas Thucydides and Aristotle describe the formation of political groups and alliances, and leave the reader to draw his own conclusions, Sallust does not hesitate to register his regret at the degeneration of Rome brought about by the elimination of the threat posed by Carthage. In Sallust's powerful account of *metus hostilis*, Saint Augustine

---

[2] Cary & Scullard, *A History of Rome*, 148.

found the evidence to show that the city of man is fallen, and that the fall of the city of Rome had begun long before its conversion to Christianity.

Machiavelli opens his own work on Rome by claiming that he is about to lead the way to a path as yet untrodden by anyone. His declaration turns out to be true, albeit in unexpected ways, since it involves a return to the ancients, whose theories seemed all too familiar. Machiavelli's most important lesson is that cities need to be returned to their beginnings, where they can be reinvigorated and reacquainted with their most basic identity. He himself shows that he has learned it by returning to the ancients and, more specifically, to Livy's account of the beginnings of Rome. He also follows his own counsel in choosing the individual, fallen or not, as the starting point of political inquiry. This twofold return to first principles leads Machiavelli to the realization that regaining the state is the best means of maintaining it. The passage of time erodes the initial vigor of the state, and individuals lose the clear sense of identity and purpose that guided them in the beginning. Eventually, priorities are reclassified, fissures develop, and internal tumult replaces external threat as the order of the day. Machiavelli notes that states everywhere have different ways of recreating something of the state of mind that characterized their beginnings, but those usually involve the reshuffling of offices and institutions, and are ultimately inadequate for the task. At the same time, he recognizes that the most effective means of achieving such a return to the beginnings, exposing the state to external threats, is also the most dangerous. If such a measure backfires, it can prove disastrous, for, instead of postponing the demise of the state, it can hasten it.

Machiavelli parted company with the Sallustian tradition insofar as he had no interest in evaluating negative association from a moral point of view. At best indifferent and at worst downright hostile to moral considerations in political matters, Machiavelli was first and foremost concerned with the efficacy of proposed measures. His examination of the benefits of drawing republics back to their beginnings is a detached and rather sober one, but in the eyes of his critics these attributes were shortcomings; they constituted further evidence of his immorality. Three such critics, Gentillet, Bodin, and Botero, stand out. These thinkers' ventures to restore morality to politics and reinstate it in a world created by a benevolent Maker display many traits that one would expect to encounter but also several that one would not. Loud denunciations of the Florentine abound, but so do suggestions for policies that are Machiavellian in all but name. Most striking among the latter are those that pertain to the use of external threats to consolidate the commonwealth and purge it of undesirable elements and bad habits. The vehemence with which these critics met Machiavelli's teachings, however, did not cloud their theories completely. This wave of reaction put Machiavelli and the issues surrounding the preservation of the state at the center of political discourse, and thereby enabled the advent of the systematic theories of the modern state that followed.

By the end of the sixteenth century, all the pieces for such a systematic theory were in place. Foremost among these were a concern with the preservation of the state, the realization that any attempt to preserve the state has to begin by taking account of human psychology, the concept of sovereignty, and the need to approach – or at least appear to approach – complex issues in a scientific way. Whatever their disagreement with Machiavelli on the moral front, political thinkers did not question his fundamental premise that the state needed to be preserved, and agreement on this principle was no small matter. Once the debate shifted from ends to means, Machiavelli's task was much simpler. His interest in human psychology as the proper foundation for the preservation of the state was equally important. Here, Machiavelli drew less fire, for, after all, Machiavellian man is not too far removed from fallen man. Although concerned exclusively with the domestic realm, Bodin's formulation of the concept of sovereignty paved the way for a comprehensive examination of the difference between the state and the natural condition of mankind. These developments converged with the rise of interest in systematic approaches to the solution of political problems, and the search for ways in which scientific method could be applied to all aspects of life.

It was this climate that Thomas Hobbes found himself in when the King of England declared his right to determine whether or not the state was in danger and was challenged by his subjects. In the political theory that he formulated in response to those events, Hobbes announced the foundation of political science. This scientific approach to politics consisted of all the raw materials bequeathed to him by the reason of state thinkers that preceded him, and Hobbes put them to good use. Following Machiavelli's lead, he began by formulating a detailed theory of human nature before moving on to consider how it affects politics. In his search for a foundation that would appeal to as broad an audience as possible, Hobbes turned to fear, a human trait as familiar as it is universal, and one that partakes as much of reason as it does of emotion. The quest for a *summum bonum* had failed again and again. Fear, he suggested, could serve as a *summum malum*, and he challenged his readers to look inside themselves for proof that he was right.

Combining this starting point with the need for a better way to achieve the psychological effects of a return to the beginnings of cities, Hobbes constructed the image of the state of nature and urged his readers to think about the consequences of life without the protection of a sovereign, life, that is, when it was "solitary, poor, nasty, brutish, and short."[3] The ingeniousness of Hobbes's construct lay not only in its capacity to move the imagination but also in the way he related it to reality. The state of nature was no mere fiction, no tale of a time that never was. He who doubted its truth had but to step beyond the protection of his sovereign and taste the dangers of a life when there is no overarching power to keep all in awe. This aspect of the state of nature rendered it familiar enough to make it credible. As such, it was the perfect solution to Machiavelli's problem. It produced the effects of a return to the beginning but with fewer of the dangers inherent in the real thing. Moreover, by adding a view of the commonwealth from without, Hobbes expanded Bodin's strictly inward-looking vision of absolute sovereignty, and made explicit what was only implicit in Bodin's conclusion that the sovereign is the absolute bearer of authority. Nothing illustrates the validity of that conclusion as vividly as the contrast between the inside of the commonwealth and the anarchic world that lies beyond its borders.

Hobbes's fundamentally conflictual vision and his union of reason with the passions gave rise to a wave of political thought centered on negative social emotions. Taking as their points of departure a wide range of previously despised human motives, such as greed, envy, and hatred, these theories brought into the mainstream the notion of negative self-definition – definition, that is, in contrast with others – and established it as an unavoidable and explicit consideration of political thought. Initially, reaction to Hobbes's teachings bore a general resemblance to the one that followed the publication of Machiavelli's political works. Just as Machiavelli left his imprint on subsequent debates, those writing from the second half of the seventeenth century forward found it impossible to ignore Hobbes. The concept of the state of nature became a staple of political thought in the eighteenth century and continued to be discussed throughout the nineteenth and twentieth centuries with reference to international relations. There was, however, an important difference as well. Whereas Machiavelli's view of human beings had been the least of his problems, Hobbes was criticized severely for depicting them in the way that he did. While he accepted Hobbes's basic construct of the state of nature, Rousseau nevertheless argued that it ought to begin further back, at a time when man was a much lonelier and tamer creature.

Much as the Anti-Machiavellists discovered that there were aspects of the Florentine's teaching that could not be dismissed, the Anti-Hobbists found out that regrettable though Hobbes's view of human nature might sound, it

---

[3] Hobbes, *Leviathan*, XIII § 9. All references to this work are to the Curley edition.

posed a serious challenge. This was especially true when it came to thinking about the state in the context of the international realm. After all, if human beings were not as dangerous as Hobbes had thought, why would states and wars be necessary? That some type of answer to a question of this sort would have to be given if Hobbes were to be proven wrong became apparent very quickly. The eighteenth century saw the publication of numerous treatises on the problem of war and the prospects for perpetual peace, and debates about federations of states and transnational unions abounded. Perhaps the two most notable efforts of this kind to emerge from this period were Saint-Pierre's and Kant's projects for perpetual peace. Widely circulated and discussed, these drew a number of responses, among which those of Rousseau, to the former, and Hegel, to the latter, reveal the extent to which Hobbes's views influenced subsequent political thought. These exchanges are striking because they show that proponents and opponents of projects for perpetual peace speak in Hobbist terms, feel the need to address Hobbist concerns, and shape their respective arguments around a fundamentally Hobbist vision of the world. Hobbes is not a thinker who is traditionally associated with this period, and yet these debates reveal the extent of his influence and thus explain why a conflictual model draped in terms of negativity, juxtaposition, and contrast became so prevalent in the budding disciplines of psychology and sociology. It also provides an explanation to one of the most baffling mysteries: Hobbes's stature among theorists of international relations. Textbooks of international relations routinely list Hobbes as one of the founders of the discipline, and yet why a thinker who devotes only a handful of lines to the relations among states should be considered a theorist of international relations is not at all clear. The reason given most often is that Hobbes's account of anarchy in the state of nature is the best metaphor for the relations between states. Another reason is that Hobbes is the best known of the theorists who depict the state as a unitary actor, not least because of the famous frontispiece of *Leviathan*. Although these reasons are significant, they are still insufficient when it comes to explaining Hobbes's standing as a theorist of international relations. The story of German Hobbism provides the missing link.

Interest in Hobbes's political thought remained strong outside his country during the eighteenth and nineteenth centuries, and by the end of the nineteenth century the most important students of Hobbes's political thought had emerged from the German world. To understand Hobbes's influence on the academic study of international relations, it is necessary to examine two particularly important examples of German Hobbism: the political theories of Carl Schmitt, who considered the friend–enemy distinction to be the fundamental political criterion, and Hans Morgenthau, who incorporated the most central aspects of Schmitt's theory into his version of political realism. Schmitt defined the sphere of the political as that in which the possibility of the negation of one's existence is what determines the enemy; this kind of existential threat is what makes a relationship political, rather than moral, economic, or aesthetic. This distinctly Hobbist outlook was the single greatest source of influence on Morgenthau during his time in Europe. With Morgenthau's emigration, it was transmitted to the United States and became the basis for the study of international relations in the second half of the twentieth century.

In times of relative peace and prosperity, security tends to lose its primacy and recede on people's lists of priorities. Calls for attention to security thus come to be associated with excessive worry or fearmongering, or to be considered window dressing for the advancement of dubious political agendas. A good deal of this skepticism and criticism is justified, and yet there are aspects of security that remain pressing and taken for granted. This is a necessary outcome of peace and prosperity that comes with some positive and some negative consequences of its own. Constant worry would be paralyzing, and yet obliviousness to actual danger and harm would be deadly. As Shklar points out, it is from recognition of fear and harm that our struggle to establish rights and political institutions begins.[4] As such, fear of harm, the emotion that triggers our concern with our preservation and security, becomes the enemy, the rallying point for political awareness, vigilance, and meaningful collective action. Even this enemy is not universal, since it pits those who oppose harm against those who threaten or inflict it, and yet it may well be the best that we can hope for.

Many of the thinkers examined in this book are known as bearers of bad news. Their views of human nature are at best "cautious" – they see human beings as "dangerous and dynamic."[5] The search for the role of negative association in the history of political thought, however, reveals that a fundamental concern with security is implicit even in the arguments of thinkers who are not usually thought of in these terms. Thus, seemingly familiar texts in the history of political thought reveal overlooked, important new sides, with surprising results. In examining what these thinkers have to say about the ways in which political associations form and respond to

[4] Shklar, *Ordinary Vices*, 5, 237–38.
[5] Schmitt, *The Concept of the Political*, 61.

the presence of common threats, this book revisits some well-trodden paths but also exposes certain unfamiliar aspects of their arguments, and often challenges established interpretations of the texts in question.

The centrality of negative association for each of these theories means that there is widespread agreement about much, and yet there are also significant differences that need to be borne in mind. An exclusive focus on similarity or one on difference each presents its own enticements, but each must be resisted as far as possible. On the one hand, the universality of negative association yields an enduring set of basic characteristics that renders it recognizable from the Peloponnesian War through the Cold War, to the "War on Terror," and beyond. On the other hand, particular circumstances raise new problems in addition to old ones, and every one of the thinkers examined herein has a set of each to contend with. That the authors in question are taken up in chronological order, therefore, is no accident. As every new hurdle emerges, old observations and methods are tested and amended to fit the demands of the times, and revisions and innovations are provided along with ample commentary on those who have come before. As a result, one way to describe the trajectory of this concept in political thought is as a series of actions followed by reactions. But to leave it at that would be to put too much stress on the differences and risk losing sight of the common ground. Behind the bold claims for innovation, and the announcements of new discoveries, there is a profound agreement that people everywhere define themselves as much by figuring out who they are as by finding out who they are not.

I

NEGATIVE ASSOCIATION

For man by nature chooseth the lesser evil...

– Thomas Hobbes[1]

NEGATIVE ASSOCIATION

The term *negative association* refers to the formation of political groups (in-groups) that is based on identification with others who are similarly situated in relation to an external entity, such as another individual or group (out-group).[2] While political groups may form for a variety of positive reasons, for example, on the basis of a common language or religion, or for the pursuit of a common, specific goal, such as the conquest of a certain piece of land, an *essential* part of what brings their members together is their common difference from an outside entity, as in the case of a common enemy. Negative association manifests itself during crucial moments in the life of political groups: at the founding and during crises that threaten the unity and continued existence of the group.[3] There will be periods of time in which negative

---

[1] *Leviathan*, XIV § 29.

[2] The terms *in-group* and *out-group* were coined by William Graham Sumner, who argues,

> All the members of one group are comrades to each other, and have a common interest against every other group. If we assume a standpoint in one group we may call that one the 'we-group' or the 'in-group'; then every other group is to us an 'others-group' or an 'out-group.' The sentiment which prevails inside the 'we-group,' between its members, is that of peace and cooperation; the sentiment which prevails inside of a group towards all outsiders is that of hostility and war. These two sentiments are perfectly consistent with each other; in fact, they necessarily complement each other ("War", 142).

Cf. Brewer & Brown, "Intergroup Relations," 559.

[3] According to Coser, "Antagonism against a common enemy may be a binding element in two ways. It may either lead to the formation of new groups with distinct boundary lines, ideologies, loyalties and common values, or, stopping short of this, it may result only in instrumental associations in the face of a common threat." Coser adds, "[t]he emergence of

association is the primary cause of individuals' identification with a group. At other times, negative association is manifest only in the background, while it is clearly identifiable positive characteristics that unite the members of a political group. Nevertheless, whether a primary, secondary, or minimally auxiliary cause, negative association is always an element of the process by which individuals form their political identities and identify with political groups.

Differentiation is built into group formation by definition. Unless a group is to be all-inclusive, in which case it would be unnecessary, the declaration of intent to form it amounts to a declaration of difference from those who are not to be included in it, and its continued existence reaffirms that difference. Such differentiation is true of all groups, whether political or not.[4] In some cases, it is only a logical extension of a union based on positive shared traits, as, for example, in the case of a group of philatelists. What brings such individuals together is their appreciation of stamps, and chances are that they think of their group mostly in terms of that appreciation and its consequences, rather than as distinct from those who either hate stamps or are completely indifferent to them. In such a case, differentiation from nonphilatelists is a fact arising from the formation and continuation of their association, but one that is in the background and unlikely to have played any role in the formation of the group or to stand out in the minds of its members afterwards. This way of thinking about the group in question would most likely change, however, if one day the government were to decide to ban stamp collecting, and to confiscate and burn all existing stamps.

Theories of groups usually focus on the purpose for which a group exists, or on the characteristics of a group, such as its size and organization.[5] Both sets of considerations are crucial in understanding a group, and yet there is an important side of each group's story that is mainly implicit in the group's nature and purpose, and which as a result often gets lost, namely the ways in which its relationship to outsiders shapes it and the identities of its members. The theory of negative association holds that this relationship is an essential part of a full understanding of a group for two reasons. First, it complements approaches that focus on the characteristics and goals of a group, by shedding

such associations of otherwise isolated individuals represents a 'minimum' of unification" (*The Functions of Social Conflict*, 140).

[4] See Walzer's discussion of membership and its implications (*Spheres of Justice*, 31–63).

[5] Olson, e.g., finds that studies of collective action focused too much on the former and failed to take the latter into consideration. He presents his account as a corrective to that trend, suggesting, among other things, that group size makes a difference (*The Logic of Collective Action*, 5, 53–65).

new light on their findings. Second, it may provide additional information that is not available through a narrow focus on the group and its goals. The importance of these two functions is obvious: knowing, for instance, that a particular group is trying to seize a piece of land is one thing, but it is quite another to know whom it is trying to take this land from, as well as who the other groups or actors are that may affect the outcome. In fact, more information about outsiders may lead to revisions of hypotheses about the group's motivation. Attempts to determine the causes of particular conflicts are especially good examples of the need for this kind of information.[6] Immediate causes may be easy to identify, but underlying causes are more difficult to locate, and research on the history of the relationship between the parties may lead to the need to revise initial explanations of the sources of a conflict.[7]

In the case of political groups, in particular, the role of outsiders is a crucial element of group identity. While the purpose of all groups is to further the interests of their members in one way or another, political groups are distinguished by the fact that their purposes revolve around the promotion of the interests of the group in relation to (and, more often than not, in opposition to) others, outside the group.[8] Groups are political because they form with reference to (i.e., in anticipation of or in response to) an antagonistic relationship with other entities. This relationship need not be the kind of radical, life-or-death conflict that Schmitt has in mind, although it has the potential

---

[6] The difficulty of such a determination is captured most famously by Thucydides, in the opening of his history (*The Peloponnesian War*, I, esp. I.23).

[7] See, e.g., Stathis N. Kalyvas, "The Ontology of 'Political Violence.'"

[8] This is a simple consequence of the observation that people join groups for a reason, and that "organizations often perish if they do nothing to further the interests of their members," as Olson suggests (*The Logic of Collective Action*, 6). Interests in this sense are broadly conceived as the motivation behind an individual's decision to join a group and remain a part of it. Thus, they may include a wide variety of things, such as the enjoyment of the company of others, the exchange of information, the shared pursuit of hobbies, improved health benefits, financial gain, and political power. This basic definition of interest thus includes the motives even of those who join groups the purpose of which is other-regarding, such as philanthropic organizations, for example (cf. Olson, *The Logic of Collective Action*, 6, note 6). In so doing, this basic understanding of interest says nothing about the relative force of motivating factors as compared with the results of the group's efforts. It need not imply, e.g., that people who join philanthropic organizations do so merely because they derive some personal benefit (e.g., satisfaction). The motive for joining such an organization might well be one's belief in the rectitude of helping others, but even in that case, it is assumed that such a person has an interest in promoting that belief and therefore a preference for more rather than less efficient means of doing so.

3

to escalate into one.[9] Thus, political groups are defined fundamentally by some relationship to others, outsiders, regardless of whether the particular objective of the group is the preservation of something possessed already, as for example in the case of defense, or the acquisition of something else, as in the case of a struggle for workers' rights.[10] By their very being, political groups make a statement with which at least some outside entity disagrees or is expected to do so. Where conflict, or at least the potential for conflict, does not exist, there is no reason for political mobilization.[11]

FEAR

Individuals and groups experience a wide variety of negative feelings towards others, and thus negative association may develop as a result of any of several social emotions, such as common envy, greed, or hatred. As economic, moral, and political theories began to extol the social benefits of such negative, and previously deemed undesirable, characteristics of human nature (in Mandeville's words, the "publick benefits" of "private vices"), negative emotions towards others came to be appreciated as important motivators of human beings and therefore worthy of earnest and serious consideration in the construction of political and social order.[12] Perhaps more notorious than other negative emotions, fear had already been recognized as an important parameter from Thucydides to Machiavelli, reaching preeminence in the political philosophy of Hobbes.[13] This degree of interest is not accidental.

[9] Schmitt, *The Concept of the Political*, 25–37. Schmitt's response to such a broader understanding of conflict would be that it *becomes* political once the underlying cause (economic, moral, etc.) leads the parties to a position in which they pose an existential threat to one another.

[10] Efforts to acquire various goods are exacerbated by the degree to which the goods sought are scarce, but as the example of a struggle for higher wages between employers and workers shows, competitions for goods can cause the solidification of groups and escalate into conflicts between "us" and "them" without being zero-sum games.

[11] As Wrong, following Simmel, puts it, in this sense, "conflict is a social relation just as much as cooperation" (*The Problem of Order*, 18); cf. Simmel, "Conflict," 13.

[12] See, e.g., Vico, *The New Science*, §§ 132–33; Mandeville, *Fable of the Bees*, I: 137–38; Hirschman, *The Passions and the Interests*, 14–20; Shklar, *Ordinary Vices*, 4–5. Rousseau, who is anxious to present as bare a conception of natural man as possible, considers pity natural and universal (*Discourse on the Origin and Foundations of Inequality*, 152). In drawing the distinction between *amour de soi-même* and *amour-propre*, Rousseau notes that the latter arises only in society, since it requires the presence of other human beings (*Discourse on the Origin and Foundations of Inequality*, note XV, p. 218).

[13] See, e.g., Thucydides, *The Peloponnesian War*, I.23, I.88; Machiavelli, *The Prince*, XVII; Hobbes, *The Elements of Law*, I.15.13, I.17.15, II.3.2; *On the Citizen*, I.2, note 2; *Leviathan*, XIII: 89.

Although any negative social emotion may be the cause of negative association at a particular juncture, it is fear that plays a crucial role in the formation
of political groups, if only because security is a prerequisite not merely for
the pursuit of positive goals, but also for the leisure required by the full range
of possible feelings towards others.[14]

The primacy of self-preservation renders fear of the threat posed by others
vital for the formation of alliances, as well as for their subsequent preservation
and consolidation, because it provides a way of overcoming barriers to group
formation and collective action that are insurmountable by positive means
alone.[15] The emergence of a threat calls for the reclassification of existing
threats and consequently for the rearrangement of one's priorities. Thus,
individuals or small social groups, such as families, who are concerned with
their self-preservation but are nevertheless unable to address the demands of
an overwhelming threat on their own, are forced to seek the assistance of
others, including those with whom they share no positive unifying characteristic, and even those towards whom they are apprehensive or hostile, but
whom they have come to see as a lesser threat, as a result of this reprioritization. The potential for the sudden and radical transformation of others from
enemies to allies and vice versa is one of the most important aspects of something akin to what Wolin refers to as "the economy of violence," something
that might be called the *political economy of fear*, in which the changing intensity of threats and the consequent fluidity of groups along the friend–enemy
continuum bring about the realignment of individuals and groups.[16]

---

[14] In studying the role of emotions in ethnic violence and discrimination, Petersen distinguishes between fear, hatred, and resentment, and attempts to determine the role of each
in ethnic conflicts in Eastern Europe (*Understanding Ethnic Violence*). Although he is correct
in emphasizing the role of these emotions as motives for collective action and the need for
distinctions between them, the distinctions that he draws are not sufficiently clear. Petersen
predicts that when fear is the predominant emotion, "[t]he *target of ethnic violence will be
the group that is the biggest threat*," whereas when there is resentment, "[t]he *predicted ethnic
target will be the group perceived as farthest up the ethnic status hierarchy that can be most surely
subordinated through violence*" (ibid., 25). As they stand, these predictions are unequal, because
fear has a more specific content (threat to security) than resentment. Knowing the source
of resentment in each case makes a big difference, and in many cases resentment may be
tied very closely to concerns for safety. Moreover, although a narrow understanding of fear
might only count immediate threats to physical safety, very often the prospect of severe
economic hardship and abject poverty has a similar effect. In such cases, it would be hard to
know precisely where fear ends and resentment begins, and vice versa. See, e.g., Inglehart
et al., "Xenophobia and In-Group Solidarity in Iraq."

[15] Montesquieu, e.g., wonders, "[w]ho can fail to see that natural defense is of a higher order
than all precepts?" (*The Spirit of the Laws*, XXVI.7).

[16] See Wolin, *Politics and Vision*, 197–200. Cf. Livy, *Ab urbe condita*, III.65; Machiavelli, *Discourses*, I.1, I.46; Hobbes, *On the Citizen*, Pref. § 10.

Fear is an emotion so familiar that for Aron "it needs no definition," and yet its very familiarity is often a barrier to a satisfactory, systematic understanding of it.[17] People use the word *fear* to describe their reaction to very different stimuli in a wide variety of contexts. This is because certain physical and emotional consequences of these various experiences are the same or at least very similar.[18] Nevertheless, the nature of the stimulus, the perceived duration of the threat, the possible existence of prior traumatic experiences with similar stimuli, and several other factors determine the precise nature of each state generally thought of as fearful, so that one can distinguish, with a greater or lesser degree of consistency and precision, between states of anxiety, stress, fright, panic, posttraumatic stress disorder, phobias, and other fear-related categories.[19] In political history and thought, the words *fear*, *panic*, and *terror* are frequent, but further explanation is rare.[20] One important exception is Hobbes, who defines *fear* generally as "*[a]version, with opinion of hurt from the object*," but explains that he means thereby "*any anticipation of future evil* [. . .] *not only flight, but also distrust, suspicion, precaution and provision against fear.*"[21]

The behavior that Hobbes describes in the latter definition is of two kinds. Both are strictly speaking "*aversion, with opinion of hurt from the object*," but

---

[17] Aron, *Main Currents in Sociological Thought*, 1: 20. Aron considers fear "a primal and, so to speak, subpolitical emotion" (*ibid.*, 20–21). Shklar argues, "[o]f fear it can be said without qualification that it is universal as it is physiological" ("The Liberalism of Fear," 29). Cf. LeDoux, *The Emotional Brain*, 11–12; Mannoni, *La peur*, 15; Rachman, *The Meanings of Fear*, 11.

[18] Despite a wide variety of definitions of fear and anxiety, there seems to be general agreement on the presence (fear) or absence (anxiety) of a specific object as the defining characteristic of each state. On the relationship between fear and anxiety, see Öhman, "Fear and Anxiety," 574, 588; May, *The Meaning of Anxiety*, 190–93, 203; Mannoni, *La peur*, 43–48; Rachman, *The Meanings of Fear*, 13. For a different perspective, see Mowrer, "A Stimulus-Response Analysis of Anxiety and Its Role as a Reinforcing Agent." On the importance of physical reactions as signals of fear, see Öhman, "Fear and Anxiety," 589–90.

[19] See Mannoni, *La peur*, 40–48.

[20] According to the *Oxford English Dictionary Online*, panic refers to a state of fear that is "sudden, wild, or unreasoning," and *terror* to "intense fear, fright, or dread." In general, *terror* became a term of interest in politics after the French Revolution, although occasional earlier references appear. Consistent fear – especially of external enemies – on the other hand, is described in some of the earliest political histories, including Thucydides', as well as various histories of Rome, for which *metus Gallicus* (fear of Gaul) and *metus Punicus* (fear of Carthage) were a widely accepted part of political life (cf. Bellen, *Metus Gallicus, metus Punicus*; Kneppe, *Metus temporum*, 54–57; Chapter 2 in this volume).

[21] Hobbes, *Leviathan*, VI § 16; *On the Citizen*, I.2, note 2. The latter work will be referred to by its original and translated titles interchangeably. All references are to the Tuck and Silverthorne edition, unless otherwise indicated.

one is quick, whereas the other is longer term, though different from what psychologists describe as anxiety, since it has a specific object.[22] Reaction to the sudden sight and sound of a snake in one's path is an example of the former, whereas a general uneasiness on the eve of a likely invasion is a case of the latter.[23] Experience with similar situations of either kind tells us that there is a difference between them, yet there are also significant similarities, not the least of which is the general tendency towards avoidance.[24] Although that tendency manifests itself in different ways, depending on the proximity, imminence, and magnitude of the threat, it nevertheless forms the common core that ties all fearful reactions together. It does so all the more when that which is to be avoided is death.

The brain perceives external stimuli in two ways: through "the low road and the high road."[25] The former course is "quick and dirty"; it allows for a swift reaction to the stimulus perceived, which in dangerous situations may make a difference.[26] The "high road," on the other hand, produces a more discriminating response to external stimuli, but takes more time. In LeDoux's example, a hiker sees a curved object in his path. The low road will lead him to treat it like a snake, whereas the high road will determine that it is a snake or a stick. LeDoux explains,

If it is a snake, the amygdala is ahead of the game. From the point of view of survival, it is better to respond to potentially dangerous events as though they were in fact the real thing than to fail to respond. The cost of treating a stick as a snake is less, in the long run, than the cost of treating a snake as a stick.[27]

The economizing quality of the low road has a parallel in the more thoughtful behavior that, depending on the circumstances, one might call prudential. Uncertainty about the possibility of harm in the future leads human beings to adopt the safety precautions that Hobbes lists in his expanded definition, even though these are not necessary most of the time. A number of considerations lead to this kind of behavior. First, as Hobbes points out, one

[22] See Mowrer, "A Stimulus-Response Analysis of Anxiety and Its Role as a Reinforcing Agent."

[23] LeDoux uses the example of the snake to illustrate the way in which such a stimulus is processed by the brain (*The Emotional Brain*, 163–65, 166).

[24] According to Rachman, "[a] mountain of laboratory evidence demonstrates a direct connection between fear and avoidance in animals" (*Fear and Courage*, 268).

[25] LeDoux, *The Emotional Brain*, 161–68.

[26] On the "low road," a stimulus goes directly from the sensory thalamus to the amygdala (LeDoux, *The Emotional Brain*, 161–65).

[27] LeDoux, *The Emotional Brain*, 165.

need not assume that all men are evil. However, because "we cannot tell the good and the bad apart, [...] even if there were fewer evil men than good men, good, decent people would still be saddled with the constant need to watch, distrust, anticipate and get the better of others, and to protect themselves by all possible means."[28] Second, the lessons that we take away from fearful situations are manifold. The encounter with the snake may lead to a general fear of snakes, but may also lead to a fear of the woods. This effect, known as "contextual conditioning," means that something associated with a previous reaction to a fearful stimulus may in turn become a fearful stimulus in the future.[29] These aspects of fear explain in part why it is such a complicated state of mind. Some of its mechanisms are clearly liabilities; they have a paralyzing effect. On the other hand, onetime liabilities may turn into benefits, since fear at the right time and for the right reasons is essential for survival. This salutary effect is not limited to the individual, but rather plays a crucial role in the formation and preservation of political associations.

GROUP FORMATION

At the start of his history of Britain, Milton observes, "[t]he beginning of Nations, those excepted of whom sacred Books have spok'n, is to this day unknown."[30] A quick survey of writings that touch on the subject of the origin of societies, both studies of particular nations and studies of the history of the nation or the state in general, reveals the extent and seriousness of the problem.[31] The historical record is generally insufficient, in that the earliest testimony of organized political groups comes at a stage that is already relatively advanced and thus removed from the period of interest.[32] This absence of earlier records is no doubt explained by the circumstances to which Hobbes ascribes the absence of philosophy, namely the lack of leisure that is required for the contemplation and recording of a sequence of events.[33]

---

[28] Hobbes, *On the Citizen*, Pref. § 12.

[29] LeDoux, *The Emotional Brain*, 167. Rachman thus distinguishes between a "core" fear (such as fear for one's health) and "secondary and conditional" fears (such as the fear of not having access to medicine or a hospital), and argues that there is a possibility that the person suffering from the former "will also learn to fear the secondary cues, by a process of conditioning" (*Fear and Courage*, 109).

[30] Milton, *The History of Britain*, 1.

[31] See, e.g., Fried, "The State, the Chicken, and the Egg; or, What Came First?," 35–46.

[32] See Oppenheimer, *The State*, 14.

[33] Hobbes, *Leviathan*, XLVI § 6.

Nevertheless, political theories look to the founding of nations and states for answers to the question of motivation for political mobilization. Where method is concerned, accounts of the formation of the first political groups belong to one of two categories that are sometimes hard to distinguish. The first consists of conjectural accounts based on very little, if any, historical evidence. Rousseau's account of the first stage of the state of nature, in the Second Discourse, is an example of this kind.[34] The second type purports to have its foundation exclusively in the historical record, although, as the more sober surveys of historical anthropology reveal, the dearth of evidence means that at one point or another these accounts too will have to resort to conjecture.[35] Ferguson's account of the rise of civil society belongs to this second type.[36]

One of the main problems that accounts of either kind face is that they have to explain the rise of political groups in a group vacuum, that is, in an environment in which no political group has taken shape. Answering the question regarding the origins of the first group is in many ways more difficult than explaining the rise of subsequent ones. For some, however, this problem never arises. Such accounts consider groups to be the natural unit of social analysis, and therefore regard the political group as the result of an agglomeration of natural groups such as families and clans.[37] In many ways, the choice between the solitary individual and the small group as the irreducible unit of social analysis determines the character and direction of a political theory, and yet the striking differences between the two points of origin tend to obscure some important elements that they have in common.[38] Both individualist and group accounts eventually agree that their respective fundamental units of analysis will sooner or later become incapable of providing for their own survival and security, and that as a result larger aggregations will have to form, in some cases even prior to the emergence of the state.[39] Thus, for example, the individualist accounts of the

---

[34] Rousseau, *Discourse on the Origin and Foundations of Inequality*, Part I.

[35] See, e.g., Rousseau, "The State of War" § 22. As Service notes, "[m]any important theories and debates connected with the origin of the repressive state have been handicapped because it is so difficult to account convincingly for its appearance out of the matrix of egalitarian primitive society" (*Origins of the State and Civilization*, 15).

[36] Ferguson, *An Essay on the History of Civil Society*, 9.

[37] See, e.g., Aristotle, *Politica*, 1252b9–27; Ferguson, *An Essay on the History of Civil Society*, 9.

[38] "Individualist" accounts are sometimes referred to as "atomistic," but this characterization is problematic because it may give the false impression of selfishness.

[39] See Hume, "Of Political Society". Ehrenreich describes this as the "Defense Hypothesis" (*Blood Rites*, 52–57).

social contract theorists all allow for the formation of temporary associations in the state of nature for the achievement of goals that are out of reach for solitary individuals.[40] On the other side, Aristotle declares famously that self-sufficiency through cooperation is the objective of the coming together of small groups in the form of the city.[41] Anthropologists tend to accept small groups such as immediate and extended families as the foundations of more complex groups, since the helplessness of the infant and its dependence on at least one adult – usually the mother – provides reasonable evidence for the emergence and formation of small, basic groups.[42] Even small groups, however, quickly reach a point at which they require the assistance of others for the attainment of goals that are beyond their reach, so the fundamental question of the motivation behind cooperation returns.

A further remarkable similarity between individualist and group accounts is that regardless of their starting point, explanations of the rise of the political association sooner or later speak of the initiation of conflict between individuals or small groups. In some cases, the source of conflict is clear, but in many it is not. Following Simmel, Coser takes conflict as an essential

[40] Contrary to conventional wisdom, this is true even of Hobbes, who argues, "if you add also how difficult it is, with few men and little equipment, to take precautions against enemies who attack with the intention to overwhelm and subdue, it cannot be denied that men's natural state, before they came together into society, was War" (*On the Citizen*, I.12); cf. *The Elements of Law*, II.1.2; *Leviathan*, XV § 5. In the Second Treatise, Locke speaks of "friends" and allies in the state of nature (*Two Treatises of Government*, II, § 13, § 16), which he describes as a state "of Peace, Good Will, Mutual Assistance, and Preservation" (*ibid.*, II, § 19), and draws a sharp distinction between the dissolution of government and the dissolution of society (*ibid.*, II, § 211). Despite claiming that "being unable to do without another" is "a situation which [...] does not obtain in the state of nature" (*Discourse on the Origin and Foundations of Inequality*, I § 50), Rousseau devotes the opening of Part II of the Second Discourse to an account of how the formerly solitary individuals that inhabited the state of nature had to band together to obtain the essentials for survival and protect themselves from natural disasters and other "difficulties" (161; cf. *Discourse on the Origin and Foundations of Inequality*, II §§ 1–24, esp. §§ 11–15).

[41] In the *Nicomachean Ethics*, Aristotle argues, "[n]ow all forms of community are like parts of the political community; for men journey together with a view to some particular advantage, and to provide something that they need for the purposes of life; and it is for the sake of advantage that the political community too seems to have come together originally and to endure" (1160a9–12; cf. *Politica*, 1152b27–1253a4).

[42] See, e.g., Service, *Origins of the State and Civilization*, 3. Even Rousseau, who exaggerates man's natural independence, has to admit that children remain with their mothers until they can fend for themselves: "as soon as they had the strength to forage on their own, [children] left even the mother" (*Discourse on the Origin and Foundations of Inequality*, I § 25; cf. *ibid.*, II § 2). In his account, families do end up under the same roof and thereby form the foundations of larger societies, but this is in response to the demands of nature, rather than to any positive social bond among the individual members (*ibid.*, II §§ 1–15).

constitutive social force, and distinguishes between "realistic" and "nonrealistic" conflict, where the former refers to conflict as a means towards the attainment of some end, and the latter to conflict as a way to release tension.[43] For Freud, "the inclination to aggression is an original, self-subsisting instinctual disposition in man."[44] Locke, on the other hand, describes an attractive natural condition in which man can find what he needs to survive and in which the dictates of the Law of Nature are accessible to all who can reason properly, and yet somehow one or more parties come to declare "by Word or Action, not a passionate and hasty, but a sedate setled Design, upon another Mans Life."[45] One may consider aggression and violence more or less important elements of human nature, but as Locke's theory of the state of nature shows, even in situations in which there is no scarcity or other apparent reason for quarrel, conflict emerges nonetheless.[46] The reason for its emergence lies in the uncertainty that Hobbes describes in his explanation of fear, an uncertainty that Schmitt sees as central to "all genuine political theories [which] presuppose man to be evil, *i.e., by no means an unproblematic but a dangerous and dynamic being.*"[47] It is the word *evil* in Schmitt's claim that draws one's attention, but his explanation makes it clear that he places emphasis on the *possibility* of evil.[48] Whether or not this is the precise reason behind the initiation of hostilities among individuals or small groups does

---

[43] Coser, *The Functions of Social Conflict*, 48–55; cf. Simmel, "Conflict," 27–28.

[44] Freud, *Civilization and Its Discontents*, 81. Cf. *ibid.*, 69. According to Wrong, "[c]onflict within the individual, as well as conflict among individuals and between the individual and the demands of society, is [. . .] a human universal" (*The Problem of Order*, 3).

[45] Locke, *Two Treatises of Government*, II, § 16. Regarding the Law of Nature, Locke argues, "yet, it is certain there is such a Law, and that too, as intelligible and plain to a rational Creature, and a Studier of that Law, as the positive Laws of Common-wealths, nay possibly plainer; As much as Reason is easier to be understood, than the Phansies and intricate Contrivances of Men, following contrary and hidden interests put into Words" (*Two Treatises of Government*, II, § 12).

[46] See Locke, *Two Treatises of Government*, II, §§ 16–21, esp. II, § 18. Cf. Van Creveld, *The Rise and Decline of the State*, 7. According to Treitschke, "Political history dawns on a world of petty States. The next step brings us to intertribal conflicts and a combination of larger masses into a common organization" (*Politics*, I: 107). Oppenheimer argues, "The State, completely in its genesis, essentially and almost completely during the first stages of its existence, is a social institution, forced by a victorious group of men on a defeated group, with the sole purpose of regulating the dominion of the victorious group over the vanquished, and securing itself against revolt from within and attacks from abroad. Teleologically, this dominion had no other purpose than the economic exploitation of the vanquished by the victors" (*The State*, 15).

[47] Schmitt, *The Concept of the Political*, 61, emphasis added. Schmitt lists Machiavelli, Hobbes, Bossuet, Fichte, de Maistre, Cortés, Taine, and Hegel among such theorists (*ibid.*).

[48] Note that Schmitt is concerned with the presuppositions of political theories regarding human nature, and that he defines "evil" man as problematic, "dangerous," and "dynamic"

not matter. What does matter is that there be at least one credible way to explain the emergence of conflict in the absence of objective reasons, such as scarce resources, for example, one that does not rely on the assumption that man is aggressive by nature.

Regardless of other differences, then, theories of man's presocial state identify two enemies: nature and others. This designation needs to be approached with some caution in both cases. First, where nature is concerned, and irrespective of the point of departure (individual or small group), it is important to bear in mind that the line between the battle *against* nature and the battle *to conquer* nature is sometimes very thin. For example, collective action to secure basic shelter for protection from the elements may indeed be an instance of negative association, but continued action by the same group for the improvement of that shelter and the addition of amenities is not, since it is no longer the desire for protection from the wind and the rain that is motivating it. In Hobbes's terms, one might refer to this difference as one between self-preservation and "commodious living."[49] Second, in the context of the political economy of fear, one's relationship to others need not be fixed, but will vary depending on the way in which the circumstances alter one's view of others. Friends may become enemies and vice versa. Nevertheless the conditions that characterize the state of nature are such that especially initially, but also subsequently, negative association will be necessary if the barriers to group formation and collective action are to be overcome.

In the language of collective action, one can explain the force of negative association in terms of the distinction between "collective goods" and "collective bads."[50] Hardin notes that "[d]espite the formal equivalence of their payoff structures, cooperation to oppose a loss may be easier than cooperation to support a gain for several reasons"; he lists six such reasons, of which four are particularly relevant here.[51] First, a collective bad is more likely to

---

(*The Concept of the Political*, 61). This interpretation is supported further by the fact that in the original text, Schmitt places the term *böse* (evil) in quotation marks (Schmitt, *Der Begriff des Politischen*, 61). Cf. Hobbes, *De Cive*, Preface to the Readers, § 12. Freud argues that human beings can detect the existence of an inclination towards aggression, and that we therefore "justly assume [it] to be present in others" (*Civilization and Its Discontents*, 69).

[49] See Hobbes, *Leviathan*, XIII § 14.

[50] See Hardin, *Collective Action*, 17–20, 61–66. An important component of the "collective" attribute of both categories is that no participant is excluded from enjoyment of the good and avoidance of the bad, respectively.

[51] Hardin, *Collective Action*, 62. Two additional reasons, Hardin's numbers four and five, concern the difference between acting in ways that avoid doing harm to others versus acting in ways that help others, and the greater likelihood that one may engage in the former kind of action even if one were averse to the latter kind, as well as the fact that some people are "contractarians," who like to play fair, respectively (cf. *ibid.*, 63–64).

be easier to identify and focus on. Second, "the gain to a group from action to regulate a bad created by an external agent may be large relative to the costs of the action." Third, collective action to avoid a collective bad "may be heightened by moral reaction to the inequity." Fourth, individuals may feel losses "more acutely than gains of comparable magnitude."[52] The most compelling general reason for negative association in the face of a collective bad, however, is simply that the cost of inaction is greater than the cost of association. Two individuals, in the state of nature, who are mistrustful of each other, need no more common ground to join forces, if temporarily, than the realization that they are being harassed by the same third party. In short, association with others similarly situated lowers the cost of participation, increases the chances of successful mobilization, and therefore renders collective action appealing, all the more so in situations in which such action is aimed at collective goods, as in the case of security from an external threat, which all successful participants can enjoy more or less equally.[53] The nature of the good to be gained through cooperation is a crucial determinant of the extent to which mobilization and cooperation will succeed and endure. Private goods are like insufficient spoils. Even if an army succeeds in defeating its enemy, it will eventually have to face the problem of dividing the loot among its members. In some cases, anticipation of such problems may give rise to internal dissention even before the in-group achieves its purpose, and may even prevent the very formation of the alliance in question. By contrast, collective goods, such as defense from a common threat, are less susceptible to the effects of this troublesome property.[54]

The discovery of the origins of the very first political associations is the hardest case, but there are two other types of large political group formation that are instructive in their own way. These cases are different in certain crucial respects from conjectural or anthropological explanations, but they can nevertheless provide us with some insight into the role of negative

[52] Hardin refers to this as "the problem of hysteresis in individuals' perceptions of the relative sizes of their gains and losses" (*Collective Action*, 62–64). On hysteresis (literally "loss"), see *ibid.*, 82–83. Interestingly, the identifiability and universality of collective bads is also what allows for comparative historical anthropology: Service cites Goldschmidt, who argues, "What is consistent from culture to culture is not the institution; what is consistent are the social problems. What is recurrent from society to society is solutions to these problems" (Service, *Origins of the State*, 9).

[53] See Hardin, *One for All*, 51–52.

[54] This difference in goods explains why despite a wealth of evidence in favor of the hypothesis that common threats unify individuals (see, e.g., Stein, "Conflict and Cohesion," 149–50), there are studies that display individualistic behavior, as, e.g., in the case of prisoners in concentration camps (cf. *ibid.*, 150, 158).

association in group formation, because historical records and other evidence about them are available. The first type includes radical transformations of the identities of subnational entities (individuals and groups) that lead to the formation of a new nation. The main difference between this situation and the previous two types (conjectural and anthropological) is that in this case, the formation of the political group in question occurs in an environment in which other, more or less clearly defined political groups exist. Processes of group identity formation and transformation are constantly underway, yet there are periods during which these processes reach a critical mass, at which point radical transformations of regimes and groups take place, as in the cases of the dissolution of empires in the late nineteenth and early twentieth centuries, the transition from colonial rule to self-rule during the twentieth century, and the dissolution of large, multiethnic states, such as the Soviet Union and Yugoslavia.[55] In those instances, in particular, negative association is a crucial element of the process of group identity formation for two sets of reasons. First, there is a status quo ante (oppression, persecution, and exploitation) that the aspiring group's constitutive elements wish to escape.[56] Second, there are out-groups, associated either with this status quo or with the efforts to change it, that the members of the potential in-group want to distinguish themselves from. Such groups could include the holders of power in the status quo ante, rival ethnic groups, foreign enemies, and various out-groups seeking to hinder the group's path towards the attainment of its goals. As the in-group forms its identity, both the situation to be avoided and the various out-groups serve as focal points. Contradistinction from these is one of the most important – in some cases, the single most important – clearly identifiable determinants of the in-group's identity. Examples of this dynamic in group formation abound. Several modern nations, the successors of empires, such as Turkey, and of colonialism, such as Indonesia, formed and consolidated their identities in opposition to others, neighbors, antagonists, enemies, and former despots.[57]

Alliances, especially between states, are the second major source of evidence for the role of negative association in group formation. According to

---

[55] See Deutsch, *Nationalism and Its Alternatives*, 49–51.

[56] The principle here is the same that guides the use of the state of nature in Hobbes and, to a lesser degree, Locke. The state of nature represents that which is to be avoided. For Hobbes, it is to be avoided at all costs (*Leviathan*, XIII), whereas for Locke, it is sometimes preferable to subjection to a despot (*Two Treatises of Government*, II §§ 123, 199–243).

[57] On Turkey, see Gökalp, *Turkish Nationalism and Western Civilization*, 71–72, 132, 260; Gökalp, *Principles of Turkism*, 12–16; Mardin, "The Ottoman Empire." On Indonesia, Bunge, *Indonesia*, 80; Zainu'ddin, *A Short History of Indonesia*, 169, 173, 205.

Walt, "[w]hen confronted by a significant external threat, states may either balance or bandwagon," where "balancing" refers to the formation of an alliance with others "against the prevailing threat," and "bandwagoning" to "alignment with the source of danger."[58] Walt's study of motivation behind alliance formation leads him to conclude that balancing "was far more common than bandwagoning, and bandwagoning was almost always confined to especially weak and isolated states."[59] What is more, threat, rather than power, was the driving force behind alliances.[60] In some instances, it is clear from the outset – and supplicants do not deny it – that the basis for the formation of an alliance is the presence of a common enemy. Thucydides, for example, captures the logic of "The enemy of my enemy is my friend" vividly in his account of the Corinthians' appeal to the Spartans and their confederates for help.[61] In other cases, realignment after the achievement of the alliance's purpose reveals that negative association was at work. As World War II was drawing to its close, Churchill realized that when German military power was destroyed, the relations between Communist Russia and the Western democracies changed fundamentally, for "[t]hey had lost their common enemy, which was almost their sole bond of union."[62] Churchill's

---

[58] Walt, *The Origins of Alliances*, 17. Cf. Waltz, *Theory of International Politics*, 125–27.

[59] Walt, *The Origins of Alliances*, 263. Walt adds, "the importance of ideological distinctions declined as the level of threat increased; ideological solidarity was most powerful when security was high or when ideological factors and security considerations reinforced each other" (*ibid.*).

[60] Walt, *The Origins of Alliances*, 263. Walt thus proposes a "balance of threat" theory, instead of the prevalent "balance of power" theory. The validity of this distinction is evident in a classic formulation of "balance of power" theory by Morgenthau, who argues,

> The struggle between an alliance of nations defending their independence against one potential conqueror is the most spectacular of the configurations to which the balance of power gives rise. The opposition of two alliances, one or both using imperialistic goals and defending the independence of their members against the imperialistic aspirations of the other coalition, is the most frequent configuration within the balance-of-power system (*Politics among Nations*, 209).

Morgenthau's examples center on the threat posed by potential conquerors and imperialists, respectively, rather than on the power of the parties involved.

[61] Thucydides, *The Peloponnesian War*, I.122; cf. *ibid.*, I.101, V.11, V.28–29, V.82, VI.79, VI.85–86, VII.77.

[62] Churchill, *Triumph and Tragedy*, 456. Churchill then listed eight "decisive, practical points of strategy and policy," of which three are particularly noteworthy:

> *First*, that Soviet Russia had become a mortal danger to the free world.
> *Secondly*, that a new front must be immediately created against her onward step. [. . .]
> *Finally, and above all*, that a settlement must be reached on all major issues between the West and the East in Europe *before the armies of democracy melted*, or the Western allies yielded

assessment of the situation surrounding the defeat of Germany received grave and familiar confirmation in the momentous realignment that followed it and resulted in the Cold War. Interestingly, the validity of this assessment is also confirmed in a small but telling way by the nomenclature of the warring parties: whereas the enemy had a name, the Axis, the ingroup was only known as "the Allies."

Christensen remarks, "[i]f politics makes strange bedfellows, then international politics makes the strangest."[63] International alliances based on negative association command attention not only because of the stark differences between their constitutive parts, but also because of their scale and consequences. Nonetheless, it is their reliance on negative association, rather than any other quality, that makes strange bedfellows at any level extraordinary and remarkable. If the short-lived feeling of solidarity generated in the wake of the 2001 terrorist attacks on the United States, among otherwise mutually suspicious parties, is strange, the fear of Arab immigrants that drove some Belgian Jews to support a far right party founded by Nazi collaborators is certainly no less so.[64] The emergence of an external threat forces the rearrangement of priorities. If the threat is seen as a collective bad and the results of group action as a collective good, then parties will come together in order to address it. If cooperation among these parties is unexpected and inexplicable on positive grounds alone – because they have a history of noncooperation, mutual suspicion, or hostility – then negative association based on fear is most likely the primary reason for group formation. Negative association, however, underpins even the strongest of positive identities.[65]

GROUP PRESERVATION: TWO VARIETIES OF XENOPHOBIA

The invocation of out-groups by in-groups seeking to consolidate is recognized so widely that it has been called "a general law" and "a founding axiom of modern political thought."[66] Among the historians who described

any part of the German territories they had conquered, or, as it could soon be written, liberated from totalitarian tyranny (*ibid.*, 456–57).

[63] Christensen, *Useful Adversaries*, 3.

[64] Sanger, "Russia, China, and the U.S.; In Terror, at Last a Common Enemy for the Big Three"; Smith, "Europe's Jews Seek Solace on the Right."

[65] Herzl, for example, concluded that the nationality of Jews "cannot be destroyed, because external enemies consolidate it" (*The Jewish State*, 18; cf. *ibid.*, 76–77).

[66] Dahrendorf, "The New Germanies," 58; Wood, "Sallust's Theorem," 181. Cf. Christensen, *Useful Adversaries*, 3.

the role of Carthage in the promotion of Roman unity, this phenomenon was known as *metus hostilis* (fear of enemies).[67] Contemporary political scientists refer to it as the "rally-round-the-flag phenomenon" or the "diversionary theory of war hypothesis."[68] In lay terms, we often speak of "scapegoats." The preservation and consolidation of groups already in existence is different, in many ways, from the formation of a group *ex nihilo*. Political groups develop a complex identity regardless of whether they came into being primarily through negative association or for positive reasons. As with groups of all kinds, this history becomes simultaneously more and less complicated as time goes by. Some aspects of a group's history become lost or forgotten. Some are covered up or beautified deliberately. As a result, there are popular versions of the genealogies and histories of political associations, such as nations and parties, that are simple and clear.[69] At the same time, however, the histories of political groups become more complicated. Alternative histories develop alongside narratives of the former kind, and simplistic accounts of events in the evolution of the group are challenged. More importantly, however, the histories of political groups are complicated by the fact that their place in the world and their relations with their members and outsiders change constantly.[70] Thus, members who might not meet the criteria for admission at one point find themselves included at others, as in the case of the full assimilation of immigrants in previously homogeneous countries or the enfranchisement of women and blacks in the United States. Conversely, former members may find themselves unwanted, as did Jews in Germany and Americans of Japanese descent in the United States, before and during World War II.

The comings and goings that are part and parcel of group life mean that for most political groups there are two very different levels at which negative association can manifest itself: internally and externally. Although this book is concerned with the latter, a word about the former is necessary. Racism, fascism, and xenophobia can assume many forms and target groups within or across borders.[71] Where consolidation by means of negative association is

---

[67] See Sallust, *The War with Catiline*, X.1–2. Cf. Chapter 2 in this volume.

[68] See Levy, "The Diversionary Theory of War: A Critique," 261; Deutsch, *Nationalism and Its Alternatives*; Russett, *Controlling the Sword*, 34; Polsby, *Congress and the Presidency*, 66.

[69] See Gellner, *Nations and Nationalism*, 56; Gellner, *Nationalism*, 72; Hobsbawm, "Introduction: Inventing Traditions." 7, 9.

[70] Hence Benhabib identifies "the fiction of a 'closed society'" ("Citizens, Residents, and Aliens in a Changing World," 101; cf. *The Rights of Others*, 74–75, 86–87).

[71] See Demetrios I. Evrigenis, *Committee of Inquiry into the Rise of Fascism and Racism in Europe: Report on the Findings of the Inquiry*, §§ 27–47.

concerned, the use of domestic minority groups as scapegoats constitutes a distinct area of study with its own peculiarities and significant differences from the equivalent use of external threats. Foreigners make compelling targets for a number of reasons. Groups of foreigners are more easily identifiable in the midst of the domestic population. Foreigners do not have a say, and therefore do not affect the established domestic political process (campaigns, elections) directly.[72] They lack the means to address a domestic audience. They are not as familiar, and are therefore more likely to be viewed with suspicion.[73] One hesitates to ascribe a universal character to these statements, but in the case of minority targeting for political purposes the vast and diverse array of examples speaks for itself.[74]

What, then, determines whether a domestic minority or an external threat will serve as the rallying point for a political group in trouble? The answer to this question will clearly depend on the circumstances, but some general observations are possible. The first consideration is opportunity: external enemies often appear of their own accord, and some political groups do not have viable internal targets on which to focus. That said, in cases in which both conditions are satisfied, one often sees both internal and external out-groups targeted. The most obvious example here is once again the persecution of Jews and Gypsies during World War II, but there are many other cases that one can point to, such as the persecution of minorities during the revolution of the Young Turks at the beginning of the twentieth century, or the events that led to the dissolution of the former Yugoslavia. It may be that this connection is no mere accident, and that the heightening of contradistinction for the purposes of group conflict is not easily manageable, for reasons that have to do with the very dynamic of consolidation that characterizes an in-group in conflict with an out-group. As noted above, one of the requirements for successful consolidation and collective action in the face of threat is that the threat itself be collective. This requirement means that the first steps towards the consolidation of a group include inquiries into that which makes it what it is. These inquiries can be seen as existential questions in hard times, but they are actually instrumental, since consolidation without some answer to the question "Who are we?" is impossible. Once this question is asked in the presence of easily identifiable minorities, their exclusion is a matter of time, and exclusion in the context of existential concerns

[72] Russett, *Controlling the Sword*, 32.
[73] Deutsch, *Nationalism and Its Alternatives*, 15.
[74] See Demetrios I. Evrigenis, *Committee of Inquiry into the Rise of Fascism and Racism in Europe: Report on the Findings of the Inquiry*, §§ 52–209, 212.

can quickly assume a nasty face. This logic is well known: "If you're not with us, you're against us."

Things are different when it comes to xenophobia writ large. Pointing to Sallust's background as a commander and the preponderance of warfare in Roman times, Wood suggests that the origins of Sallust's Theorem are military: "[w]ar against a hostile enemy was the normal situation, and fear in the struggle for survival was endemic to the Roman way of life."[75] Wood himself wrote of *metus hostilis* at a time of unprecedented peace and prosperity, and for an audience largely unaccustomed to war. As a consequence, his observation might have seemed like an interesting historical proposition. Its force, however, is far greater. As historians and political theorists recognize time and again, in most places, most of the time, the choice between peace and war as the descriptor of the normal state of affairs is at best a matter of perspective, but in altogether too many cases war is the norm. Nevertheless, Sallust's Theorem is significant because its lesson extends into times of peace. When threats to security are distant, the pursuit of private goods rises on the list of individuals' priorities. This rearrangement harbors the potential for trouble. In fragile societies, it may mean civil war.[76]

The dual capacity of *metus hostilis* as a cure for dissent and a means for the achievement of collective ends renders Sallust's Theorem "easily translatable into a prudential precept of government."[77] In conventional wisdom, this precept has axiomatic status. Shakespeare's Henry IV encapsulates it when he counsels his son and heir to "busy giddy minds / With foreign quarrels; that action, hence borne out, / May waste the memory of the former days."[78] One year before the September 11, 2001 terrorist attacks, a think tank published a report on the defense of the United States that urged the Department of Defense to transform the country's armed forces, but noted that "the process of transformation, even if it brings revolutionary change, is likely to be a long one, absent some catastrophic and catalyzing event – like a new Pearl Harbor."[79] Several of the main contributors to the report became members of the administration that took office in January 2001, and leading strategists in the "War on Terror." The dual nature of fear makes the implementation of Sallust's Theorem a challenging matter, since invoking it can unleash its

---

[75] Wood, "Sallust's Theorem," 182.
[76] According to Machiavelli, "the cause of the disunion of republics is usually idleness and peace; the cause of union is fear and war" (*Discourses on Livy*, II.25). Cf. Wood, "Sallust's Theorem," 182; Bodin, *The Six Bookes of a Commonweale*, V.5, 602.
[77] Wood, "Sallust's Theorem," 183.
[78] Shakespeare, *The Second Part of King Henry IV*, Act IV, Scene 5.
[79] Project for the New American Century, "Rebuilding America's Defenses," 51.

adverse effects.[80] When the right balance is struck, however, external threats increase the cohesion of the in-group, place leaders in a favorable light, and even allow for the passage of otherwise unpopular measures.[81]

Fear is seen as irrational when it produces a disproportionate reaction to the stimulus that gave rise to it. From uncontrollable physical symptoms to panicking mobs, this side of fear is most troubling but all too familiar. Even in its mildest forms, however, fear is an unpleasant feeling. As such, it belongs at the head of a notorious list of human characteristics that have occupied the attention of political theorists and will continue to do so. But just as pain, another unpleasant fact of life, exists to alert us to dangers to our health and well-being, so too does fear have a salutary side. At the level of the individual, it alerts the mind to dangers near and far. At the level of the political group, it contributes to cohesion. In both cases, it may lead to paralysis, but short of that, it bridges the gap between the irrational and the rational, and thus allows us to continue to move forward.[82]

The universe that surrounds us is too vast and complex for the human brain to comprehend fully. In making their way in it, human beings develop mechanisms to help them manage this otherwise overwhelming complexity, and use external entities as signposts.[83] Through a combination of such tricks, the mind is able to create a semblance of order and treat a world beyond its

---

[80] Russett argues, "[t]he trick is to produce a moderate amount of concern (or fear), but not so much as to induce people simply to avoid thinking or acting about the problem" (*Controlling the Sword*, 76–77). Cf. Robin, *Fear*, 155–60.

[81] Polsby argues, "[i]nvariably, the short-run popular response to a President during an international crisis is favorable, regardless of the wisdom of the policies he pursues" (*Congress and the Presidency*, 66). According to Christensen, this was the strategy that Truman and Mao adopted when they faced the difficulty of implementing unpopular policies: "[t]he manipulation or extension of short-term conflict with the other nation, while not desirable on straightforward international or domestic grounds, became useful in gaining and maintaining public support for the core grand strategy" (*Useful Adversaries*, 6). Churchill's case confirms the hypothesis. When the threat of the Axis had been eliminated and the impending threat of the Soviet Union had not become apparent, the effects of his domestic policies took their toll and he lost the election of 1945. Levy discusses some research that challenges the "diversionary theory of war" hypothesis and concludes that the problem lies with the "limitations of the quantitative empirical literature" ("The Diversionary Theory of War: A Critique," 282). Cf. Robin, "Why Do Opposites Attract?"; *Fear*, esp. 155–60, 249–52.

[82] Tocqueville urges, "[l]et us therefore have that salutary fear of the future that makes one watchful and combative, and not that sort of soft and idle terror that wears hearts down and enervates them" (*Democracy in America*, II.iv.7, p. 673).

[83] See Breyer, *Breaking the Vicious Circle*, 35.

control as though it were predictable and controllable.[84] Conflict conceived broadly as antagonistic interaction with others, at all levels, has been called a universal characteristic of the human condition. In many of its forms, it is one of the principal features that make that condition regrettable. That side is known only too well. Yet, there is another side that motivates individuals to act, causes groups to form and pursue collective goals, and in so doing provides human beings with an essential part of their identity. Dahrendorf observes, "it appears that not only in social life, but wherever there is life, there is conflict," and suggests, "[m]ay we perhaps go so far as to say that conflict is a condition necessary for life to be possible at all?"[85] Political thinkers of all shades answer this question in the affirmative, and proceed to build their theories on this foundation. This book shows that conflict gives life to political groups, and thereby shapes their identities and those of their members.

[84] Cf. Pittman, "Motivation," 551.
[85] Dahrendorf, *Class and Class Conflict in Industrial Society*, 208.

2

"CARTHAGE MUST BE SAVED"

Now it may be possible to find a country, in which, as it is recorded of Crete, there are no wild animals, but a government which has not had to bear with envy or jealous rivalry or contention – emotions most productive of enmity – has not hitherto existed. For our very friendships, if nothing else, involve us in enmities.

– Plutarch[1]

According to a Greek proverb that has its roots in Hippocrates' *Decorum*, "leisure is the mother of all evil."[2] The absence of leisure denotes the existence of a higher priority, of attention to more pressing concerns, such as security and the procurement of the essentials for survival. Accounts of the origins of states usually begin with such circumstances. Individuals band together because alone they are unable to defend themselves and provide everything that they need to stay alive. Once threats are dealt with, enemies repelled, and the essentials secured, leisure permits human beings to rearrange their priorities and pursue less pressing objectives. At such times, original alliances dissolve, allegiances shift, actors are reshuffled, factions form, and bad habits return. Such is Hobbes's account of the rise of philosophy. He claims that in the beginning, men were busy "procuring the necessities of life, and defending themselves against their neighbors." Once their efforts bore fruit and great commonwealths arose, however, leisure became possible, and with it philosophy, which

was not risen to the *Grecians*, and other people of the west, whose *commonwealths* (no greater perhaps than *Lucca* or *Geneva*) had never peace, but when their fears of one another were equal, nor the *leisure* to observe anything but one another.

---

[1] "How to Profit by One's Enemies," 86c.
[2] "Ἀργία μήτηρ πάσης κακίας." Cf. Hippocrates, *Decorum*, I.7–8: "Idleness and lack of occupation tend – nay are dragged – towards evil."

At length, when war had united many of these *Grecian* lesser Cities into fewer and greater, then began *seven men*, of several parts of *Greece*, to get the reputation of being *wise* [...][3]

War, according to Hobbes's account, gave rise to the first self-sufficient political communities. Perhaps paradoxically, its cessation initiated the process of dissolution of those communities. Hobbes's choice to attribute the process of decay to philosophy is one of several possibilities. Following the different lead of Saint Augustine, who in turn follows the Sallustian tradition of Roman history, Bodin sees the distancing of threat as leading to vice.[4] Although these applications differ from one another in their particulars, they are based on the same principle, the old idea of ἔξωθεν φόβος, the fear of external threats. Supreme emergencies, during which the very existence of a state is threatened from the outside, draw attention away from lesser domestic disputes and thus contribute to the consolidation of the political community within which individuals and parties exist. In such times, disagreements are set aside temporarily and unlikely alliances emerge, often driven by nothing more than fear of the same enemy. Guided by the age-old maxim "The enemy of my enemy is my friend," individuals and factions rearrange their priorities to secure their preservation.

If Rome's *metus hostilis* for Carthage was the symbol of the political significance of the fear of enemies, then Sallust's account of it was the model for subsequent political thought. Only very small fragments of Sallust's *Histories* survive, and those come to us through quotations or references found in the works of other writers. Wood concentrates his inquiry on one such passage that comes from Saint Augustine's *City of God*, and explains that he has "simply chosen 'Sallust's Theorem' as a point of departure, a heuristic device encapsulating and emphasizing an important notion of ancient antecedents which, together with its ramifications, may possibly illuminate a significant and neglected aspect of early modern political thought."[5] Wood recognizes that the principle in question predates Rome, yet he is justified in naming it after the Roman historian because on the one hand Sallust and Augustine

---

[3] Hobbes, *Leviathan*, XLVI § 6. In the same passage, Hobbes explains the sequence of events thus: "*Leisure* is the mother of *philosophy*; and *Commonwealth*, the mother of *peace* and *leisure*."

[4] Bodin argues, "[t]here is yet an other reason of great moment, to shew that it is necessarie to entertaine martiall discipline, and to make warre, for that there is no citie so holy, nor so well governed that hath not in it many theeves, murtherers, idle persons, vagabonds, mutins, adulterers, and diceplayers, which leade a wicked life, and corrupt the simplicitie of good subiects; neither can lawes, magistrates, nor any punishment keepe them in awe" (*The Six Bookes of a Commonweale*, V.5, 602).

[5] Wood, "Sallust's Theorem," 175.

23

were undeniably important for the intellectual formation of the West, and on the other hand it was in Rome and Roman historiography that the fear of enemies received its most consistent and explicit treatment.[6]

A separate issue arising from Wood's treatment of *metus hostilis* deserves particular attention. Wood concentrates on the importance of the fear of external enemies as a unifier and enforcer of communities. Although this is a crucial element of the way in which the fear of others shapes politics, it is only part of the story. Another, prior, element concerns negative association, especially where the *formation* of communities, not just their *preservation*, is concerned. This distinction is important because even though the general device employed in both cases is the same, the different circumstances raise the possibility of different manifestations and means. Failure to take this distinction into account has serious consequences. For example, Wood sees Sallust's Theorem as "essentially a military axiom, probably originating in the tactical shrewdness of the military commander."[7] This hypothesis, however, presupposes the existence of political communities with organized military units, which does not account for the existence of *metus hostilis* at the very founding of those communities. Evidence of the latter would suggest that negative association due to the fear of enemies constitutes a fundamental element of self-definition, and therefore of political identity formation, which is itself constitutive of community rather than its product. Indeed, an analysis of key Greek texts, such as Thucydides' history of the Peloponnesian War and Aristotle's *Politics* shows that ἔξωθεν φόβος is recognized as an important part of group formation *and* preservation by political thinkers who exercised considerable influence on Sallust and his followers, and that Roman fear of Carthage is important for its symbolic power and subsequent influence rather than for its originality.

POLITICS AMONG NATIONS FIRST

There is hardly a history of international relations that does not include Thucydides among the progenitors of the discipline. Similarly, there is widespread consensus in studies of realism in international relations that

---

[6] See, e.g., Wood's opening footnote, in which he makes a brief case for the extent to which Sallust was known to prominent political philosophers (Wood, "Sallust's Theorem," 174, n. 1). Cf. Burke, "A Survey of the Popularity of Ancient Historians, 1450–1700"; Worden, "English Republicanism," 446.

[7] Wood, "Sallust's Theorem," 183.

Thucydides' history is the school's founding text.[8] Some international relations scholars debate the extent to which such attributions are accurate, but usually investigations of this kind take place in reverse chronological order. Thus, Thucydides' realist credentials are assessed on the basis of what late twentieth century international relations theorists take to be realism of one variety or another.[9] However, there is a fundamental, if relatively straightforward, characteristic of realism that precedes such considerations as the differences between classical and neorealism, and that is a concern with what Machiavelli calls "the effectual truth."[10] Definition on the basis of an interest in the effectual truth might strike one as superfluous. After all, who is not thus concerned? There is, nevertheless, good reason why Machiavelli and others like him take this concern seriously, and that is none other than the fact that it distinguishes them from those who are interested in normative questions and ideal situations at the expense of reality. According to this line of argument, human beings share certain basic characteristics, and awareness of that fact will permit one to see things as they really are, and therefore to understand politics and history, and perhaps draw some useful lessons from them.[11] It is in this sense that Thucydides is first and foremost a realist. He does not write to delight, but rather for the reader who "desires to look into the truth of things done and which (according to the condition of humanity) may be done again, or at least their like."[12]

---

[8] See, e.g., Clark, "Realism Ancient and Modern," 491; Donnelly, *Realism and International Relations*, 1, 23; Doyle, *Ways of War and Peace*, 90–92; Forde, "International Realism and the Science of Politics"; Gilpin, "The Richness of the Tradition of Political Realism," 305, 306; Garst, "Thucydides and Neorealism," 3–8; Keohane, "Theory of World Politics," 507; Kokaz, "Moderating Power," 27–29, esp. note 8; Orwin, *The Humanity of Thucydides*, 8–9; Rahe, "Thucydides' Critique of Realpolitik," 105–07; Romilly, *Thucydides and Athenian Imperialism*, 256–57; Smith, *Realist Thought from Weber to Kissinger*, 4–10; Waltz, *Theory of International Politics*, 66.

[9] One instance can be found in Johnson, "The Use and Abuse of Thucydides in International Relations," 132–33.

[10] Machiavelli, *The Prince*, XV: 61.

[11] See Thucydides, *The Peloponnesian War*, III.82. This belief in an unchanging core of human nature is also shared by subsequent realists, such as Schmitt and Morgenthau (see Chapter 7 in this volume), so that grouping Thucydides with the realists is also justified for this reason. This, of course, is also true of Hobbes. Cf. Schlatter, "Thomas Hobbes and Thucydides," 357; Orwin, *The Humanity of Thucydides*, 4–5, 10–11; Romilly, *Thucydides and Athenian Imperialism*, 256–57.

[12] Thucydides, *The Peloponnesian War*, I.22; cf. III.82; Bolotin, "Thucydides," 17; Forde, "International Realism and the Science of Politics," 151; Ahrensdorf, "The Fear of Death and the Longing for Immortality," 587; Ioannis D. Evrigenis, "Hobbes's Thucydides."

Such a reader, he claims, will find enough in his history to make it "profitable."[13]

For an understanding of negative association, Thucydides' history is doubly useful, as it sheds light on the onset of war and the formation of political associations, both phenomena driven by fear.[14] In what is perhaps the best-known part of his account of the war, Thucydides argues that "the truest [cause], though least in speech, I conceive to be the growth of the Athenian power, which putting the Lacedaemonians into fear necessitated the war."[15] As Thucydides' "truest cause" is a conjecture, he supplements his account with the justifications offered by the participants, all of which refer to particular episodes claimed as the reasons for the initiation of the hostilities.[16] Yet, throughout the rest of the history, Thucydides returns to the connection between fear and war.

The first part of Thucydides' "truest cause," the growth of Athenian power, was a direct consequence of negative association in response to the coming Persian threat.[17] In Thucydides' account, this explanation is first introduced by the Corinthians, in their address to the Peloponnesian League.[18] When the Athenian ambassadors take it upon themselves to explain to the Lacedaemonians their involvement in the dispute between Corinth and Corcyra, they claim that Athens began to expand its dominion "to what it is out of the nature of the thing itself, as chiefly for fear, next for honour, and lastly for profit."[19] The presence of honor and profit in the

---

[13] On the benefits from reading Thucydides' history, see Hobbes's epistle dedicatory of his translation, to Sir William Cavendish (Thucydides, *The Peloponnesian War*, xix–xx); cf. Ioannis D. Evrigenis, "Hobbes's Thucydides." Thucydides' emphasis on power also satisfies Morgenthau's main criterion for his classification as a realist (see, e.g., *The Peloponnesian War*, I.76, V.105; cf. Morgenthau, *Politics among Nations*, 4–14. See also Chapter 7 in this volume).

[14] Grene calls the Peloponnesian War "great in its political and psychological implications for us as well as its contemporaries" (*Greek Political Theory*, 3).

[15] Thucydides, *The Peloponnesian War*, I.23. This translation follows Grene's in reading "truest cause" instead of Hobbes's "truest quarrel." Thucydides repeats this claim at I.88 and I.118, among other places. On Spartan fear, see Rahe, *Republics Ancient & Modern*, I: 127–28.

[16] On the relationship between the "truest cause" and the particular provocations, see Gomme, *A Historical Commentary on Thucydides* I, 152–54. Cf. Hornblower, *A Commentary on Thucydides*, I, 64–66; Kagan, *The Outbreak of the Peloponnesian War*, 354.

[17] Thucydides describes the rise of Athens in the first part of the period known as the *pentakontaetia* (*The Peloponnesian War*, I.89–96). Cf. Kagan, *The Outbreak of the Peloponnesian War*, 31–49; Grene, *Greek Political Theory*, 51–52.

[18] Thucydides, *The Peloponnesian War*, I.68–69. The Mytileneans offer the same explanation later on (III.10); cf. VI.82.

[19] Thucydides, *The Peloponnesian War*, I.75. Cf. Hobbes, *On the Citizen*, I.2.

list of motivations supplied by the Athenian ambassadors, coupled with the increasingly arrogant and imperialistic attitude of Athens following the defeat of the Persians, has caused some commentators to take fear for granted and focus instead on the latter two elements of the list. Such a line of interpretation is supported further by the fact that when the Athenian delegates return to the motives for their city's expansion, they change the order and list the "three greatest things, honour, fear, and profit."[20] It is clear that, over time, the rise of Athens' power corresponded to a lessening of its fear.[21] Nevertheless, Thucydides' repeated emphasis on the importance of the fear of an enemy as a motivation for political mobilization reminds us of another way to look at the three greatest things.[22] In his description of the civil unrest that spread after the events at Corcyra, he calls attention to the ways in which war necessitates that one resort to otherwise undesirable actions:

For in peace and prosperity as well cities as private men are better minded because they be not plunged into necessity of doing anything against their will. But war, taking away the affluence of daily necessaries, is a most violent master and conformeth most men's passions to the present occasion.[23]

---

[20] Thucydides, *The Peloponnesian War*, I.76. In their speech before the Peloponnesian League, the Corinthians cite only fear and profit as motives behind alliances (I.123). With regard to the relationship between imperialism and the "three greatest things," Grene argues, "[t]hat men struggle to live and then to dominate one another individually and nationally is a recurrent theme but does not attain any precision of form until their concerted and collective efforts have built a great monument to their individual greed and fear" (*Greek Political Theory*, 84). Orwin ("Justifying Empire," 77) finds this transposition "breathtaking" and sees it as indicative of the shift in the relative weight of each motive. Cf. Strauss, *The City and Man*, 183; Orwin, *The Humanity of Thucydides*, 47, note 36.

[21] As Romilly points out, the Mytilenean speech in Book III reveals this gradual shift: "[Athens'] imperialism begins little by little (by attacking the weakest) and hypocritically (by disguising itself with fine reasons)" (*Thucydides and Athenian Imperialism*, 38).

[22] Ahrensdorf, for example, argues that Thucydides' description of the civil unrest at Corcyra is evidence that the fear of violent death was no longer the top priority, as individuals began to engage in behavior that is not compatible with such a fear ("The Fear of Death and the Longing for Immortality," 587–88). This interpretation, however, ignores Thucydides' own judgment about the climate of the time and the demands of necessity (see Thucydides, *The Peloponnesian War*, III.82; VI.83). Bruell points out correctly that fear is the only one of the three reasons mentioned by the Athenians that makes for an acceptable defense ("Thucydides' View of Athenian Imperialism," 13); cf. Romilly, *Thucydides and Athenian Imperialism*, 253–55.

[23] Thucydides, *The Peloponnesian War*, III.82; cf. III.45: "For poverty will always add boldness to necessity; and wealth covetousness to pride and contempt." Cf. Aristotle, *Politica* 1334a.

Leisure – the absence of threat – allows men to rearrange their priorities and begin to think loftier thoughts.[24] The transposition of the motives, then, is a sign of Athens' growing imperialism and corresponding viewpoint only insofar as these resulted from the distancing of the threat that followed from the defeat of the Persians and the consequent increase of Athenian power vis-à-vis other city-states.[25] The Athenian delegates themselves are aware of the relative standing of fear among the three greatest things; they know that only once the Persians were defeated, and the common enemy ceased to pose a threat, were they able to turn their attention to their erstwhile allies, the other city-states.[26] They warn the Spartans that were they to topple Athens and assume hegemony of the Greek city-states, they would lose the support of all those who had allied themselves with Sparta only for fear of Athens.[27] The Athenian ambassadors' account of the rise of Athenian power as a result of the fear of the Persians is also corroborated by the Mytileneans, who in their appeal to the Peloponnesian League for assistance explain their earlier alliance with Athens on the basis of the common Persian threat, and add that after the happy conclusion of that expedition, the confederates "through the multitude of distinct counsels unable to unite themselves for resistance" fell into the subjection of the Athenians.[28]

The second component of Thucydides' "truest cause," the fear of Athenian power, dominates the early stages of the war, as it is the basic motivating factor behind appeals to Sparta for the formation of alliances. This emphasis on the fear of Athens, which is necessitated by the chronological order of the events, however, turns out to be merely paradigmatic, since, as the war progresses, the fear of enemies leaves no party unaffected. The perpetual movement of actors and the shifting of allegiances are crucial to the

---

[24] Strauss suggests that in terms of expansionism "Sparta was moderate because she had grave troubles with her Helots; the Helots made her moderate" (*The City and Man*, 191–92). Aristotle likens the Helots to enemies waiting for a Spartan disaster to rise up (*Politica*, 1269a38–39).

[25] As Strauss notes rightly, at a later point in the war, Euphemus "justifies both the Athenians' empire and their Sicilian expedition by their concern with their salvation or security alone, by their fear alone" (*The City and Man*, 183–84; cf. Thucydides, *The Peloponnesian War*, VI.83–87).

[26] Thucydides, *The Peloponnesian War*, I.75. Cf. Orwin, "Justifying Empire," 75–76.

[27] See Thucydides, *The Peloponnesian War*, I.77: "Insomuch as you also, if you should put us down and reign yourselves, you would soon find a change of the love which they bear you now for fear of us if you should do again as you did for awhile when you were their commanders against the Medes." The Athenians' prediction was proven correct after the end of the war; cf. Grene, *Greek Political Theory*, 60–61.

[28] Thucydides, *The Peloponnesian War*, III.10.

development of the Peloponnesian War, and it is clear that Thucydides takes a particular interest in alliance formation. This interest is also indicated by the fact that although he is mainly concerned with the behavior of states and much less so with the actions of nameless men within the confines of the polis, he nevertheless takes the time to reflect on the tendency of human beings to band together in times of need. The force of this tendency was such that factions went after the neutrals, he tells us, "partly because they would not side with them and partly for envy that they should so escape."[29]

Thucydides' exploration of this fear is striking because it conveys the readiness with which envoys admit their fearfulness when they plead for help and because it makes it abundantly clear, time after time, that neutrality is not an option.[30] In all these speeches, fear is ever present. When the Peloponnesian city-states gather to consider their course of action with respect to Athens, the Corinthians argue that Athens has become "too strong for us" and caution, "unless we oppose them jointly and every nation and city set to it unanimously, they will overcome us asunder without labour."[31] Similarly, in their appeal to the Spartans for help against the Athenians, the Mytileneans advance a brilliant argument for the complex role of fear in alliances. They point out that "the equality of mutual fear is the only band of faith in leagues."[32] To illustrate the validity of their assertion, they point to their erstwhile confederacy with Athens. That union, they argue, was held together by mutual fear, since the Athenians would refrain from attacking them whilst they needed them for war, and the Mytileneans would in turn remain faithful whenever Athens' attention was not diverted by another threat.[33] Mutual fear, then, is not only the reason why they associated with the enemy of the state to which they have now turned for help, it is also the reason why this state should nevertheless help them. They thus urge the Spartans to admit

---

[29] Thucydides, *The Peloponnesian War*, III.82. Cf. Aron, *Peace and War*, 138.

[30] Of this, too, the Melian dialogue is the most famous example.

[31] Thucydides, *The Peloponnesian War*, I.122. A similar argument is put forth by the Thebans during their dispute with the Plataeans (III.63–64).

[32] Thucydides, *The Peloponnesian War*, III.11. Hornblower finds the juxtaposition of Athenian and Mytilenean fears here to be "[a] neat antithesis, the first part of which (as Gomme remarks) serves to 'screen' the Mytileneans' own discreditable flattery" (*A Commentary on Thucydides*, I: 396).

[33] See Thucydides, *The Peloponnesian War*, III.12: "What friendship then or assurance of liberty was this when we received each other with alienated affections: when whilst [the Athenians] had wars, they for fear courted us; and when they had peace, we for fear courted them: and whereas in others good will assureth loyalty, in us it was the effect of fear? So it was more for fear than love that we remained their confederates; and whomsoever security should first embolden, he was first likely by one means or other to break the league."

them into their league and send aid, "thereby the better at once both to defend those [they] ought to defend and to annoy [their] enemies."[34]

Thucydides' references to fear in the formation of alliances, however, extend far beyond the confines of the fear of Athens and the "truest cause" and show that no party is immune to such considerations. At the very initiation of the hostilities, when the Corcyreans appeal to the Athenians for help in their struggle against the Corinthians, they begin their plea with the realization that their attempt to remain neutral in the past has failed them, since it has resulted in their inability to find help. The Corcyrean ambassadors admit that this has been an "error in judgment" on their part (I.32) and proceed to request the help of the Athenians by making use of a double specter of fear, on the one hand invoking the dangers of a Spartan threat, but on the other pointing out that

[i]f any here think that the war wherein we may do you service will not at all be, he is in an error and seeth not how the Lacedaemonians, through fear of you, are already in labour of the war; and that the Corinthians, gracious to them and enemies to you, making way for their enterprize, assault us now in the way to the invasion of you hereafter, that we may not stand amongst the rest of their common enemies, but that they may be sure beforehand either to weaken us or to strengthen their own estate. It must therefore be your part, we offering and you accepting the league, to begin with them and to anticipate plotting rather than to counterplot against them.[35]

At a later stage in the war, it is two Athenians, Alcibiades and Athenagoras, who invoke the fear of harm as a justification for preemptive action.[36] Nor are these the only examples of this practice. Thucydides' history is riddled

---

[34] Thucydides, *The Peloponnesian War*, III.13. Orwin notes that the Mytileneans' explanation of their alliance with Athens is insufficient, since Mytilene had greater reason to fear Athens than vice versa, and argues that that alliance too was held together also by the fear of enemies inspired by the Persians. This observation leads him to the conclusion that "[f]ear reemerges as the only reliable basis of alliance, but it is common fear of a third party rather than a mutual fear of each other" (*The Humanity of Thucydides*, 69). He also points out that if we search for the inclination of the Mytileneans to honor their alliance with Athens, "we will find it in subjection to constraint of yet another kind, that imposed by fear of a common enemy," the Medes (68).

[35] Thucydides, *The Peloponnesian War*, I.33.

[36] According to Thucydides, Alcibiades told the Athenians, "[f]or when one is grown mightier than the rest, men use not only to defend themselves against him when he shall invade, but to anticipate him, that he invade not at all" (*The Peloponnesian War*, VI.18). Athenagoras argued similarly, "[f]or one must not only take revenge upon an enemy for what he hath already done, but strike him first for his evil purpose; for if a man strike not first, he shall first be stricken" (VI.38).

with appeals for the formation of alliances based on the specter of a common enemy.[37]

The persistence with which alliances among individuals and states form and dissolve on the basis of the fear of external threats in Thucydides' history is not surprising given his claim that the horrific events that transpired during the *stasis* "have been before and shall be ever as long as human nature is the same," and his announcement that his history is a possession for all time.[38] This constant flux of alliances illustrates one of the central elements of negative association, the existence of a political economy of fear, a hierarchy of threats that determines the behavior of actors towards others. The inability of human beings to address simultaneously and effectively all threats leads them to a necessary classification of those threats in relation to one another, depending on their urgency. The formation of alliances leads to a rearrangement of threats, which in turn means that previously pressing situations become downgraded so that more urgent new demands can be addressed first, and new alliances form as necessary. Nothing reflects this reordering better than the readiness to accept hitherto unthinkable allies.[39] In their own calculations, Thucydides' actors may classify only external threats and alliances, but the same basic logic extends to choices between internal political groups and external threats.[40] Romilly argues that Thucydides' focus is

---

[37] In addition to those mentioned already, see, e.g., Thucydides, *The Peloponnesian War*, I.101, V.11, V.28–29, V.82, VI.79, VI.85–86, VII.77. Cf. Brown, "Thucydides, Hobbes, and the Derivation of Anarchy," 54.

[38] Thucydides, *The Peloponnesian War*, I.22, III.82. Thucydides allows for minor differences due to time and place, but these affect only the particular manifestation of a certain behavior or situation rather than its core character. Hornblower argues that this is "[a]n important sentence for the understanding of Th.'s method, and a pioneering scientific statement in itself" (*A Commentary on Thucydides*, I: 481).

[39] While advising the Spartans not to rush into war, Archidamus nevertheless recommends that they "make friends both of Greeks and barbarians," arguing, "nor are they to be blamed that being laid in wait for, as we are by the Athenians, take unto them not Grecians only but also barbarians for their safety" (Thucydides, *The Peloponnesian War*, I.82). The terms of the treaty between the Spartans and the Athenians that followed the Peace of Nicias (*ibid.*, V.23) are another striking example of realignment.

[40] Thus, as Slomp points out, "Thucydides' twin description of ancient Greece and of the plague in Athens implicitly sets political philosophy the task of solving the following dilemma: given a world where fear is the overwhelming passion (as in ancient Greece) is as unbearable and as ungovernable as a world without fear altogether (such as Athens during the plague), how is fear to be channeled so as to result in a stable social order?" ("Hobbes, Thucydides and the Three Greatest Things," 572). Cf. Ahrensdorf, "The Fear of Death and the Longing for Immortality," 588.

fixed firmly on the city and that he never calls its existence as a political unit into question. This observation leads her to the conclusion that "whether consciously or not, it is the defeat of the city as such which Thucydides is recording."[41] In that period of mounting challenges to the very existence of the city-state, the determination of the proper amount of fear for the preservation of the state assumed a new significance.

PRESERVING THE STATE: A BALANCING ACT

For Romilly, the century that followed the Peloponnesian War was characterized by a move away from the city and towards either a Panhellenic union or a moral regeneration.[42] In fact, even Thucydides' account, opening as it does with the juxtaposition between the war against the Persians and the Peloponnesian War, points to an awareness of the tension that Romilly writes of. As Grene observes, "within the memory of a single man, a Greek could see the two great powers so readily united in the cause of freedom against Persian despotism, each trying to destroy the other and acquire its empire"; the cynical realism resulting from this development "drove men to ask whether the morality of the Persian Wars was a fiction, after all."[43] The record of extant works from the fourth century shows orators struggling to deal with the rising threat of conquest from the north, and philosophers attempting to address the moral degeneration that they saw as the source of the city-state's decay. These two strands of thought, however, need not be separate, and one of the points at which they connect is the fear of external threats, which is simultaneously a matter of foreign policy and the preservation of the state from without *and* a cure for social dissention within the walls. Nowhere is this more clear, in the period following Thucydides' history, than in Aristotle's *Politics*, a work that begins by raising the issue of the naturalness of the polis and then devotes considerable attention to the preservation of the regime.

Aristotle begins his political treatise with the very question that Romilly considers the central concern of political theory in the period after the Peloponnesian War. Is association between men by nature, and, if so, what

---

[41] Romilly, *Thucydides and Athenian Imperialism*, 357–58.

[42] Romilly, *Thucydides and Athenian Imperialism*, 358–59. Bradley concurs: "For a century or more before the *Politics* was written, the traditional Greek view had been called into question, and ideas had been opposed to it which strike us at once by their modern air" ("Aristotle's Conception of the State," 19).

[43] Grene, *Greek Political Theory*, 4. Cf. Cartledge, *The Greeks*, 3, 11, Chapter 3.

is the natural form of association? The answer to this question given at the very beginning of the *Politics* is notorious for the amount of attention it has received. Aristotle pronounces man a "political animal" and the polis the highest form of association and by nature.[44] To demonstrate the reasons for his claims, Aristotle proposes to consider the matter from the beginning and trace the transformation of human associations from their elementary stages to the polis.[45] His examination reveals that the first association of human beings is the union of man and woman that results from their natural urge to reproduce and thus gives rise to the family.[46] The very next association is simultaneously necessary and political, and is usually overlooked because it is out of place.[47] Aristotle argues that those who should rule by nature unite with those who should be ruled "διὰ τὴν σωτηρίαν," that is, for their safety, salvation, security, or preservation.[48] As this union follows in order that of man and woman, commentators usually interpret it as the union of master and slave.[49] There is good reason to think, however, that Aristotle means "ἄρχον" and "ἀρχόμενον" in the broader sense of the ruling and ruled elements, rather than in the limited sense of rule within the confines of the household. Although the association between the ruling and the ruled is followed by a discussion of slaves, Aristotle follows that with another list that includes the family, the village, and the city.[50] This repetition of the family – first mentioned as man, woman, and their offspring, and then as "family" – points to the likelihood that the union of ruling and ruled, which is mentioned between the former, is intended as a formal category, rather than a specific one. Such an interpretation is corroborated by Aristotle's insistence on the general principle of ruling and being ruled as essential for political habituation among equals, which thus includes not only the master-slave relationship, but also relationships of authority of all kinds.[51] It is also

[44] Aristotle, *Politica*, 1253a1–3, 1252b27–31 1252a1–7.

[45] Aristotle, *Politica*, 1252a24–26.

[46] Aristotle, *Politica*, 1252a26–30. Cf. 1252b12–15.

[47] Saunders, e.g., mentions this association, but limits his commentary to the union between man and woman (Aristotle, *Politics Books I and II*, 63–64).

[48] Aristotle, *Politica*, 1252a30–31.

[49] Bradley, for example, refers to "master" and "slave," but his analysis shows that he means these in the broader sense of "ruling" and "ruled" elements ("Aristotle's Conception of the State," 23).

[50] Aristotle, *Politica*, 1252b9–30. Thus, a schematic representation of his list of associations is as follows: (1) man, woman, offspring; (2) ruling, ruled; (3) family; (4) village; (5) polis. The similarity between (1) and (3) renders (2) problematic. The interpretation proposed here is supported by the fact that the terms in question (ἄρχον and ἀρχόμενον) are neuter.

[51] See, e.g., Aristotle, *Politica*, 1252a14–16, 1261a39–1262b6.

33

supported further by the fact that Aristotle characterizes the relationship of ruling and ruled as aimed at the σωτηρία of the two elements. However one interprets σωτηρία, it would have to include security in addition to the normal duties of slaves, such as the procurement of food and other essentials.[52]

The transition, in Aristotle's summary history of the development of human associations from the village to the city, is swift, and his statement that the city is aimed at the *good* life, rather than simply life, tends to draw attention away from the preceding statement, according to which the city is the culmination of human association because it is the height of self-sufficiency.[53] *Self-sufficiency* here refers to the many goods and services that a village is unable to provide, and these cannot but include security from external threats, which is a necessary prerequisite for the conditions that will permit individuals to seek the good life.[54] Self-sufficiency is also a reason why, for Aristotle, the whole is prior to the parts. Only gods and beasts can exist by themselves, outside the city. An individual human being cannot, because first and foremost he cannot be safe.[55] Emphasis on the ends does not imply a neglect of the means, and when Aristotle returns to this matter in Book VII of the *Politics*, he argues that peace is the end of war and leisure the end of work.[56] That despite his interest in the life of εὐδαιμονία, Aristotle never loses sight of the most basic demands of communal life is also manifest in what he has to say about the preservation of the polis.

Much like Thucydides, Aristotle recognizes that fear can work both for and against a group. On the one hand, he caricatures Socrates' argument

---

[52] The Liddell and Scott dictionary lists "safety," "security," and "preservation" among the primary meanings of the word, and gives *salus* as the Latin equivalent (*An Intermediate Greek–English Lexicon*, 789). According to Bradley, "Master and slave are united by the desire for security" ("Aristotle's Conception of the State," 23). Cf. Aristotle, *Politica*, 1253b24–25: "for it is impossible, without the essentials, both to live and to live well"; 1261b9: "Surely the good of each thing is that which preserves it." On the equivalent conception of *salus populi* in Hobbes, see Chapter 5 in this volume.

[53] Aristotle, *Politica*, 1252b27–1253a1.

[54] See, e.g., Aristotle, *Politica*, 1253b24–25, 1261b10–15, 1325a5–15. In the *Nicomachean Ethics*, Aristotle argues, "[n]ow all forms of community are like parts of the political community; for men journey together with a view to some particular advantage, and to provide something that they need for the purposes of life; and it is for the sake of advantage that the political community too seems both to have come together originally and to endure, for this is what legislators aim at, and they call just that which is to the common advantage" (1160a8–14).

[55] Aristotle, *Politica*, 1253a19–29.

[56] Aristotle, *Politica*, 1334a15–16.

in the *Republic* that the city be one, arguing instead that diversity and differentiation are necessary for self-sufficiency and survival.[57] On the other hand, such diversity may also be dangerous, as it may lead to the formation of factions around particular interests. Thus, in his inquiry into the causes of conflict and regime change in the *Politics*, Aristotle draws attention to the dangerous polarization that arises from demagoguery. There, he warns that "a common fear brings together even the worst of enemies."[58] This principle of negative association should be guarded against when it concerns the formation of domestic parties that harbor the possibility of civil war, but should be embraced by those in power when it can be used at a higher level, to unite otherwise antagonistic domestic groups in defense of the state from external threats. In one of his several criticisms of Plato, Aristotle takes issue with the suggestion in the *Laws* that the legislator look to the country and the people in legislating, and argues that it is advisable that the legislator also look at neighboring places.[59] The reason for this advice is that for Aristotle it is essential that a city inspire fear in its enemies, whether in defending itself or in attacking them.[60] There are other reasons to look outwards, however, and Aristotle is mindful of the fact that domestic benefits begin abroad. In a little-noticed passage from the *Politics* that anticipates the style of the reason of state writers, he advises,

Constitutions are preserved not only by keeping their destroyers at a distance, but also sometimes by keeping them near, because being afraid, [the people] will keep a better grip on the constitution. Thus, those who care for the constitution should manufacture fears and bring that which is far near, so that [the people] will guard the constitution like night watchmen, without relaxing.[61]

The inclusion of this advice in his list of recommendations for the preservation of the state shows a recognition, on Aristotle's part, that positive goals and shared identities will eventually require an element of negative association to

---

[57] Aristotle, *Politica*, 1261a10–b15; cf. 1261b10–15. On the issue of the coexistence of the constitutive elements of the city in Socrates' argument, see Ioannis D. Evrigenis, "The Psychology of Politics," 590–610, esp. 596.

[58] Aristotle, *Politica*, 1304b23–24.

[59] Aristotle, *Politica*, 1265a18–22.

[60] Aristotle, *Politica*, 1265a25–28. Aristotle uses "πολεμίοις" here; cf. Schmitt, *The Concept of the Political*, 28; Chapter 7 in this volume.

[61] Aristotle, *Politica*, 1308a24–30. I follow most translators in rendering πολιτεία as "constitution" in this passage, but it should be borne in mind that the Greek term also means "state," a translation that would also fit the passage well.

complement existing shared characteristics or even supersede them, in times of conflict, by means of a greater and more urgent threat.

METUS HOSTILIS

The political identities of states and their constituents faced new pressures as the relatively homogeneous Greek city-states gave way to larger and more diverse forms of political association. Conquered by Philip and Alexander the Great, and eventually by Rome, the world of Thucydides and Aristotle became part of a political structure in which the pressures of dissention and conflicting interests were acute and often overbearing. In this long and complex history of tumult, the fear of external enemies acquired a new significance, and came to be symbolized by Rome's antagonism with Carthage, the city to which Rome owed its life.[62]

Of the Roman historians, Polybius is the first to mention the fear of external enemies. In his *Histories*, he examines the relations between the various elements of Roman society and their corresponding relationships to the state's political institutions, and observes that

Such being the power that each part has of hampering the others or co-operating with them, their union is adequate to all emergencies, so that it is impossible to find a better system than this. For whenever the menace of some common danger from abroad compels them to act in concord and support each other, so great does the strength of the state become, that nothing which is requisite can be neglected, as all are zealously competing in devising the means of meeting the need of the hour, nor can any decision arrived at fail to be executed promptly, as all are co-operating both in public and in private to the accomplishment of the task they have set themselves.[63]

---

[62] In the *Aeneid*, Virgil ties the fates of the two cities together from the outset, when he singles out the eventual danger of Rome for Carthage as the reason for Aeneas's sufferings, and makes it quite clear that Carthage was necessary for Rome to come into being (I.520 ff.). Levene argues, "[f]or the Roman historians, no passion is more prominent than fear," adding, "[f]ear for them is perhaps the single most important influence on the behaviour of individuals and states" ("Pity, Fear and the Historical Audience," 128). In addition to Wood's "Sallust's Theorem," there are several studies of fear in Roman politics, such as Heinz's *Die Furcht als politisches Phänomen bei Tacitus*, Kneppe's *Metus temporum*, Bellen's *Metus Gallicus, metus Punicus*, and Bonamente's "Il metus Punicus." Although there are studies of courage in Greek thought, there is none of fear in politics. The closest thing to an exception is Romilly's *La crainte et l'angoisse dans le théâtre d'Eschyle*.

[63] Polybius, *The Histories*, VI.18.1–3.

Polybius is nevertheless aware of the danger inherent in such a union, and is quick to add that once the specter of the external threat has gone, the classes that compose the state "are corrupted by flattery and idleness and wax insolent and overbearing."[64] It is then that the system of checks and balances of the Roman constitution comes in handy, as it preserves domestic tranquility.

Polybius's faith in the institutional ability of the Roman system of government to check the discord that follows the elimination of an external threat was not shared by all; other historians who seem to have taken their cue from Posidonius are much more skeptical. As one might expect, there is broad agreement that the menacing presence of Carthage had certain salutary effects upon Roman unity; these effects became all the more evident once that threat and its consequent fear were eliminated. Despite the fact that the Numidians under Masinissa had managed to defeat the Carthaginians in 150 BC, "the specter of Hannibal still haunted Rome": "Nurses told fractious children that Hannibal was coming to fetch them; politicians conjured up the same dread name to throw the Senate into a thoroughly un-Roman panic."[65] The most famous of the latter was Marcus Porcius Cato, a veteran of the Second Punic War, immortalized for his conviction that Carthage must be destroyed.[66] As we shall see, however, his famous dictum was only part of the story.

The stoic philosopher and historian Posidonius ($c.135$–$c.51$ BC) was one of the most important intellectual figures of his time. Originally from Apamea, he moved to Rhodes, of which he became a citizen and founded a school that became "the leading center of Stoicism, and a general mecca not only for intellectuals, but for the great and powerful of the Roman world such as Pompey and Cicero."[67] Posidonius studied an "astonishing" range of subjects, but no complete work of his survives. His influence is nevertheless known to us through the numerous references that subsequent writers make to his works.[68] The similarity of various passages in histories of Rome that

---

[64] Polybius, *The Histories*, VI.18.5.

[65] Cary & Scullard, *A History of Rome*, 148.

[66] The popular version "Carthago delenda est" does not come from any contemporary source but is a Latin rendition of the Greek account of Diodorus (34/35, 33). Willy Theiler cites the research of Silvia Thülermann (*Gymnasium* 81 [1974], 465–75), who shows that the Latin version has its origin in the 1821 work of F. Fiedler, who in turn found it in Florus, I, 31, 4 (Posidonius, *Die Fragmente II: Erläuterungen*, 109). Cf. Bellen, *Metus Gallicus, metus Punicus*, 3–4.

[67] Kidd, "Posidonius," 1231.

[68] Kidd, "Posidonius," 1231–32.

tell the story of Cato's views on Carthage, coupled with the fact that many of these writers acknowledge a debt to Posidonius, raises the likelihood that his *History* was a common source of the story.[69]

In his *Library of History*, Diodorus of Sicily recounts the controversy between the consul Nasica and Cato regarding Carthage. There, he explains that after the war with Hannibal, Cato "made it his practice to remark on every occasion, when stating his opinion in the senate, 'Would that Carthage did not exist,' and he kept repeating that," regardless of the subject matter of the discussion.[70] On the other hand, Diodorus adds, Nasica "always expressed the contrary wish, 'May Carthage exist for all time.'"[71] Diodorus claims that both points of view seemed worthy of consideration, but Nasica's was seen as better because Rome should compare herself only to the greatest, but more importantly,

so long as Carthage survived, the fear that she generated compelled the Romans to live together in harmony and to rule their subjects equitably and with credit to themselves – much the best means to maintain and extend an empire; but once the rival city was destroyed, it was only too evident that there would be civil war at home, and that hatred for the governing power would spring up among all the allies because of the rapacity and lawlessness to which the Roman magistrates

---

[69] According to Kidd, Posidonius's *History*

> was a major work in its own right of 52 books covering the period from 146 BC probably to the mid-80s and possibly unfinished.... It was packed with formidable detail of facts and events, both major and minor, global and local, and of social and environmental phenomena. But the unifying factor of the huge canvas, factually drawn and sharply critical of credulous legend was [...] a moralist's view of historical explanation, where events are caused by mind and character in the relationship between ruler and ruled, and by tribal and racial character in social movement and motives ("Posidonius," 1232).

> There are two general approaches to the attribution of fragments to Posidonius. The first, exemplified in Posidonius, *I. The Fragments*, ed. Ludwig Edelstein & Ian Gray Kidd, attributes to Posidonius only those fragments "attested by ancient writers." Thus, according to this principle, and despite his remarks in the *Oxford Classical Dictionary* regarding Posidonius's *History*, Kidd, the surviving editor, chose to adhere to Edelstein's wishes and to leave out passages like that from Diodorus below. This approach, however, although cautious is not universally accepted, as both Felix Jacoby (*Die Fragmente der griechischen Historiker*) and Willy Theiler (*Poseidonios: Die Fragmente I: Texte*), who follows Reinhardt, find that there is sufficient justification for including the passages listed here. See Theiler's explanation of his general method (xi), as well as his reasons for including the passage from Diodorus (145–46). Cf. Earl, *The Political Thought of Sallust*, 48–49; McGushin, C. *Sallustius Crispus, Bellum Catilinae, A Commentary*, 88.

[70] Diodorus of Sicily, *Library of History*, XXXIV/XXXV.33.3.

[71] Diodorus of Sicily, *Library of History*, XXXIV/XXXV.33.4.

would subject them. All this did indeed happen to Rome after the destruction of Carthage [. . .].[72]

Combining, as it did, the most pressing domestic with the greatest foreign policy questions, the dilemma encapsulated by the exchange between the two Senators was elevated by Sallust to a matter of the utmost importance in his own influential histories.

Sallust's account of the war with Catiline begins in a manner highly reminiscent of Thucydides. He tells his readers that his cherished purpose was to write "a history of the Roman people, selecting such portions as seemed [. . .] worthy of record"; and that he "was confirmed in this resolution by the fact that [his] mind was free from hope, and fear, and partisanship."[73] As Scanlon notes, "Sallust's pervasive imitation of Thucydides in themes, style and passages in the *Bellum Catilinae* suggests that the imitation cannot be construed as incidental."[74] Several commentators, from Velleius Paterculus and Quintilian to the present have often remarked on the similarity between Sallust and Thucydides.[75] For the present purposes, three areas of affinity are worth noting. First, like Thucydides, Sallust is interested in human nature and the way in which the actions that he records stem from specific human traits. He too pays particular attention to man's *libido dominandi*. Although in his own "archaeology," at the beginning of *The War with Catiline*, Sallust refers to a time when "men's lives were still free from covetousness," the rest of his account leaves one with the impression that the lust for power is a permanent characteristic of human nature.[76] In what could very well be a reference to Thucydides' history, the opening lines of *The War with Catiline* tell us that that initial, happy time was ended by the exploits of Cyrus in Greece and the negative association of the Athenians and the Lacedaemonians. Second, both historians exhibit a significant interest in *stasis*. Although Thucydides devotes only a small part of his history to *stasis* explicitly, the description of the events at Corcyra and eventually throughout Greece is a crucial part of his account.[77] For Sallust, conflict within Rome and its

---

[72] Diodorus of Sicily, *Library of History*, XXXIV/XXXV.33.5–6.
[73] Sallust, *The War with Catiline*, IV.2–3. Cf. Thucydides, *The Peloponnesian War*, I.1, I.21–22.
[74] Scanlon, *The Influence of Thucydides on Sallust*, 50.
[75] See Velleius Paterculus, *Compendium of Roman History*, II.36.2; Quintilian, *Institutio oratoria*, X.101–102; Scanlon, *The Influence of Thucydides on Sallust*, 11–12.
[76] Sallust, *The War with Catiline*, II.1. Cf. *The War with Jugurtha*, VI.3; *The War with Catiline*, II.1–4, V.6; *The Histories*, I.8 (volume I, pp. 24, 74–76 of the McGushin edition); Thucydides, *The Peloponnesian War*, I.76, III.82–84, V.105.
[77] According to Price, "[t]he analysis of *stasis* contains Thucydides' own fullest, most concentrated and profoundest reflections on historical truths" (*Thucydides and Internal War*, 11), and

39

dominions is the primary subject matter.[78] Third, and most important, even though their respective treatments differ, both Thucydides and Sallust identify negative association as a crucial dynamic in the formation of political associations.

Both historians consider the effects of war and foreign policy on the internal affairs of states, yet Thucydides emphasizes the external, whereas Sallust focuses on the internal. After all, the former recounts the history of a war involving several states, without adopting the point of view of any one, whereas the latter writes a "history of the Roman people."[79] This difference in perspective in turn explains the particular role that negative association plays in each account. For Thucydides, the fear of enemies is crucial mainly in the formation of alliances among states. In Sallust's history, *metus hostilis* becomes the primary explanation for the emergence of factions and civil strife in Rome. Both accounts, however, demonstrate the importance of negative association by means of the same technique: they focus primarily on the void left by the removal of the external threat and from there project forward to explain the onset of conflict among previously allied parties. This is Thucydides' explanation for the deterioration of cooperation among Greek city-states after the defeat of the Persians, and the same is true of Sallust with respect to the utility of Carthage for Rome: in all three of his major histories, the defeat of Carthage marks the commencement of the deterioration of Rome. In *The War with Catiline*, Sallust argues, "when Carthage, the rival of Rome's sway, had perished root and branch, and all the seas and lands were open, then Fortune began to grow cruel and to bring confusion into all our affairs."[80] In a similar vein, in his history of the war with Jugurtha, Sallust writes:

before the destruction of Carthage the people and senate of Rome together governed the republic peacefully and with moderation. There was no strife among the citizens either for glory or for power; fear of the enemy preserved the good morals of the

the account of *stasis* at III.81–82 is the model for the entire history of the Peloponnesian War (see, e.g., *Thucydides and Internal War*, 11–22; 73–78). Cf. Scanlon, *The Influence of Thucydides on Sallust*, 99–102, 110–11.

[78] Mindful of the differences resulting from the diverse settings, Scanlon draws attention to the fact that both accounts of civil strife cite greed and ambition as the chief causes (*The Influence of Thucydides on Sallust*, 99–102).

[79] Sallust, *The War with Catiline*, IV.2.

[80] Sallust, *The War with Catiline*, X.1–2. Cf. *The Histories*, I.10, 12. McGushin argues, "[s]ince the Cato-Nasica debate was famous and the theory of *metus hostilis* a rhetorical commonplace it seems feasible to assume that this type of material was probably S's source" (*C. Sallustius Crispus, Bellum Catilinae, A Commentary*, 88).

state. But when the minds of the people were relieved of that dread, wantonness and arrogance naturally arose, vices which are fostered by prosperity. Thus the peace for which they had longed in time of adversity proved to be more cruel and bitter than adversity itself. For the nobles began to abuse their position and the people their liberty, and every man for himself robbed, pillaged, and plundered. Thus, the community was split into two parties, and between these the state was torn to pieces.[81]

As several commentators point out, the relationship between *metus hostilis* and domestic harmony is clearly crucial for Sallust.[82] In his commentary on Sallust's *Histories*, McGushin argues that it is possible to attribute to Sallust "a deep scepticism concerning the nature of man," although it is also possible to conclude that he "could simply be pointing to an innate perversity in man which renders him always dissatisfied with the fruits of the struggles for liberty and national glory."[83] For Earl, the explanation is more concrete and lies at the intersection of human nature and necessity. Recall that Sallust writes of an early period in human history in which men were free of *libido dominandi*. Earl argues that the transition from that innocent time to a period characterized by constant struggles for power occurs at the point at which *metus hostilis* ceases to be the first priority. Roman history affords many examples of this kind of transition, but it is the destruction of Carthage that figures most prominently among these, and this is perhaps the reason why Sallust treats it as symbolic of the beginning of Rome's decay. As Earl notes, after the *concordia* of the Roman Republic, "came the destruction of Carthage, removal of the *metus hostilis*, *otium* and a superfluity of good

---

[81] Sallust, *The War with Jugurtha*, XLI.2–5. Sallust does not attribute this argument to Nasica in any of his histories, but according to Paul, "[t]he choice of this event was perhaps influenced by the tradition concerning the debate between Cato Censorius and Scipio Nasica" (*A Historical Commentary on Sallust's Bellum Jugurthinum*, 124). Cf. Earl, *The Political Thought of Sallust*, 13, 47–48.

[82] Wood, "Sallust's Theorem." 178. Cf. Earl, *The Political Thought of Sallust*, 13; Scanlon, *The Influence of Thucydides on Sallust*, 33, 122; Paul, *A Historical Commentary on Sallust's Bellum Jugurthinum*, 124–25; Bellen, *Metus Gallicus, metus Punicus*, 4–5; among others.

[83] Sallust, *The Histories* I, 75. McGushin compares the various formulations of *metus hostilis* in Sallust and finds that the historian's choice to concentrate on the destruction of Carthage marks his rejection of a long tradition in Roman historiography that attributed Rome's degeneration to "processes already at work." McGushin finds Sallust's view "over-simplified" and remarks that Sallust's "idealized view [. . .] made him overlook other factors of a very complex situation – factions among the nobility, increase in public and private wealth and the like are ignored" (commentary on Sallust, *The Histories* I.9–10, volume I, page 79 of the McGushin edition), which seems unduly strong given that Sallust hints at these in *The War with Jugurtha*, XLI.

things, with the result that *lubido* seized men's minds."[84] This vital, symbolic power, then, explains why Sallust, who was well aware of the many forces that contributed to the decline of Rome, chose to put such weight on the role of *metus hostilis*. This is the reason why Sallust's *metus hostilis* explanation strikes some commentators as too simplistic, but also the reason why "subsequent writers adopted Sallust's choice of 146 as an epochal year in Roman history."[85]

Two examples of such writers are Velleius Paterculus and Plutarch. The former, in his *History of Rome*, repeats the observation attributed to Posidonius and formulated by Sallust:

> For, when Rome was freed of the fear of Carthage, and her rival in empire was out of her way, the path of virtue was abandoned for that of corruption, not gradually, but in headlong course. The older discipline was discarded to give place to the new. The state passed from vigilance to slumber, from the pursuit of arms to the pursuit of pleasure, from activity to idleness.[86]

Plutarch brings up the fear of enemies in his life of Marcus Cato, wherein he recreates the antagonism between Cato and Nasica. According to Plutarch's account, Cato's insistence on his view that Carthage should be destroyed was "savage." Commenting on Nasica's opposition, Plutarch remarks,

> He saw, probably, that the Roman people, in its wantonness, was already guilty of many excesses, and in the pride of its prosperity spurned the control of the Senate, and forcibly dragged the whole state with it, whithersoever its mad desires inclined it. He wished, therefore, that the fear of Carthage should abide, to curb the boldness of the multitude like a bridle, believing her not strong enough to conquer Rome, nor yet weak enough to be despised.[87]

Plutarch adds, however, that the disagreement between Cato and Nasica was not about whether Rome was in trouble and needed a cure for its political ills, but rather about whether the fear of Carthage was the right way to go about it. Plutarch ascribes to Cato the view that it would be better for Rome to do away with the threat of Carthage, and then turn to its domestic problems, to deal with them in peace.[88]

---

[84] Earl, *The Political Thought of Sallust*, 15.

[85] McGushin, Commentary, *The Histories*: I, 79. For an assessment of the *metus hostilis* explanation see Cary & Scullard, *A History of Rome*, 602, note 12. On the adequacy of Sallust's *metus hostilis* explanation, see Earl, *The Political Thought of Sallust*, 41–50; Paul, *A Historical Commentary on Sallust's Bellum Jugurthinum*, 124–25.

[86] Velleius Paterculus, *Compendium of Roman History*, II.I.1–2.

[87] Plutarch, *Lives* II, XXVII.2.

[88] Plutarch, *Lives* II, XXVII.3. Cf. "How to Profit by One's Enemies," 88a.

NEGATIVE ASSOCIATION

Thucydides has been praised by generations of commentators for his ability to present a detached account of the events he is chronicling, and yet allow for the passions of the speakers to shine through. Through this combination, the mechanisms that unite to produce negative association are illuminated in his account, and the reader is left to draw his own conclusions about the desirability and merits of the resulting alliances.[89] Aristotle departs from Thucydides in that he does not hesitate to indicate his approval of negative association when he encounters it, but his explicit references to this aspect of political organization are few and far between. What is interesting in his account of it is what he omits. The magnitude and significance of the rivalry between Rome and Carthage changed the status of negative association, and forced historians of Rome to bring it to the fore and consider its implications openly. Sallust is exemplary of this tradition not only because of the primacy that he accords to negative association, but also because he is the first to color his history with a tone of regret. That negative association would be necessary in the first place is bad enough. What happens in its absence, however, is even worse.

Sallust's lament rendered his history particularly appealing to Saint Augustine, for whom Rome's depravity predated its conversion to Christianity and sack by the Visigoths. Augustine put Sallust's account of *metus hostilis* to use in his argument against the pagans, and thereby ensured not only the survival of some parts of Sallust's work that would have been otherwise lost, but also the perpetuation of this Sallustian lesson well into Christian times.[90] Augustine goes through a number of instances in Sallust's *Histories*, wherein the historian lists fear of an external enemy as the preserver of order in the state.[91] These include the period between the Second and Third Punic Wars, during which the cause of the Roman morality was "not the love of justice, but the fear that peace was unreliable while Carthage still stood."[92]

---

[89] See Ioannis D. Evrigenis, "Hobbes's Thucydides."

[90] Fragments I.10 and I.13 (see Sallust, *The Histories*, I: 24–5) of Sallust's *Histories* survive only in Saint Augustine's *Concerning the City of God against the Pagans*, II.xviii.

[91] Saint Augustine, *Concerning the City of God against the Pagans*, II.xviii.

[92] Saint Augustine, *Concerning the City of God against the Pagans*, II.xviii. Augustine adds, "and that was why Nasica resisted the annihilation of Carthage, so that the wickedness should be restrained by fear, immorality checked, and the high standard of conduct preserved"; cf. *ibid.*, II.xix. As Wood notes, any assessment of the role of Sallust's history in Augustine's *City of God* must not lose sight of how convenient the concept of *metus hostilis* is for Augustine's own thesis regarding the depravity of Rome ("Sallust's Theorem," 179).

Augustine cites the rest of the passage from Sallust, according to which it was the wars of Tarquin and the Second Punic War that served as intervals in the strife between the patricians and the people, although as Wood notes, Augustine extends Sallust's argument even further, since he disagrees with the "view that the half century between the Second and Third Punic Wars was a golden age of harmony and unity."[93]

The foregoing survey shows that picking any one moment as the point of origin of the idea of negative association in the history of political thought is bound to prove problematic. In opting for Sallust's histories as paradigmatic, Wood is careful to acknowledge that the origins of the idea of *metus hostilis* probably lie in Thucydides, and yet one can locate them just as easily in Herodotus's history, for example.[94] The difficulty involved in choosing a starting point has two significant consequences. On the one hand, it shows that negative association for fear of enemies is a universal phenomenon with no shortage of examples. On the other hand, however, it gives added significance to the choice of a symbolic moment. Here, too, one could pick from a series of excellent candidates, and yet each choice carries certain limiting consequences of its own for the full appreciation of negative association. Thus, given the central role of the Roman historians for centuries of subsequent historiography and political philosophy, Wood's choice of Sallust is justified. As Wood shows, in addition to his indirect influence through Saint Augustine, Sallust is likely to have been on the reading list of an educated individual, and was read and cited by such theorists as Aquinas, Marsilius of Padua, More, Machiavelli, Bodin, Hobbes, and Locke.[95] Sallust's particular influence, coupled with the broader significance of Roman history in the education of subsequent political thinkers, thus render Wood's choice a good one. Nevertheless, just as one can trace Sallust's influence on Saint Augustine and Bodin, one can easily document Thucydides' influence on Sallust.[96] As noted above, such a corrective is important for at least two reasons that go beyond lineage.

---

[93] Wood, "Sallust's Theorem," 179. See Saint Augustine, *Concerning the City of God against the Pagans*, V.xii. It is convenient for Augustine's argument that these crucial events all took place before the coming of Christ, a fact of which he is keenly aware and which enables him to ask his adversaries why it was that during that time their gods failed to intervene and stop the decay of Rome (Saint Augustine, *Concerning the City of God against the Pagans*, II.xviii).

[94] Wood, "Sallust's Theorem," 188. See, e.g., Herodotus, *Historiae*, I.4.13–15, VIII.144.

[95] See Wood, "Sallust's Theorem," 174, note 1. According to Earl, "Sallust's choice of the destruction of Carthage as the turning-point of Roman history set a fashion" (*The Political Thought of Sallust*, 47).

[96] See Scanlon, *The Influence of Thucydides on Sallust*. Cf. Wood, "Sallust's Theorem," 176.

First, a fuller history of negative association will lead to a better understanding of it, by providing evidence of the ways in which particular instances are similar to or different from one another. Where the period examined above is concerned, whether dealing with ἔξωθεν φόβος or *metus hostilis*, instances of negative association are usually presented in epigrammatic fashion, with little detail. Moreover, identification of negative association at work usually takes place in hindsight, and is presented in that order. That is, both Thucydides and Sallust conclude that negative association was at work by comparing a subsequent state of affairs with what preceded it and identifying the addition or removal of a previously important actor as the crucial variable that accounts for the change. It is this procedure that has led commentators of Sallust, in particular, to characterize his *metus hostilis* explanation as overly simplistic, since in his histories emphasis on a dominant enemy tends to overshadow other socioeconomic factors at work.[97]

Second, a greater range of examples attests to the wider applicability of negative association. The description of a phenomenon in similar terms by Thucydides, Sallust, Bodin, Hobbes, and Schmitt points to the likelihood that the phenomenon in question is not parochial or particular to a certain period. In the case of *metus hostilis*, evidence of universality is especially important, because it combats the impression given by the existing literature that it is a distinctly modern phenomenon. Students of reason of state, in particular, have argued that devices such as the manipulation of the fear of enemies are outside the scope of ancient political philosophy, which is primarily concerned with virtue.[98] As the passages examined above show, however, there is a significant amount of attention devoted by ancient political philosophers to the study of mechanisms that may be mere prerequisites for the pursuit of virtue, but are nonetheless essential to a full account of a politics concerned with virtue.

Indeed, the frequency with which one encounters references to negative association in pre-Sallustian thought should come as no surprise, given the Greeks' preoccupation with group formation by juxtaposition to outsiders. In Plato's *Statesman*, a dialogue that is an exercise in division and dichotomy, Socrates asks the Stranger to explain why their procedure has failed them at a particular juncture. The Stranger's response sums

---

[97] See, e.g., Earl, *The Political Thought of Sallust*, 46–51.

[98] See, e.g., Friedrich, who considers the Athenians' claim that "might makes right" an anomaly (*Constitutional Reason of State*, 15–16). While acknowledging its premodern origins, Wood nevertheless considers the theory of *metus hostilis* a founding principle of modern political thought ("Sallust's Theorem," 175–76, 188).

up the pervasiveness of negative association in the formation of political identity:

It was very much as if, in undertaking to divide the human race into two parts, one should make the division as most people in this country do; they separate the Hellenic race from all the rest as one, and to all the other races, which are countless in number and have no relation in blood or language to one another, they give the single name "barbarian"; then, because of this single name, they think it is a single species.[99]

The uneasy union of Greek city-states in the face of the common Persian enemy that Herodotus and Thucydides describe in their histories is but the most famous example of a puzzling aspect of Greek political life. If city-states were the primary forms of political association, then what is the meaning of the common appellation *Hellene*? As Finley points out, this question pressed itself with particular force upon the historians and political theorists of the nineteenth and twentieth centuries, who sought to learn from the past and apply those lessons to their own experience in nation formation. Finley is probably correct that in their zeal to reap such benefits, nineteenth and twentieth-century historians attributed to the Greeks a goal – national unity – that they most likely did not have.[100] Nevertheless, one cannot help but be struck by the fact that although the city-state remained the dominant element of one's political identity, one's identification as a Hellene extended far beyond linguistic and religious affinities, and came with its own set of political consequences.[101] This dual political identity is a consequence of the simple fact that an individual has several group affiliations, each of which plays a more or less important role depending on the circumstances.[102]

The earliest accounts of negative association illustrate this political economy of fear through examples of the ways in which vital interests become threatened and actors or groups feel the need to rearrange their priorities in response. Later accounts, such as Sallust's, mark a shift from illustration by example to the extraction of a general principle that can be presented in the form of a succinct law of politics. As such, these accounts pave the way for the inclusion of negative association among the principles of statecraft that are offered in the more systematic theories of Machiavelli and Hobbes. They are also striking for calling things as they see them, a quality all the

---

[99] Plato, *Statesman*, 262c10–d7. Cf. Herodotus, *Historiae*, I.4.13–15; Hall, *Inventing the Barbarian*, 1–2, 161.

[100] Finley, *The Use and Abuse of History*, 121–22. Cf. Cartledge, *The Greeks*, 54.

[101] See, e.g., Thucydides, *The Peloponnesian War*, I.82.

[102] Finley, *The Use and Abuse of History*, 127.

more conspicuous in a period allegedly concerned exclusively with loftier thoughts.[103] Herodotus's, Thucydides', and Sallust's accounts are riddled with instances in which individuals and delegations show no reluctance in confessing that fear for their safety and preservation is their chief motivation. Their teachings would form the point of departure for Machiavelli, the first writer to address matters of government in some 1200 years.[104]

---

[103] See Xenophon, *Oeconomicus*, I.15.
[104] Bodin, *Method*, 153.

3

ENEMIES AT THE GATES: MACHIAVELLI'S
RETURN TO THE BEGINNINGS OF CITIES

For the cause of the disunion of republics is usually idleness and peace; the cause of union is fear and war.

— Niccolò Machiavelli[1]

There is a striking dissonance between the promise of the title of Machiavelli's *Discourses on Livy* and the one that he makes at the start of the preface to Book I. Even though the work seems to be a commentary on an ancient historian, Machiavelli promises "to take a path as yet untrodden by anyone".[2] The explanation lies in the lamentable way in which his contemporaries admire things ancient but fail to imitate them. This is particularly true in matters of government, where "neither prince nor republic may be found with recourse to the examples of the ancients."[3] It is, of course, no lack of ancient thoughts on politics that is to blame for this condition, but rather the mistaken impression that they can offer only diversion and not practical advice, as though human nature had somehow changed. As it turns out, this fairly cryptic diagnosis foreshadows one of the central problems in the *Discourses*, the loss of identity. With ancient tools in hand, the reader of the *Discourses* will follow Machiavelli's path towards its retrieval.

Machiavelli's new path requires a return to first principles, albeit an unconventional one. To demonstrate the misuse of things ancient and the benefits of a periodic return of this kind, Machiavelli proposes to reexamine the foundation of Rome. Much of the ground that he will cover will thus seem familiar, but this familiarity will prove deceptive in large measure, as Machiavelli will often draw quite unexpected conclusions from it. On occasion, an

---

[1] *Discourses*, II.25 § 1.
[2] Machiavelli, *Discourses*, I. Pref. § 1.
[3] Machiavelli, *Discourses*, I. Pref. § 2.

ancient maxim or episode will be used in precisely the way one would expect it to be. At other times, however, the conclusion that Machiavelli will draw departs from the tradition and comes as a complete surprise. The reason for this complex and irregular method lies in Machiavelli's fundamental concurrence with the Hippocratic warning against idleness.[4] Among the many ills that spring from idleness is complacency, which leads men to rely on established rules rather than exhibit resourcefulness in response to necessity. At best, the state will thus wither away, unable to meet the challenges of the times. At worst, its decay will be hastened by the active involvement of individuals who are otherwise insufficiently occupied. Ultimately, Machiavelli's willingness to take his own advice and go where the evidence takes him results in the fulfillment of his promise to innovate by means of ancient things. In psychological terms, the alertness that results from the reexamination of seemingly familiar territory and the questioning of accepted views approximates the feelings that individuals experience during the founding of states. Machiavelli identifies the state of mind at the time of the founding as the one to which it is necessary to return every so often. More than an act of reanimation of the state, the return to its beginnings serves to remind its constituents who they are and why they owe it their allegiance, by reminding them who they are not.

Where his predecessors noted with regret the moments during which the identity of the state was in crisis, Machiavelli sought to provide a solution. That solution is a daring one, as it involves the judicious combination of two mechanisms that by themselves are highly combustible, tumult and war. Although each of these can bring the state to its knees, Machiavelli proposes that if pitted against each other they can pull it out of a crisis and prolong its life. Machiavelli's pessimistic view of human nature is by no means the first of its kind, but his is the first political theory that does not shy away from that pessimism, and instead confronts it openly and attempts to harness it in some constructive way. Hence, he argues, "prudence consists in knowing how to recognize the qualities of inconveniences, and in picking the less bad as good."[5] Machiavelli's grounding of politics in psychology forced a reconfiguration of the terms in which political debates could be conducted. Admirers and detractors alike realized quickly that it was impossible to circumvent him. Whether to agree or disagree with him, one simply had to confront him. The magnitude of his innovation is most apparent in

---

[4] See, e.g., Machiavelli, *Discourses*, I.1 § 4, I.2 § 1, I.25 § 1, I.37 § 1, III.1, III.16 § 2, III.21 § 2, III.30 § 1.
[5] Machiavelli, *The Prince* XXI: 91; cf. *Discourses*, I.38 § 2.

the degree to which even his most vehement critics are forced to agree with him on the unlikeliest of points.

HUMAN NATURE

Machiavelli's remarks on human nature are scattered throughout his writings. This dispersal, however, is not tantamount to inconsistency. From the multiplicity of seemingly unconnected comments, one can glean a basic theory of human psychology and motivation that is coherent, if not systematic.[6] At times, he offers general maxims that seem to apply to all men, regardless of where and when they live, and yet at other times he seems to distinguish between different types of men.[7] A distinction of the latter

---

[6] Cf. Germino, "Machiavelli's Thoughts on the Psyche and Society," 59, 74; Hirschman, *The Passions and the Interests*, 13.

[7] Arguments against a theory of a single human nature in Machiavelli's thought usually center on passages that draw explicit distinctions between categories of human beings. Among these, one of the most famous, and one that pervades Machiavelli's political theory, is that between the *grandi* and the people. In *The Prince*, Machiavelli argues, "[f]or in every city these two diverse humors are found, which arises from this: that the people desire neither to be commanded nor oppressed by the great, and the great desire to command and oppress the people" (IX: 39). This distinction, however, is one that arises from circumstances, as Machiavelli explains to Lorenzo in *The Prince* (Ded. Let.: 4). There is no reason to think that a member of either group displays these qualities because of innate characteristics. Machiavelli returns to this issue and addresses it explicitly, in *Discourses*, I.58 § 3: "The variation in their proceeding arises not from a diverse nature – because it is in one mode in all, and if there is advantage of good, it is in the people – but from having more or less respect for the laws within which both live." See also *Discourses*, I.4 § 1, where Machiavelli discusses the need for modes in every city "with which the people can vent its ambition." Cf. *ibid.*, I.5; *Florentine Histories* II.12, III.1.

In fact, in the Preface to Book I of the *Discourses*, Machiavelli writes, "as if heaven, sun, elements, men had varied in motion, order, and power from what they were in antiquity". Cf. *Discourses*, I.12 § 5; I.37; I.46; II. Pref.; III.43. According to Acton, Machiavelli "represents more than the spirit of his country and age" (Introduction to *Il Principe*, ed. L. A. Burd, xix). Coleman argues, "there is no historicism here. We can reduce these species-specific characteristics which demonstrate human nature to the following: men are by nature primarily self-interested, and what they take to be their interest is material wealth and glory (reputation, the esteem of others). All their actions are aimed at self-betterment *as they perceive it*. They are inclined by their nature to live in societies such that they are fearful of threats to perceived self-interest" ("Machiavelli's *Via Moderna*", 51). Mansfield notes that Machiavelli "does not confine his view to his own time, nor does he respect the conventional opinions of that time; and he frequently speaks of *virtù* transhistorically, as pertaining to the nature of man" (*Machiavelli's Virtue*, 7). Cf. Strauss, *Thoughts on Machiavelli*, 11, 14. For evidence to support these claims see *Discourses*, I.39: "Whoever considers present and ancient things easily knows that in all cities and in all peoples there are the same desires and the same humors, and there always have been. So it is an easy thing for

kind perhaps explains why he proceeds in the way that he does. He argues that men have "three kinds of brains: one that understands by itself, another that discerns what others understand, the third that understands neither by itself nor through others."[8] On the face of it, this observation means that brains of the third type cannot be helped, that those of the first kind do not need any help, and that works like Machiavelli's are therefore intended for those in the middle. There are good reasons, however, to care about the first and third types as well. Where the former are concerned, confirmation of one's correct understanding never hurts, and agreement with brains of this sort brings with it glory. If the latter understand neither by themselves nor through others what one would want them to understand, then it is necessary to do something about their misunderstanding; it cannot be ignored and may well have to be checked somehow.

Machiavelli offers no equivalent distinction between human beings when it comes to the emotions and their role in determining behavior, however. Here, his pronouncements are universal. In the infamous chapter on "Cruelty and Mercy, and Whether It Is Better to Be Loved than Feared, or the Contrary," Machiavelli considers men "ungrateful, fickle, pretenders and dissemblers, evaders of danger, eager for gain." "While you do them good," he argues, "they are yours, offering you their blood, property, lives, and children, [. . .] when the need for them is far away; but, when it is close to you, they revolt."[9] A man-turned-pig in Machiavelli's unfinished poem the *Golden Ass* compares his erstwhile and newfound states and realizes that

Only man is born stripped of any kind of defense: he has neither leather-hide, nor quills, nor feathers, wool, silk, nor shell that would serve to shield him.

whoever examines past things diligently to foresee future things in every republic and to take the remedies for them that were used by the ancients, or, if they do not find any that were used, to think up new ones through the similarity of accidents." See also *The Prince*, Ep. Ded.: "I have found nothing in my belongings that I care so much for and esteem so greatly as the knowledge of the actions of great men, learned by me from long experience with modern things and a continuous reading of ancient ones"; *Mandragola*, Prologue: "You see the scene / which is now shown to you: / this is your Florence; / another time it will be Rome or Pisa: / a thing to break your jaws with laughter." In the *Discourses*, Machiavelli maintains "That Men Who Are Born in One Province Observe Almost the Same Nature for All Times" (*Discourses*, III 43). Cf. Gentillet, *Anti-Machiavel*, esp. 29–32, Figgis, *Political Thought from Gerson to Grotius*, 96; Wood, "Machiavelli's Humanism of Action," 45; Gilbert, *Machiavelli and Guicciardini*, 170; Skinner, *Machiavelli*, 42; Parel, *The Machiavellian Cosmos*, 105–06; Mansfield, *Machiavelli's New Modes and Orders*, 428–31; Spackman, "Machiavelli and Maxims," 137–44; Nederman, "Machiavelli and Moral Character," especially p. 356–57; Hörnqvist, *Machiavelli and Empire*, 265–66, 274 and n. 24.
[8] Machiavelli, *The Prince*, XII: 92.
[9] Machiavelli, *The Prince*, XVII: 66.

In crying he enters life, and so feeble and so plaintive are his first sounds that it causes nothing but pity to behold. If one examines the length of his life, it is certainly quite brief, compared to that enjoyed by a deer, a crow, or even a goose.... You have at once ambition, luxury, tears, and avarice, the true itch of this existence that causes you so much distress. There is no animal whose life is so fragile, who is so possessed of such a great desire to live, who is subject to more fears and more rage.

A pig does not torment another pig, a deer leaves other deer in peace: there are only men who massacre men, who crucify and strip him bare.

Now consider if you could wish that I become human once more.[10]

These two examples are unusual in that they summarize views that are normally scattered. They are quite typical, however, in the views they contain. Alongside his occasional remarks – judiciously repeated at important junctures throughout his writings – they emerge as fragments of a coherent view of men and their nature, a suspicion confirmed by Machiavelli's persistence that men are always and everywhere fundamentally the same, so that a good observer and careful student of history may draw valuable lessons from the actions of men past and present, for the future.

---

[10] Quoted in Delumeau, *Sin and Fear*, 142. See also the characters' comments on human nature, and especially the songs, at the beginning, and after each act, as well as the Prologue, in Machiavelli's *Mandragola*. Machiavelli's pessimism may strike one as excessive, and the way in which it is presented may appear novel by virtue of its bluntness, but in this respect too the shock is deceptive. Delumeau argues that Machiavelli is following a "pessimistic meditation that had already appeared, though in a fragmentary and attenuated state, in earlier humanist writings," and Skinner shows that *The Prince* exhibits key characteristics of humanist writings in general and of the mirror-for-princes genre in particular, even if Machiavelli departs from these in many ways and criticizes them (Delumeau, *Sin and Fear*, 142; Skinner, *The Foundations of Modern Political Thought*, I: 128–29). Cf. Strauss, *Thoughts on Machiavelli*, 10. This gloomy view of human nature has led Isaiah Berlin to pronounce Machiavelli's psychology "excessively primitive," because it refuses altruism its due, and ignores exceptions for the sake of the rule. Berlin attributes Machiavelli's fame more to the shocking nature of his writings than to the depth of his insight into human nature. In an extraordinary passage, he claims, "[Machiavelli] has no historical sense and little sense of economics. He has no inkling of the technological progress which is about to transform political and social life, and in particular the art of war. He does not understand how either individuals, communities or cultures develop and transform themselves" (*Against the Current*, 73). At the very least, Berlin's pronouncements here are strange. Machiavelli's self-professed reliance on history as a source of equal weight with experience figures prominently in the Epistles Dedicatory of both *The Prince* and the *Discourses*, and his use of historical examples in both works is staggering. On Machiavelli's sense of economics, see De Grazia, *Machiavelli in Hell*, 7; Wood, "Machiavelli's Humanism of Action," 41. On military matters, see Lynch, Introduction to *Art of War*.

These passages are also important because they capture the centrality, for Machiavelli, of selfishness and fear.[11] Ingratitude, inconstancy, pretence, and trickery are all characteristics of self-interested behavior. When one shies away from acknowledging one's gratitude to another, one is refusing to pay one's dues. When another shifts and pretends, he is using deceit either to cover up some deficiency or to conceal intentions or actions that are dishonest, improper, or shameful, but almost without exception self-serving. The more explicitly selfish propensities to avoid danger and to seek personal gain need no explanation. In portraying man's predicament as it does, the second passage provides an explanation of sorts for the behavior described in the first. A multitude of endless desires seated in a weak and exposed being makes for an uncomfortable amount of uncertainty, and the description of the human condition from the *Golden Ass* conveys the consequent anxiety very well. The centrality of this characteristic in this passage is a reflection of its larger significance in Machiavelli's thought.

The uncertainty summed up so eloquently by the man-turned-pig calls for a versatile toolbox. Ideally, therefore, one would want to have recourse to both love and fear, but the reality is that "because it is difficult to put them together, it is much safer to be feared than loved, if one has to lack one of the two."[12] Fear is the safer of the two for a number of reasons. First, it speaks to our highest priorities.[13] Whereas a promise plays on our natural desire for further acquisition, a threat speaks to our aversion to harm or the loss of something already possessed.[14] In such a ranking of priorities, preservation trumps acquisition for reasons that are as natural as they are logical: life and health are necessary prerequisites for the acquisition of material goods, and material goods necessary to the preservation of life and health take precedence over items of luxury. Only very few human beings are not

---

[11] Cf. Wood, "Machiavelli's Humanism of Action," 40, 43; Wood, Introduction to *The Art of War*, l-liii; Coleman, "Machiavelli's *Via Moderna*," 51–52; Rebhorn, *Foxes and Lions*, 94–105.

[12] In *The Prince*, Machiavelli argues, "men have less hesitation to offend one who makes himself loved than one who makes himself feared; for love is held by a chain of obligation, which, because men are wicked, is broken at every opportunity for their own utility, but fear is held by a dread of punishment that never forsakes you" (XVII: 66). On the degree to which this claim marks a departure from conventional wisdom, see Skinner, *The Foundations of Modern Political Thought* I, 135–36; Skinner *Machiavelli*, 46.

[13] Machiavelli lists and ranks these, in the *Discourses*, as follows: matters of "blood" ("nel sangue," that is, pertaining to self-preservation and avoidance of injury), matters of property, and matters of honor (*Opere* I, 427, 1075).

[14] Cf. Machiavelli, *Discourses*, III.6 § 2, III.23.

afraid of death, and therefore fear of death is a credible and powerful threat for the rest.[15] Second, it does not go away. One can rid oneself of it only temporarily and by transferring it to others.[16] Third, it does not depend on the voluntary cooperation of the other party. Because "men love at their own convenience and fear at the convenience of the prince, a wise prince should found himself on what is his, not on what is someone else's."[17] For these reasons, fear is the primary means by which the prince founds his dominion and maintains it both against internal challenges and against external threats. Like much of Machiavelli's advice, this too comes with qualifications. In general, fear provides more control than love, but not all means of fear afford the same amount of independence. Of the two principal means of instilling fear, punishment and external threats, the prince exercises far greater control in the case of the former than he does in the latter. Both, however, reveal further why fear works as well as it does.

In the opinions of ancient writers on punishment, Machiavelli finds arguments both in favor of and against it as a means of controlling a multitude. His own view is that the value of punishment depends on the relationship between the ruler and the subjects. When those commanded are "partners with you, one cannot use punishment entirely, nor that severity on which Cornelius [Tacitus] reasons"; if, on the other hand, they are subjects, then one "ought to turn rather to punishment than to compliance so that they do not become insolent and do not trample on you because of too much easiness from you."[18] Once again, however, Machiavelli cautions that one must not be led into excess, because it is important, if possible, to avoid hatred. For example, multitudes are known for criticizing the decisions of their rulers, but Machiavelli argues that once they are faced with the specter of punishment, they retreat in an orderly fashion, and obey.[19] Yet, this effect is by no means limited to the many. Even among those of the outstanding

---

[15] "[A]nyone who does not care about death can hurt him; but the prince may well fear them less because [such men] are very rare" (*The Prince*, XIX: 79). Callimaco is one such example: "But there's no remedy here, and if I don't hold on to hope through some course, I'll die no matter what; and seeing I have to die, I'm not afraid of anything, but will take any course – bestial, cruel, nefarious . . ." (*Mandragola* I, iii).

[16] In *The Prince*, Machiavelli argues, "fear is held by a dread of punishment that never forsakes you" (XVII: 67). In the *Discourses*, he adds, "when men seek not to fear, they begin to make others fear; and the injury that they dispel from themselves they put upon another, as if it were necessary to offend or to be offended" (I.46). Cf. Althusser, *Machiavelli and Us*, 100.

[17] Machiavelli, *The Prince*, XVII: 68.

[18] Machiavelli, *Discourses*, III.19 § 1. Cf. *ibid.*, I.24 § 1.

[19] Machiavelli, *Discourses*, I.57.

who attempt to conspire and seize power, it is hard to find men whose benevolence towards the ringleader will surpass their fear of punishment.[20] Once again, however, the virtuous prince will need to remember to shy away from excess; punishment is no panacea. On the one hand, it needs to be tangible if it is to be credible. On the other hand, the holding of "the spirits of subjects in suspense and fearful with continual penalties and offenses" defeats the purpose, since those who grow accustomed to constant threats and danger grow more audacious and thus more likely to behave in unexpected ways.[21] At this juncture, the prudent prince will trade in one fear for another, so as to avoid the indifference that may follow too much exposure to any single threat. The surest cure for this ailment lies in taking the state back to its beginnings.

BEGINNINGS

At the outset of the *Discourses*, Machiavelli makes it clear that the beginnings of cities are crucial for their subsequent development. Anyone who encounters the glorious history of Rome, he argues, will understand how it came about by examining its birth.[22] Because Rome is but the most illustrious example of a more general point about the foundations of cities, however, Machiavelli begins his case with a classification of the different types of founders and foundings.[23] The primary division is between cities that have a "free" beginning and those that do not. The former category, which includes Rome, contains two important considerations, the choice of site and the ordering of laws. Machiavelli takes these up in order of priority, and puts an interesting twist on this traditional starting point of treatises on foundings. Invariably, these treatises encounter the question of the richness or poverty of the site.[24] Some, following the idea encapsulated in Hippocrates' observation that leisure is the mother of all evil, recommend a barren site to induce men "to be industrious and less seized by idleness, live more united,

[20] Machiavelli, *Discourses*, III.6 § 4. That no one is exempt from fear of punishment, for Machiavelli, is apparent in the example of Themistocles, "a very excellent man" (*Discourses*, II.31 § 2).

[21] Machiavelli, *Discourses*, I.45 § 3.

[22] Machiavelli, *Discourses*, I.1 § 1; cf. I.2 § 1; I.49.

[23] Machiavelli, *Discourses*, I.1 § 1. The title of this chapter reads "What Have Been Universally the Beginnings of Any City Whatever, and What Was That of Rome." On the significance of beginnings in republican theories, see Pocock, *The Machiavellian Moment*, 184–86.

[24] Plato addresses this issue implicitly at the founding of the city in speech, in the *Republic* (369b5–374a2) and more explicitly in the *Laws* (704a1-b6). Cf. Aristotle, *Politica*, 1326b26–1327b18, 1330a34-b19; Cicero, *De re publica*, II.iii-v; Machiavelli, *Florentine Histories*, II.2.

having less cause for discord, because of the poverty of the site."[25] Machiavelli grants this connection but dismisses the solution because it is not far-reaching enough. A sterile location would force its inhabitants to work hard, thereby making them too busy to argue with one another, but only if men "were content to live off their own and did not wish to seek to command others."[26] Because the desire to command others is part of man's nature, however, and the power through which it is achieved is the only thing that makes men feel secure, Machiavelli recommends that founders opt for fertile locations, because they will need all the help they can get to defend themselves from invaders and expand their dominion over others.[27]

A fertile site, then, can provide several advantages in the future, but what about the disadvantages in the short term? By granting that poverty and hardship constrain men's tendency towards idleness, Machiavelli acknowledges their roles in forming communities and keeping them together. His simultaneous agreement with the political implication of the Hippocratic maxim that too much free time leads to more discord and preference for fertile sites, however, means that he now has to explain how the danger of discord from abundance will be dealt with in the newly founded community. Machiavelli's answer here is laconic but clear: "the laws should be ordered to constrain [idleness] by *imposing* such necessities as the site does not provide."[28] Machiavelli thus urges founders to imitate those who have settled fertile lands but had the wisdom to prevent idleness from taking root in their edifices. Interestingly, the only examples that he offers concern "imposing a necessity to exercise on those who had to be soldiers, so that through such an order they became better soldiers there than in countries that have naturally been harsh and sterile."[29] Machiavelli's military examples here are far from accidental. In his account of the origin of societies, he singles out the need for defense as the impetus behind the rise of government.[30] New

---

[25] Machiavelli, *Discourses*, I.1 § 4. Cf. Hippocrates, *Decorum*, I.7–8; Chapter 2 in this volume.

[26] Machiavelli, *Discourses*, I.1 § 4. Machiavelli thus concludes that "men cannot secure themselves except with power," which is why he opts for a fertile site, which will provide the means for expansion. Cf. *Discourses*, I.46; Livy, *Ab urbe condita* III.65. For evidence of Machiavelli's agreement with the Hippocratic view, see *Discourses*, I.6 § 4, I.46; II.25 § 1.

[27] Machiavelli, *Discourses*, I.1 § 4. Cf. *ibid.*, II.3, where Machiavelli adds that a rich site by itself is insufficient, if not supplemented by large numbers of citizens.

[28] Machiavelli, *Discourses*, I.1 § 4, emphasis added.

[29] Machiavelli, *Discourses*, I.1 § 4. Machiavelli lists only the Ancient Egyptians and the order of the Mamelukes. Cf. *Opere*, I, 201, 901.

[30] Machiavelli, *Discourses*, I.2 § 3. Cf. *The Prince*, XII: 48: "there cannot be good laws where there are not good arms, and where there are good arms there must be good laws." In the preface to *The Art of War*, Machiavelli argues, "all the arts that have been introduced

states, he argues in *The Prince*, are "full of dangers," and so a new prince will find it impossible to avoid being considered cruel.[31] To back up his claim, Machiavelli can summon no more apt a witness than Dido, the legendary founder of Carthage and, according to Virgil, lover of Aeneas, forefather of the founders of Rome. Her words capture the founder's predicament: "The harshness of things and the newness of the kingdom compel me to contrive such things, and to keep a broad watch over the borders."[32] Machiavelli considers the violence that accompanies the founding of cities so crucial that he keeps returning to it.[33]

This intense interest in beginnings, however, is but one part of a story that is somewhat more complicated than those initial paragraphs of the *Discourses* might lead one to think. Machiavelli closes the first chapter of Book I by promising the reader more detailed discussions of the ways in which various founders constructed the laws in such ways that they would check the inhabitants of fertile sites by imposing necessities upon them.[34] The founders of durable states will therefore be mindful of the occasional need for necessities, and will see to it that where a fertile site and other advantages make for a deficit in natural necessities, a store of artificial ones will be available to keep the population in check. Machiavelli cites Romulus as the first example of such a founder, and this much is unsurprising, but he also cites Numa, and this second example complicates matters even further, because the side-by-side mention of Romulus and Numa expands the scope of means that can produce artificial necessities.[35] Whereas for most of the first chapter these necessities concerned military matters of the kind that Romulus was faced with, Numa's contribution to the preservation of Rome was of a very different kind. Machiavelli explains that even though Rome owes its birth and

---

into society for the common benefit of mankind, and all the ordinances that have been established to make them live in fear of God and in obedience to human laws, would be in vain and insignificant if they were not supported and defended by a military force," and concludes, "[b]ut the best ordinances in the world will be despised and trampled under foot when they are not supported, as they ought to be, by a military power" (4); cf. *ibid.* I:30. As Mansfield points out, "[a]ccording to Machiavelli, [. . .] protection is the first and last goal of cities" (*Machiavelli's Virtue*, 71); cf. *ibid.*, 63.

[31] Machiavelli, *The Prince*, XVII: 66.

[32] Machiavelli, *The Prince*, XVII: 66; Machiavelli quotes Virgil's Latin, "res dura et regni novitas me talia cogunt / moliri et late fines custode tueri" (Virgil, *Aeneid*, I, 563–64; Machiavelli, *Opere*, I, 163); cf. *Opere*, I, 871.

[33] In addition to the detailed discussion in *Discourses*, III.1, examined below, Machiavelli returns to the salutary effects of poverty and war in III.16 § 2.

[34] Machiavelli, *Discourses*, I.1 § 5.

[35] Machiavelli, *Discourses*, I.1 § 5.

education to Romulus, it has to acknowledge an equally important debt to Numa, who supplied those arrangements that were necessary for the survival of the new state that his predecessor had left out:

> As he found a very ferocious people and wished to reduce it to civil obedience with the arts of peace, he turned to religion as a thing altogether necessary if he wished to maintain a civilization; and he constituted it so that for many centuries there was never so much fear of God as in that republic, which made easier whatever enterprise the Senate or the great men of Rome might plan to make.[36]

By superimposing the fear of God onto the fear of man, Numa provided a far more versatile and threatening, and therefore more potent, means for the creation of necessity. It is for this reason that, if forced to rank them, Machiavelli would put Numa above Romulus as the individual to whom Rome owes the greatest debt.[37] Machiavelli argues that the very nature of extraordinary (emergency) laws makes recourse to God necessary, because a justification of this magnitude is the only thing that will make such laws accepted by the people.[38] If this highest and most effective of the legitimizing sources of emergencies fails, then the fear of the prince is the only thing standing between the state and its ruin.[39] The security that any one prince – however virtuous – can provide is nevertheless ephemeral, compared to the lasting effects that orders, and especially religious orders, can have on the state.

Machiavelli's preference for Numa over Romulus, however, turns out to be fleeting. For all the praise that he heaps upon the founder of the Roman religion, a few chapters later, Machiavelli finds that he has occasion to reconsider. Machiavelli deems it a "very great fortune" for Rome that Numa was followed by Tullus, a king "similar in ferocity to Romulus and more a lover of war than of peace."[40] After its foundation, Rome needed an orderer of civil life, and it was this need that Numa supplied by introducing religion. Had Rome continued along this path, however, it "would have become effeminate and the prey of its neighbors."[41] In explaining what accounts for the difference between Romulus and Tullus, on the one hand, and Numa, on the other, Machiavelli informs the reader that Numa's reign

---

[36] Machiavelli, *Discourses*, I.11 § 1.
[37] Machiavelli, *Discourses*, I.11 § 2.
[38] Machiavelli, *Discourses*, I.11 § 3. Cf. Critias's account of the emergence of belief in the divine, in Rahe, *Republics Ancient & Modern*, I: 98–99.
[39] Machiavelli, *Discourses*, I.11 § 4.
[40] Machiavelli, *Discourses*, I.19 § 1.
[41] Machiavelli, *Discourses*, I.19 § 1.

marked the end of Romulus's *virtù*. Were it not for Tullus, who picked up where Romulus had left off, the kingdom would necessarily have come to ruin.[42] According to the language that Machiavelli uses in this chapter, Romulus and Tullus were "excellent" princes, whereas Numa was "weak," because for Machiavelli weak princes are "those who do not rely on war"; this deficiency exposes them to danger in situations in which fortune is not on their side.[43] He who is armed with weapons and prudence, on the other hand, will be able to hold onto his kingdom "in every mode unless it is taken from him by an obstinate and excessive force."[44] As Machiavelli's assessment of the contributions of the first three kings shows, a complete separation of the internal from the external is impossible, and yet his apprehension regarding the one whose focus was primarily internal and his preference for those mainly concerned with the external illuminate his views regarding the right ordering of a state's priorities further, and explain why Machiavelli returns again and again to the beginnings of cities.

BEGINNINGS, ANEW

The first treatment of beginnings, in Book I, leaves the reader unsure about Machiavelli's precise view. Although he began by stating that beginnings were crucial in their formative capacity and therefore essential in understanding the trajectory of a city in time, he closed the first chapter of Book I by making it sound as though all beginnings were created equal; Numa was listed alongside Romulus, and both were followed by other, unnamed, founders to be examined in the rest of the work.[45] As we have seen, however, a few chapters later, Machiavelli checks that final impression of Book I by qualifying his earlier, glowing assessment of Numa and placing him clearly below Romulus for lacking his predecessor's *virtù*. In explaining the structure of the *Discourses*, Machiavelli had announced that Book I was going to deal with internal matters and Book II with the external.[46] In light of this structure, Machiavelli's choice to begin Book III not with a preface, but with another chapter on the

---

[42] Machiavelli, *Discourses*, I.19 § 1, 3.

[43] Machiavelli, *Discourses*, I.19 § 2, 4. In Chapter III of *The Prince*, Machiavelli argues that one of the main advantages of the Romans lay in their readiness to wage war, "because they knew that war may not be avoided but is deferred to the advantage of others" (12–13).

[44] Machiavelli, *Discourses*, I.19 § 4.

[45] Machiavelli, *Discourses*, I.1 § 5: "quelle alterazioni sono a salute che le riducano inverso i principii loro" (*Opere*, I, 416). In discussing the natural cycles of regimes, Machiavelli claims, "all states have some reverence in the beginning" (*Discourses*, I.2 § 3).

[46] Machiavelli, *Discourses*, I.1 § 6; II. Pref. § 3.

importance of the beginnings of cities may strike one as strange.[47] Whereas
in I.1, Machiavelli had considered the founding of Rome and the importance
of foundings in general, in Book III, he begins by advising, "If One Wishes
a Sect or a Republic to Live Long, It Is Necessary to Draw It Back Often
toward Its Beginning."[48] According to this second formulation, therefore,
beginnings have an active role to play throughout the life of a state, for no
other reason than that a state, too, is a living thing.

The natural condition of bodies is one of motion towards decay. Every living thing dies, so the question for Machiavelli is which survives the longest.
His answer is a puzzling one: heaven ordains how long a life will be, but
whether or not something lives up to that potential depends on the way in
which it can cope with change. The condition in which mixed political bodies, such as republics find themselves at birth is the strongest; it is sufficient to
launch them and marks the beginning of a process of natural deterioration.[49]
It would be ideal to be able to maintain that condition and resist change,
but the harsh reality is that changes have to be introduced in order to halt
decay, postpone death, and maintain them. If republics are strongest at their
beginnings, then the changes that make them safe are those that return them
to their beginnings or first principles.[50] The reputation and momentum that
were sufficient to launch a republic are also the forces that ought to be used
to rejuvenate it in times of crisis, "because the end of the republic is to
enervate and to weaken all other bodies so as to increase its own."[51] This
rejuvenation can come about in two ways: a sect or republic can renew itself
either by means of its orders, namely its systems and institutions, or by some
accident "outside" of these orders.[52]

---

[47] Books I and II each have a preface, but Book III does not.

[48] Machiavelli, *Discourses*, III.1. The title of the original reads "A volere che una sètta o una republica viva lungamente, è necessario ritirarla spesso verso il suo principio" (*Opere*, I, 416). It should be noted that in addition to "beginning," *principio* also means "principle." Despite the title, Machiavelli devotes only a single paragraph (§ 4) to sects. The rest of the chapter deals with states (§§ 1–3 with republics and § 5 with kingdoms; § 6 contains a summary of his conclusions).

[49] Machiavelli, *Discourses*, III.1 §§ 1–2.

[50] Machiavelli, *Discourses*, III.1 § 1: "i principii loro" (*Opere*, I, 416).

[51] Machiavelli, *Discourses*, III.1 § 2: "la prima riputazione ed il primo augumento loro" (*Opere*, I, 416; cf. *ibid.*, 1065, 2); *ibid.*, II.3 § 4.

[52] Machiavelli, *Discourses*, III.1 § 2: "E però quelle sono meglio ordinate ed hanno più lunga vita che mediante gli ordini suoi si possono spesso rinnovare, ovvero che per qualche accidente fuori di ditto ordine vengono a detta rinnovazione" (*Opere*, I, 416; cf. *ibid.*, 1065, 6). Just below, Machiavelli calls these "external accidents" ("accidente estrinseco") and "internal prudence" ("prudenza intrinseca") (*Opere*, I, 417).

So, what are these "external accidents"? Machiavelli illustrates by using the example of the first conquest of Rome by the Gauls.[53] He thinks it "was necessary that Rome be taken by the French, if one wished that it be reborn and, by being reborn, regain new life and new virtue, and regain the observance of religion and justice, which were beginning to be tainted in it."[54] Evidence of this decay is to be found in Livy's account of numerous instances of Roman neglect of religious duties and the demands of justice. The "external beating" that Rome received on that occasion provided a temporary respite to the ongoing conflict between its Orders.[55] The Gallic threat forced the Romans to pay attention once more to the demands of piety and justice, and also made them realize that they should pay attention to the virtue rather than the shortcomings of individuals. After rectifying their earlier mistakes, the principal actors were able to "put aside all envy," readmit Camillus into their ranks, and put him in charge once more.[56] The meaning of Machiavelli's example is clear enough: rather than focus on one another, the Orders turned to the Gauls. By means of negative association, Rome presented a united front in a time of internal upheaval and thereby saved itself. When Machiavelli's earlier discussion of the utility of beginnings is placed alongside the story of the Gallic invasion, it becomes clear that beginnings provide safety because they are fraught with danger, and because the beginnings of republics are responses to insecurity and vulnerability, responses to threat. What is most interesting about Machiavelli's insistence on the importance of beginnings, however, is not so much his alignment with the tradition that recognizes the inevitability of negative association, but more so the particular – and quite novel – way in which he identifies the process at work. In explaining the moral of the story of the Gallic invasion,

---

[53] Machiavelli, *Discourses*, III.1 § 2. This reference is to the Gallic invasion of 391 BC. Cf. Livy, *Ab urbe condita*, V.37–48; Cary & Scullard, *A History of Rome*, 73–74.

[54] Machiavelli, *Discourses*, III.1 § 2. In II.29, Machiavelli claims that "to make Rome great and lead it to that greatness it came to, fortune judged it was necessary to beat it [. . .] but still did not wish to ruin it altogether (§ 2).

[55] According to Cary and Scullard,

> During the century that followed the Gallic invasion the Romans, while continuing to hammer out a compromise between the claims of the two Orders, also completed the main stage in the development of their republican constitution. But these internal developments were achieved against a background of severe external threats and wars which inevitably affected not only economic life but also the tempo of the pressure which the plebeians could exert upon the patricians. (*A History of Rome*, 75)

[56] Machiavelli, *Discourses*, III.1 § 2. Cf. Livy, *Ab urbe condita*, V.46. Marcus Furius Camillus, the general who had captured Veii (19–22) and was driven into exile, only to return and aid in the liberation of the city from the Gauls (*ibid.*, V.19–22, 32, 46).

Machiavelli advises that men who live together in whichever order use this type of internal or external accident often, to examine and get to know themselves anew.[57] Whether by means of these external threats, good laws, or the illustrious example of a leader, republics must engage in this re-examination and rediscovery of their identity if they are to withstand the forces of decay.

The reacquaintance with first principles occasioned by external threats is but one of the ways in which a republic can be drawn back toward its beginning. Machiavelli suggests that virtuous individuals or virtuous orders can intervene to check the ambition and insolence of men, and thus halt a republic's disintegration, by reviving those orders that were at work in the beginning.[58] To illustrate this point, Machiavelli offers an odd list of seven incidents from Roman history: six involving executions and one involving an accusation, which he breaks down into two chronological groups, one on either side of the Gallic invasion.[59] These events were exceptional in two ways. They were both rare and striking breaks from the ordinary. As he had noted at the beginning of III.1, Machiavelli believes that once born, republics, like all living things, begin to march towards their death. Extraordinary events such as these constrain men, and the rarer they become, the more space they give "men to corrupt themselves and to behave with greater danger and more tumult."[60] Machiavelli advises that no more than ten years should pass without such an event, because "[u]nless something arises by which punishment is brought back to their memory and fear is renewed in their spirits, soon so many delinquents join together that they can no longer be punished without danger."[61] Under Medici rule, in Florence, the

---

[57] Machiavelli, *Discourses*, III.1 § 2: "È necessario adunque, come è ditto, che gli uomini che vivono insieme in qualunque ordine, spesso si riconoschino, o per questi accidenti estrinseci o per gl'intrinseci" (*Opere*, I, 417). Literally, the term that Machiavelli uses (*riconoschino*) means to recognize something, which in this case fits well with a return to first principles, a sense reinforced by the fact that the term has overtones of reacquainting oneself with something, in this case the identity of Rome as "ordered by Romulus and by the other prudent princes" (III.1 § 2).

[58] Machiavelli, *Discourses*, III.1 § 3. Machiavelli speaks of "executing" these orders against those who seek to violate them. His choice of term here is interesting, in light of the list of examples that follows.

[59] Machiavelli, *Discourses*, III.1 § 3.

[60] Machiavelli, *Discourses*, III.1 § 3.

[61] Machiavelli, *Discourses*, III.1 § 3. When he considers the prospects of a corrupt people, Machiavelli concludes, "[i]f one individual of very long life or two virtuous ones continued in succession do not arrange it, when they are lacking [...] it is ruined, unless indeed he makes it be reborn with many dangers and much blood" (*Discourses*, I.17 § 3). Recall also the discussion of succession, at I.19, where Machiavelli argues that two "weak" princes in a row will prove detrimental to the state. Cf. I.20.

recommended interval was even shorter – five years. According to Machi-avelli, when the Medici spoke of regaining the state, they meant "putting that terror and that fear in men that had been put there in taking it, since at that time they had beaten down those who, according to that mode of life, had worked for ill."[62]

Whether external threats or internal checks against upheaval in the form of laws, orders, or virtuous individuals, to Machiavelli all means of returning a state to its beginnings are "accidents."[63] This curious choice of term points to their common purpose but also to the fact that the ruler stands between his subjects and dangers, be they internal or external. Earlier in the *Discourses*, Machiavelli had advised the new ruler to upset everything, introduce changes with every opportunity, so as to make it perfectly clear to his subjects that all they enjoy comes from him.[64] At the end of III.1, Machiavelli compares the internal and external means and draws an interesting conclusion. He argues that "nothing is more necessary in a common way of life [...] than to give back to it the reputation it had in its beginnings," but he advises that one prefer good orders or good men rather than an external force to that end, because the latter is too dangerous a solution.[65] Machiavelli's reluctance to recommend that one depend on external threats to combat domestic upheaval follows from his broader insistence on self-sufficiency.[66] Dependence on the means of others is a precarious and unpredictable state. Dependence on their plans against one's state is all the more so. If by his actions one can have any kind of control over the actions of an enemy, this control is only fleeting and minimal. In this sense, the threat of an enemy is at least as dangerous as the most unreliable tools of policy belonging to others. Beyond this danger, however, such threats are also pregnant with the danger that they may prove ultimately detrimental to one's internal goals. The man-agement of external threats is a balancing act of the most delicate kind, and at

---

[62] Machiavelli, *Discourses*, III.1 § 3. Cf. *ibid.*, I.26; *Florentine Histories*, V.1, 4; Guicciardini, *Opere*, II, 253.

[63] Machiavelli, *Discourses*, III.1 § 2. In his description of the natural cycle of regimes, in I.2, Machiavelli claims that the popular state "was maintained for a little while, but not much, especially once the generation that had ordered it was eliminated; for it came at once to license, where neither private men nor public were in fear, each living in his own mode, a thousand injuries were done every day" (§ 3).

[64] Machiavelli, *Discourses*, I.26. With respect to the "execution" of internal "accidents" by someone, Mansfield points out correctly that "[t]he execution, is, or should be, managed by his prudence, but he must manage it to appear as a sign of the terror from which he or the government protects the people" (*Machiavelli's New Modes and Orders*, 302).

[65] Machiavelli, *Discourses*, III.1 § 6.

[66] See, e.g., Machiavelli, *Discourses*, I.43, II.10 § 1, II.20; *The Prince*, XII, XIII.

the one end of the spectrum of possible outcomes lies not just the failure of the policy to achieve its domestic purpose but also the potential enslavement or destruction of the state at the hands of its enemies. This is the reason why even though an external threat is sometimes "the best remedy," Machiavelli considers it ultimately "so dangerous that it is not in any way to be desired."[67] Despite this recognition of the dangers inherent in external threats, however, it turns out that one may not be able to avoid resorting to them after all. Machiavelli admits as much when he points out that there can be no good laws unless there are good arms, as well as when he counsels the prince that the only art he need concern himself with is that of war.[68] Since notions of good and bad arose only after men came together and formed communities, good arms are not only prior to good orders but also necessary for their very existence.[69] Machiavelli knows that men ought to settle their differences by means of the laws and that force is the province of beasts, but he also knows that because the laws are often not enough, the prince should "know well how to use the beast and the man," and employ force where necessary.[70]

A SALLUSTIAN NECESSITY

Machiavelli's rejection of a barren site is thus deceptive. Although he grants that human nature needs to be constrained by necessity, he nevertheless disagrees that such a site is the best means of bringing this about. His reason has to do with what he sees as an equally fundamental characteristic of human beings, albeit one that is overlooked by those who recommend hard work as

---

[67] Machiavelli, *Discourses*, III.1 § 6. When he discusses the utility of religion "well used," Machiavelli wonders whether that too should be classified as an external force (*Discourses*, I.15).

[68] Machiavelli, *The Prince*, XII: 48, XIV: 58. Further along, in the same work, Machiavelli also argues that a new prince never disarms his people and that if he finds them unarmed he arms them (XX: 83–84). Cf. *The Art of War*, where Machiavelli justifies his interest in the subject matter as follows: "For all the arts that have been introduced into society for the common benefit of mankind, and all the ordinances that have been established to make them live in fear of God and in obedience to human laws, would be vain and insignificant if they were not supported and defended by a military force" (Pref., 4). Machiavelli advances this argument repeatedly in the *Discourses*, (I.4 § 1, I.21, III.31 § 4). On the latter occasion, he defends the utility of repeating it by identifying it "at every point in this history."

[69] Machiavelli, *Discourses*, I.2 § 3. Cf. I.11 § 2.

[70] Machiavelli, *The Prince*, XVIII: 69. Machiavelli believes that this is the meaning of the ancient story of Achilles and other princes, whose education was entrusted to the centaur Chiron.

the solution to the problem of order. Machiavelli agrees that human beings can become unruly and destructive if not checked somehow, but he also thinks that they have a desire for security that is satisfied only by dominion over others.[71] If this need for domination of others were true only of a certain segment of the population, then the acquisition of domestic power by that group would solve the problem. Machiavelli argues quite clearly, however, that this is not the case. Every individual moves from one ambition to the next, and even the people as a whole have ambitions that they need to vent.[72] This is, therefore, a matter that cannot be solved within the confines of the state; a solution will have to be sought elsewhere, and this is why Machiavelli opts for a more far-reaching response to the Hippocratic maxim, and recommends that founders choose a richer site, so that they can afford to expand and thus satisfy the *animus dominandi* of their subjects. In adopting the position that he does at the beginning of the *Discourses*, therefore, Machiavelli is not expressing any misgivings regarding external necessity as a constraint, but is in fact setting his sights higher, by proposing recourse to necessity conceived far more broadly, since it involves a combination of internal and external pressures, which he sees as a state's only real means towards stability and growth.[73]

Machiavelli's view of this matter is noteworthy for three reasons. First, although internal conflict among the various socioeconomic orders of a state is one of the principal difficulties of political life, Machiavelli's assessment of it and recommendation concerning how it should be addressed mark a

---

[71] The choice of a poor site for the founding of a city, argues Machiavelli, "would without doubt be wiser and more useful if men were content to live off their own and did not wish to seek to command others," and concludes, "[t]herefore, since men cannot secure themselves except with power, it is necessary to avoid this sterility in a country and to settle in the most fertile places" (*Discourses*, I.1 § 4). Cf. Livy, *Ab urbe condita*, III.lxv.11: "while insuring themselves against fear, men actually render themselves fearful to others; and having defended ourselves from an injury, we proceed – as though it were necessary either to do or suffer wrong – to inflict injury upon our neighbor."

[72] Machiavelli, *Discourses*, I.5 § 1, I.46. Cf. Hörnqvist, *Machiavelli and Empire*, 73–74. Commentators are often misled by Machiavelli's distinction between the great and the people in *The Prince*, where he argues that the former wish to "command and oppress" and the latter wish "neither to be commanded nor oppressed" (IX: 39). Because the mixing of these two humors results in "principality, liberty, or license," however, it is clear that the people's desire to not be ruled by the great is a reference to self-government. Cf. *Discourses*, I.16 § 5.

[73] See Kluxen, *Politik und menschliche Existenz bei Machiavelli*, 77. Machiavelli cites the "verdict of the ancient writers that men are wont to worry in evil and to become bored with good" (*Discourses*, I.37 § 1; cf. III.21 § 2).

departure from the mainstream. Second, Machiavelli's advice regarding *metus hostilis* for the purposes of negative association is somewhat unexpected. His theory of negative association turns out to be more expansive than those of his predecessors; whereas they presented it as an exceptional solution, Machiavelli introduces it into the repertoire of normal politics. At the same time, his view of negative association is also much more sober and restrained than one might expect in light of the shocking and provocative nature of some of his other recommendations. Third, his theory draws the closest connection between the two sources of "necessity." Although previous accounts of the mechanics of *metus hostilis* recognize the external problem as a solution to the internal problem, they stop short of identifying the relationship between the two as potentially cyclical, let alone necessary on a regular basis. For Machiavelli, by contrast, the two fundamental problems of the state – internal disorder and external security threats – are best solved when they are pitted one against the other, in a chain reaction that allows the state to vent, acquire, and maintain, again and again.

Near the beginning of Book I of the *Discourses*, after having considered the importance of foundings, Machiavelli turns his attention to the "disunion" between the Senate and the plebs. Expanding on a distinctly Sallustian theme, Machiavelli sees this internal conflict as both a natural fact and fortune's contribution to Rome's greatness.[74] Given the success of capitalism in the market and of checks and balances in government, the idea of desirable consequences flowing from the pitting of one set of interests against another may not sound earth shattering to us, but in Machiavelli's time the argument in favor of tumults was quite extraordinary.[75] Among Machiavelli's

---

[74] Machiavelli, *Discourses*, I.2 § 7: "Notwithstanding that [Rome] did not have a Lycurgus to order it in the beginning in a mode that would enable it to live free a long time, nonetheless so many accidents arose in it through the disunion of the plebs and the Senate that what an orderer had not done, chance did." Machiavelli's main departure from Sallust here concerns his assessment of the internal conflict. Whereas Sallust sees it as a sign of moral decay, Machiavelli proposes a more optimistic interpretation, according to which the conflict among the orders was one of the principal forces that propelled the state to greatness. See also his discussion of the Orsini and Colonna factions in Rome, in chapters VII and IX of *The Prince*, as well as *Florentine Histories*, VII.1, where Machiavelli distinguishes between internal divisions that are helpful and harmful to the city, and cf. Wood's distinction between "corrupt" and "ordered" conflict (Introduction to *The Art of War*, li), as well as Fontana, "Sallust and the Politics of Machiavelli," 101–02.

[75] Machiavelli criticizes those who damn tumults "inconsiderately" (*Discourses* I.4 § 1). Cf. Hamilton, Madison, & Jay, *The Federalist Papers*, esp. numbers 10 and 51; Hirschman, *The Passions and the Interests*, esp. p. 33.

contemporaries, Guicciardini remarked that the divisions among the Orders of Rome "cannot be worthy of praise, and it cannot be denied that they were harmful," and protested that "praising discord is like praising a sick man's illness, because the remedy that has been used on him was the right one."[76] In *Leviathan*, Hobbes criticized severely those who learn from ancient authors to favor tumults.[77] More recently, Pocock has called Machiavelli's argument "daring," "arresting," "shocking," and "incredible to minds which identified union with stability and virtue, conflict with innovation and decay," and Skinner has pointed out the "radical nature of Machiavelli's attack on the prevailing orthodoxy."[78] Shocking though Machiavelli's approval of the tumults may be, it is but a part of his broader and even more provocative solution to the problems of the state.

According to Machiavelli, the founder of a state would have to order it after Rome, and ensure that internally it is marked by "tumults and universal dissensions," because these allow states to expand and then preserve themselves.[79] The objection from those who view conflict as potentially disastrous for the unity of the state is obvious: if unchecked, it will lead to civil strife and, eventually, to dissolution. Whereas most would proceed thence to conclude that internal conflict ought to be eliminated so as to prevent it from destroying the state, Machiavelli argues instead that it must merely be controlled. Disorder must have its limits: too little will prevent the state from reaching its full potential, but too much will lead to civil war and ruin.[80] Some sort of balance between the two would be "the true political way of life and the true quiet of a city," according to Machiavelli, but how does one strike such a balance? Unfortunately, as things are by nature in constant motion, a balance of this sort is impossible, unless it is imposed artificially.[81]

---

[76] Guicciardini, *Considerations*, I.4, p. 393 (*Opere*, II, 436–37). Cf. Guicciardini, *Dialogue*, 143–54 (*Opere* II, 650–61); Pocock, *The Machiavellian Moment*, 245–47.

[77] Hobbes, *Leviathan*, XXI § 9. This, and a reference to "successful wickedness [that] hath obtained the name of virtue" (*ibid.*, XV § 4), is as close as Hobbes comes to referring to Machiavelli.

[78] Pocock, *The Machiavellian Moment*, 194; Skinner, *The Foundations of Modern Political Thought* I, 181–82; Skinner, "Ambroggio Lorenzetti," 8–9, 32–34; Skinner, *Visions of Politics*, II: 45–46, 69–70. Cf. Gilbert, "The Concept of Nationalism in Machiavelli's *Prince*," 42; Gilbert, *Machiavelli and Guicciardini*, 158–60, 170; Kahn, *Machiavellian Rhetoric*, 48–50; Hörnqvist, *Machiavelli and Empire*, 38, 73–75; Fischer, "Machiavelli's Rapacious Republicanism," xxxiv-viii.

[79] Machiavelli, *Discourses*, I.6 § 4. Cf. Wood, "Machiavelli's Humanism of Action," 41.

[80] In Bock's words, civil discords are "both the life and the death of the republic" ("Civil Discord in Machiavelli's *Istorie Fiorentine*," 201).

[81] Machiavelli, *Discourses*, I.6 § 4. Cf. *Florentine Histories*, V.1.

The search for its attainment, according to Machiavelli, begins with the realization that "[i]n all human things [...] one inconvenience can never be suppressed without another's cropping up."[82] The answer, therefore, is to find inconveniences that move in opposite directions, so that one cancel the other out and an equilibrium be found:

So when a republic that has been ordered so as to be capable of maintaining itself does not expand, and necessity leads it to expand, this would come to take away its foundations and make it come to ruin sooner. So, on the other hand, if heaven were so kind that it did not have to make war, from that would arise the idleness to make it either effeminate or divided; these two things together, or each by itself, would be the cause of its ruin. Therefore, since one cannot, as I believe, balance this thing, nor maintain this middle way exactly, in ordering a republic there is need to think of the more honorable part and to order it so that if indeed necessity brings it to expand, it can conserve what it has seized.[83]

Because no single solution can produce a middle path, the "honorable" thing to do is to prepare the state to meet the demands of necessity. Inward pressure from tumults will lead it to seek outlets for its *animus dominandi*, and will therefore lead it to expand. At that point, its encounter with the outside world will require its constituent parts to rearrange their priorities, set their differences aside, and focus on what unites them rather than on what divides them. Thus, one of the many things that a state must do to maintain internal peace will be to expand, that is, to wage war.[84]

Given the importance that he attributes to the beginnings of cities, Machiavelli's choice of Livy as his primary source for the history of Rome is not surprising. Nevertheless, in his diagnosis of the mechanics of internal conflict among the Orders and his identification of *metus hostilis* as the mechanism by which that conflict was kept in check, Machiavelli acknowledges a distinct, if indirect, debt to Sallust.[85] Roman history is riddled with cycles of

---

[82] Machiavelli, *Discourses*, I.6 § 2. Cf. *ibid.*, I.38 § 2; *The Prince*, XXI: 91: "For in the order of things it is found that one never seeks to avoid one inconvenience without running into another; but prudence consists in knowing how to recognize the qualities of inconveniences, and in picking the less bad as good."

[83] Machiavelli, *Discourses*, I.6 § 4. See Kahn, *Machiavellian Rhetoric*, 53; Sullivan, *Machiavelli, Hobbes, & the Formation of a Liberal Republicanism in England*, 36.

[84] See Machiavelli, *The Prince*, III: 12–13; *The Art of War*, Preface, Book I; Armitage, "Empire and Liberty"; Hörnqvist, *Machiavelli and Empire*, 80, 87–89, 93–94; Fischer, "Machiavelli's Rapacious Republicanism"; cf. Viroli, *From Politics to Reason of State*, 164.

[85] As Burke shows, Sallust was by far the most popular ancient historian during Machiavelli's lifetime ("A Survey of the Popularity of Ancient Historians, 1450–1700"). On Sallust's influence on Machiavelli, see Whitfield, *Machiavelli*, 139–42; Wood, "Machiavelli's

internal conflict followed by external conflict, so in this sense Machiavelli's treatment of the Gallic invasion and other similar incidents is not extraordinary. Despite not invoking Sallust explicitly in this respect, Machiavelli sees the internal turmoil as checked primarily by means of negative association.[86] In so doing, he employs a time-honored tool, but once again gives it an unexpected twist, just as in the case of internal tumults.[87] In the Sallustian tradition, negative association in the face of external threats was recognized as something of a necessary evil at best. There was no doubt that it checked internal conflict before it escalated into full-scale civil war, but it was a nasty solution to the even nastier problem of internal moral and political decay. In Machiavelli's cyclical solution to the problems of the state – where one problem (*metus hostilis*) checks another (tumults), and thus the state remains strong and united, and continues to survive – recourse to negative association is recommended as a matter of course. Whether at fixed intervals or as mandated by necessity, every now and then the state will have to be brought back to its beginnings.

Machiavelli's view of negative association is also surprising for its moderation. It is not necessary to delve into the contentious issue of his motivation in order to conclude that the character of his teaching is scandalous and that some of the measures he recommends were shocking to the moral sense of his contemporaries and beyond. The reaction that they have elicited suffices, and there are enough easily identifiable examples of such teachings in all of his writings. Those teachings, however, tend to obscure a more measured side of Machiavelli, one that involves a pragmatic approach to difficult political problems and seeks solutions to them in earnest. In the context of this view, Machiavelli's sober discussion of the role of tumults and negative association is less surprising than it might be to someone who expects to hear the views of the Devil incarnate.

Concept of *Virtù* Reconsidered," 161–62; Sasso, *Machiavelli e gli antichi e altri saggi*, I: 451–59, 490–99; Skinner, "Machiavelli's *Discorsi* and the Pre-Humanist Origins of Republican Ideas"; Osmond, "Sallust and Machiavelli," esp. 421–30; Wood, "Sallust's Theorem," 174, 184; Fontana, "Sallust and the Politics of Machiavelli"; Armitage, "Empire and Liberty," 30–32.

[86] This is true even in the domestic example of the Tarquins, whom Machiavelli identifies as the common enemy of the nobles and the plebs. Althusser identifies a similar domestic dynamic at work in a prince's alliance with the people against the nobles, which he considers a manifestation of fear without hatred, of the kind that Machiavelli favors in chapter XVII of *The Prince* (Althusser, *Machiavelli and Us*, 100–01).

[87] Gilbert identifies this approach as Machiavelli's primary innovation (see, e.g., "The Concept of Nationalism in Machiavelli's *Prince*," 42; *Machiavelli and Guicciardini*, 159).

NEW MODES AND ORDERS

Commonwealths are paradoxical entities. To fulfill their purpose, they require the coexistence of individuals and groups with some common and some conflicting interests. The conflicting interests lead to the tumult that animates political life and gives states the momentum to move forward, but too much tumult may be destructive and has to be checked. At that point, demarcation from outsiders steps in and assumes the burden of cohesion. External threats provide the other side of the coin, the force that counterbalances internal turmoil and ensures that only that portion of it which contributes to the advancement of the state will be allowed to materialize.[88] If it is true that people feel secure only when they can dominate others, and that this is the case for all human beings, then it is not sufficient to address the ways of satisfying the *animus dominandi* of those in power. Machiavelli claims in passing that the difference between the few and the many is that the former wish to rule whereas the latter wish not to be ruled.[89] This picture, however, is once again deceptive, for what does it mean to wish to not be ruled, but to rule, if only over oneself?[90] Because it is impossible for everyone's *animus dominandi* and desire for the goods of others to be satisfied within the confines of a single state, a state that knows human nature will seek to vent by dominating others. This is why Machiavelli prefers a fertile site over a barren one, and this is why Rome is his favorite example.[91]

At the outset of the *Discourses*, Machiavelli promises to put ancient materials to new uses. His treatment of negative association attests to the fact that he keeps that promise. Although Machiavelli's version of this device displays some familiar traits, it also bears the marks of significant innovation. Beyond the subtle transformation of traits recognized by Thucydides and

---

[88] See Kahn, "Reduction and the Praise of Disunion in Machiavelli's *Discourses*," 15.

[89] Machiavelli, *The Prince*, IX: 39. Machiavelli notes that the great desire to command and oppress the people, whereas the people do not wish to be commanded or oppressed by the great, and concludes that from the combination of these appetites results "principality, liberty, or license."

[90] See Machiavelli, *Discourses*, I.4 § 1, where Machiavelli discusses the ambition of the people. Cf. *ibid.*, I.5 § 2; *Florentine Histories*, III.1.

[91] According to Machiavelli, "a city that lives free has two ends – one to acquire, the other to maintain itself free" (*Discourses*, I.29 § 3). Wood characterizes Machiavelli's conception of violence as "the dynamic of [the] universal chaos of intramural and inter-state contention" ("Machiavelli's Humanism of Action," 41); Sullivan, *Machiavelli, Hobbes, & the Formation of a Liberal Republicanism in England*, 34–38. As Sullivan points out, "The Rome [Machiavelli] embraces is marked by its dividedness, by its aggressiveness, and by its acquisitiveness" (*ibid.*, 31). Cf. Hörnqvist, *Machiavelli and Empire*, 74–75.

Sallust before him, Machiavelli locates the very origins of the state in negative association, and rather than lament its implications for human nature, recommends that it be sought after as a source of renewal, an opportunity for individuals to become reacquainted with themselves and their collective identity. In so doing, he paves the way for two seminal developments in the history of political thought.[92]

The first is the reemergence of an explicit connection between the psychology of the individual and the formation of a political association, a connection that had remained more or less dormant since Plato's analogy between the city and the soul, in the *Republic*.[93] Although a full and systematic exploration of the relationship between individual psychology and political community would have to wait for Hobbes, Machiavelli's political writings send a clear message that the latter is dependent upon the former.

The second, and related development, stems from Machiavelli's insistence that states be made to return to their beginnings periodically. These periodic returns seek to capture some of the strength that states display during their founding, the time during which there is the least doubt about their identity.[94] Machiavelli examines a series of measures aimed at such a return, from Florence's fairly innocuous periodic reshuffling of positions and institutions, to reliance on potent external threats. While the latter simulate the feelings experienced during the state's founding best, they are also risky because they leave the state dependent on the most dangerous plans of others.[95] Machiavelli's search for a means of achieving the same effect but without many of the undesirable side effects would also have to wait for the arrival of Hobbes's state of nature, the vision of what life would be like in the absence of the state. By planting this image in the minds of individuals, Hobbes provided the surest and most enduring means of achieving Machiavelli's return to the beginnings of cities. Hobbes's innovation, however, would have to wait until the tempest of reactions to Machiavelli's teachings had passed.

---

[92] See Strauss, *Natural Right and History*, 177–83; Rahe, *Republics Ancient & Modern*, II: 33.
[93] See Ioannis D. Evrigenis, "The Psychology of Politics."
[94] See Machiavelli, *Discourses*, III.1 §§ 1–2.
[95] Machiavelli concludes that reliance on an external force is "sometimes the best remedy, as it was in Rome, [but] it is so dangerous that it is not in any way to be desired" (*Discourses*, III.1 § 6).

4

THE ENEMY OF MY ENEMY IS MY FRIEND: NEGATIVE ASSOCIATION AND REASON OF STATE

It is a wicked prayer to ask to have someone to hate or to fear, so that he may be someone to conquer.

So if it was by waging wars that were just, not impious and unjust, that the Romans were able to acquire so vast an empire, surely they should worship the Injustice of others as a kind of goddess? For we observe how much help "she" has given towards the extension of the Empire by making others wrong-doers, so that the Romans should have enemies to fight in a just cause and so increase Rome's power.

– Saint Augustine[1]

Just as "Sallust's Theorem" did not originate in Sallust's history, but can be seen wherever there are political associations, Machiavellism "existed before Machiavelli, and is as old as politics itself."[2] Nevertheless, for reasons that

---

[1] *Concerning the City of God against the Pagans*, IV.xv.

[2] Gilbert, "Machiavellism," 116. In his famous study, Meinecke explains his choice of Machiavelli as his point of departure by arguing that the notion of sinfulness in the ancient world was neither sufficiently developed nor powerful enough to make reason of state as serious a problem as it was to become in the context of Christianity. Meinecke thus finds it "a historical necessity that the man, with whom the history of the idea of *raison d'état* in the modern Western world begins and from whom Machiavellism takes its name, had to be a heathen; he had to be a man to whom the fear of hell was unknown, and who on the contrary could set about his life-work of analysing the essence of *raison d'état* with all the naïvety of the ancient world" (*Machiavellism*, 29). There are certainly good reasons, of which Machiavelli's forcefulness and persuasiveness are only the most obvious, to take his claims of novelty at face value, but any demarcation of this kind is bound to be problematic. Friedrich, for example, disagrees with Meinecke's choice and argues that "the very cast of [Machiavelli's] thought kept him from 'discovering' the problem of the reason of state" (*Constitutional Reason of State*, 22). Friedrich is correct that a rigid distinction between means and ends misses the fundamental role that the state plays in Machiavelli's thought. The significance of the state, however, does not free Machiavelli completely of the need to justify the means required for building and maintaining it, as Friedrich claims (*ibid.*, 23). Machiavelli's radical departure from conventional moral frameworks is dependent nevertheless upon terms whose meaning he is seeking to change. This difficulty manifests itself

become apparent to any reader of *The Prince*, Machiavelli's name became synonymous with immoral political action very quickly. A few years after his death, the term *reason of state* made a reluctant appearance on the political stage. From the beginning, it was used to refer to political considerations that lie outside the bounds of ordinary circumstances, especially those foreseen and addressed by the law.[3] The relationship of the term *reason of state* to Machiavellism is a complicated one, and the date of birth of the former only adds to the complication. Reason of state became popular at the same time that reaction – mostly, but not exclusively, negative – to Machiavelli's teachings was mounting.[4] The precise details of that relationship are not as important as the fact that thinkers who identify themselves as concerned with reason of state find it impossible to avoid confronting Machiavelli.[5]

Machiavelli's alleged atheism, as evidenced in his less than respectful critique of Christianity, his view that religion ought to be harnessed in the service of the state, and his numerous suggestions for action that contravene even the most rudimentary understanding of religious morality, form the primary target. In their polemics, self-proclaimed defenders of religion and morality declare their intention to counter the pernicious teachings of Machiavelli, even though on occasion they have not read him.[6] Usually, these attacks focus

---

throughout his writings, whenever he attempts to redefine a term of this kind or to use it in an unconventional sense. See, e.g., his discussion of men's inability to be "honorably wicked or perfectly good" (*Discourses*, I.27 § 1), as well as his suggestion that the use of fraud in war is a "glorious thing" (III.40). For a discussion of the problems involved in choosing any single point of departure for Machiavellism, see Post, *Studies in Medieval Legal Thought*, 241–47.

[3] See Burke, "Tacitism, Scepticism, and Reason of State," 480. The consensus is that the first recognizable form of the term occurs in Giovanni Della Casa's 1547 oration to Charles V. Della Casa distinguishes between two types of reason: one false, called "reason of state" and another "simple, direct, and constant" (Della Casa, *Rime et prose*. This discussion begins on a page marked "69," but it is one of several pages in this edition that are numbered incorrectly; it follows page 64).

[4] On positive reactions, see Bireley, *The Counter-Reformation Prince*, 24.

[5] As Burke notes, "[t]he problem for Botero, as for later writers in the genre, was that, much as they might dislike Machiavelli's recommendations, they could not do without his ideas" ("Tacitism, Scepticism, and Reason of State," 483); cf. Kelley, "Murd'rous Machiavel in France," 555, 559; Gilbert, "Machiavellism," 122. Machiavelli's influence, direct and indirect, thus extends to a wide variety of unlikely reason of state thinkers, including Jesuits, such as Contzen and Possevino. See Bireley, *The Counter-Reformation Prince*; Höpfl, "Orthodoxy and Reason of State."

[6] See Horrocks, "Machiavelli in Tudor Political Opinion and Discussion," esp. pp. 202, 204, 208, 210; Weissberger, "Machiavelli and Tudor England," 589–90; Allen, "An Unmentioned Elizabethan Opponent of Machiavelli," 92. There is widespread consensus that this was also the case with Possevino (Villari, *The Life and Times of Niccolò Machiavelli*, II: 191;

on Machiavelli's approval of the actions of individual rulers, especially those that are flagrant violations of the most basic moral injunctions, such as those condemning theft, murder, and deceit. Even at this level, however, the results of these various polemics are often strange. Anti-Machiavellists of all kinds often end up sounding quite Machiavellian, finding it difficult to disagree in spirit with their opponent, even if they cannot bring themselves to admit it. In part this is because Machiavelli was right about one fundamental point, the realization that the standards that apply to conduct necessary for the foundation and preservation of the state cannot be the same as those applied to individual actions within the state. This problem, which lies at the heart of reason of state, is evident in the efforts of even its most pious defender. The tension between reasons of state and individual morality is also the reason why Machiavelli proves far more irresistible when it comes to matters of policy on the grandest scale, as in the case of foreign policy and war.

Machiavelli's military thought has an interesting history. The *Art of War* was one of only two works to be published during his lifetime.[7] A second edition of this work was issued in 1529, two years after Machiavelli's death, and prior to the publication of the first editions of the *Discourses* and *The Prince*. Together, all three works remained popular until their prohibition, both in the original, and in translation.[8] The *Art of War*, however, is important not just because it was the first – and for a while the only – work to offer the public a taste of Machiavelli's views on political matters, but also because it was the first work to state Machiavelli's view that political and military affairs are inextricably intertwined, a position that he would repeat in his political works proper.[9] Commentators have pointed out often that some of the recommendations contained in the *Art of War* show a surprising lack of acumen regarding the state and future of matters military.[10] The significance of the work, however, lies not so much in what it tells us about martial minutiae, but

---

Panella, *Gli antimachiavellici*, 54; De Mattei, *Dal premachiavellismo all'antimachiavellismo*, 240; Stewart, *Innocent Gentillet*, 128–29). Panella credits Conring with the observation. On the varieties of Anti-Machiavellism, see Bireley, *The Counter-Reformation Prince*, 24–25.

[7] The *Art of War* was published in 1521, as was the other work, *Mandragola*.

[8] According to Anglo, prior to their inclusion in the Index of prohibited books, in 1559, Machiavelli's works were published at least seventy-one times, including at least fourteen editions of the *Art of War*, compared with seventeen of *The Prince* (*Machiavelli*, 6). On the numerous translations, see Bowen, "Sixteenth Century French Translations of Machiavelli"; Wood, Introduction to *The Art of War*, xxix–xxx; Kahn, *Machiavellian Rhetoric*, 94–96; Anglo, *Machiavelli*, 32–33, 521.

[9] Machiavelli, *The Art of War*, 4; cf. *The Prince*, XIV; *Discourses*, I.19.

[10] See Berlin, *Against the Current*, 73. For the opposite view, see Lynch, Introduction to *Art of War*, xxvi–xxxiv.

rather in what it says about Machiavelli's views on politics.[11] Taken together, the multitude of editions, translations, and references to Machiavelli's military maxims tells us that during the sixteenth century, he was seen as someone to be reckoned with when it came to the study of war.[12]

It was in this area, more than any other, that Machiavelli posed a serious challenge to his adversaries. Even those who saw him as a teacher of tyranny could not disagree that the survival of the state was of the utmost importance. After all, their mission was not to deny the existence of reason of state, but to rescue it from the hands of the Devil. If individual immoral actions within the confines of the state are relatively easy to assess and condemn, however, those surrounding the conduct of foreign policy and war are far less so. The reconciliation of war with the demands of morality and piety is hard enough without the danger of sounding Machiavellian. Beyond the usual challenges, the thinkers who sought to respond to Machiavelli had to provide justifications for war and violence that contributed to such a reconciliation without ceding any ground to their opponent. The results of their efforts are often surprising.[13] In one way or another, their justifications had to incorporate war into God's plan for mankind. Thus, some argued that God created enmities in order to keep vices in check, whereas others suggested that war was God's way of making man social.[14] As a result of the challenges faced in this task, the arsenal of explanations of and justifications for human conduct in general, and war in particular, broadened to include attributes that in the past had often been passed over in silence.[15]

Keeping these constraints in mind goes some way towards explaining why reason of state thinkers are often dismissed as second rate.[16] The

---

[11] See, e.g., Wood, Introduction to *The Art of War*; Mansfield, *Machiavelli's Virtue*, 191–218; Colish, "Machiavelli's *Art of War*." Machiavelli's reliance on ancient sources for the specific recommendations in *The Art of War* was apparent to readers from the outset (cf. Anglo, *Machiavelli*, 523).

[12] See Anglo, *Machiavelli*, 528; Lynch, Introduction to *Art of War*, xxvi–xxvii.

[13] See Walzer, *The Revolution of the Saints*, chapter 8; Johnson, *Ideology, Reason, and the Limitation of War*, 160–63.

[14] See, e.g., Mariana, *The King and the Education of the King*, 113; Commynes, *Memoirs* I, 355; cf. Hale, "Sixteenth-Century Explanations of War and Violence," 51. Such explanations are part of a long tradition of attempts by Christian thinkers to understand and explain war. See, e.g., Saint Augustine, *Concerning the City of God against the Pagans*, I.i.

[15] As Hale notes, "[t]he shift from analysing human motivation in terms of a balance of virtues and vices to investigating the working of qualities like ambition, greed and fear enabled biographical case studies to enhance the objective study of human behavior" ("Sixteenth-Century Explanations of War and Violence," 12–13).

[16] In an oft-quoted footnote, Meinecke remarks, "[t]here are real catacombs here of forgotten literature by mediocrities" (*Machiavellism*, 67, note 1).

single-mindedness with which they approach their task, coupled with their often questionable sources of information about Machiavelli's views, prevents them from paying serious attention to his focus on the psychology of the individual and his consequent insistence that states be reminded of their beginnings. The result is thus curious, since a crucial line of argument that underpins Machiavelli's political thought is unaccounted for, and the consequences of this absence are evident even in the most sophisticated theories of the period. The extent of the problem becomes apparent when one considers the three most noteworthy exemplars of the genre: Gentillet, whose treatise singled out Machiavelli and in many cases served as the only source of information about his prohibited writings; Bodin, whose attempt to wrest politics away from Machiavelli yielded the concept of sovereignty; and Botero, who paradoxically branded his anti-Machiavellism "reason of state." In some ways, their reactions to Machiavelli's work display characteristics of the first wave of responses to negative association. Thus, it is not surprising that their views of *metus hostilis* are reminiscent of Saint Augustine's. All three, for example, note with approval that fear of external threats and mobilization for war distract individuals from sinful behavior and cleanse the state of undesirable elements. Their matter-of-fact acceptance of their importance, however, signals their defeat, for in granting negative association a role in the preservation of the state, they concede Machiavelli's central claim.

ANTI-MACHIAVELLISM

In 1576, Innocent Gentillet, a Huguenot jurist, published a critique of Machiavelli's political theory that came to be known as *Anti-Machiavel*.[17] Gentillet's work, first published anonymously, is divided into three parts, the first dealing with the counsel of a prince, the second with religion, and the third with *policy*, a term used often during this period as a synonym for reason

[17] The full title of the work is *Discours sur les moyens de bien gouverner et maintenir en bonne paix un royaume ou autre principauté. Divisez en trois parties: asavoir, du conseil, de la religion & police que doit tenir un prince. Contre Nicolas Machiavel Florentin*, but it is commonly referred to as *Anti-Machiavel*. Patrick's English translation of 1602 conveys the title of the original accurately. Cf. [Gentillet], *A Discourse upon the Meanes of Well Governing and Maintaining in Good Peace, a Kingdome, or Other Principalitie. Divided into Three Parts, namely, the Counsell, the Religion, and the Policie, which a Prince Ought to Hold and Follow. Against Nicholas Machiavell the Florentine*; Rathé, "Innocent Gentillet," 186–88; D'Andrea, "The Political and Ideological Context of Innocent Gentillet's *Anti-Machiavel*," 397, note 1. On Gentillet's place in anti-Machiavellism, see Beame, "The Use and Abuse of Machiavelli," 41–43; Anglo, *Machiavelli*, esp. 283–84, 322–24.

of state.[18] Each section of the book contains maxims drawn from Machiavelli's writings on the subject, which Gentillet proceeds to examine and refute by means of evidence drawn from Homer, Greek and Roman historians, and historians of France.[19] This method produces odd results, however, because despite Gentillet's frequent defamatory remarks about Machiavelli, his examination of the latter's maxims results quite frequently in agreement, in essence, rather than refutation.[20] This is especially true of the third – and largest – section, wherein Gentillet treats matters of policy internal and external.

At the outset of Part III, Gentillet tackles a fundamental problem in Machiavelli's thought – the intersection of politics and morality. He begins

[18] See, e.g., Rathé, "Innocent Gentillet," 198–99; Burke, "Tacitism, Scepticism, and Reason of State," 479–80.

[19] Gentillet does not employ scriptural references for this purpose (cf. Bireley, *The Counter-Reformation Prince*, 17; Anglo, *Machiavelli*, 303–04). He explains his choice of sources in the Preface of *Anti-Machiavel* (39–40; *Discours*, 17–18). On his choice of method, see Rathé, "Innocent Gentillet," 200.

[20] Part of the difficulty involved in assessing Gentillet's position has to do with the maxims themselves. Although in some cases they represent an accurate summary of Machiavelli's views of a certain matter, in others they are clearly oversimplifications, outright errors, or distortions. Particularly striking examples of Gentillet's unwitting concurrence with Machiavelli may be found in maxims 1, 9, 10, and 12 of Part III. In his consideration of maxim 12, e.g., Gentillet disputes the validity of Machiavelli's claim that the prince should be both a lion and a fox, arguing, "[i]f the prince hath reason on his side, and he with whom hee hath to doe, refuseth to come to reason, then the prince may justly constraine him by force of armes: and this is not called to fight like a beast, not like a Lion, but it is to fight as a man using reason, who employeth his owne corporall force, and the force of his horses, of his armies and walls, and of all other things offensive and defensive, to serve for instruments and meanes to execute that which reason commandeth and ordaineth: so that force employed to his right use, is no other thing but a servant of reason, which obeyeth her in all her commandements: and therefore therein there is nothing of a beast, and they which thus employ their forces, doe nothing that holds of a beast" ([Gentillet], *A Discourse*, 223–24). Gentillet's disagreement with Machiavelli here, then, is nominal rather than essential. The prevalent tendency among scholars has been to dismiss Gentillet's Machiavellian maxims as simplistic and tendentious. For examples of this view, see Villari, *The Life and Times of Niccolò Machiavelli*, II, 194–95; Meyer, *Machiavelli and the Elizabethan Drama*, 8–9; Meinecke, *Machiavellism*, 54; Whitfield, *Machiavelli*, 6; Rathé, "Innocent Gentillet," 216 and note 3; Stewart, *Innocent Gentillet*, 49–76; D'Andrea, "The Political and Ideological Context of Innocent Gentillet's *Anti-Machiavel*," 400–01; Salmon, *Renaissance and Revolt*, 41. Anglo, on the other hand, discusses the shortcomings of contemporary French translations and notes that Gentillet had never read Machiavelli's works in the original ("Le plus gentil esprit'", esp. 209–10, but cf. De Mattei, *Dal premachiavellismo all'antimachiavellismo*, 230). Anglo also takes Gentillet's maxims more seriously, both substantively and within their context, in which the use of maxims "was both desirable and normal" (*Machiavelli*, 298; cf. *ibid.*, 296–303, 316–22 and note 72). Compare also Kahn, "Reading Machiavelli," esp. 542, 546, 552–53.

by attributing to Machiavelli a maxim taken from Livy, namely that a necessary war is a just war, and that arms are "reasonable" when one has no hope of employing other means.[21] Gentillet counters that there is a distinction between just and unjust wars, and that princes should not take war lightly, but engage in it only when necessity commands them to do so and only for as long as they have to.[22] Above all, argues Gentillet, a prince should try to quell wars, whether civil or external, taking place in his own country. Foreign wars, he adds, are not so bad, especially if the prince happens to rule over a military people.[23] That Gentillet has negative association in mind here is apparent both from the fact that he cites Sallust on the ills of internal conflict and from his conclusion, which could well have been extracted from Machiavelli's writings: "[t]herefore, a war abroad, in a foreign country, appears not to be very damaging, but rather something necessary to a prince, to occupy and exercise his subjects."[24]

Spurred by Machiavelli's shocking preference for fear over love, Gentillet argues that a prince who oppresses his subjects cannot hope to retain power for long. He agrees with Machiavelli that it is necessity and force that make fear a compelling motivation, but attempts to draw a different conclusion. He argues, "because no violent thing lasts long by nature, disagreeable commandments will not be observed for long, and [. . .] obedience founded upon fear will be broken beyond repair."[25] The realization that necessity is fleeting marks the end of Gentillet's thoughts on the matter, whereas for Machiavelli it is but the first step; it is precisely because necessity does not last long, that it is necessary to renew it.

Machiavelli is well aware of the dangers involved in renewing necessity, since recourse to the wrong means is likely to have an adverse effect. Excessive use of punishment, for example, or abuse of one's powers with respect to the property of one's subjects are likely to incur hatred, which is a source of instability for the prince and thus a method to be avoided at all costs.[26] With these concerns in mind, Machiavelli turns instead to his broader conception

---

[21] "La guerre est juste qui est necessaire, et les armes raisonnables, quand on ne peut avoir esperance d'ailleurs" (Gentillet, *Anti-Machiavel*, 272; *Discours*, 217). As the editors of both editions of Gentillet's work point out, this maxim comes from Livy (*Ab urbe condita*, IX.i 10–11: "Iustum est bellum, Samnites, quibus necessarium, et pia arma quibus nulla nisi in armis relinquitur spes").

[22] Gentillet, *Anti-Machiavel*, 282; *Discours*, 226.

[23] Gentillet, *Anti-Machiavel*, 284; *Discours*, 227.

[24] Gentillet, *Anti-Machiavel*, 284; *Discours*, 227.

[25] Gentillet, *Anti-Machiavel*, 387; *Discours*, 315.

[26] Cf. Machiavelli, *The Prince*, XVII, XIX.

of necessity as manifested in the beginnings of cities. This move puts Gentillet in an awkward position. Even if he believes that he has dealt adequately with Machiavelli's maxim regarding fear and love, Gentillet discovers quickly that he has by no means dealt with the issue of necessity. Machiavelli knows well that necessity through fear can assume many guises, and Gentillet realizes as much when he comes to consider the maxim, "The prince should always nourish some enemy against himself, so that having oppressed him he may be considered all the greater and more formidable."[27] This maxim, drawn from Chapter XX of *The Prince*, focuses on Machiavelli's observation that "princes become great when they overcome difficulties made for them and opposition made to them," and his agreement with those who hold that "a wise prince, when he has the opportunity for it, should astutely nourish some enmity so that when he has crushed it, his greatness emerges more from it."[28] Gentillet's first objection to this suggestion is that it too is based on a preference for fear over love. After all, Gentillet notes, a prince who follows Machiavelli's advice will not want for enemies.[29] To illustrate this point, Gentillet uses an irrelevant example of Nero's suppression of a conspiracy against him.[30] The choice of example might be considered merely unfortunate, but it betrays a more serious problem with Gentillet's assessment of Machiavelli's views on negative association.

This problem manifests itself right away. As it turns out, it is not just tyrants who have their fair share of enemies, but all princes. Once again, Gentillet's choice of evidence to support his claim is curious, for he cites Monsieur Philippe de Commynes, a man known as the "French Machiavelli."[31] Gentillet seems not to be troubled in the least either by Commynes' reputation or by the fact that his "very good discourse" actually confirms Machiavelli's point. He thus attempts to answer Machiavelli by citing Commynes' observation

That God wished to give every prince, kingdom, and republic a contrary and opposite, to keep the one and the other bound to their duties, just as England has France, Scotland has England, Portugal has Castile, Grenada has Portugal, the princes of Italy have one another, and thus with all the countries and seigniories of the earth.

---

[27] Gentillet, *Anti-Machiavel*, 428; *Discours*, 352.

[28] Machiavelli, *The Prince*, XX: 85.

[29] Gentillet, *Anti-Machiavel*, 428; *Discours*, 352.

[30] The example is from Tacitus's *Annals*, 15.54–71. As Rathé points out, all of Gentillet's examples in this section are irrelevant to the point he is trying to make (Gentillet, *Anti-Machiavel*, 429, note 1).

[31] Kelley, "Murd'rous Machiavel in France," 553. According to Bakos, Machon refers to Commynes as "the French Tacitus" (quoted in "'*Qui nescit dissimulare, nescit regnare*,'" 408).

For, if there were a prince or republic that had no opposite to hold it in fear, one would see it come to tyranny and excess forthwith. But God, in His wise providence, has given each seigniorie and each prince his opposite, so that each keep the other on the right track. And there is nothing (he says) that keeps a prince bound to his duties, nor that keeps him in line more than the fear of his opposite and contrary. For, neither the fear of God, nor the love of his neighbor, nor reason (about which very often he does not care), nor justice (for there is none above himself), nor any other similar thing can bind him to his duties, but only the fear of his contrary.[32]

The fact that Commynes' opinion, as summarized here by Gentillet, confirms Machiavelli's view is not as surprising as the fact that Gentillet proceeds to characterize it as "truly Christian."[33] Gentillet finds that Commynes has far more impressive credentials than Machiavelli, who is but a "pettie burn-paper" and whose history covers the insignificant affairs of a single house of Florence.[34]

Although Meinecke sees Gentillet's *Anti-Machiavel* as an important signpost in the history of nascent Machiavellism, he dismisses it as "clumsy, garrulous, and full of misconceptions."[35] Despite this judgment, Meinecke nevertheless notes that *Anti-Machiavel* contains recommendations that could well be considered Machiavellian.[36] To the reader who takes Gentillet's anti-Machiavellian proclamations seriously, such teachings may come as a surprise. Nevertheless, Gentillet's inability to dismiss central elements of Machiavelli's

---

[32] Gentillet, *Anti-Machiavel*, 430; *Discours*, 353. Gentillet conveys the substance of Commynes' argument well. In the *Memoirs*, Commynes writes, "[a]ll things considered, it seems to me that God has created neither man nor beast in this world without establishing some counterpart to oppose him, in order to keep him in humility and fear" (I, 353). Commynes proceeds to cite several examples of such oppositions in Europe and adds that according to his limited information about the other two parts of the world, Asia and Africa, this phenomenon seems to be universal, and concludes "that these divisions are necessary in all the world and that these dissensions and oppositions, which God has given and ordered for every estate and almost for every person [...] are also necessary" (I, 355).

[33] Gentillet, *Anti-Machiavel*, 432; *Discours*, 355.

[34] Gentillet, *Anti-Machiavel*, 432; *Discours*, 355; *A Discourse, etc.*, 246. Gentillet repeats here a comparison first made in the preface of the work (*Anti-Machiavel*, 40; *Discours*, 18). On Commynes, cf. Huppert, *The Idea of Perfect History*, 21–22; Keohane, *Philosophy and the State in France*, 28–29.

[35] Meinecke, *Machiavellism*, 54. Meinecke concludes his section on Gentillet as follows: "Neither the Christian in him, nor the knight, wanted to have anything to do with the cold monster of *raison d'état*" (*ibid.*, 56).

[36] Meinecke notices, e.g., Gentillet's treatment of maxim 1, of part 3, where Gentillet concedes the value of foreign wars (*Machiavellism*, 55–56). Cf. Kahn, "Reading Machiavelli," 541; Anglo, *Machiavelli*, 284.

views on foreign policy and war betrays a fundamental problem with the development of a moral reason of state, one that every other serious exponent of the genre would have to struggle with as well. Ultimately, the conclusions of the Anti-Machiavellists on foreign policy and war turn out to be silent acknowledgments of Machiavelli's vision.

A MYOPIC VISION OF ABSOLUTE SOVEREIGNTY

In addition to *Anti-Machiavel*, 1576 saw the publication of Bodin's *Six livres de la république*. In his earlier work, *Method for the Easy Comprehension of History*, written just after Machiavelli's works began to be placed on the indexes of prohibited books, Bodin offers a mix of praise and blame for Machiavelli. He considers him "the first" writer on matters of government "for about 1,200 years after barbarism had overwhelmed everything" and acknowledges that his sayings "are on the lips of everyone," but he adds, "there is no doubt but that he would have written more fully and more effectively and with a greater regard for the truth, if he had combined a knowledge of the writings of the ancient philosophers and historians with experience."[37] In the preface to *Six livres de la république*, Bodin is less charitable.[38] He singles Machiavelli out as the exemplar of everything that is wrong with writing on politics:

We have a Machiavelli, for example, who has been fashionable among the agents of tyrants. Paulus Jovius places him in the ranks of remarkable men, yet calls him an atheist, and ignorant of good literature. As for atheism, he glorifies it in his writings. As for knowledge, I believe that those who are accustomed to discuss learnedly, to assess wisely and to resolve subtly important matters of state will agree that he never explored the terrain of political science. The latter is not a matter of tyrannical ruses, such as he sought out from all the nooks and crannies of Italy and poured like a slow poison into his book, *The Prince*. In it he uplifts to the skies, and sets out as a model for all kings, the most perfidious son of a priest that ever lived. Yet this man, for all his trickery, was ignominiously cast down from the high and slippery rock of tyranny on which he was ensconced, and in the end exposed like a beggar to the mercy and derision of his enemies. The same

---

[37] Bodin, *Method*, 153. The latter criticism is all the more striking given that this is precisely what Machiavelli claims to have done in the *Discourses* (Ep. Ded., p. 3) as well as *The Prince* (Ep. Ded., p. 3).

[38] Bodin produced a Latin version of this work ten years after the French edition. The two differ in some ways, and Knolles's translation of 1606 was produced from both, so neither by itself corresponds fully to the English version. For an explanation of the various editions, see McRae's introduction to his edition of the Knolles translation (*The Six Bookes of a Commonweale* [1962]).

has since befallen other princes who have followed in his footsteps, and prac-
ticed those goodly precepts of Machiavelli, who laid down the twin foundations
of Commonweals impiety and injustice, and condemned religion as hostile to the
state.[39]

In light of the fact that the use of Machiavelli as an adversary was becoming more frequent by this time, Bodin's choice to introduce his work by
renouncing the immoral Florentine atheist is unsurprising.[40] The main body
of the work itself contains only six references to Machiavelli or his works,
but Machiavelli's influence on Bodin is omnipresent. More broadly, Bodin's
main themes resemble those of Machiavelli and are often treated in the same
order.[41] More specifically, Bodin's choice and treatment of episodes from
Roman history very often mirrors Machiavelli's own. By itself, the former
similarity does not mean very much, but coupled with the second and given
that Machiavelli's course through Roman history is quite idiosyncratic, there
is good reason to think that Bodin's dependence on Machiavelli is greater
than either his prefatory disclaimer or the paucity of explicit references to
Machiavelli might indicate.[42] As in the case of Gentillet, in Bodin's work
the anti-Machiavellian rhetoric clashes with the author's own views regarding the relationship between morality and politics. Although there is good

---

[39] Bodin, *The Six Bookes of a Commonweale* (McRae ed.), A69–70 (*Six livres* [1583], preface,
áiij–áiijv). Bodin returns to Machiavelli's treatment of Borgia in V.vi (*The Six Bookes of a
Commonweale*, 629v). Bodin's judgment that Machiavelli is no political scientist is not as
unusual as it may sound to a contemporary reader. At the time, and especially outside Italy,
Machiavelli was primarily known as a historian and tactician, through his *Florentine Histories*
and *Art of War*, respectively (cf. Cardascia, "Machiavel et Jean Bodin," 130, 134).

[40] This is especially true in France, where Italian influence, as personified in Catherine de'
Medici, was blamed for a wide range of political problems, including, most notably, the St.
Bartholomew's Day Massacre (see, e.g., Cardascia, "Machiavel et Jean Bodin," 131–32, 149;
Bowen, "Sixteenth Century French Translations of Machiavelli," 313; Kelley, "Murd'rous
Machiavel in France," 556–57; Gilbert, "Machiavellism," 117–18; Anglo, "Le plus gen-
til esprit,'" 208–09; Anglo, *Machiavelli*, 229–31). Bodin's prefatory declarations regarding
Machiavelli are frequently taken at face value. Baudrillart, e.g., suggests that Bodin argues as
much against Machiavelli as against the anti-monarchical pamphleteers (*Bodin et son temps*,
225).

[41] Compare, for example, their respective discussions of fortresses (Machiavelli, *Discourses* II.24;
Bodin, *The Six Bookes of a Commonweale*, 596–614; cf. Anglo, *Machiavelli*, 548–49). Also
striking is Bodin's approval of a certain amount of internal discord (*Six livres de la république*,
IV.5: 419–24; cf. Keohane, *Philosophy and the State in France*, 77–78; Waszink, Introduction
to *Politica*, 93).

[42] This similarity is noted by students of Bodin's work. See, e.g., Chauviré, *Jean Bodin*, 192–
207, esp. 196–97; Garosci, *Jean Bodin*, 189–90, 234; Panella, *Gli antimachiavellici*, 49–51;
Cardascia, "Machiavel et Jean Bodin," 133–51, esp. 150–51.

reason to think that Bodin's fundamental disagreement with Machiavelli over the dissociation of politics and morality was genuine, the substance of his theory shows him to be at least an unconscious Machiavellian.[43]

In chapter 5 of book V, for example, Bodin proposes to consider "whether it bee more conuenient to trayne up the subiects in armes, and to fortifie their townes or not," which he considers "one of the highest questions of State" and most difficult to answer.[44] He announces his intention to present both sides and leave the resolution "to the wise politicians." He begins by dismissing the simple but extreme Aristotelian position in favor of fortifications and of a site inaccessible to the enemy, because he believes that different regimes call for different measures. Yet, Bodin fulfills his promise to supply arguments for both sides only in the most nominal sense. His presentation results in an unqualified endorsement of military training and a somewhat less enthusiastic endorsement of fortifications.[45] Despite an impassioned rejection of war and soldiers at the outset of the chapter, Bodin calls for a broader definition of just war, one that includes any war resulting from a "necessarie" cause, such as those waged to "defend the liues of innocents."[46]

Immediately thereafter, his argument takes a curious turn. He states that there are other particular considerations besides the ones he has just addressed, and begins a lengthy discussion of negative association.[47] The best means to preserve a state and ensure it against rebellions and civil wars, while maintaining its subjects in a state of concord, is to have an enemy to whom they may oppose themselves.[48] Bodin finds this to be universally true, "by the example of all Commonweales, and namely of the Romans, who never could find a more safe and surer remedie against ciuill warres, than to affront the subiects with an enemie."[49] The universality of this realization cannot be overstated. After reviewing a wide-ranging series of more recent cases, Bodin proposes to consider some more ancient examples, to demonstrate that it is well-nigh

---

[43] The phrase is Cardascia's ("Machiavel et Jean Bodin," 152).

[44] Bodin, *The Six Bookes of a Commonweale*, 596.

[45] Bodin, *The Six Bookes of a Commonweale*, 596–601. For example, after making a series of unconvincing and sometimes unintelligible claims in connection with arguments against military training, Bodin concludes, "I see no reason why wee should instruct citisens in this cruell and execrable kind of life, or to arm them, but to repulse violence in time of extreame necessitie" (*ibid.*, 599). Cf. Anglo, *Machiavelli*, 548–49.

[46] Bodin, *The Six Bookes of a Commonweale*, 601.

[47] Bodin, *Les six livres de la république*, 760.

[48] Bodin, *Les six livres de la république*, 760.

[49] Bodin, *The Six Bookes of a Commonweale*, 601.

impossible "to maintain subjects in peace and amity when they are not at war with the enemy."[50] The obvious example is once again Rome. After Rome defeated all its enemies, the Senate found itself forced to entertain wars and forge enemies where there were none. Having expanded to the ends of the world and unable to find further enemies, Rome's parts turned on one another.[51]

In addition to preventing internal conflict, however, external wars also help keep the city free of undesirable elements. Because there is no city so holy that it does not have its share of "theeues, murtherers, idle persons, vagabonds, mutins, adulterers, and dice players, which leade a wicked life, and corrupt the simplicitie of good subiects; neither can lawes, magistrates, nor any punishment keepe them in awe." The solution must be sought elsewhere, among enemies, for "[t]here is no better meanes then to purge the Commonweale of this infectious filth, then to send them to the warre, the which is as it were a purging medicine to expell corrupted humors out of the vniuersall bodie of the state."[52]

Despite his initial hesitation, Bodin now feels ready to declare that war is not only necessary but a part of God's plan. Without referring to Machiavelli, Bodin nevertheless agrees that "all nations" should adopt the military discipline of the Romans, which makes "a coward valiant, an intemperate man modest, a slothful man actiue, a prodigall man frugall, and a licentious man continent."[53] This military discipline teaches the soldier more than the art of fighting. It renders him industrious, resolute, temperate, and prevents lust, licentiousness, impiety, and sloth from taking hold. "Besides," adds Bodin, "there is nothing that containes the people within the dutie of honor and vertue more then the feare of a warlike enemie."[54] To support this claim, Bodin cites Polybius's account of the reign of virtue in Rome while enemies were at its gates, and praises Nasica for standing before the Senate and warning of the dangers of discord and civil war that would follow the destruction of Carthage.[55] Bodin concludes his thoughts on negative association through *metus hostilis* with an arresting statement:

for euen as moderate libertie puffes men vp, and makes them proane to all vices, so feare retaines them in their duties: and we must not doubt but the great polititian and

[50] Bodin, *Les six livres de la république*, 761.
[51] Bodin, *Les six livres de la république*, 761.
[52] Bodin, *The Six Bookes of a Commonweale*, 602. Cf. Meinecke, *Machiavellism*, 57–58.
[53] Bodin, *The Six Bookes of a Commonweale*, 603.
[54] Bodin, *The Six Bookes of a Commonweale*, 603.
[55] Bodin, *The Six Bookes of a Commonweale*, 603.

gouernour of all the world as he hath giuen to euery thing his contrarie, so hath he suffred warres and hatred among the nations to punish one by an other, and to keep them all in feare, which is the only comptroller of vertue, as *Samuell* in an oration which he made vnto the people said, That God had stirred them vp enemies, to keep them in awe, try them, and punish them.[56]

These considerations lead Bodin to conclude that military training is undoubtedly necessary, both for waging war and for keeping one's subjects in check.

Bodin never cites Sallust, Machiavelli, or Commynes in this chapter, but their influence is abundantly clear. His prefatory declaration of war against the immorality of Machiavelli perhaps explains why he chooses Polybius as his main source of evidence regarding the political utility of *metus hostilis*, but his procedure betrays his agreement with the sources that he would rather not name. Bodin's emphasis of the moral utility of *metus hostilis* in purging the city of undesirable elements and corrupting behavior follows the Sallustian interpretation that Saint Augustine emphasized in *City of God*.[57] More telling, perhaps, is Bodin's approach to the issue of military training, which has left students of his works with an unmistakable impression that Machiavelli is his primary source of influence.[58] Perhaps the most striking feature of Bodin's examination of *metus hostilis*, however, is his conclusion. Whereas Bodin had begun the chapter in question by listing the evils of war and emphasizing the degree to which peace was the only way of life in accordance with God's will, he concludes by referring to God as the "great politician," in whose plan war plays a central role.[59]

---

[56] Bodin, *The Six Bookes of a Commonweale*, 603.

[57] In the lengthiest of four references to Sallust, in *Method for the Easy Comprehension of History*, Bodin writes, "Concerning Sallust, since almost all his writings have perished, we cannot judge so easily. Yet from those which we have it is evident that he was a most honest author and possessed experience of important affairs. In order that he might write more truthfully about the great war with Jugurtha, he journeyed as far as Africa. He made rather frank statements, however. What is bolder than to lodge in Caesar and in Cato alone the valor of all the Romans of that age?" (56–57). Bodin refers to Sallust once in the Latin edition of the *Six livres*. He refers several times to Saint Augustine in both works.

[58] Chauviré, e.g., concludes that Bodin borrows Machiavelli's military theories "almost word for word" (*Jean Bodin*, 207). Cardascia notes that despite Bodin's repeated disavowal of policy centered on *salus populi*, "[t]out le machiavélisme est chez lui" ("Machiavel et Jean Bodin," 153. Cardascia notes that the idea of *metus hostilis* is "une idée bien machiavélique" that Bodin uses on several occasions (*ibid.*, 155). Cf. Meinecke, *Machiavellism*, 57–58.

[59] Bodin, *The Six Bookes of a Commonweale*, [598]–599. If Bodin's contention that God created oppositions and enmities to keep the nations in check is reminiscent of the "French Machiavelli," Philippe de Commynes, the similarity is once again far from accidental. Bodin cites Commynes several times in the *Six Bookes*. Just a few pages below his discussion of

REASON OF STATE

In some ways, Giovanni Botero's 1589 work, *Della ragion di stato*, marks a turning point in the history of reason of state thought. It is the first work to bear the name of that tradition in its title. It is also the first work to try to break the term's association with Machiavelli.[60] *Della ragion di stato* is also one of two prominent works published that year that connect Machiavelli's name with that of Tacitus.[61] Despite these innovations, however, Botero's work is also highly conventional. In his dedicatory letter, the author reports, "I have been greatly astonished to find Reason of State a constant subject of discussion and to hear the opinions of Niccolò Machiavelli and Cornelius Tacitus frequently quoted," and "amazed that so impious an author and so wicked a tyrant [Tiberius] should be held in such esteem that they are thought to provide ideal examples of the methods by which states should be governed and administered."[62] Botero proposes to restore conscience to government by wresting reason of state away from Machiavelli. His identification of Machiavelli as the enemy thus puts him squarely in the same camp as Gentillet and Bodin, and just as their attacks on the Florentine left them more Machiavellian than not, Botero's does too.[63]

Botero, who was highly influenced by Bodin's work, seems well aware of what will be necessary to fight Machiavelli.[64] He therefore begins by defining the central terms of the debate in such a way as to distance himself from the Florentine. Thus, he describes the state as "a stable rule over a people" and reason of state as "the knowledge of the means by which a dominion may be founded, preserved, and extended," and yet notes immediately that "although in the widest sense the term includes all these, it is concerned *most nearly* with preservation, and more nearly with extension

---

metus hostilis, in a section in which Bodin discusses the dangers of neutrality, he invokes the authority of Commynes and Livy, respectively (*ibid.*, 622).

[60] Cf. Viroli, *From Politics to Reason of State*, 252.

[61] The other one is Lipsius's *Six Books of Politics*. Lipsius's interest in Tacitus, however, predates this work (see Schellhase, *Tacitus in Renaissance Political Thought*, 117–26; Salmon, *Renaissance and Revolt*, 51; Bireley, *The Counter-Reformation Prince*, 50; Burke, "Tacitism, Scepticism, and Reason of State," 489).

[62] Botero, *The Reason of State*, Ep. Ded., xiii.

[63] See Schellhase, *Tacitus in Renaissance Political Thought*, 123; cf. Mansfield, "On the Impersonality of the Modern State," 855; Burke, "Tacitism, Scepticism, and Reason of State," 483.

[64] On Bodin's influence, see Chabod, *Scritti sul Rinascimento*, 298–99, 308 and note 4, 311–12, 340; De Luca, *Stato e chiesa nel pensiero politico di G. Botero*, 49–54; Schellhase, *Tacitus in Renaissance Political Thought*, 126; Bireley, *The Counter-Reformation Prince*, 47.

than with foundation."[65] Yet, his attempt to eliminate from the discussion one of Machiavelli's central tenets, the importance of beginnings, backfires instantaneously because he realizes that "the art of foundation and of extension is the same because the beginnings and the continuations are of the same nature."[66] This inability to move too far from the kinds of situations that Machiavelli sees as equivalent to beginnings becomes apparent throughout Botero's study of the requirements of reason of state.[67] Rehearsing this repertoire, he too cannot avoid making the occasional comment regarding the utility of enemies for the preservation of the state.

In considering the connection between the size of the state and its chances of survival, Botero notes that greatness makes a state overconfident in its powers, which in turn leads to "negligence, idleness and contempt both of subjects and of enemies."[68] In such cases, the state survives at best through its reputation, but that foundation is an uncertain one. It is a short step from this lesson to the utility of *metus hostilis*, and Botero takes it almost imperceptibly. He lists several examples of states that began to decline after vanquishing their main enemies, and observes that after valor has won the day, "it is immediately stifled by riches, enervated by pleasure, and degraded by sensuality; it weathers severe storms and threatening tempests on the high seas, but shipwrecks and is lost in harbour."[69] The reason for this counter-intuitive observation lies in the familiar Hippocratic realization that idleness leads to vice. Botero finds that "because the common people are by nature unstable and long for novelty they will seek it out for themselves, changing even their government and their rulers if their prince does not provide some kind of diversion for them."[70] One ought to keep the ship on the high seas as long as possible, therefore, and nothing does so as well as military enterprises. Botero observes that these are "the most effective means of keeping a people occupied, for nothing arouses their interest so much as an important war."[71] In a shocking reversal of his moralistic overture, Botero notes that regardless of the reason for which a war is waged, "everyone who is able is ready to

---

[65] Botero, *The Reason of State*, I.1: 3, emphasis added.
[66] Botero, *The Reason of State*, I.1: 3. This realization accords well with Botero's conclusion to his *The Cause of the Greatnesse of Cities, etc.*, where he argues, "[f]or the Causes of the production of things, and conservation of them, are assuredly the same" (177).
[67] This is an issue that Botero addresses also in *The Cause of the Greatnesse of Cities, etc.*, where he uses terms reminiscent of Machiavelli's (see, e.g., 6–7, 20).
[68] Botero, *The Reason of State*, I.6: 7.
[69] Botero, *The Reason of State*, I.6: 8.
[70] Botero, *The Reason of State*, III.1: 74.
[71] Botero, *The Reason of State*, III.3: 76.

play his part either in council or in action, and all discontent is vented on the common enemy." "The rest of the people," he adds,

either follow the camp to bring supplies and to perform similar necessary services, or remain at home to offer prayers and vows to God for ultimate victory, or at least are so stirred by expectation and by news of the progress of the war that there is no place for thoughts of revolt in their minds: either in thought or in deed everyone is preoccupied by the war

The Romans frequently had recourse to this remedy which served as a sort of sheet-anchor when the multitude seemed to threaten revolt. The army was led into action against some enemy, and the bad feelings of the common people toward the aristocracy were dissipated.[72]

Just as Gentillet and Bodin had done before him, Botero views Rome as the most notable example of negative association through *metus hostilis*. He too offers other examples, but he also gives his argument a peculiar twist. He concludes by citing the example of the Swiss, whose government is "popular and thereby liable to disturbance," and argues that they have managed to secure internal peace by serving as mercenaries for others![73]

While those who lack other occupations should thus seek out war, even if someone else's, a state should do its utmost to avoid having to use the services of mercenaries.[74] When he comes to the question that Bodin identified as central to politics, in the *République*, namely "[w]hether or not a ruler should make warriors of his people," Botero too turns to the Romans for examples and joins his predecessors once more in dismissing mercenaries as detrimental to the health of the state.[75] He too considers the disadvantages of armed subjects and acknowledges that in some instances, warlike peoples turn against their own when their enemies have been vanquished. Despite this danger, Botero favors military training much as Machiavelli and Bodin did.[76] His justification for this choice is striking. It is based on two of Machiavelli's most fundamental maxims, that one will always be forced to choose between the lesser of two evils, and that reliance on the means of others is to be avoided

---

[72] Botero, *The Reason of State*, III.3: 77. Botero's list includes quite matter-of-factly those wars waged "simply to win glory and riches" (*ibid.*, III.3: 76).

[73] Botero, *The Reason of State*, III.3: 77. According to Hale, de la Noue recommended joining the Knights of Malta for similar reasons ("Sixteenth-Century Explanations of War and Violence," 22).

[74] Cf. Machiavelli, *Discourses*, I.43, II.20; *The Prince*, XII, XIII.

[75] See Bodin, *The Six Bookes of a Commonweale*, V.5; Botero, *The Reason of State*, IX.2.

[76] His agreement with Machiavelli on military matters is extensive and includes such unlikely positions as a preference for infantry over cavalry (*The Reason of State*, X.8).

at all costs. In terms that could have been extracted from the *Discourses*, Botero argues, "in human affairs and especially in handling and governing men, it is impossible to avoid all ill consequences; the business of the wise prince is to escape the greatest and most dangerous of these, and to be dependent upon the power of others is the greatest evil to which the state can be subject."[77] Given this position, his conclusion that alliances last "only so long as the partner is useful" is not entirely unexpected.[78] Botero concludes his thoughts on military training by proclaiming it an "excellent plan [...] to keep a fleet of galleys, so that those who are of a restless disposition can find an outlet for their youth and courage in fighting the true enemies, for this also serves as a diversion and a remedy for peccant humours."[79]

If these signs of agreement with Machiavelli appear surprising in light of his self-proclaimed anti-Machiavellism, *The Reason of State* concludes with two further unexpected Machiavellian elements. The first is Botero's startling claim that in addition to using military forces for its defense, the state may also use them to expand "In the defense of the public good."[80] This position, which comes close to summarizing Machiavelli's reasons for choosing a fertile site and cultivating tumult within the state, is made all the more astonishing by Botero's rationale, according to which "[d]efensive warfare has such absolute justification that offensive warfare is only justified by defence, and in no circumstances can offensive action be lawful except for purposes of defence."[81] Even though Botero identifies heretics as the worst offenders against peace, he argues that war cannot be waged against them, except as the last resort. "But he who wishes to fight," he adds, "cannot claim that there is no public enemy against whom he may prove his valour."[82] This bold transgression of Saint Augustine's admonition in the epigraph to this chapter paves the way for Botero's *coup de grâce*, "[w]e have the Turks at our gates and on our flanks: could there be juster and more honorable argument for war?"[83]

---

[77] Botero, *The Reason of State*, IX.2: 171. Cf. Machiavelli, *Discourses*, I.6 § 2: "In all human things [...] one inconvenience can never be suppressed without another's cropping up"; *The Prince* XXI: 91: "For in the order of things it is found that one never seeks to avoid one inconvenience without running into another; but prudence consists in knowing how to recognize the qualities of inconveniences, and in picking the less bad as good."

[78] Botero, *The Reason of State*, VIII.13: 163.

[79] Botero, *The Reason of State*, IX.2: 172–73.

[80] Botero, *The Reason of State*, X.9: 221.

[81] Botero, *The Reason of State*, X.9: 221.

[82] Botero, *The Reason of State*, X.9: 222.

[83] Saint Augustine, *Concerning the City of God against the Pagans*, IV.15; Botero, *The Reason of State*, X.9: 222.

Botero's concluding appeal to the Christian powers to unite against the Turks follows a long tradition of Christian claims for unity with a strong measure of negative association, and it is part of an agenda that Botero himself has expressed repeatedly.[84] At this juncture, the invocation of the Turkish specter is noteworthy not only because it marks the culmination of the first treatise on reason of state but also because it signals the increasing importance of negative association in the context of calls for Christian unity.[85] Given the trajectory of the idea of negative association outlined herein, it should come as no great surprise that Botero would choose to end the chapter and the book by paralleling the Turkish threat to that posed by Carthage for Rome, and by referring to Cato.

MACHIAVELLISM

When Rousseau accused Frederick the Great of having begun his Machiavellism by refuting Machiavelli, he captured in a sentence a practice that had dominated reactions to Machiavelli in the sixteenth and seventeenth centuries.[86] In his essay "Of Evil Means Employed to a Good End," Montaigne focuses almost exclusively on such matters. He, too, builds his case around the inescapable topos, the Roman recourse to *metus hostilis*, and observes,

[t]here are many in our times who reason in like fashion, wishing that this heated passion that is among us might be deflected into some war with our neighbors, for fear that these peccant humors which dominate our body at the moment, if they are not drained of elsewhere, may keep our fever still at its height and in the end bring on our total ruin. And indeed, a foreign war is much milder than a civil war."[87]

---

[84] See, e.g., Botero, *Relations*, C 1 r., 233–34. Earlier in *The Reason of State*, Botero writes, "There are only two ways of uniting against the Turk with any hope of success. Either the rulers of all the countries which border upon his dominions should attack him at the same moment on all sides, not with limited strength but using all available resources – and in this way all the parties would have an equal interest in ultimate victory. Or another and more noble way would be for many princes to unite together with no other interest than the honour of God and the exaltation of the Church, and to attack the Turk at one or several points" (VIII.13: 163–64). The attempt to distinguish between the motives of one approach and the other is only nominally successful, at best. Cf. Mastnak, "Abbé de Saint-Pierre: European Union and the Turk," 575; Chapter 6 in this volume.

[85] Negative claims of this sort will come to play an increasingly important role in discussions of European unity in the eighteenth century. See, e.g., the discussion of Saint-Pierre, in Chapter 6 in this volume.

[86] Letter to M. Lenieps, 4 October 1758 (*Correspondence générale de J.-J. Rousseau* IV, no. 584: 150).

[87] Montaigne, *The Complete Essays*, II.23: 517–18.

Montaigne doubts that this type of activity would be favored by God, but is nevertheless forced to concede that it is part of the human condition to resort to the use of evil means towards a good end. Rousseau's observation, then, captures the nature of anti-Machiavellism, whereas Montaigne's conveys its magnitude and focus. When defenders of morality and religion took it upon themselves to combat Machiavelli's central teaching that the ends justify the means, nowhere did they encounter greater difficulties than when it came to matters of foreign policy and war. In this respect, they differed neither from the long tradition seeking to reconcile war with Christianity nor from the broader tradition of those whom Wolin identifies as trying to "weave ingenious veils of euphemism to conceal the ugly fact of violence."[88] Among the many and quite varied religious and moral justifications offered for war, however, the ones provided by the so-called Anti-Machiavellists stand out for their inventiveness. This is no small feat, considering the difficulty inherent in the task under any circumstances.

The thinkers in question had to walk a very fine line between extreme naïveté – a world in which the fact of violence is simply ignored – and Machiavellism. In this balancing act, adherents to reason of state were forced to accept the existence of enmity as part of the reality of the natural world, and to find ways to include it among the most essential tools for the preservation of domestic order. This and other such concessions regarding foreign policy and war in turn explain some of the other unexpected positions on matters of individual conduct that can be found in their writings. Wolin argues that although Machiavelli's predecessors had considered the effects of violence on those who administer it, they "rarely faced up [...] to the problem of the cumulative effect on society of the consistent application of coercion and the not infrequent use of violence."[89] Machiavelli's innovation, in this sense, is twofold: he is concerned not only with the effects of violence on the society at large, but also with the effects of its absence.[90] His serious attention to the effects of war on a society includes the unusually vociferous, and therefore scandalous, suggestion that a certain amount of it is both necessary and good for domestic tranquility. Coupled with his radical and shocking approval of internal tumult, this attention made for an astonishing political theory.

Machiavelli's simple and yet revolutionary realization is summed up in his observation that when confronted with the kind of necessity that character-izes the beginnings of states, the people come to reacquaint themselves with

---

[88] Wolin, *Politics and Vision*, 197.
[89] Wolin, *Politics and Vision*, 197.
[90] Machiavelli discusses both in *Discourses*, II.2 § 2.

their identity.[91] The powerful effects of this return to first principles, where one's political identity receives its ultimate justification, are the reason why Machiavelli focuses his advice on the recreation of such encounters.[92] This is why it is a good idea to take away necessity from one's enemy and to impose it on one's own troops, and why "a prince should have no other object, nor any other thought, nor make anything else his art but that of war and its orders and discipline."[93] When it turned blood into wine, Christianity removed the terror that made the ancients greater lovers of freedom than his contemporaries.[94] Interestingly, Machiavelli argues that this cowardly transformation was the result of interpreting the new religion "according to *idleness* and not according to virtue."[95] To Machiavelli, this comes as no surprise, since he knows well that religion is necessary but not sufficient for the preservation and greatness of the state.[96] This is why despite his admiration for Numa's contribution to the development of Rome, Machiavelli ultimately sees him as a weak prince, and prefers to entrust the future of the state to a Romulus or Tullus.

Before Machiavelli, negative association was viewed with trepidation. The manner in which Thucydides, Sallust, and Saint Augustine approached it was cautious and, occasionally, regretful. This is nowhere more true than in Sallust's emblematic treatment of *metus hostilis*, in which the absence of negative association marks the beginning of the end for Rome, but even its

---

[91] Machiavelli, *Discourses*, III.1 § 2.

[92] Mansfield notes that in *Discourses*, I.1, Machiavelli wishes to show that men are forced to make the fundamental political distinction between natives and foreigners and adds, "If they could rely on the protection of nature or God, they would not have to separate themselves into natives and foreigners. If they could consider themselves natives of a mother earth or of an intended home, they could regard themselves as brothers. But necessity forbids it . . ." (*Machiavelli's Virtue*, 69).

[93] Machiavelli, *The Prince*, XIV: 58. Cf. *Discourses*, III.12; *The Art of War*, II, 76–80, IV, 129, VI, 174–75. It is also why one ought to expose them to the enemy through hand-to-hand combat (II.17 § 5), as well as why fortresses are a bad idea (*The Prince*, XX).

[94] Machiavelli claims that the difference between them "arises from the same cause that makes men less strong now, which [. . .] is the difference between our education and the ancient, founded on the difference between our religion and the ancient" (*Discourses*, II.2 § 2). The spectacle of the sacrifices in the latter, "being terrible, rendered men similar to itself." Cf. Machiavelli, *Discourses*, I. Pref. § 2. Moreover, fear of the Gods, as a supplement to political order, was sufficiently present through Numa's arrangements (*Discourses*, I.11 § 1). If anything, Machiavelli thinks that Christianity seems to have diluted that too.

[95] Machiavelli, *Discourses*, II.2 § 2, emphasis added.

[96] Machiavelli argues, "[f]or where the fear of God fails, it must be either that the kingdom comes to ruin or that it is sustained for fear of a prince, which supplies the defects of religion" (*Discourses*, I.11 § 4; cf. *ibid.*, I.19).

presence meant that the state remained united in spite of the natural tendencies of its constitutive parts; even under the best of circumstances, the
lesson to be drawn regarding human nature was a pessimistic one. Machiavelli's innovation came in the form of his dispassionate approach to *metus
hostilis* and many other facts of political life. Freed from the need to justify,
reconcile, or excuse these facts, he was able to locate them in individual and
collective behavior, trace their development and manifestation, and write
openly about ways in which they could be understood and dealt with.[97]
Thus, he came to the conclusion that tumult should not be avoided at all
costs, and that empire ought to be pursued neither for the glory of the prince
nor for the glory of the God but for the survival of the state. This realization made it impossible to ignore him, and forced both Machiavellists and
Anti-Machiavellists to take seriously the psychological bases of political life.
Through this prism, it becomes possible to understand the full significance
of his insistence on the importance of returning states to their beginnings.
There, individuals are exposed to necessity and are reminded, thereby, of the
source of their allegiance to those with whom they have chosen to identify.
This is the ultimate justification of the state, and in many ways the origin of
its modern instantiation.[98] It is also the groundwork, political and psychological, for the construction of Hobbes's theory, in which the return to the
beginning becomes the return to the state of nature.

---

[97] See Figgis, *Political Thought from Gerson to Grotius*, 96–98.

[98] Wood sees an analogy between "Sallust's Theorem" and sovereignty, "between fear of a
ruler and fear of an external enemy." He suggests that the "concept of sovereignty is the
domestication of Sallust's Theorem. Indeed, the very structure of the state – as conceived by
early modern theorists – to which the principle of sovereignty was so vital, institutionalizes
and follows the psychological and political logic of Sallust's Theorem" ("Sallust's Theorem,"
184). Kahn captures well the mechanism by which this transformation comes about. She
argues, "[o]bedience to the state requires the forced remembrance of drastic actions," and
adds, "[t]he violence of war remains an external accident until it is internalized: until, that
is, it is imitated and appropriated by being used deliberately and theatrically" ("Reduction
and the Praise of Disunion in Machiavelli's *Discourses*," 14–15).

5

SURVIVAL THROUGH FEAR: HOBBES'S
PROBLEM AND SOLUTION

It is true that the advantages of this life can be increased with other people's
help. But this is much more effectively achieved by Dominion over others
than by their help. Hence no one should doubt that, in the absence of fear,
men would be more avidly attracted to domination than to society. One must
therefore lay it down that the origin of large and lasting societies lay not in
mutual human benevolence but in men's mutual fear.

– Thomas Hobbes[1]

However else they may have felt about Machiavelli's views, reason of state
theorists found themselves in the awkward position of having to concede, if
only tacitly, the validity of his fundamental concern with the survival of the
state. Yet, acceptance of this goal put many of these theorists in a difficult
position. In Burke's words, these were "men who could neither accept reason
of state nor do without it."[2] If the survival of the state is necessary, how far
can one go to ensure it? When do measures of the kind proposed in *The
Prince* become unacceptable? In some cases, such as those examined above,
responses to Machiavelli's challenge took the form of essential agreement
clothed in vocal polemic. In yet others, more innocuous theories with similar
views were used as proxies. The most widespread tendency of this kind was
the increasing interest in the histories of Tacitus, which had yielded a new
variety of reason of state thought and, by the end of the sixteenth century,
had led to the almost mechanical association of Tacitus with Machiavelli
recorded by Botero in his dedication of *The Reason of State*.[3] As Tuck notes,

---

[1] *On the Citizen*, I.2; cf. *ibid.*, I.13.
[2] Burke, "Tacitism, Scepticism, and Reason of State," 491.
[3] Botero, *The Reason of State*, Ep. Ded., xiii. See also Schellhase, *Tacitus in Renaissance Political
Thought*, 3–16; Burke, "Tacitism, Scepticism, and Reason of State," 484–85; Waszink,
Introduction to *Politica*, 44–47. The first part of the *Annals*, which contains the account of
Tiberius, was rediscovered in 1515. According to Burke, this was the part that "commentators
tended to concentrate on" ("Tacitism, Scepticism, and Reason of State," 486–87).

"this *ragion di stato* culture was clearly what the young Hobbes was most at home in," and the events that unfolded during Hobbes's long life only served to confirm its significance.[4]

Enemy fleets played a formative role in Hobbes's life on two occasions. The first of these, related famously by Hobbes himself in the short verse autobiography that he composed towards the end of his life, coincided with his birth, on April 5, 1588. According to this account, his mother was so frightened by the rumored approach of the Spanish Armada that she gave birth to twins, Hobbes and fear.[5] The second came some fifty years later, in the form of the ship-money controversy, culminating in the trial of John Hampden. Beginning in 1634, on the basis of the alleged threat posed by the Dutch fleet, King Charles I issued a series of ship-money writs demanding that his subjects contribute to their defense by providing warships for the Royal Navy. Before Charles I, Elizabeth I had also demanded and collected ship-money from those of her subjects who lived along the coast. Initially, Charles I followed her example, but in August 1635, went further by extending the application of the policy to cover inland communities as well.[6] Two years later, when the local authorities were asked to report the names of those who refused to pay, the sheriff of Buckinghamshire gave the name of John Hampden.[7] The Crown brought suit against Hampden, and eventually the ship-money writ was found by a high court to have been legal by a narrow margin of seven to five.[8] Accounts of the Hampden case, from the opinions of the judges and contemporary pamphlets down to the assessments of twentieth-century historians, leave little doubt that the ship-money case generated a great deal of controversy, and that despite the wide range of possible legal technicalities that one could concentrate on, the central issue

---

[4] Tuck, *Philosophy and Government*, 282; cf. "Hobbes and Tacitus," esp. 107–10; Malcolm, *Aspects of Hobbes*, 458. Hobbes cites Lipsius ("Of the Life and History of Thucydides," 586; *The English Works of Thomas Hobbes*, 5: 245) and Bodin (*The Elements of Law*, II.viii.7) with approval. Compare, e.g., Bodin's language in *The Six Bookes of a Commonweale*, 602 with Hobbes's in *Leviathan*, XIII § 8. See also Chappell, ed., *Hobbes and Bramhall on Liberty and Necessity*, 29, note 37; Malcolm, *Aspects of Hobbes*, 540–41; Skinner, *Visions of Politics*, 3: 44, 65, 255–56. See also Salt, "Sir Simonds D'Ewes and the Levying of Ship Money," 285.

[5] "metum tantum concepit tunc mea mater, / Ut pareret geminos, méque metúmque simul" (*Thomae Hobbesii Malmesburiensis vita*, 2).

[6] Kishlansky, *A Monarchy Transformed*, 121. On the difference between the writs of Elizabeth I and Charles I, as well as the evolution of the policy, see Keir, "The Case of Ship-Money," 550–57.

[7] Keir, "The Case of Ship-Money," 549.

[8] See Keir, "The Case of Ship-Money," 546 and Kishlansky, *A Monarchy Transformed*, 138, but cf. *State Trials* III, column 1251, where the minority is composed of four.

was who should decide whether there was an emergency and what should be done about it.[9]

Hobbes's writings contain abundant evidence to suggest that "the particular issue which [. . .] lay behind [his] decision to explore the political implications of post-sceptical philosophy, is likely to have been the Ship Money case."[10] The problem of the authority to declare emergencies is central in Hobbes's first political treatise, *The Elements of Law*, which was completed in 1640. In the preface to *De Cive*, which was published in 1642, Hobbes claims to have developed his ideas because his country "was already seething with questions of the right of Government and of the due obedience of citizens, forerunners of the approaching war."[11] Documentary evidence from this period of Hobbes's life is sparse, but what little there is does indeed support this connection. Hobbes's surviving correspondence contains only eight letters written by him between the second ship-money writ and the end of the trial of John Hampden. Although between August 1635 and October 1636, Hobbes was traveling on the Continent, and the collection of ship-money was proceeding without any serious objections, his correspondence shows that he was quite interested in the intellectual and political debates surrounding the English, Spanish, and Dutch claims to ownership of the sea that had caused Charles I to issue the writs.[12]

---

[9] Where the existence or not of an emergency is concerned, Keir claims that "[a]ll the judges agree in principle that the King is the sole judge of dangers from abroad, and of the means requisite to avert them," that "[t]he prerogative to judge of unusual danger from abroad [. . .] implied a correlative duty – that of making adequate defensive preparations," and that "this obligation fell to the King," but that they disagreed on the issue "of deciding by what means the King acquired powers commensurate with his responsibilities" ("The Case of Ship-Money," 562–63). This assessment, however, implies a greater degree of agreement than that warranted by the opinions of the judges. Keir himself proceeds immediately to consider the different positions that judges took with respect to the issue of the proximity of the threat, as well as whether the King had a right to request the assistance of his subjects in cases in which the danger was *apprehended*, rather than *immediate*. Keir quotes Jones, who asked characteristically "Will you have the danger so apparent as Hannibal *ad portas*? Will you suffer an enemy to come in before you prepare to resist?" (*State Trials* III, column 1188, quoted in Keir, "The Case of Ship-Money," 564). With respect to what is to be done, Henry Parker, argues "That the King ought to have aid of his subjects in time of danger, and common aid in case of common danger, is laid down for a ground, and agreed upon by all sides, But about this aid there remains much variety and contrariety of opinion amongst the greatest Sages of our Law" (*The Case of Shipmony Briefly Discoursed*, 2).

[10] Tuck, *Philosophy and Government*, 298; cf. Tuck, *Hobbes*, 23–24.

[11] Hobbes, *On the Citizen*, Pref. § 19; cf. Tuck, *Hobbes*, 23.

[12] See Hobbes to William Cavendish, Byfleet, October 16/26, 1636, in Hobbes, *Correspondence*, I: 37, wherein Hobbes announces his return. On the trip itself, see Martinich, *Hobbes*, 89–93. On the collection of ship-money, see Gordon, "The Collection of Ship-Money in the

In 1609, Grotius had published *Mare liberum* at the behest of the Dutch East India Company, in an attempt to provide ammunition for Dutch claims to trade in Southeast Asia, although the work had "global" implications and was "taken by the English and the Scots as an assault on their fishing rights in the North Sea and by the Spanish as an attack on the foundations of their overseas empire."[13] Among the various responses generated by *Mare liberum* was John Selden's *Mare clausum*, which was composed independently around 1616–17, but was not published until the end of 1635, when it was deemed useful by the Crown in its confrontation with the Dutch that ultimately led to the ship-money controversy.[14] Selden's book, which was "published as effectively an official statement of the English government view" and was also "quoted in the government's defense" in the Hampden trial, had caught Hobbes's interest to such an extent that he writes of it in two of his eight letters that survive from the first period of the ship-money controversy.[15] In a letter to Mr. Glen, in April 1636, Hobbes declares, "I desire also to see *Seldens Mare clausum*, having already a great Opinion of it."[16] Apparently, Hobbes managed to find a copy of the book in Paris soon thereafter, because in a letter written two months later, he reports to William Cavendish, "[a]ll I study is a nights, and that for a little while is yᵉ reading of Certayne new bookes, especially mʳ Seldens Mare Clausum [...]."[17] Hobbes's early interest in the legal aspects of the dispute over the dominion of the sea appears to have developed into a much larger fascination with the determination of threat. In *Behemoth*, Hobbes lists the ship-money controversy as the first link in the chain of events that led to the English Civil War, and in his *A Dialogue between a Philosopher and a Student of the Common Laws of England*, the section on "Sovereign Power" is devoted to a discussion of whether "a King should have Right to take from his Subjects, upon the pretence of Necessity what he pleaseth."[18]

Reign of Charles I," 142–43; Salt, "Sir Simonds D'Ewes and the Levying of Ship Money," 253–54; Kishlansky, *A Monarchy Transformed*, 122.

[13] Armitage, Introduction to *The Free Sea*, xi. Cf. Tuck, "Grotius and Selden," 504; Tuck, *Philosophy and Government*, 170, 178.

[14] On the story of the composition and function of *Mare clausum*, see Tuck, "Grotius and Selden," 524; *Philosophy and Government*, 212–13; *The Rights of War and Peace*, 116.

[15] See Tuck, *The Rights of War and Peace*, 116; "Grotius and Selden," 524, especially note 20.

[16] Hobbes to Mr. Glen, London, April 6/16, 1636 (letter 17) (Hobbes, *Correspondence*, I: 30). Hobbes writes to Glen that he expects to be able to find a copy of Selden's book in Paris, his next destination (*ibid.*, I: 31).

[17] Hobbes to William Cavendish, Earl of Newcastle, Paris, June 13/23, 1636 (letter 18) (Hobbes, *Correspondence*, I: 32).

[18] Hobbes, *Behemoth*, 60; *A Dialogue between a Philosopher and a Student of the Common Laws of England*, 65.

Similarly, Hobbes concludes the fourth part of the Latin version of *Leviathan* by urging, "we should all take pains to see that by our internal disagreements we do not allow ourselves all to be oppressed by an external enemy."[19]

Machiavelli was well aware of the magnitude of his project, as well as his limitations. Having outlined his difficult enterprise in the *Discourses*, he concluded, "I believe I can carry it far enough so that a short road will remain for another to bring it to the destined place."[20] That other was destined to be Hobbes.[21] Machiavelli's advice that rulers be attuned to the psychology of their subjects and that cities be returned to their beginnings had been lost in the noise raised by the furious reaction to his shocking views. By Hobbes's time, however, the dust had settled sufficiently to allow for the emergence of a theory of politics that took both pieces of advice seriously. Hobbes was uniquely positioned to bring this about. The combination of the reason of state culture that Hobbes found himself in with the questions of sovereignty that were emerging at the beginning of the seventeenth century might have been enough to fuel a sustained interest in the subject and produce another important moment in the evolution of the genre, but in Hobbes's case these were coupled with an attendant fascination with scientific method and the possibilities for its application to the study of politics.[22] As a result of this constellation of factors, Hobbes was able to fuse the two elements of Machiavelli's advice and produce a science of politics in which the return to the beginnings of cities would take place by means of a thought experiment: the contemplation of life before the emergence of government, life in the state of nature. By painting this picture in vivid terms, anchoring it sufficiently in reality, and implanting it in the minds of men, Hobbes substituted the messy, dangerous, and crude means of instilling the fear that was there at the founding with a device that will always lurk in the background and that, when awakened, will perform its task in a neat and orderly fashion. To do so, Hobbes himself had to return to the beginning, the first principle of a commonwealth, man.[23]

---

[19] Hobbes, *Leviathan*, XLVII § 29, p. 488.

[20] Machiavelli, *Discourses*, I. Pref. § 2.

[21] On Hobbes's connection to Machiavelli, see Strauss, *Natural Right and History*, 177–81; Tuck, "Hobbes and Tacitus," 110.

[22] See, e.g., Strauss, *The Political Philosophy of Hobbes*, Chapter VIII, esp. p. 136; Tuck, *Hobbes*, 42–43; Malcolm, *Aspects of Hobbes*, 6, 9, 12, 153–55; Skinner, *Visions of Politics*, 3: 75.

[23] In *De Cive*, Hobbes explains his method as follows:

> Rather I should begin with the matter of which a commonwealth is made and go on to how it comes into being and the form it takes, and to the first origin of justice. For a thing is best known from its constituents. As in an automatic Clock or other fairly complex device, one cannot get

HUMAN NATURE

In Chapter IX of the first part of *The Elements of Law*, Hobbes presents his definitions of the passions of the mind. At the end of that chapter, he suggests that the comparison of man's life to a race is a convenient, if not perfect, mnemonic device by which to remember those passions, and adds that this race has "no other goal, nor other garland, but being foremost."[24] There are at least two reasons why this metaphor is important in understanding Hobbes's philosophy of man. First, the race itself, as well as the goal that Hobbes ascribes to those in it, reveals the extent to which man's existence is determined by what is around him; life, according to Hobbes, is social, and the race illustrates this very well.[25] Second, although Hobbes claims that the goal of the race is to be ahead of every other runner, the race itself has no finish line. It continues forever, and it is only by forsaking the course, that is, dying, that one can exit it. For these two reasons, Hobbes's metaphor is perhaps even more successful than he is willing to acknowledge, for it captures two crucial determinants of man's life and identity: others and death.[26]

Hobbes begins *The Elements of Law* by stating that his subject requires the knowledge of what is (i) human nature, (ii) a body politic, and (iii) a law.[27] He

> to know the function of each part and wheel unless one takes it apart, and examines separately the material, shape and motion of the parts, so in investigating the right of a commonwealth and the duties of its citizens, there is a need, not indeed to take the commonwealth apart, but to view it as taken apart, i.e. to understand correctly what human nature is like [...] (*On the Citizen*, Pref. § 9).

[24] Hobbes, *The Elements of Law*, I.9.21.

[25] Cf. Hobbes, *Leviathan* VIII § 1. According to Oakeshott, the effect of others can also be seen in the difference between Hobbes's view of death and death at the hands of another human being, specifically. Thus, being killed by another man,

> signified failure in the 'race' for precedence which constitutes human life — failure, not in competition with the natural world, but in competition with other human beings. And this I take to be the central point; and this is what is meant by shameful death. To be killed by another man is eo ipso shameful or dishonourable because it signified that inferiority vis-à-vis other men which is at the centre of all human *aversion* (Oakeshott, Letter to Watkins, 24 May 1963, 834).

[26] Strauss considers the race metaphor the conclusion of Hobbes's "earliest and most perfect exposition of the passions," and notes that fear has no place in it. He argues, "fear, which moderates the unchecked race of the state of nature, in which force and fraud are the two cardinal virtues, to reasonable competition, to the regulated 'play' of the civil state, is for that very reason exalted above the passions, and, therefore, replaces reason" (*The Political Philosophy of Hobbes*, 150, note 1). Strauss also notes the general antithetic character of Hobbes's political philosophy (*ibid.*, 149–50). Cf. Wolin, *Hobbes and the Epic Tradition of Political Theory*, 29–30.

[27] Hobbes, *The Elements of Law*, I.1.1.

is mindful of the difficulties involved in acquiring such a knowledge, however, because he recognizes that these matters are controversial, insofar as they have consequences for men's interests.[28] To avoid the pitfalls of controversy, he proposes to lay the foundation of his inquiry on a ground that his readers will find beyond dispute: they will be able to confirm what he tells them by referring to their experience.[29] Hobbes puts his method to work right away, by considering the ways in which human beings conceive of the world around them and then classify their conceptions of it. He argues that contrary to received theories of sense perception, "[o]riginally all conceptions proceed from the actions of the thing itself, whereof it is the conception."[30] Thus, the particular attributes that we sense in external objects are the results of the effect that the actions of these objects have on our organs of sense. The physical consequence of this claim is that what we perceive is not inherent in the object of perception, but is rather the result of the particular effect, within a given set of circumstances, of that object on our organs of sense. Indeed, experience confirms that a reflection of the sun in a puddle of water is something other than the sun itself, that the same object can have different colors depending on one's point of view, or even that the same individual's view of a certain object may be blurry or double as a result of some illness.[31] The bottom line, for Hobbes, is "the great deception of sense," namely that although these properties are "seemings and apparitions only," we nevertheless are tricked into believing that they are real. In actuality, however, the only things that are real are the motions that give rise to these false impressions.[32]

---

[28] Cf. Hobbes, *The Elements of Law*, Ep. Ded., p. xv.

[29] Hobbes, *The Elements of Law*, I.1.2. Cf. *Leviathan*, "A Review, and Conclusion" § 13; *Of Liberty and Necessity*, § 33; *The Elements of Law*, I.5.11: "for there be few men which have not so much natural logic, as thereby to discern well enough, whether any conclusion I shall hereafter make, in this discourse, be well or ill collected." Cf. also Machiavelli, *The Prince*, XV: 61.

[30] Hobbes, *The Elements of Law*, I.2.2. Cf. *Leviathan*, I § 2. Hobbes outlines the mechanics of sight in greater detail in *De Corpore*, in *The English Works of Thomas Hobbes*, 1: 78–79, and treats sense more generally later in the same work, at 390–94. Malcolm argues that this part of the theory has its origin in Hobbes's enthusiastic adoption of the "Galilean principle of the subjectivity of secondary qualities" ("Hobbes and Spinoza," 532). The consensus is that the target of Hobbes's attack here is Aristotle (Tuck, "Optics and Sceptics," 251; *Philosophy and Government*, 298; Malcolm, *Aspects of Hobbes*, 5, 17; Rahe, *Republics Ancient & Modern*, II: 140–41; Skinner, *Reason and Rhetoric in the Philosophy of Hobbes*, 406–07); cf. Leijenhorst, *The Mechanisation of Aristotelianism*.

[31] Hobbes, *The Elements of Law*, I.2.1–9. Cf. *De Corpore* in *The English Works of Thomas Hobbes*, 1: 75–76.

[32] Hobbes, *The Elements of Law*, I.2.10.

Although our organs of perception are constantly challenged by new stimuli, the effects of earlier perceptions remain with us in the weaker form of "PHANTASY or IMAGINATION."[33] Hobbes argues that the constant effect of new stimuli on the brain causes the gradual decay of conceptions stored earlier, so that remembrance of things past becomes obscure with time, and details fade away.[34] He adds that the mind tends to group conceptions together based on the extent to which such a grouping is coherent at the time of the last conception. Thus, it is possible for the mind to "run almost from any thing to any thing," but "for the most part" the mind does pay attention to the relationship between cause and effect, both at the time of the initial perception and afterwards, in "imagination."[35] This is a crucial part of the story, for two reasons. First, it is a central component of the formation of strategy. Once the object of one's appetite is known, Hobbes argues, the means to that object are chosen backwards, on the basis of existing information about the relationship between cause and effect.[36] Whether the relationship between antecedents and consequents or causes and effects has been determined on the basis of a voluntary series of actions by someone or simply observed has no significance for the relationship itself, so Hobbes refers to the remembrance of such successions as "experiments."[37] A larger pool of these means that there will be a better likelihood of finding a connection that suits a particular goal, which is why Hobbes argues,

they shall conjecture best, that have most experience: because they have most signs to conjecture by; which is the reason that old men are more prudent, that is, conjecture better, *cæteris paribus*, than young. For, being older, they remember more; and experience is but remembrance. And men of quick imagination, *cæteris paribus*, are

---

[33] Hobbes, *The Elements of Law*, I.3.1. Cf. *Leviathan*, II § 2; *De Corpore* in *The English Works of Thomas Hobbes*, 1: 396.

[34] Hobbes, *The Elements of Law*, I.3.7.

[35] Hobbes, *The Elements of Law*, I.4.2. Cf. *De Corpore* in *The English Works of Thomas Hobbes*, 1: 397–98; *ibid.*, 4: 449. In *Leviathan*, Hobbes argues, "[w]hen a man thinketh on any thing whatsoever, his next thought after, is not altogether so casual as it seems to be" (III § 2).

[36] Hobbes, *The Elements of Law*, I.4.2. Cf. *Leviathan*, III § 4: "From desire, ariseth the thought of some means we have seen produce the like of that which we aim at; and from the thought of that, the thought of means to that mean; and so continually, till we come to some beginning within our own power." Cf. *Leviathan*, VIII § 16: "For the thoughts are to the desires, as scouts and spies, to range abroad, and find the way to the things desired." In *De Corpore*, he argues: "For the thought or phantasm of the desired end brings in all the phantasms that are means conducing to that end, and that in order backwards from the last to the first, and again forwards from the beginning to the end" (*The English Works of Thomas Hobbes*, 1: 398).

[37] Hobbes, *The Elements of Law*, I.4.6.

more prudent than those whose imaginations are slow: for they observe more in less time.[38]

Second, the mind uses various mechanisms to simplify the processing of new information. One of these is activated when the object is perceived. At that time, the mind uses experience amassed from relevant instances already perceived, so that "[f]rom the experience and the recollection of there being good and evil consequences of a similar object, the mind-picture *is modified* through our expecting, in turn, good or evil."[39] Both the very perception of an object, then, and its ensuing classification are tainted by previous experience with similar objects in a way that transforms our image of it. So, for example, an individual whose first sighting of a bear takes place in the context of an uneventful circus performance has a very different mind-picture of bears than one who first saw a bear as it was mauling a human being.

THE SEEDS OF CONFLICT

No single element of this initial account of the mechanics of perception explains why different individuals would perceive the same object differently, to say nothing of coming to blows over their differing perceptions. The synthesis of those elements, however, tells a different story, and Hobbes is now prepared to explain why perceptions differ. He sees two causes of this: passions and words. The latter arise from the need to manage the endless stream of information grasped by one's senses, as well as the connections between different bits of information new and old.[40] As mnemonic devices,

---

[38] Hobbes, *The Elements of Law*, I.4.10. Cf. *De Cive*, XIII.17; *Leviathan*, III § 8:

> A *sign* is the event antecedent of the consequent, and contrarily, the consequent of the antecedent, when the like consequences have been observed before; and the oftener they have been observed, the less uncertain is the sign. And therefore he that has the most experience in any kind of business has most signs, whereby to guess at the future time; and consequently is the most prudent; and so much more prudent than he that is new in that kind of business, as not to be equalled by any advantage of natural and extemporary wit, though perhaps many young men think the contrary.

> In his brief biography, Aubrey relates that Hobbes declared that he would prefer to be treated by an old woman with experience than by a learned physician (Hobbes, *The Elements of Law*, edited by J.C.A. Gaskin, 240). See also Rahe, *Republics Ancient & Modern*, II: 150–51.

[39] Hobbes, *Thomas White's De Mundo Examined*, Fol. 410v: 447, emphasis added. Cf. *On the Citizen*, XIII.17: "For we gauge the future from the past, rarely expecting what rarely happens."

[40] Hobbes, *The Elements of Law*, I.5.1–2. Cf. *Leviathan*, IV; *De Corpore* in *The English Works of Thomas Hobbes*, 1: 79–80.

the names of things are arbitrary, and, given that conceptions take place in varying circumstances and in no order that we can control, there are often many names for a single thing, as for example in the use of adjectives to describe the same person when he is being just, valiant, and so on, at different times.[41] Given his concern with exactitude, Hobbes's explanation here may seem puzzling, since it does not point to what it is precisely that is labeled just, valiant, and so forth.[42] However, this otherwise inauspicious illustration marks a turning point in his theory, for it signals the transition from similarity and order to difference and conflict. Because the classification of a perception depends not only on the character of the perception itself, but also on the information already possessed, to which it is to be compared, it is possible for one to classify the same object differently.[43] For example, seeing a friend get burned as a result of touching a hot dish could be classified with burns or accidents, but could also be classified with other memories of that friend. This seemingly innocuous possibility opens the door to the further chance of disagreement, since what is possible for a single individual is certainly also possible for the perceptions of two or more individuals.[44] What is more, if disagreement is introduced at the ostensibly objective level of the mere description of the outside world, then it is undoubtedly to be expected at least as much in the realm of valuation.[45] Indeed, in *Leviathan* Hobbes adds this consideration to his account of the effect of names:

[. . .] in reasoning a man must take heed of words which, besides the signification of what we imagine of their nature, have a signification also of the nature, disposition,

---

[41] See Hobbes, *The Elements of Law*, I.5.2; *Leviathan*, IV § 1. Cf. Hobbes, *The Elements of Law*, I.5.1–5. Cf. I.5.7: "[. . .] there is scarce any word that is not made equivocal by divers contextures of speech, or by diversity of pronunciation and gesture."

[42] Socrates captures this intricacy well in Plato's *Republic* (436c).

[43] Cf. Hobbes, *The Elements of Law*, I.4.2.

[44] Hobbes stresses this point in *The Elements of Law*: "This equivocation of names maketh it difficult to recover those conceptions for which the name was ordained; and that not only in the language of other men [. . .] but also in our own discourse" (I.5.8). In *Leviathan*, Hobbes argues, "divers men differ not only in their judgment on the senses (of what is pleasant and unpleasant to the taste, smell, hearing, touch, and sight), but also of what is conformable or disagreeable to reason in the actions of common life. Nay, the same man in divers times differs from himself" (XV § 40); Cf. *Leviathan*, IV § 4.

[45] Cf. Hobbes, *The Elements of Law*, I.4.11: "As in conjectural things concerning past and future, it is prudence to conclude from experience, what is likely to come to pass, or to have passed already; so it is an error to conclude from it, that it is so or so called. That is to say, we cannot from experience conclude, that any thing is to be called just or injust, true or false, nor any proposition universal whatsoever, except it be from remembrance of the use of names imposed arbitrarily by men."

and interest of the speaker, such as are the names of virtues and vices; For one man calleth *wisdom*, what another calleth *fear*, and one *cruelty*, what another *justice*; one *prodigality*, what another *magnanimity*; and one *gravity*, what another *stupidity*, &c.[46]

The likelihood that different individuals will form different perceptions even of the same object under the same circumstances is increased by the second complicating factor, the passions:

if we consider the power of those deceptions of sense [...] and also how unconstantly names have been settled, and how subject they are to equivocation, and how diversified by passion, (scarce two men agreeing what is to be called good, and what evil; what liberality, what prodigality; what valour, what temerity) and how subject men are to paralogism or fallacy in reasoning, I may in a manner conclude, that it is impossible to rectify so many errors of any one man, as must proceed from those causes, without beginning anew from the very first grounds of all our knowledge, sense; and, instead of books, reading over orderly one's own conceptions: in which meaning I take nosce teipsum for a precept worthy of the reputation it hath gotten.[47]

The connection between conceptions and the passions is direct. Hobbes argues that the motion that affects the organs of sense perception proceeds to the heart, and "of necessity must there either help or hinder that motion which is called vital."[48] Hobbes calls the incoming motion "Delight" or "Pain," depending on whether it helps or hinders the vital motion of the body.[49] The pleasure or pain that results from this incoming motion invites the subject to "draw near the thing that pleaseth, or to retire from the thing that displeaseth," the tendencies that we commonly refer to as "appetite"

---

[46] Hobbes, *Leviathan*, IV § 24. Compare Hobbes's translation of Thucydides' description of the effects of the civil war in Corcyra: "The received value of names imposed for signification of things was changed into arbitrary. For inconsiderate boldness was counted true-hearted manliness; provident deliberation, a handsome fear; modesty, the cloak of cowardice; to be wise in everything, to be lazy in everything. A furious suddenness was reputed a point of valour" (Thucydides, *The Peloponnesian War*, III: 82). In *De Cive*, Hobbes observes that *"as things are, [...] a man now approves what at another time he condemns, and gives a different judgement of an action when he does it than when someone else does the very same thing"* (Ep. Ded., § 7). Cf. *Behemoth*, 45: "For several men praise several customs, and that which is virtue with one, is blamed by others; and, contrarily, what one calls vice, another calls virtue, as their present affections lead them"; *Leviathan*, "A Review, and Conclusion" § 1. See also Ioannis D. Evrigenis, "Hobbes's Thucydides."

[47] Hobbes, *The Elements of Law*, I.5.14.

[48] Hobbes, *The Elements of Law*, I.7.1. Hobbes defines vital motion as "the motion of the blood, perpetually circulating (as hath been shown from many infallible signs and marks by Doctor Harvey, the first observer of it) in the veins and arteries" (*De Corpore* in *The English Works of Thomas Hobbes*, 1: 407).

[49] Hobbes, *The Elements of Law*, I.7.1; Cf. *De Corpore* in *The English Works of Thomas Hobbes*, 1: 406–07.

and "aversion."[50] It is telling, and noteworthy for the present purposes, that Hobbes distinguishes between appetites and aversions in two steps. First, he lumps all pleasing things into the former group, but separates the latter into two quite distinct categories. Thus, whereas things that are pleasing are all subject to appetite, things that are immediately displeasing are subject to aversion, but things that are *expected to displease in the future* give rise to fear.[51] This will turn out to have serious consequences for subsequent parts of the theory, two of the most important of which are that (i) it paves the way for the claim that man is insatiable and (ii) it draws a meaningful and quite complex and sophisticated distinction between fright and fear.[52] The latter is as crucial an element of Hobbes's theory as it has been misunderstood, and his separation of it from aversion at this juncture is an important corrective of a host of misunderstandings of his theory that have resulted in the uncritical association of Hobbes with omnipresent and exaggerated fear.

This breakdown, however, is not the end of the matter. Hobbes's next claim is one of his most controversial and misunderstood. He declares,

> Every man, for his own part, calleth that which pleaseth, and is delightful to himself, GOOD; and that EVIL which displeaseth him: insomuch that while every man differeth from other in constitution, they differ also one from another concerning the common distinction of good and evil. Nor is there any such thing as ἀγαθὸν ἁπλῶς, that is to say, simply good.[53]

---

[50] Hobbes, *The Elements of Law*, I.7.2. The consequences of this process are outlined by Hobbes in the sections in which he considers some of the causes of a state of war. Tricaud finds it difficult to understand how it could be possible that a passion such as the desire to fight in response to slander "can arise in a psychic machine where a pleasant thing is that which helps the vital motion" ("Hobbes's Conception of the State of Nature from 1640 to 1651," 118), but Hobbes's account here is clear: disagreement signals sudden opposition in one's perceived course towards one's ends, it signals competition for those ends, and it challenges one's perception of the world on a fundamental level. Considerations such as outward appearances and reputation are also important in one's pursuit of one's ends, and therefore only add to the gravity of the hindrance.

[51] Hobbes, *The Elements of Law*, I.7.2. This does not come across as clearly in the equivalent definition in *Leviathan* ("*Aversion* with opinion of *hurt* from the object, FEAR" [VI § 16]) although there is nothing in the latter that signals a departure from the definition in *The Elements of Law*.

[52] Hobbes, *On the Citizen*, Ep. Ded., § 10; *Leviathan*, XI § 1; *De Homine*, X.3 (*Man and Citizen*, 40); *A Dialogue between a Philosopher and a Student of the Common Laws of England*, 65–66.

[53] Hobbes, *The Elements of Law*, I.7.3. The last line of this passage in the Molesworth edition of *Human Nature* reads: "Nor is there any such thing as absolute goodness, considered without relation" (*The English Works of Thomas Hobbes*, 4: 32); cf. Saint Augustine, *Concerning the City of God against the Pagans* VIII.iii.

To the reader familiar with *Leviathan*, this passage echoes Hobbes's infamous statement therein that "there is no such *Finis ultimus* (utmost aim) nor *Summum Bonum* (greatest good) as is spoken of in the books of the old moral philosophers."[54] This passage, supported by an earlier statement in the same work, has been interpreted as tantamount to a declaration of moral relativism, but such an interpretation misses the context within which the statement is made, and consequently the purpose that it serves in Hobbes's theory, which is an important one.[55]

Before accusing Hobbes of being inconsistent, a careful reader has to wonder how it could be possible for him to claim that there is no *summum bonum* and, at the same time, that there are universal responses to stimuli, as for example in the case of the fear of violent death.[56] After all, if there is a *summum malum*, violent death, then presumably the preservation of life from such violent death would be a *summum bonum*. There are two answers to this question. The first, hinted at above, lies in the metaphor of the race, which teaches us that there is no ultimate victory; all gains and losses acquire their meaning in relation to the performance of others. The second answer

[54] Hobbes, *Leviathan*, XI § 1.

[55] In Chapter VI, Hobbes argues:

> whatsoever is the object of any mans appetite or desire that is it which he for his part calleth *good*; and the object of his hate and aversion, *evil*; and of his contempt, *vile* and *inconsiderable*. For these words of good, evil, and contemptible are ever used with relation to the person that useth them, there being nothing simply and absolutely so, nor any common rule of good and evil to be taken from the nature of the objects themselves, but from the person of the man (where there is no commonwealth), or (in a commonwealth) from the person that representeth it, or from an arbitrator or judge whom men disagreeing shall by consent set up, and make his sentence the rule thereof (*Leviathan*, VI § 7).

> See, e.g., Tuck, *Philosophy and Government*, 304; *Hobbes*, 52–53. Tuck argues that Hobbes treats "*moral* terms in exactly the same way as he had treated colour terms: though common language and common sense might lead us to think that something is really and objectively good, in the same way that something is really and objectively red, in fact such ideas are illusions or fantasies, features of the inside of our heads only" (*Hobbes*, 53). Although tempting, this analogy between secondary qualities, such as color, and moral terms is also misleading. As will be shown later, the existence of a multitude of claims regarding good and evil does not preclude the possibility of the existence of good and evil. For Hobbes, this is true on two levels. First, an individual acts on his self-interest as he perceives it; his will is an expression of what he takes to be good for himself. The subjectivity of perception renders his judgment on this matter paramount, as there is no basis on which someone else could question it. Second, there are facts stemming from primary qualities, such as that all human beings hunger, which are simply true and universal (see, e.g., *Leviathan*, VI § 1, on vital motions), and which have consequences for the designation of means and ends and the determination of the extent to which those are useful and desirable. Cf. Malcolm, *Aspects of Hobbes*, 436.

[56] See, e.g., Hobbes, *On the Citizen*, Ep. Ded., § 10; I.7; II.18; *Leviathan*, XI § 4.

lies in an important but usually overlooked distinction that Hobbes draws between two kinds of appetites and aversions: "some [...] born with men, as appetite of food, appetite of excretion and exoneration [...]. The rest, which are appetites of particular things, proceed from experience and trial of their effects upon themselves or other men."[57] Hobbes sees two sets of appetites, then: a set of primary, formal appetites that are innate and related to the Law of Nature, and particular appetites that are the result of particular circumstances and experiences.[58] Thus, for example, all men become hungry and desire food, but they then disagree widely about what in particular will satiate their desire to eat. Disagreement about the latter in no way diminishes the universality of the former. Indeed, this interpretation is supported by the fact that immediately after having discussed appetite and aversion, in *The Elements of Law*, Hobbes turns to consider the difference between immediate and farther ends, which he sees as means and ends, respectively.[59] It is important here to also bear in mind that Hobbes's distinction between proximate and ultimate ends is fully consistent with his theory of perception, since formal desires, such as the desire to eat or to stay alive are radically different from particular ones, in that the former do not require the presence of any particular good, whereas the latter do. Thus, even if one has never seen a piece of food, he will nevertheless feel hunger, whereas it is impossible for someone who has never seen or heard of steak and kidney pie to desire one.[60]

To the extent, then, that our formal appetites – for food, survival, and so forth – are insatiable, it makes no sense to speak of an utmost end, and this Hobbes sees as an important deficiency in the philosophies of the ancients that speak of felicity as such an end.[61] One might object, as many have, that it is nevertheless possible to find oneself in a state of felicity even though one would still be plagued by the demands of desires that can never be put to

---

[57] Hobbes, *Leviathan*, VI § 4.

[58] These appetites are formal both in the sense that they are to be found in all human beings as well as in the sense that they are devoid of specific content. Where their connection to the Law of Nature is concerned, see *Leviathan*: "A LAW OF NATURE (*lex naturalis*) is a precept or general rule, found out by reason, by which a man is forbidden to do that which is destructive of his life or taketh away the means of preserving the same, and to omit that by which he thinketh it may be best preserved" (XIV § 3).

[59] See the difference between *propinqui* and *remoti*, in *The Elements of Law*, I.7.6.

[60] In *De Cive*, Hobbes argues, "men do not usually compete for public office, until they have won the battle against hunger and cold" (*On the Citizen*, V.5). Later, in the same work, he adds, "[b]y nature all men compete for honors and reputation, but those most of all who are least distracted by worry about ordinary necessities" (XII.10). Cf. Strauss, *The Political Philosophy of Hobbes*, 132–33.

[61] Hobbes, *The Elements of Law*, I.7.6.

rest, and that it is possible to declare oneself happy overall, despite pockets of hunger, greed, and discontentment. There is no reason to think that Hobbes would disagree with these observations, but there is considerable evidence that he would consider them to be beside the point. Strictly speaking, having lived a life that one can call happy in hindsight cannot really have been the result of the conscious pursuit of a goal. Here and elsewhere Hobbes renounces ancient philosophy, but he is generally fond of ancient history, and it is Herodotus's story of Solon and Croesus that is an apt illustration of this point in more ways than one.[62] Croesus, the richest man in the world, wants Solon, one of the wisest men in the world, to tell him who the happiest man in the world is, all the while hoping that it will be he. Solon lists Tellus and Cleobis and Biton before he is stopped by the angry Croesus who wants to know why unknown, dead men are ranked happier than he. Solon replies that he is unable to pronounce someone happy or unhappy unless he has found out the ending. Hobbes's objection here seems similar to Solon's, who proclaims: "man is entirely what befalls him."[63] Although Hobbes does not provide any strong evidence for his insistence upon man's insatiability here, it is worth remembering that he has repeatedly urged his reader to test his claims by introspection and observation.[64] Interestingly, he does cite the examples of Nero and Commodus, who were very similar to Croesus, in that despite their enormous power and wealth, they too were dissatisfied.[65]

Having explained the relationships between antecedents and consequents on the one hand and means and ends on the other hand, Hobbes now combines the two, to examine how we make decisions about the future. He argues that there are three types of conception: (i) sense, or conception of things present; (ii) remembrance, or conception of things past; and (iii) expectation, or conception of things future.[66] The latter, Hobbes explains, is "but a supposition of the same, proceeding from remembrance of what is past; and we so far conceive that anything will be hereafter, as we know there is something at the present that hath power to produce it."[67] This power

---

[62] Herodotus, *Historiae*, I: 30–33. Schlatter argues that Hobbes saw Thucydides' history as a corrective of the seditious teachings of the ancient philosophers ("Thomas Hobbes and Thucydides," 359).

[63] Herodotus, *The History*, I: 32.

[64] See, e.g., Hobbes, *The Elements of Law*, I.1.2; I.5.11. Cf. *Of Liberty and Necessity*, § 33; *On the Citizen*, Pref. § 9.

[65] Hobbes, *The Elements of Law*, I.7.7. Hobbes's position here is also consistent with his image of the race that cannot be won. Cf. *Decameron Physiologicum* in *The English Works of Thomas Hobbes*, 7: 73.

[66] Hobbes, *The Elements of Law*, I.8.2.

[67] Hobbes, *The Elements of Law*, I.8.3.

includes not only the powers of the body and the knowledge accumulated by the mind, but also wealth, honor, and everything else that can be acquired by means of these. Where the assessment of those powers is concerned, Hobbes is explicit that their worth emerges from the fact that the relations between individuals are a zero-sum game: "because the power of one man resisteth and hindreth the effects of the power of another: power simply is no more, but the excess of the power of one above that of another."[68] Furthermore, it is one subset of these powers that gives rise to the passions, for according to Hobbes the passions arise as a result of the pleasure or displeasure that men feel in response to honor and dishonor, respectively.[69] As noted above, the individual passions turn out to receive their definitions *in toto* through some comparison to other individuals, and this is no surprise, given Hobbes's theories of sense perception and conception, both of which see the perceiver as an object bombarded by stimuli from the outside world.[70] Hence, life is like the race that cannot be won but must be run in competition not only with other runners, but also with a set of needs and desires that cannot be quenched.

In the end, however, the introduction of complicating factors, such as differences in accumulated experience and circumstances, may not have made for a sufficient explanation of why different individuals will act differently. After all, if life is a zero-sum game and desires are never ending, then ultimately all individuals will want the same things, since they will want everything. To complicate matters further, the impression of similarity is compounded further by the constant reminders of the ultimate equality of human beings. Hobbes seems aware of the need for further explanation, so in Chapter 10 of the first part of *The Elements of Law*, he attributes diversity to the fact that "joy and grief proceed not in all men from the same causes, and that men differ much in constitution of body, whereby, that which helpeth and furthereth vital constitution in one, and is therefore delightful, hindereth and crosseth it in another, and causeth grief."[71]

[68] Hobbes, *The Elements of Law*, I.8.4; cf. I.14.5; *On the Citizen*, I.6.

[69] Hobbes, *The Elements of Law*, I.8.8.

[70] Interestingly, in what turns out to be a relatively detailed examination of the main passions, in *The Elements of Law*, Hobbes does not provide an explicit definition of fear, except in the context of negative definitions of certain aspects of other emotions, such as dejection and hope (cf. I.9). In *Leviathan*, too, fear figures prominently in the definitions of other emotions, but is also defined independently (VI § 16).

[71] Hobbes, *The Elements of Law*, I.10.2. This is in accordance with the exposition of the fourth precept of nature in *De Cive*, wherein Hobbes argues "when men enter into society there are differences of opinion among them which spring from the diversity of their passions" (*On the Citizen*, III.9).

WILL

The influx of percepts into the mind and the effects of those on the vital motion give rise to an initial reaction of appetite or aversion. The succession of appetites and aversions in reaction to a stimulus is "deliberation," and the will is but the last of these.[72] This is true of all actions, so that even so-called "spontaneous" actions are no less willful than ones that follow long deliberations; actions signify the will of the actor, and in cases in which the actor has had no time to deliberate extensively, he acts on the basis of "all the precedent time of his life."[73] As expressions of the will, all actions are therefore indications of what the actor considers to be in his best interest.[74] This important step paves the way for one of Hobbes's most contentious and misunderstood claims. He argues infamously that the difficulty of the choice has no bearing on the extent to which it may be deemed free, and uses Aristotle's example from the *Nicomachean Ethics*, wherein an individual at sea, caught in a storm, is throwing his belongings overboard, so as to save the vessel.[75] For Hobbes, then, necessity and absence of free will are distinct considerations. The former is true of any action in the sense that

That which [...] necessitates and determinates every action [...] is the sum of all those things which, being now existent, conduce and concur to the production of that action hereafter, whereof if any one thing now were wanting, the effect could not be produced. This concourse of causes, may well be called (in respect they were all set and ordered by the eternal cause of all things, God Almighty) the decree of God. [...]

The last dictate of the judgment, concerning the good or bad that may follow on any action, is not properly the whole cause, but the last part of it; and yet may be said to produce the effect necessarily, in such manner as the last feather may be said to break a horse's back, when there were so many laid on before as there wanted but that to do it.[76]

---

[72] Hobbes, *The Elements of Law*, I.12.1–2; cf. *Leviathan*, VI §§ 49–54; *Of Liberty and Necessity*, §§ 25–27.

[73] See Hobbes, *Of Liberty and Necessity*, § 23: "the will follows the last opinion or judgment immediately preceding the action, concerning whether it be good to do it or not, whether he have weighed it long before or not at all." Cf. *Ibid*. §§ 8, 25; *The Elements of Law*, I.12.4, as well as I.4, especially as regards the coherence of thoughts, experience, and prudence.

[74] Cf. Hobbes, *The Elements of Law*, I.12.6; *Of Liberty and Necessity*, § 14.

[75] Aristotle, *Ethica Nicomachea*, 1110a8–9. Hobbes uses this example in *The Elements of Law* (I.12.3) as well as in *Of Liberty and Necessity* (§ 19) and *Leviathan* (XXI § 3).

[76] Hobbes, *Of Liberty and Necessity*, § 11.

Thus, in the example of the man at sea, while most would side with Bramhall and consider that the man in the example had no choice but to do what he did, Hobbes thinks that the action may have been necessitated by the circumstances, but was nonetheless the result of deliberation between two alternatives, and hence the expression of a preference in light of the actor's self-perceived best interests, since "by necessity of nature all men choose what is apparently good for themselves."[77] These self-perceived best interests define groups just as much as they define individuals, since "what is sought in every society is an Object of will, i.e. something which seems to each one of the members to be Good for himself."[78] As we have seen above, Hobbes distinguishes between primary and secondary appetites, and thus between primary and secondary goods.[79] One such primary good – security – in particular defines political associations from their formation and throughout their duration, and it is by examining man's natural state and juxtaposing it to political society that Hobbes can best illustrate this.[80]

THE STATE OF NATURE

The state of nature is the "most widely known of Hobbes's concepts" and the "notion which is the main premiss of his whole ethical and political

---

[77] Hobbes, *On the Citizen*, VI.4. Cf. *A Briefe of the Art of Rhetorique*, I.10: 38: "*Voluntary* is that which a man does with knowledge; and without compulsion." Hobbes takes the actor's self-perceived interests so seriously that in *De Cive* he refers to them as "right reason" (see Hobbes's note to II.1, on pp. 33–34).

[78] Hobbes, *On the Citizen*, I.2. Although Hobbes is at pains to distance himself from Aristotle, there is nothing in this part of his reasoning that puts his account of the formation of groups at odds with Aristotle's. As has been shown in Chapter 2 in this volume, Aristotle's account emphasizes the positive contributions of the individuals who come together to form a society every bit as much as Hobbes's does here. Hobbes's earlier statement, "for they who shall more narrowly look into the Causes for which Men come together, and delight in each others company, shall easily find that this happens not because naturally it could happen no otherwise, but by Accident" (*De Cive* [Warrender, ed.], I.2), should not be read as contradicting the present claim, since it is intended merely as a counter to any claims for the existence in man of a natural, positive sociability not driven by need. Leijenhorst argues, "The main 'paradigm shift' probably lies in the very fact that the moderns style their philosophy as 'new' and 'modern.' Upon delving deeper, the patient historian detects but few of the announced radical ruptures" (*The Mechanisation of Aristotelianism*, 222). This is an accurate reflection of the actual relationship between Aristotle and Hobbes's theories, the differences of which are often exaggerated.

[79] See Hobbes, *Leviathan*, XI § 4.

[80] See Hobbes, *The Elements of Law*, I.14.2: "In this chapter it will be expedient to consider in what estate of security this our nature hath placed us, and what probability it hath left us of continuing and preserving ourselves against the violence of others." Cf. *On the Citizen*, Pref. §§ 9–10; *Leviathan*, XIII.

system."[81] The concept is, in some of its attributes, an old one. The reference to a state of affairs antecedent to political organization calls to mind images of man outside the polis, as in the accounts of Aristotle and Lucretius, as well as of man in the Garden of Eden, before and after the Fall.[82] By the 1640s, when Hobbes began to use the concept, the state of nature was becoming a part of what we have come to think of as the social contract tradition.[83] The term, however, as it appears in Hobbes's theory, seems to be his own.[84] Those who know nothing else of Hobbes and his theories often know at least some of the adjectives of that infamous description from Chapter XIII of *Leviathan*, according to which life in the state of nature is "solitary, poor, nasty, brutish, and short," a war in which "every man is enemy to every man."[85] For all its rhetorical merit, and despite the fact that it captures certain essential characteristics of the state of nature, this description is also misleading. Interpreters of Hobbes have struggled for a long time to determine whether a state of nature fitting this description can possibly have been an actual historical state, or whether it is merely a mental image, a thought experiment.[86]

The present interpretation departs from such accounts in a number of ways. First, as the subsequent analysis will show, even the most cursory reading of Hobbes's chapters on man's natural condition will immediately reveal several examples of actual situations, both historical and contemporary, that Hobbes equates (to a greater or lesser extent) with the state of nature in his theory. The real question, then, is not whether Hobbes thinks that the state of nature exists, but rather how far reaching it is. As will be shown below, Hobbes offers a series of historical, sociological, and psychological

---

[81] Tricaud, "Hobbes's Conception of the State of Nature from 1640 to 1651," 107.

[82] See Aristotle, *Politica*, 1253a25–31; Lucretius, *On the Nature of Things*, V.925–1457; Bailey, *Lucretius*, 14. Klosko & Rice, "Thucydides and Hobbes's State of Nature," as well as Curley (*Leviathan*, p. 76, note 4) point to the similarities between Hobbes's description in *Leviathan* XIII and the opening of Book I of Thucydides' *History*. The language in the famous passage from *Leviathan* XIII is also strikingly similar to that in Hobbes's rendition of Homer's description of the land of the Cyclopes in *Odysses*, Book IX (101).

[83] Most notably Grotius. For a brief summary of the concept of the state of nature in Grotius, Pufendorf, Burlamaqui, and other social contract theorists, see Derathé, *Jean-Jacques Rousseau et la science politique de son temps*, 125–31.

[84] The first instance is in *De Cive*, Pref. § 14.

[85] Hobbes, *Leviathan*, XIII § 9.

[86] Mintz, for example, dismisses seventeenth-century readings of Hobbes's state of nature as a normative state, but he then proceeds to proclaim "[i]t is neither a historical picture nor a practical guide to conduct" (*The Hunting of Leviathan*, 33). As will be shown later, neither claim has any basis in Hobbes's texts.

examples of the state of nature. Second, commentators fault Hobbes with having provided scant and vague references to the state of nature, as a result of which, they hold, it is impossible to come away with a clear and concise understanding of what it is. The second of these accusations (vagueness) is correct, but the first (scarcity) is misplaced. In fact, it will be shown that the state of nature is intended to reach farther than most commentators are willing to grant, and that some of its manifestations are to be found in unusual parts of Hobbes's theory. As a result, there are more, rather than fewer, instances of it throughout his writings, and these will help the reader get a firmer grasp of the centrality of this concept. Third, through its multiplicity of manifestations, the state of nature preserves Hobbes's concern with security from enemies as the defining element of political power.[87] Ultimately, misunderstandings of Hobbes's theory of the state of nature can be seen to result from insufficient attention to the role that he ascribes to fear and war.

People dislike bearers of bad news, and Hobbes's account of the natural condition of man has a long history of misreading stemming, it seems, from the forceful way in which it bears such news about who we are.[88] Reactions to such news are often so visceral and forceful that they tend to confirm, even if inadvertently, some of the claims they purport to disprove.[89] The publication of *Leviathan*, which contains the most succinct and powerful description of the state of nature, gave rise to a stream of polemics and mockery that eventually made "Hobbist" a term of abuse.[90] In *De Cive*, Hobbes commented on the profound ability of the emotions to cloud one's judgment, and it seems that the only explanation for some of the reactions to Hobbes's theory is that his depiction of the state of nature gives rise to emotions of this

[87] The primary sources of information regarding the state of nature are: *The Elements of Law*, I.14; *De Cive*, I; *Leviathan*, XIII. Although the most widely known, the latter is also the least informative, as it presents only the basic elements of Hobbes's argument. Nevertheless, the accounts are consistent with one another, and in examining them we will draw from all three, as well as from other relevant works.

[88] Clarendon, for example, claims "[n]or had Mr. *Hobbes* any other reason to degrade [man] to this degree of Bestiality, but that he may be fit to wear those Chains and Fetters which he hath provided for him" (*A Brief View and Survey of the Dangerous and Pernicious Errors to Church and State, in Mr. Hobbes's Book Entitled Leviathan*, 28). See also Chapter 6 in this volume.

[89] See Hobbes, *On the Citizen*, Pref. §§ 11–12: "All commonwealths and individuals behave in this way, and thus admit their fear and distrust of each other. But in argument they deny it, i.e. in their eagerness to contradict others they contradict themselves."

[90] Cf. Rogers, Introduction to *Perspectives on Thomas Hobbes*, 3–4; Rogers, "Hobbes's Hidden Influence," 190–94; Mintz, *The Hunting of Leviathan*, 147–56, Appendix (157–60).

potency.[91] Unfortunately, some of the misunderstandings that have emerged out of such interpretations have proven to be persistent, and are largely responsible for a mainstream, street-level perception of Hobbesian political thought that is hard to dispel.[92] This perception affects various aspects of Hobbesian political theory, but it is the main two, war and fear, that we are concerned with here.

On the basis of his observations regarding the universality of human nature, Hobbes concludes that human beings in the state of nature are equal for all intents and purposes; no one is completely secure from the possibility of getting killed by another.[93] In the analysis of the faculties of perception and will formation, Hobbes offered a glimpse into the mechanisms by which conflict between individuals might arise. In his description of the state of nature, he moves further to provide the structural framework that explains why conflict will in fact take place. Each individual, we are told, is commanded by the Law of Nature to preserve his life.[94] To facilitate adherence

---

[91] Hobbes, *On the Citizen*, IV.26.

[92] One noteworthy example of a curious branch of commentary on Hobbes is that which concerns itself with determining whether or not his theory is "egoistic." Although Hobbes himself is not concerned with this question, commentators anxious to exonerate human nature have taken it upon themselves to determine whether men are selfish or not. This line of investigation has a long lineage, beginning with such works as Eachard's (*Mr. Hobbs's State of Nature Considered*), wherein Hobbes is portrayed as "Philautus" (self-lover or egoist), who is so timid as to require seven pages' worth of convincing just to take a walk with "Timothy" (the one who honors God). More recently, Gert ("Hobbes, Mechanism, and Egoism") tried to show that the dependence of Hobbes's theory of motion makes it pointless to speak of motives. McNeilly ("Egoism in Hobbes") argued in response that Hobbes is inconsistent, presenting an egoistical theory in *The Elements of Law* but one devoid of egoism in *Leviathan*. In his reply, Gert ("Hobbes and Psychological Egoism") changed his mind about both the extent to which Hobbes is consistent and the connection between Hobbes's mechanism and man's actions. In his analysis of the connection between Hobbes's natural and political philosophies, Verdon puts the issue of egoism into perspective by pointing out that Hobbes's emphasis on motion renders the question irrelevant to his program ("On the Laws of Physical and Human Nature," 659–60).

[93] In both *The Elements of Law* and *De Cive*, Hobbes begins his account of the state of nature by pointing to his conclusions about the faculties of human nature, examined above: "*Physical force, Experience, Reason, Passion*" (*De Cive*, I.1). Cf. *The Elements of Law*, I.14.1. Schlatter argues that the idea of a fixed, unchanging human nature is one of the reasons that made Thucydides so appealing to Hobbes ("Thomas Hobbes and Thucydides," 357–58); cf. Ioannis D. Evrigenis, "Hobbes's Thucydides". On equality, see Hobbes, *The Elements of Law*, I.14.2; *De Cive*, I.3; *Leviathan*, XIII §§ 1–2.

[94] Hobbes, *Leviathan*, XIV § 3. Cf. *The Elements of Law*, I.14.6:

And forasmuch as necessity of nature maketh men to will and desire *bonum sibi*, that which is good for themselves, and to avoid that which is hurtful; but most of all that terrible enemy of nature, death, from whom we expect both the loss of all power, and also the greatest of bodily

to this command, individuals also have a right of nature that consists of the following components: (i) to use their own power to preserve themselves, (ii) to judge what will be necessary for their preservation, and (iii) to use anything else that they might consider necessary for their preservation.[95] In a setting that prizes self-preservation to such an extent, and given the multiplicity and insatiability of desires as well as the zero-sum game that these give rise to, the prospect of conflict always lurks in the horizon.[96]

This brings us to the two central concepts in the description of the state of nature, war and fear, both of which suffer the same type of abuse all too often. Hobbes was doubtless well aware of the fact that the mere mention of war invokes images of savagery and bloodshed, and that the element of anticipation is likely to get lost in the fog of such a state of affairs. As we shall see, Hobbes was eager to reap the benefits of this first reaction to the word *war*, but he is also at pains to draw his reader's attention to the other, more distant and calculating meaning of the word. Thus,

WAR consisteth not in battle only, or the act of fighting, but in a tract of time wherein the will to contend by battle is sufficiently known. And therefore, the notion of *time* is to be considered in the nature of war, as it is in the nature of weather. For as the nature of foul weather, lieth not in a shower or two of rain, but in an inclination thereto of many days together, so the nature of war consisteth not in actual fighting, but in the known disposition thereto during all the time there is no assurance to the contrary.[97]

This emphasis on the *prospect* of conflict is supported by Hobbes's explanation of what he means by *fear*. Much like *war*, readers have always been quick to interpret *fear* in Hobbes's theory as fright leading to flight. As a result,

---

pains in the losing; it is not against reason that a man doth all he can to preserve his own body and limbs, both from death and pain.

[95] See Hobbes, *Leviathan*, XIV § 1 for (i) and (ii); (iii) is explained in § 4: "in such a condition every man has a right to everything, even to one another's body." This right is often interpreted literally, but one need not go so far as to assert that Hobbes means that an individual in the state of nature will in fact go after everything. Rather, it is enough that once any single thing is seen by one as necessary to one's survival, that individual will have a right to that particular thing.

[96] On conflict, see Hobbes, *The Elements of Law*, I.14.3–5; *De Cive*, I.4–6; *Leviathan*, XIII §§ 4–7. On the zero-sum game arising out of the combination of insatiable desires and finite amounts of goods, see *The Elements of Law*, I.14.5; *De Cive*, I.6; *Leviathan*, XIII § 3.

[97] Hobbes, *Leviathan*, XIII § 8. Cf. *De Cive*, I.12: "For what else is WAR but that time in which the will to contend by force is made sufficiently known by words or actions?"; *The Elements of Law*, I.14.11: "For WAR is nothing else but that time wherein the will and intention of contending by force is either by words or actions sufficiently declared."

Hobbes's name has become synonymous with timidity in a way similar to that in which Machiavelli's came to be synonymous with evil.[98] Upon its publication in 1642, *De Cive* generated enough of a response to cause Hobbes to add a series of explanatory notes that appeared in the second edition of 1647 and have been considered a part of the text ever since.[99] In one of those notes, Hobbes addresses those who misunderstood his use of the word *fear:*

The following objection is made: it is not true that men could combine into society through mutual fear; to the contrary, if they had been so afraid of each other, they could not even have borne the sight of each other. The objectors believe, I think, that fearing is nothing but being actually frightened. But I mean by that word any anticipation of future evil. In my view, not only flight, but also distrust, suspicion, precaution and provision against fear are all characteristic of men who are afraid. On going to bed, men lock their doors; when going on a journey, they arm themselves because they are afraid of robbers. Countries guard their frontiers with fortresses, their cities with walls, through fear of neighbouring countries. Even the strongest armies, fully ready for battle, open negotiations from time to time about peace, because they fear each other's forces and the risk of being beaten. Men take precautions because they are afraid – by running away and hiding if they see no alternative but most often by using arms and instruments of defence; the result is that when they do risk an advance, each tries to probe the other's mind. And if they do fight, a commonwealth comes into being as the result of victory; and if they make an agreement, a commonwealth comes into being through an accord.[100]

Combined, Hobbes's definitions of war and fear indicate the extent to which Hobbes is concerned with the *prospect* of violence rather than with actual fighting. This interpretation is supported further by what he *actually* says about human beings. Many of his readers, Hobbes predicts, will object that all this distrust leads to the conclusion that

all Men are evil (which perhaps, though harsh, should be conceded, since it is clearly said in Holy Scripture), but also (and this cannot be conceded without impiety) that they are evil by nature. However it does not follow from this Principle that men are

---

[98] See, e.g., [Eachard], *Mr. Hobbs's State of Nature Considered,* 1–7.

[99] This history follows the usual practice of numbering only the printed editions, even though the manuscript was first circulated among Hobbes's friends in 1641; it was not until 1642 that an edition, also limited, appeared in print. On the history of these editions, as well as the status of the notes, see the Introduction to *On the Citizen,* viii–ix, esp. note 4. Cf. Martinich, *Hobbes,* 177–80. On the significance of *De Cive,* see Hobbes, *Considerations upon the Reputation, Loyalty, Manners, and Religion of Thomas Hobbes* in *The English Works of Thomas Hobbes,* 4: 415; *Thomae Hobbesii Malmesburiensis vita,* 6.

[100] Hobbes, *On the Citizen,* I.2, note 2. Cf. *Leviathan,* XIII § 10. By contrast, in *De Cive,* Hobbes describes a "kind of supreme stage of fearfulness" in which one sees the harm threatening him as the worst possible (injury or death), and "must be expected to look out for himself either by flight or by fighting" (*On the Citizen,* II.18).

evil by nature. For we cannot tell the good and the bad apart, hence even if there were fewer evil men than good men, good, decent people would still be saddled with the constant need to watch, distrust, anticipate and get the better of others, and to protect themselves by all possible means.[101]

The very possibility of harm from another is sufficient to divert one from any sustained pursuit of constructive activity, and it is for this reason that in the state of nature it makes no sense to speak of industry, agriculture, commerce, building, and so forth.[102]

This list of the basic characteristics of the state of nature brings us to a crucial question, one that Hobbes anticipates from his readers: whether or not such a state has ever existed.[103] Hobbes's first response is that "it was never generally so," but this turns out to be deceptively restrictive, given the examples that he provides.[104] In both *The Elements of Law* and *De Cive*, Hobbes follows the strategy of Thomas Hariot, in citing side by side the examples of contemporary savages and the condition of the ancestors of the civilized nations of his day. Anyone wanting a first glimpse of what the state of nature is like has but to look at the natives of America or the "old inhabitants of Germany."[105] Both these examples share the absence of an all-powerful, commonly accepted authority to "keep [...] all in awe," and the lack of "all the comforts and amenities of life which *peace* and society

---

[101] Hobbes, *On the Citizen*, Pref. § 12. Cf. *ibid.*, Ep. Ded. § 2. As Hardin points out rightly, this passage provides an interesting corrective to those accounts that characterize Hobbes's view of human nature as strictly and simply misanthropic (*Collective Action*, 185). Cf. Walzer, *Politics and Passion*, 111.

[102] See Hobbes, *Leviathan*, XIII § 9. Hobbes's famous description of the barrenness of the state of nature receives a similar reception as his description of the extent of natural right. Tricaud, however, seems to be right in arguing that one should not read too much into it ("Hobbes's Conception of the State of Nature from 1640 to 1651," 108). There is no reason to think that Hobbes means that individuals have no dwelling, no clothes, and no weapons. Rather, Hobbes's point seems to be that what artifice exists in such a state will remain rudimentary because of the insecurity that prevails. This interpretation is supported by *De Cive*, I.13, as will be shown later.

[103] Hobbes, *Leviathan*, XIII § 11.

[104] Hobbes, *Leviathan*, XIII § 11.

[105] Cf. *The Elements of Law*, I.14.12; *De Cive*, I.13. This technique is first employed by Thomas Hariot, in his *A Briefe and True Report of the New Found Land of Virginia, etc.* (1590), where detailed sketches and descriptions of the way of life of the Virginia natives are compared to alleged equivalent accounts of the Picts, early inhabitants of eastern and northeastern Scotland. Hariot's account, supplemented by John White's sketches, was very popular, and Hobbes was surely familiar with it as well as other sources of information about Virginia, given his membership in the Virginia Company (see Malcolm, "Hobbes, Sandys, and the Virginia Company," 298–99; Martinich, *Hobbes*, 60–64).

afford."[106] They do not, however, as some commentators have claimed, mean that it is impossible for individuals to band together, even if temporarily, to deal with external threats.[107] Hobbes makes this abundantly clear in *De Cive*, where in describing how two equally rightful claims to something will lead to conflict he explains that "if you add also how difficult it is, *with few men and little equipment*, to take precautions against enemies who attack with the intention to overwhelm and subdue, it cannot be denied that men's natural state, before they came together into society, was War."[108] Even in his most famous formulation, in *Leviathan*, where one's attention is usually captured by the powerful emphasis on solitude, destitution, and fear, Hobbes is quite explicit about the possibility of temporary associations aimed at security. Indeed, he bases his argument for equality in part on the existence of such associations: "[f]or as to the strength of body, the weakest has strength enough to kill the strongest, either by secret machination, *or by confederacy with others that are in the same danger with himself*."[109] Nor is this passage an isolated example. In *The Elements of Law*, Hobbes concludes the chapter on the state of nature by emphasizing the insecurity that arises from equality. A man who perceives this equality, he argues, will be convinced by reason to "seek after peace, as far forth as there is hope to attain the same; and to strengthen himself with all the help he can procure, for his own defence

---

[106] Hobbes, *Leviathan*, XIII § 8; *De Cive*, I.13. Cf. *The Elements of Law*, I.14.12: "... where we find people few and short lived, and without the ornaments and comforts of life, which by peace and society are usually invented and procured."

[107] Kavka ("Hobbes's War of All against All," esp. 297–99), e.g., constructs an influential argument for the applicability of the prisoner's dilemma in Hobbes's state of nature that is based entirely on a misreading of Hobbes's argument, as it considers the formation of any coalition in the state of nature impossible, despite Hobbes's explicit statements to the contrary, in *Leviathan* (XIII § 1) and elsewhere (e.g., *The Elements of Law*, I.14.14; *De Cive*, I.13).

[108] Hobbes, *De Cive*, I.12; emphasis added. Cf. *Leviathan*, XV § 5: "in a condition of war wherein every man to every man (for want of a common Power to keep them all in awe) is an enemy, there is no man can hope by his own strength, or wit, to defend himself from destruction without the help of confederates (where every one expects the same defence by the confederation that any one else does); and therefore, he which declares he thinks it reason to deceive those that help him can in reason expect no other means of safety than what can be had from his own single power." Although Hobbes uses the word *covenant* to describe the means by which these associations are formed, *pace* Forsyth ("Thomas Hobbes and the External Relations of States," 203–04), the context makes it clear that he is speaking of expectations based on reciprocity, rather than actual contractual obligations.

[109] Hobbes, *Leviathan*, XIII § 1, emphasis added.

against those, from whom such peace cannot be obtained."[110] The same principle appears in *De Cive*, where Hobbes gives the clearest statement of how negative association leads men out of the state of nature: "we are driven by mutual fear to believe that we must emerge from such a state and seek allies [*socii*]; so that if we must have *war*, it will not be a war against all men and without aid."[111]

As we have seen above, experience plays a key role in the classification of our perceptions and the formation of our will, and it is experience in the state of nature that teaches one how to strike a balance between complete mistrust of others, which leads to insecurity, and participation in some joint endeavors towards security that make it possible to survive. In the state of nature, all this is achieved initially by means of negative association, since at the beginning each is the enemy of everyone. This balance is interrupted once the same individual becomes an enemy to more than one. Two individuals who otherwise have nothing in common and have every reason to be apprehensive towards each other are now threatened by the same enemy, and given that they value their self-preservation above all else, they have to address the immediate threat before they deal with other, more distant ones. As soon as they join forces, the balance of power that made for complete equality ceases to exist, and in the temporary security afforded by their success the potential benefits of alliance formation begin to dawn on the previously solitary and suspicious individuals.[112] Thus transformed by the experience of their cooperation, they are ready to consider a longer-term association that will provide more permanent security and thereby pave the way for commodious living.

---

[110] Hobbes, *The Elements of Law*, I.14.14.

[111] Hobbes, *On the Citizen*, I.13. Cf. *De Cive*, II.9–11; Tuck, *The Rights of War and Peace*: "No conventions or covenants are *secure* in the state of nature, since at any time they may be trumped by the force of the right of self-preservation or private judgment; but in the absence of such disruption they can maintain a weak existence" (133).

[112] It is this security that allows one some distance from the pressing demands of the emotions: "It is true that *hope, fear, anger, ambition, greed, vainglory* and the other emotions do impede one's ability to grasp the laws of nature, while they prevail. But no one is without his calmer moments, and at those times, nothing is easier to grasp, even for the ignorant and the uneducated" (*On the Citizen*, III.26). Cf. *Leviathan*, XV § 5, where Hobbes explains that it is not against reason to perform in the state of nature when another has done so already, as well as *Leviathan*, XXVI § 8: "For the laws of nature, which consist in equity, justice, gratitude, and other moral virtues on these depending, in the condition of mere nature [...] are not properly laws, but qualities that dispose men to peace and to obedience."

THE STATE

There is good reason to think that for Hobbes the fundamental political question is "who decides?"[113] Historically, that question seems to have been the crux of the ship-money controversy and the ensuing civil war, and philosophically it is at the center of Hobbes's theory of man and his perception of the world.[114] In his political theory, this issue emerges in every discussion of the means of transition from the state of nature to the commonwealth. This should come as no surprise, since man is fundamentally the same in the state of nature and in society with others, and submission to the laws is intended as a remedy for a problem that persists for as long as man is around.[115] Towards the end of *The Elements of Law*, Hobbes paints a dramatic picture of the potential extent of disagreement absent a standard imposed by a commonly accepted authority:

> In the state of nature, where every man is his own judge, and differeth from other concerning the names and appellations of things, and from those differences arise quarrels, and breach of peace; it was necessary there should be a common measure of all things that might fall in controversy; as for example: of what is to be called right, what good, what virtue, what much, what little, what *meum* and *tuum*, what a

---

[113] Tuck argues that in *The Elements of Law*, Hobbes's "whole argument was directed against the notion that citizens might retain private judgement about the occasions when the security of the realm was in question" (*Philosophy and Government*, 313). Cf. *De Cive*, VI.7, XII; *Leviathan*, XXIX § 6; Mansfield, "Hobbes and the Science of Indirect Government," 108.

[114] Hobbes tells his readers that the turmoil leading up to the civil war was the reason he skipped the parts of his theory dealing with the body and man (what later became *De Corpore* and *De Homine*, respectively) and wrote *De Cive* first (*De Cive*, Pref. §§ 18–19).

[115] Hobbes, *On the Citizen*, Ep. Ded., §§ 6–7. In "The Utopianism of *Leviathan*," Tuck sees Hobbes as arguing that universal peace may result from the transformation of human nature (126–27), but this interpretation is based on only the first part of the passage in question. As the very next sentence shows, Hobbes is here lamenting the way "things are." His contribution, as he goes on to explain in the rest of the Epistle, lies in his ability to extract two postulates from his observation of the way things are, from which he demonstrates the need of "*agreements and of keeping faith*" (*On the Citizen*, Ep. Ded., §§ 9–10).

Hegel captures this element of the state of nature in his short but perceptive lecture on Hobbes:

> The expression nature has a double significance: In the first place the nature of man signifies his spiritual and rational Being; but his natural condition indicates quite another condition, wherein man conducts himself according to his natural impulses. In this way he conducts himself in conformity with his desires and inclinations, while the rational, on the contrary, is the obtaining supremacy over the immediately natural (*Lectures on the History of Philosophy* III, p. 318).

See Chapter 6 in this volume.

pound, what a quart, &c. For in these things private judgments may differ and beget controversy.[116]

Hobbes's use of *meum* and *tuum* is quite interesting. To show the extent of the inconveniences that may arise out of such a state of affairs, he appeals to disagreement about something as simple and fundamental as property. This strategy is grounded in his theory of primary and secondary desires, or means and ends, and directed at the ship-money controversy.[117] The presence of a fundamental threat posed by the challenge to one's property, one's means of survival, is perhaps the aptest illustration of the state of nature, and the ground upon which the experience of the English Civil War and Hobbes's theory can combine to convince his audience of the truth of his claims.[118] This is why Hobbes sees the English Civil War as a further manifestation of the state of nature.[119] In such a condition, in which there seems to be no basis for consensus, individuals can at least agree that they are in mutual danger from a common enemy.

The possibility of longer-term collaboration, however, brings with it the need to make the temporary peace achieved in the state of nature through *metus hostilis* more lasting. This, according to Hobbes, can only be brought about by a common power, the fear of which will compel these individuals to maintain peace with one another and thereby remain an effective collective

---

[116] Hobbes, *The Elements of Law*, II.10.8. This picture is reproduced, in essence, in *Leviathan*, XIII § 13. Cf. *The Elements of Law*, I.14.10, II.1.2; *De Cive*, Pref. § 7, VI.9.

[117] This connection is illustrated very well by the Hampden case. Royalists would emphasize the threat posed by the enemy as the real issue, to support the King's case, whilst blaming Hampden of being too stingy to part with a small amount of his money. Hobbes himself makes this argument in *Behemoth* (4). Opponents of the ship-money would downplay the extent of the threat and emphasize instead the violation of the citizens' property rights (see, e.g., Parker, *The Case of Shipmony Briefly Discoursed*). Cf. *De Cive*, VI.7, XII.5, XII.7, XIII.8.

[118] In *A Dialogue between a Philosopher and a Student of the Common Laws of England*, when discussing property (*Meum, Tuum, Alienum*), the lawyer agrees with the philosopher's assessment of the importance of laws in settling disputes, and points to experience: "for without Statute-Laws, all Men have Right to all things; and we have had Experience when our Laws were silenced by the Civil War, there was not a Man, that of any Goods could say assuredly they were his own." The two interlocutors therefore conclude that by itself such a right is meaningless: "what are you better for your Right, if a rebellious Company at home, or an Enemy from abroad take away the Goods, or dispossess you of the Lands you have a right to? Can you be defended, or repair'd, but by the strength and authority of the King?" (73). Cf. *Leviathan*, XIII § 13.

[119] On civil war as the state of nature, see *Leviathan*, XVIII § 20. On the English Civil War as the motivation behind Hobbes's political writings, see *De Cive*, Pref. §§ 18–19, 24; *Leviathan*, "A Review, and Conclusion" § 17.

of defense against external enemies.[120] Hobbes is clear that man never frees himself from his social emotions. The fear of others that drives individuals into temporary associations for defense against common enemies thus becomes a necessary element of what transforms the temporary associations of the state of nature into enduring political communities, since preservation is always the primary concern. At the end of the first part of *The Elements of Law*, Hobbes sums up the pervasiveness of that fear as follows:

> The cause in general which moveth a man to become subject to another, is (as I have said already) the fear of not otherwise preserving himself. And a man may subject himself to him that invadeth, or may invade him, for fear of him; or men may join amongst themselves to subject themselves to such as they shall agree upon for fear of others.[121]

This awareness is enough to transform solitary and suspicious individuals into beings willing to cooperate temporarily to fight off the common enemy, but Hobbes realizes that such associations are nevertheless impossible to sustain. In the best-case scenario, once the immediate threat has been eliminated or fended off, individuals will be forced to rearrange their priorities and reclassify their erstwhile collaborators as potential threats.[122] Regardless of the success of any particular joint endeavor of this sort, then, the individuals in question will realize that temporary, small associations are unlikely to be of much help overall, because "it is evident: that the mutual aid of two or three men is of very little security; for the odds on the other side, of a man or two, giveth sufficient encouragement to an assault."[123] The precariousness of these temporary alliances will lead natural man to the conclusion that

> in small numbers, small additions on the one side or the other make the advantage of strength so great as is sufficient to carry the victory; and therefore gives encouragement to an invasion. The multitude sufficient to confide in for our security is not determined by any certain number, *but by comparison with the enemy we fear*, and

---

[120] See Hobbes, *The Elements of Law*, I.19.6: "consent [. . .] is not sufficient security for their common peace, without the erection of some common power, by the fear whereof they may be compelled both to keep the peace amongst themselves, and to join their strengths together, against a common enemy." Cf. *ibid.*, I.19.8; *Leviathan*, XIII § 8, XVII § 1, XVII § 12; *De Cive*, V.4–8.

[121] Hobbes, *The Elements of Law*, I.19.11.

[122] Hobbes argues that individuals who participate in such short-term defensive associations "though they obtain a victory by their unanimous endeavour against a foreign enemy, yet afterwards, when either they have no common enemy, or he that by one part is held for an enemy is by another part held for a friend, they must needs by the difference of their interests dissolve, and fall again into a war amongst themselves" (*Leviathan*, XVII § 5).

[123] *The Elements of Law*, I.19.3. Cf. *ibid.*, I.19.4; *De Cive*, V.4.

is then sufficient, when the odds of the enemy is not of so visible and conspicuous moment, to determine the event of war, as to move him to attempt.[124]

It is the enemies that remain, then, that determine the size and scope of the commonwealth under formation, and this, as we shall see, is a formative influence that never ceases to exert itself upon the state. This *metus hostilis* too, however, becomes transformed by the covenant that gives rise to the state, because along with the right to decide and the means to enforce it, it passes from the constituent individuals into the hands of the sovereign.

In the state of nature, the individual's ability and right to judge who poses a threat and what is necessary to protect himself from this threat was simultaneously the means to self-preservation and the cause of conflict. It is in this judgment that Hobbes locates the essence of politics, and it is by the transfer of this judgment that the sovereign emerges and the commonwealth is instituted. The individual's will, which expresses his appetite and aversion to things as they appear to him to be in and against his self-interest, respectively, is what needs to be tamed if temporary associations are to be turned into more permanent ones. In *Leviathan*, Hobbes argues, "[t]he only way to erect such a common power as may be able to defend [men] from the invasion of foreigners and the injuries of one another" is to give up their power to a sovereign, who may then "reduce all their wills [...] unto one will."[125] Absent this surrender, the only thing that will keep individuals from pursuing their self-interests by waging war on one another is the presence of a common enemy.[126] The transfer of each individual's right to judge against whom to use his power is captured in the very words of the hypothetical contract that signals the birth of the *Leviathan*. The solitary individuals promise to one another that they will give up their right to govern themselves to the sovereign. Thus deprived of the ability to judge, they place their power at

[124] Hobbes, *Leviathan*, XVII § 3, emphasis added. Cf. *The Elements of Law*: "before men have sufficient security in the help of one another, their number must be so great, that the odds of a few which the enemy may have, be no certain and sensible advantage" (I.19.3).
[125] Hobbes, *Leviathan*, XVII § 13. Hobbes lists the right to decide what opinions and doctrines "are averse, and what conducing to peace" among the rights of the sovereign, and bases it on the danger posed by those that "they dare take up arms to defend or introduce an opinion." Such men are effectively in the state of nature: "still in war; and their condition not peace, but only a cessation of arms for fear of one another; and they live, as it were, in the precincts of battle continually" (*Leviathan*, XVIII § 9); cf. *On the Citizen* I.5, V.5. On disagreement as a manifestation of the state of nature, see Peleau's letter to Hobbes of [December 25, 1656]/January 4, 1657 (*Correspondence*, I, letter 110: 422–23), as well as Tuck, *The Rights of War and Peace*, 136–38.
[126] Hobbes, *Leviathan*, XVII § 4.

the disposal of the sovereign, who "*may use the strength and means of them all, as he shall think expedient, for their peace and common defence.*"[127] Hobbes is quite clear about the status of this surrender: it is *required* for "the preservation of peace and stable defence."[128]

Thus armed with the power of all the erstwhile solitary individuals who have become his subjects, and with the now unique capacity to determine the existence of a threat, the sovereign begins to provide security, the primary good, from which flow all the benefits of commodious living that were unattainable in the state of nature.[129] It is well known that according to Hobbes, the sovereign achieves and maintains security by means of his awe-inspiring power, but it is less noticed and seldom remarked upon that he supplements this power with other means, the most important of which is the preservation of the image of the state of nature. In his discussion of the train of imaginations in *Leviathan*, Hobbes claims that "the impression made by such things as we desire or fear is strong and permanent, or (if it cease for a time) of quick return; so strong it is sometimes as to hinder and break our sleep."[130] Inside the state of society, the state of nature returns through this mechanism and operates at two different levels. For Hobbes's readers, it is an image so powerful and frightful that it seems to be the one thing that is sure to stay with anyone who has ever heard of or read *Leviathan*. On the level of actual politics, for any sovereign's subjects the fear of enemies becomes a constant reminder of the most basic reason for

---

[127] Hobbes, *Leviathan*, XVII § 13. On the transfer of individual wills as the passage from the state of nature to the state of society, see *The Elements of Law*, II.1.3. Hobbes provides biblical evidence for the sovereign's right to judge in *De Cive*, XI.2.

[128] Hobbes, *De Cive*, V.6, VI.3.

[129] Hobbes presents the advantages of civil society and the disadvantages of the state of nature side by side in *De Cive*, X.1. On security and the benefits that flow from it, see *On the Citizen*, XIII.6:

> Regarding this life only, the good things citizens may enjoy can be put into four categories: (1) defence from external enemies; (2) preservation of internal peace; (3) acquisition of wealth, so far as this is consistent with public security; (4) full enjoyment of innocent liberty. Sovereigns can do no more for the citizens' happiness [*felicitas*] than to enable them to enjoy the possessions their industry has won them, safe from foreign and civil war.

> Cf. *The Elements of Law*, II.9.1, II.9.9; *On the Citizen*, Ep. Ded., §§ 1–2; *Leviathan*, Introduction § 1, XIII §§ 8–9, XVII § 13, XXX § 1; *Behemoth*, 67–68; *A Dialogue between a Philosopher and a Student of the Common Laws of England*, 63, 102. Hobbes is also clear that the list of benefits from security is not limited to material possessions: "*Philosophy* was not risen to the *Grecians*, and other people of the west, whose *commonwealths* [...] had never peace, but when their fears of one another were equal, nor the *leisure* to observe any thing but one another" (*Leviathan*, XLVI § 6).

[130] Hobbes, *Leviathan*, III § 4.

remaining loyal to a political association, no matter what grievances one may have. As holder of the right to determine threats and of the coercive power to back up those judgments, the sovereign remains in the state of nature, since he is the only one who has not surrendered his natural right to punish.[131] Moreover, we know that the sovereign remains in the state of nature with respect to other sovereigns, but this is also the case when it comes to transgressors against civil law, who have to be punished, since by violating the laws, these individuals question the judgment of the sovereign, whose exclusive right it is to determine the laws and property, and thereby render themselves enemies of the commonwealth.[132] When punished by the sovereign, these individuals are put in a situation to a certain degree reminiscent of the state of nature, albeit made worse by the magnitude of the punitive power of the sovereign.[133] More importantly, however, they also give reason to everyone else to remember what life was or would be like in a condition in which everyone is a potential enemy. Hobbes argues that the Law of Nature commands that in revenge or punishment one *"consider future good, not past evil* [...] in order to correct the wrongdoer or so that others may be reformed by taking warning from his punishment."[134] In a commonwealth whose primary purpose is the preservation of the lives of its members, those subjects who by their transgressions become candidates for corporal and capital punishment thereby return themselves to the state of nature.[135] For those of the rest who may entertain the possibility of breaking the law, the revival of the image of the state of nature through the example of the punishment of another is enough to trigger that healthy, long-term fear that Hobbes speaks of in *De Cive*.[136] Thus, traces of the state of nature

---

[131] Hobbes, *Leviathan*, XXVIII § 2.

[132] See Hobbes, *De Cive*, Ep. Ded., §§ 1–2, V.2, XIII.7; *Leviathan*, XIII § 12, XXX § 30. Cf. *Leviathan*, XXVII § 54: "in almost all crimes there is an injury done, not only to some private men, but also to the commonwealth." Theft is a good example of the extent to which the injury affects the entire commonwealth, since in stealing one does not only deprive another of his property, but he also disputes the sovereign's judgment about what belongs to whom. See, e.g., *Leviathan*, XVIII §§ 10–11; *A Dialogue between a Philosopher and a Student of the Common Laws of England*, 73. Cf. ibid., 101–22, 140–68, on judgment and punishment.

[133] Although he does not attribute this to Hobbes, Locke considers it one of the best reasons against absolute submission to the sovereign (*Two Treatises of Government*, II § 138).

[134] Hobbes, *De Cive*, III.11. Cf. *Leviathan*, XXVIII § 10, XXX § 23, XXXVIII § 1.

[135] See Hobbes, *Leviathan*, XV § 5, XXVII § 1. It is for this purpose that individuals transfer their right to punish to the sovereign. Cf. *De Cive*, VI.5–6.

[136] Hobbes, *De Cive*, I.2, note 2.

live on in the state of society as reminders of what individuals escaped from and of what lies outside the boundaries of the fragile order in which they coexist. The most vivid and potent manifestation of that external threat, however, comes in the form of the countless enemies that still lie outside the actual boundaries of even the most stable of states, and it is because of his unique capacity to determine threats and therefore pronounce enemies that the sovereign is able to keep his subjects truly "in awe."

THE STATE OF NATURE, ONCE MORE

The moment of the emergence of the commonwealth marks the last time that individuals exercise their natural right to designate their enemies. At that very moment of institution, Hobbes argues, those who refuse consent are left outside, and the newly formed commonwealth "retains its original Right against the dissenter, i.e. the *right of war*, as against an enemy."[137] As this foundation implies, the sovereign's outward gaze is inseparable from the inward. He is the bearer of the sword of war just as he is the bearer of the sword of justice, "*essentially and from the very nature of the commonwealth.*"[138] The extent of this inseparability becomes apparent when Hobbes lists the causes that tend towards the dissolution of commonwealths, among which are the belief that there can be private judgments about good and evil, that sovereign power can be divided, and that the citizens' property rights are absolute and therefore inviolable, even in cases of emergency.[139] In analyzing each of these and other cases, Hobbes demonstrates that the responses to internal and external threats to order are inextricably intertwined. This is because for those who have agreed to give up their right to all things, the formation of the commonwealth constitutes a space in which they hope "to be able to live as pleasantly as the human condition allows," but beyond those boundaries the world remains in the state of nature.[140]

---

[137] Hobbes, *De Cive*, VI.2.
[138] Hobbes, *De Cive*, VI.7, emphasis added. Cf. *The Elements of Law*, II.1.8; *Leviathan* XVIII § 4.
[139] On private judgments, see Hobbes, *De Cive*, Pref. § 7, XII.1; *Leviathan*, XXIX § 8. On whether sovereign power can be divided, see *The Elements of Law*, II.8.7; *De Cive*, XII.5; *Leviathan*, XXIX § 12. On property rights, see *The Elements of Law*, II.8.8, II.9.8; *De Cive*, XII.7; *Leviathan*, XXIX § 10.
[140] Hobbes, *De Cive*, XIII.4. Cf. *A Dialogue between a Philosopher and a Student of the Common Laws of England*, 66: "To think that our Condition being Humane should be subject to no Incommodity, were Injuriously to Quarrel with God Almighty for our own Faults."

In Chapter XIII of *Leviathan*, Hobbes offers the most famous example of the existence of an actual state of nature, the condition of sovereigns over whom there is no superior power, and who assume vis-à-vis one another the posture of gladiators, with weapons pointed and garrisons armed and at the ready.[141] This image, which calls to mind the general state of foul weather that is the state of war, is usually taken as a direct analogy between individuals and states, and yet it is what distinguishes states from individuals that is most illuminating. Hobbes argues that the difference between individuals in the state of nature and sovereigns is that because the latter, by means of "forts, garrisons, guns upon the frontiers of their kingdoms, and continual spies upon their neighbours, which is a posture of war [. . .] uphold *thereby* the industry of their subjects, there does not follow from it that misery which accompanies the liberty of particular men."[142] Hobbes's emphasis on the power that keeps all in awe makes it tempting to see the sovereign as a new enemy of sorts, a new threat for the individuals who have united into the commonwealth. As bearer of the sword of justice, the sovereign will indeed inspire such feelings, and to a certain extent they are necessary for the maintenance of internal order. As this passage shows, however, the temptation to see the relationship between individuals and the sovereign as one of enmity should be treated with caution. For Hobbes, "the motive, and end" for which individuals renounce and transfer their right is "nothing else but the security of a man's person, in his life and in the means of so preserving life as not to be weary of it."[143] The sovereign who provides such security, then, cannot be the enemy of the individuals who have submitted to it for two reasons. First, they have renounced their right to judge who their enemy is.[144] Second, although security is the primary goal of the association, it is not an end in itself. It is also the means towards commodious living, that is, everything desirable but absent from the state of nature because of the prevailing uncertainty.[145] Enmities between individual members of the commonwealth must be quashed if their

[141] Hobbes, *Leviathan*, XIII § 12. Cf. *Leviathan*, XXX § 30, XXXI § 1; *De Cive*, Ep. Ded., §§ 1–2, Pref., § 11, II.18, V.2, XIII.7–8, 13.
[142] Hobbes, *Leviathan*, XIII § 12, emphasis added.
[143] Hobbes, *Leviathan*, XIV § 8.
[144] See, e.g., Hobbes, *The Elements of Law*, II.1.16. In the case of a commonwealth by acquisition, this determination was made *de facto* at the initiation of the conflict. Upon submission to the conqueror, the defeated individuals renounce their right to judge just as they would in the case of a commonwealth by institution. See, e.g., *The Elements of Law*, II.3.2. Cf. Skinner, "Thomas Hobbes's Antiliberal Theory of Liberty," 163.
[145] See Forsyth, "Thomas Hobbes and the External Relations of States," 206–07.

association is to have any meaning, but Hobbes insists that this order of business is second to defense from external threats.

Indeed, in *Leviathan* Hobbes explains that domestic order itself is preserved first for the purpose of defense against external enemies. When the sovereign expresses his will in the form of legislation, he does so with this principle in mind, for "law was brought into the world for nothing else but to limit the natural liberty of particular men, in such manner as they might not hurt, but assist one another, and join together against a common enemy."[146] In fulfilling this duty, the sovereign finds himself in a condition of hostility, since among nations there will be either open warfare or "an intermission during which each watches the motion and aspect of its enemy and *gauges its security not on the basis of agreements but by the strength and designs of the adversary.*"[147] The state of nature, then, is a very different place for individuals and nations. Whereas the former are helpless in it, the latter are not.

FREEDOM THROUGH FEAR

For Hobbes, liberty means the absence of external impediments.[148] In the state of nature, where in the beginning there is complete liberty, such external impediments emerge in the form of physical opposition and violence from others who are similarly free to do as they think fit. Thus individuals find themselves in the paradoxical position in which the excess of liberty gives rise to a series of constraints that limit severely the extent to which each can enjoy his liberty.[149] We have also seen that for Hobbes, liberty and necessity are compatible, so even though one may be free to choose between two alternatives, these alternatives need not therefore be equally attractive.[150] Strictly speaking, individuals in the state of nature are faced with two alternatives, to remain as they are or to join others and form a defensive association.[151]

---

[146] Hobbes, *Leviathan*, XXVI § 8. Cf. *A Dialogue between a Philosopher and a Student of the Common Laws of England*: "the scope of all humane law is Peace, and Justice in every Nation amongst themselves, and defence against Forraign Enemies" (57).

[147] Hobbes, *On the Citizen*, XIII.7, emphasis added. In either of these two conditions, a nation can find itself in a temporary alliance with one or more other nations, but the absence of an overarching authority means that such alliances are good only as long as there "ariseth no just cause of distrust" (*Leviathan*, XXII § 29).

[148] See, e.g., Hobbes, *Leviathan*, XIV § 2, XXI § 1.

[149] See Hobbes, *Leviathan*, XIV § 4.

[150] See, e.g., Hobbes, *Leviathan*, XXI § 3; *Of Liberty and Necessity*, §§ 3, 6, 11.

[151] In *Leviathan*, Hobbes argues, "[f]ear of oppression disposeth a man to anticipate or to seek aid by society; for there is no other way by which a man can secure his life and liberty" (XI § 9).

Hobbes argues that the assurance that comes from knowing that "the danger is extended to more, or greater than us" will lead these individuals to opt for the latter, even though the formation of a permanent association will require the surrender of some of their natural liberty.[152] The trade-off, however, is appealing because natural liberty cannot supply the conditions for commodious living.[153] Under the sovereign, the specter of punishment keeps the memory of the state of nature alive, but otherwise the laws serve as hedges, meant "not to bind the people from all voluntary actions, but to direct and keep them in such a motion as not to hurt themselves," and further, to allow them to cooperate in providing the commonwealth with the means of its defense.[154]

The sovereign's exclusive right to judge and use his power and that of his subjects makes for a significant part of the apparatus that maintains order inside the commonwealth and keeps enemies at bay. Hobbes also devotes some attention to the sovereign's right to determine the doctrines that are admissible in the commonwealth and the ways in which he can shape the conscience of his subjects through education.[155] As Meinecke points out, despite the emphasis that Hobbes places on the power of the state, he cannot be classified with the tradition of reason of state proper; his theory is better described as belonging to the "utilitarian middle ground of *raison d' état*."[156] The reason for this classification is that for all his emphasis on state power, Hobbes never loses sight of the reason for the Leviathan, which is *salus populi* broadly conceived, driven by "[t]he passions that incline men to peace, [. . .] fear of death, desire of such things as are necessary to commodious living, and a hope by their industry to obtain them."[157] The state must be preserved, then, not for its own sake and glory, but rather as a remedy to the problems stemming from the very basic psychological motives of the individuals that make it up.

By constructing his edifice in the way that he did, Hobbes fulfilled Machiavelli's prophecy at the end of the preface to Book I of the *Discourses*.[158]

---

[152] [Hobbes], *A Briefe of the Art of Rhetorique*, 7: 85.

[153] In the Preface to *De Cive*, Hobbes pleads with the readers as follows: "[m]y hope is that when you have got to know the doctrine I present and looked well into it, you will patiently put up with some inconveniences in your private affairs (since human affairs can never be without some inconvenience) rather than disturb the state of the country" (*On the Citizen*, Pref. § 20). Cf. Hobbes, *Leviathan*, XIV § 29: "For man by nature chooseth the lesser evil."

[154] Hobbes, *Leviathan*, XXX § 21.

[155] See, e.g., Hobbes, *Leviathan*, XXX §§ 1–14.

[156] Meinecke, *Machiavellism*, 212.

[157] Hobbes, *Leviathan*, XIII § 14.

[158] Machiavelli, *Discourses*, I. Pref. § 2.

Machiavelli had broken with tradition in many ways, but one of the most important of these was his insistence on dealing with the effectual truth of things.[159] His consequent study of human beings as they are brought him infamy, but it also paved the way for a more systematic study of human nature. In carrying out this study, Hobbes too broke new ground by observing that the always problematic gap between reason and the passions can be bridged by fear, a universal human trait that partakes of both, and is thus capable of serving as an Archimedean Point.[160] His return to human nature also enabled Hobbes to seek the motives that cause individuals to unite in pursuit of their goals, and thus to construct an image of what life might look like prior to the formation of the commonwealth, in the state of nature.[161] Machiavelli had argued that sometimes the threat of an external force was the best remedy for a state's problems, but had also pointed out that it was dangerous.[162] By implanting the image of life in the state of nature deep in the minds of men, Hobbes managed to retain everything that was useful in Machiavelli's remedy while eliminating much of the attendant danger. By using it, further, to describe the world that lies beyond the boundaries guarded by sovereigns, Hobbes expanded Bodin's inward-looking concept of sovereignty, gave his specter some flesh, and provided the tools that would shape the debate about sovereignty, the state, and international relations for centuries to come.

[159] Machiavelli, *The Prince*, XV: 61.
[160] See Strauss, *The Political Philosophy of Hobbes*, 149–50; Wolin, *Hobbes and the Epic Tradition of Political Theory*, 29–30; Mansfield, "Hobbes and the Science of Indirect Government," 101. In celebratory poems published during his lifetime, Cowley hails Hobbes as the "great *Columbus* of the golden Lands of new Philosophies" (Blackburne, *Thomæ Hobbes Angli Malmesburiensis philosophi vita*, A6), and Bathurst likens him to Archimedes (*ibid.*, A7v).
[161] See Hobbes, *On the Citizen*, Pref. § 9.
[162] Machiavelli, *Discourses*, III.1 § 6.

6

HOBBISM

It is not so much what is horrible and false as what is just and true in his politics that has made it odious.

            — Jean-Jacques Rousseau on Thomas Hobbes[1]

In a 1939 lecture delivered before the British Academy, George P. Gooch declared, "Hobbes is the earliest, the most original, and the least English of our three great political thinkers."[2] This statement might appear curious in light of the fact that Hobbes's political thought is often seen as inseparable from the events that characterized English political life in the seventeenth century, but it was quite accurate from Gooch's vantage point. Although Hobbes's writings on politics and religion had engendered considerable controversy in England in the latter half of the seventeenth century, by the middle of the eighteenth century there was very little English interest in Hobbes's political thought.[3] By the late nineteenth century, English scholarship on Hobbes's political writings was a rarity; Hobbes still appealed to his countrymen as a philosopher, literary stylist, translator, and historian, but not as a political thinker.[4] In Europe, however, Hobbes's reception was

---

[1] *Of the Social Contract*, IV.viii § 13.

[2] Gooch, *Hobbes*, 3.

[3] On the immediate reaction, see Bowle, *Hobbes and His Critics*; Mintz, *The Hunting of Leviathan*, as well as Rogers, ed., *Leviathan: Contemporary Responses to the Political Theory of Thomas Hobbes*, esp. vii, note 1. On the history of reactions to Hobbes's political thought, see Mintz, *The Hunting of Leviathan*, 147–49. Mintz also discusses Hobbes's subsequent, but indirect, influence on his countrymen (*ibid.*, 149–56). Cf. Rahe, *Republics Ancient & Modern*, II: 172.

[4] There are few exceptions to this trend, among which are Maitland's *A Historical Sketch of Liberty and Equality as Ideals of English Political Philosophy* (1875), Robertson's *Hobbes* (1886), and Graham's *English Political Philosophy from Hobbes to Maine* (1899). The dawn of the twentieth century saw two more studies, Stephen's *Hobbes* (1904) and Taylor's *Thomas Hobbes* (1908). The limited degree to which Hobbes's political thought attracted English

quite different. As Hobbes himself notes in his autobiographical poem, his political theory received immediate attention there.[5] French, Italian, and German interest, in particular, continued for the next two centuries, and by the end of the nineteenth century, the majority of scholarship on Hobbes's political thought was of German origin.[6] Hobbes's political views had been branded totalitarian repeatedly, but this line of criticism assumed a special significance in the 1930s.[7] By the time Gooch came to deliver his lecture, Italy and Germany, countries in which Hobbes's political thought was alive and well, had produced alarming fascist regimes.[8]

In the intervening period, the reception of Hobbes's political thought displayed some of the characteristics of Machiavellism. When writing on themes that Hobbes had addressed, subsequent thinkers found it hard to avoid confronting him. Many of those confrontations were violent, some imputed to Hobbes views that he had never held, and still others used the semblance of disagreement to conceal agreement and, on occasion, advance views that were more extreme than Hobbes's own. As in Machiavelli's aftermath,

interest can be seen in Robertson's response to a review of his *Hobbes* ("*The Quarterly Review* on Hobbes"). The most significant influence that Hobbes's political thought had during this period was on Bentham and the Utilitarians (see, e.g., Rosenblum, *Bentham's Theory of the Modern State*, 10–11, 39–47).

[5] Hobbes, *Thomae Hobbesii Malmesburiensis vita*, 6–7; cf. Rahe, *Republics Ancient & Modern*, II: 172–79; Malcolm, *Aspects of Hobbes*, 459–62.

[6] A Hobbist vocabulary and conceptual framework pervades political theories as diverse as those of Sieyès (*What Is the Third Estate?*), Fichte (*Addresses to the German Nation*), Mazzini ("The Duties of Man"). Where the scholarly study of Hobbes's works is concerned, the examples best known to English-speaking audiences are Tönnies' studies, including his *Hobbes: Leben und Lehre*, and his editions of *Behemoth* (1889) and *The Elements of Law Natural and Politic* (1889), as well as Strauss's *The Political Philosophy of Hobbes: Its Basis and Its Genesis*, which was written in German but was first published in English translation, in 1936, by Oxford University Press. During the early 1930s, and while still in Germany, Strauss produced several articles on Hobbes's political theory, and was engaged in an exchange over Hobbes with Carl Schmitt (see Chapter 7 in this volume). The magnitude of Tönnies' contributions to Hobbes scholarship is reflected in Robertson, "*The Quarterly Review* on Hobbes" and "Leibniz and Hobbes" as well as in his review of Tönnies' editions of *The Elements of Law* and *Behemoth*.

[7] The most notable interpretation of this kind is concealed in Locke's *Two Treatises of Government*. Other examples include Cumberland's *A Treatise of the Laws of Nature*, Lawson's *An Examination of the Political Part of Mr. Hobbs His Leviathan*, and Feuerbach's *Anti-Hobbes*. Mintz lists some of the literature published against Hobbes between 1650 and 1700 (*The Hunting of Leviathan*, 157–60). For a series of accusations from the 1930s, see Tarlton, "Rehabilitating Hobbes," 419–22.

[8] Tarlton suggests that for these reasons Taylor's renewed interest in Hobbes's political thought in the mid- to late 1930s may well have been an attempt to rescue Hobbes from being associated with fascism ("Rehabilitating Hobbes," esp. 416–29).

however, regardless of how subsequent thinkers might situate themselves vis-à-vis Hobbes, there were aspects of his thought that they could not ignore. The first was the crucial role of the emotions, which were usually seen in a negative light. Although the idea of pitting one passion against another was not new, Hobbes's treatment of fear made it possible to consider the social roles of negative emotions in a new light.[9] Perhaps because of the very controversy that it occasioned, Hobbes's demonstration was followed by an increasing stream of political writings that located the symptoms of social relations in the psychology of the individual, and placed negative emotions at their center.[10] Hobbes's second, and related, contribution was the concept of the state of nature. As the psychological device designed to replace Machiavelli's return to the beginnings of cities, the state of nature draws much of its potency from the contrast between the international and domestic realms. In *Leviathan*, Hobbes devotes a mere two sentences to this contrast, but its effect has been a deep and lasting one.[11] In the quest to address the challenges posed by state sovereignty, international relations, war, and the possibility for a lasting peace, Hobbes's contrast became the force to be reckoned with. This was because Hobbes extended Bodin's inward-looking concept of sovereignty to include a view of what takes place outside the boundaries of the state.[12] To those who agreed with him, the dividing line between the state and the state of nature was the ultimate boundary between order and chaos. To those who did not, it was the necessary starting point for any attempt to move beyond the state, and replace chaos with order.

The eighteenth and nineteenth centuries saw powerful arguments from both sides. It was two exchanges, however – one direct, the other indirect – that stood out and shaped the debate for years to come. The first was that between Rousseau, who situated his views explicitly, albeit deceptively, against Hobbes's, and the Abbé de Saint-Pierre, who sought to transcend the boundary that Hobbes found impenetrable. Rousseau's comments on what most saw as a utopian scheme for international peace are valuable because they contain his views on international relations, views that he promises at the end of the *Social Contract*, but never delivers. The second debate was between Kant, who also named Hobbes as the man to beat, and Hegel,

---

[9] See Hirschman, *The Passions and the Interests*, 31.
[10] Among the more familiar were La Rochefoucauld's *Maxims* (1665) and Mandeville's *The Fable of the Bees* (1714).
[11] Hobbes, *Leviathan*, XIII § 12.
[12] See Franklin, *Jean Bodin and the Rise of Absolutist Theory*, Chapters 4, 5.

for whom Hobbes's method and observations were the right starting points. These thinkers are known for many reasons that are unrelated to Hobbes, and yet their positions on international relations, the touchstone of the state, reveal a deep indebtedness to Hobbes's conceptual apparatus. More importantly, although their aims and proposals are very different, they concede, however reluctantly, that Hobbes's fundamental observation regarding political groups is correct: negative association is essential to their formation and preservation. Coming as it did at a time of deep and increasing interest in state sovereignty and the international realm, the development of negative association through these debates contributed to the emergence of attempts at systematic thought about conflict in all its aspects and manifestations. Hegel's choice to center his theory on opposition and negation exposed further the effects of negative association on the individual, and paved the way for a variety of new approaches to conflict at all levels that saw the birth of modern economics, sociology, and psychology, and, eventually, of the academic study of international relations.

HOBBISM CONCEALED

Rousseau's account of the natural condition of mankind is quite unlike Hobbes's. It is more detailed and complicated, and some of its characteristics seem diametrically opposed to Hobbes's equivalents. Their differences are no doubt accentuated by Rousseau's several direct attacks against Hobbes. After all, Rousseau lists several errors related to previous attempts to describe human nature, but names few of the perpetrators and none as frequently as he does Hobbes, whom he accuses of using the right method to reach the wrong conclusions and of applying social traits to natural man.[13] Rousseau's bark, however, is worse than his bite. For one thing, he finds it necessary to construct his own account around the Hobbesian concept of the state of nature, if only to use it properly.[14] The result of this procedure is a curious one because Rousseau's account of the state of nature differs markedly from

---

[13] See, e.g., Rousseau, *Discourse on the Origin and the Foundations of Inequality among Men*, hereafter cited as "Second Discourse," Exordium § 5, I § 6, I § 25, I § 35, and Rousseau's note XII § 7. One particularly interesting example has to do with the degree to which natural man is fearful. Rousseau ascribes to Hobbes the view "that man is naturally intrepid, and seeks only to attack, and to fight" (Second Discourse, I § 6), but Hobbes makes no such claim in *De Cive*. If anything, in Rousseau's view man is potentially more aggressive than in Hobbes's. He argues that if initially apprehensive, natural man soon discovers that he has little to fear (Second Discourse, I § 6). Cf. "The State of War" § 15.

[14] Rousseau, Second Discourse, Exordium § 5 and Rousseau's note XII § 7.

Hobbes's in certain key respects but their conclusions are very nearly the same. For example, Rousseau's account has no place for conflict and, hence, no room for defense against common enemies. The main reason for this, Rousseau claims, is that individuals in the state of nature will hardly come into contact with one another and will have little, if any, reason to fight.[15] Thus, even though Rousseau argues repeatedly that self-preservation is natural man's primary concern, he is clearly at pains to avoid equating it with defense. As a result, most of his examples concern sustenance and the collection of food.[16] This tendency is nowhere more apparent than in his attempt to strike a rhetorical blow against Hobbes's central claim about the natural condition of mankind, that it is a state fraught with the fear of violent death. Rousseau contends, "[t]he only goods [natural man] knows in the Universe are food, a female, and rest; the only evils he fears are pain, and hunger; I say pain, *and not death*; for an animal will never know what it is to die, and the knowledge of death, and of its terrors, is one of man's first acquisitions on moving away from the animal condition."[17] Why, however, even these primitive and relatively isolated beings cannot come to know death by witnessing others succumb to it is nowhere made clear. After all, the natural ability to feel pity that Rousseau ascribes to human beings requires contact with others, and some such contact there must have been, for "[a]lthough others of his kind were not for [natural man] what they are for us, and he had scarcely more dealings with them than with the other animals, they were not neglected in his observations."[18] Indeed, if he is capable of perceiving "that they all behaved as he would have done in similar circumstances," soon thereafter he should also be able to conclude that the reverse would also be true.[19]

Certain other aspects of Rousseau's view of the state of nature display clearer signs of agreement with Hobbes. Although at the outset he pronounces natural man virtually intrepid, Rousseau depicts the state of nature as a rather uncertain place. Thus, industry is impossible and foresight makes

---

[15] Rousseau, Second Discourse, I § 35, II § 7.

[16] The main exception is Second Discourse, I § 13: "Alone, idle, and always near danger, Savage man must like to sleep and be a light sleeper like the animals which, since they think little, sleep, so to speak, all the time they do not think: Self-preservation being almost his only care, his most developed faculties must be those that primarily serve in attack and defense, either in order to overcome his prey or to guard against becoming another animal's prey." Cf. *ibid.*, I § 15, and Rousseau's note XV; *Of the Social Contract*, I.ii § 2.

[17] Rousseau, Second Discourse, I § 19, emphasis added.

[18] Rousseau, Second Discourse, II § 7; cf. I §§ 35–38.

[19] Rousseau, Second Discourse, II § 7.

no sense, which is why the only cooperative associations that are likely to emerge will be temporary, certain to be abandoned at the first opportunity for personal, short-term advantage.[20] As man gains a fuller understanding of those like himself and begins to acquire new skills, solitary individuals and temporary associations give way to families, which in turn become small societies.[21] Even at this stage, however, Rousseau is unwilling to concede that conflict might emerge. The transition to the next level of social organization thus comes about by means of negative association not with reference to common enemies, but rather in response to natural calamities. Earthquakes, floods, and the movement of the earth's plates force these small associations closer together and lead to the formation of particular nations.[22]

Rousseau insists on distinguishing between man's solitary state and this subsequent stage, and locates his disagreement with Hobbes precisely on the latter's inability to do the same. He argues that since solitary man knows only self-love and not vanity, and his self-preservation at the earliest stage "is least prejudicial to the self-preservation of others, it follows that this state was the most conducive to Peace and the best suited to mankind."[23] The sources of conflict that Hobbes identifies in the state of nature, argues Rousseau, are products of society and therefore not present at this first stage, when one man hardly sees another.[24] With increasing proximity and interaction, however, these sources of conflict finally rear their heads. Rousseau does not mention fear among them, but he speaks of the transformation of love into "impetuous frenzy" and the birth of jealousy, vanity, contempt, shame, and envy.[25] These emotions added insult to injury and thus "vengeances became terrible, and men bloodthirsty and cruel."[26] In this account, then, conflict plays no part in the formation of the first societies. Response to common natural threats contributes to the formation of larger societies, but

---

[20] Rousseau, Second Discourse, I § 22, II §§ 7–9; cf. Hobbes, *Leviathan*, XIII § 9. In *Of the Social Contract*, Rousseau argues, "[t]he stronger is never strong enough to be forever master" (I.iii § 1). The primary distinction between the two accounts is that Rousseau considers the likelihood of competition among individuals at this stage extremely low (Second Discourse, II § 8).

[21] Rousseau, Second Discourse, II §§ 11–12.

[22] Rousseau, Second Discourse, II §§ 14–15; cf. "The State of War," §§ 15–18.

[23] Rousseau, Second Discourse, I § 35; cf. Rousseau's note XV to the Second Discourse; "The State of War" § 12; "Geneva Manuscript" I.ii, p. 162.

[24] Rousseau, Second Discourse, I § 35.

[25] Rousseau, Second Discourse, II §§ 15–16.

[26] Rousseau, Second Discourse, II § 17.

not to the transition from solitude to family. Anxious to maintain that stage as the distinguishing characteristic between his account and that of Hobbes, Rousseau declares at the opening of the *Social Contract* that the family is "the first model of political societies."[27] The details that comprise the rest of the picture, however, tell a different story.

A further objection to Hobbes's depiction of the state of nature has to do with equating it to a state of war. Because "war is a permanent state that presupposes lasting relations, and such relations rarely obtain between man and man," the first stage of the state of nature cannot be called a state of war.[28] Nevertheless, Rousseau argues that man's "first law is to attend to his own preservation," and agrees that once the individual has reached the age of reason, "he is the sole judge of the means proper to preserve himself."[29] He also concedes a general equality among individuals.[30] Furthermore, and perhaps most importantly, he changes his mind about the extent of natural man's desires, and thereby opens the door to conflict. He argues, "[a]nd if I do not say, along with Hobbes, everything is mine, why wouldn't I at least recognize as mine in the state of nature all that is useful to me and that I can get hold of?"[31] Rousseau thus comes close to leaving fear out of his account of the state of nature, but not quite. In a mocking paragraph in the beginning of the *Social Contract*, where he derides theories of divine right, he concludes by acknowledging that "Adam was Sovereign of the world as Robinson was of his island, as long as he was its sole inhabitant; and what made this empire convenient was that the monarch, secure on his throne, had neither rebellions, nor wars, nor conspirators to fear."[32] It is ironic that Rousseau's criticism of the degree of solitude described here applies also to the first stage of his own state of nature.

When individuals can no longer resist the "obstacles that interfere with their preservation in the state of nature," and because they "cannot engender new forces, but only unite and direct those that exist, they are left with no other means of self-preservation than to form, by aggregation, a sum of forces that might prevail over those obstacles' resistance, to set them in motion by a

---

[27] Rousseau, *Of the Social Contract*, I.ii § 3.
[28] Rousseau, "The State of War" § 18. This objection, however, overlooks the fact that Hobbes bases his decision to refer to it as a state of war on the uncertainty that follows from the fact that it is continuous and against all.
[29] Rousseau, *Of the Social Contract*, I.ii § 2.
[30] Rousseau, *Of the Social Contract*, I.iii § 1: "The stronger is never strong enough to be forever master." Cf. Hobbes, *Leviathan*, XIII § 1.
[31] Rousseau, "Geneva Manuscript," II.iv, p. 191.
[32] Rousseau, *Of the Social Contract*, I.ii § 9.

single impetus, and make them act in concert."[33] Moreover, the formation of this union sets in motion that of every other.[34]

Whatever form this pact may assume eventually, at its inception it is the result of a unanimous decision.[35] Everyone who joins it agrees with its formation. Everyone who disagrees stays out. Rousseau's description of the implications of this transition from individual to collective identity is expressed in strikingly Hobbesian terms: "[i]t is agreed that each man alienates by the social pact only that portion of his power, his goods, his freedom, which it is important for the community to be able to use, but it should also be agreed to that the Sovereign is alone judge of that importance."[36]

PERPETUAL PEACE

Rousseau acknowledges that *Of the Social Contract* is incomplete. Having examined the manner in which it ought to be founded on political right, the work ends with the author's admission that "it would remain to buttress the State by its external relations."[37] Rousseau's otherwise strange conclusion nevertheless accords with his general tendency to avoid discussing conflict in both that work and the Second Discourse. The absence of such a discussion in *Of the Social Contract* is all the more strange when one considers that a first version of the work, known as the "Geneva Manuscript," contains several illuminating statements on international relations. For example, in one of the most famous articles of the *Encyclopédie*, "Natural Right," Diderot argued that mankind comprises one community with a single general will.[38] In the Geneva Manuscript, Rousseau attacked that assertion, arguing, "[i]f the general society did exist somewhere other than in the systems of philosophers, it would be [. . .] a moral being with qualities separate and distinct from

---

[33] Rousseau, *Of the Social Contract*, I.vi §§ 1–2.

[34] Rousseau explains,

> With the first society formed, the formation of all others necessarily follows. One must either belong to it or unite to resist it. One must either imitate it or let oneself be swallowed by it ("The State of War" § 22).

[35] Rousseau, *Of the Social Contract*, I.v § 3. On the difference between fundamental acts of this kind and subordinate rules, cf. *ibid.*, II.xii; III.xvii. In *ibid.*, III.ix, Rousseau contends that the aim of the political association is "the preservation and prosperity of its members" (§ 4).

[36] Rousseau, *Of the Social Contract*, II.iv § 3. Cf. Chapter 5 in this volume, esp. "The State of Nature, Once More."

[37] Rousseau, *Of the Social Contract*, IV.ix.

[38] See Diderot, "Droit naturel," 296–301, esp. §§ 6–9.

those of the particular beings constituting it."[39] For Rousseau, Diderot and those like him, who proclaim the existence of a global community, commit a serious error in projecting the social order to which they belong onto a larger scale. What is more, Rousseau questions their motives for doing so. He calls them "supposed cosmopolites," who love their fatherland only insofar as it is a part of the human race; they "boast of loving everyone in order to have the right to love no one."[40]

Diderot and his fellow *encyclopédistes* never moved from the abstract realm of universal reason to more tangible suggestions for the institutionalization of a supranational union, but one of their acquaintances did. Along lines very similar to those of Botero, the Abbé de Saint-Pierre proposed an international federation of European states as the only means for the achievement of perpetual peace in Europe.[41] In his *Project*, Saint-Pierre proposed articles for the formation of a federation of states centered on the need to eliminate war. Saint-Pierre's project drew the sympathy of Kant and the ridicule of Frederick the Great and Voltaire, as well as the sometimes cautious and at other times scathing criticism of Rousseau.[42] Among reactions, Rousseau's *Abstract* and *Judgment* deserve special attention for two reasons. First, they are widely known; many readers know of Saint-Pierre and his proposal only through Rousseau. Second, Rousseau uses the *Abstract* and *Judgment* as an opportunity to expound his own views on supranational unions.

Rousseau begins the *Abstract* with generous praise for the man who conceived of and devoted so much energy to a project as worthy of serious consideration as perpetual peace through a federation of nations. He admits,

---

[39] Rousseau, "Geneva Manuscript," I.ii, p. 159.

[40] Rousseau, "Geneva Manuscript," I.ii, pp. 161–62. Cf. *Émile*: "Distrust those cosmopolitans who go to great length in their books to discover duties they do not deign to fulfill around them. A philosopher loves the Tartars so as to be spared having to love his neighbors" (39); Herder, *Another Philosophy of History*, 29–30; Hume, *A Treatise of Human Nature*, 3.2.1.

[41] Saint-Pierre, *Projet pour rendre la paix perpétuelle en Europe*; cf. *A Project for Settling an Everlasting Peace in Europe*, a contemporary translation of the first volume of the original. For a history of the project and its relationship to previous works along the same lines, such as Sully's, see Mastnak, "Abbé de Saint-Pierre: European Union and the Turk," 573–75. Saint-Pierre's proposal is often considered a source of inspiration for supranational institutional unions such as the European Community.

[42] On Voltaire's reaction, see Riley, "The Abbé de St. Pierre and Voltaire on Perpetual Peace in Europe," esp. 186, 191–93. Cf. Leibniz, *The Political Writings of Leibniz*, 176–84; Kant, "On the Proverb: That May Be True in Theory, but Is of No Practical Use", 89; Keohane, *Philosophy and the State in France*, 324; Archibugi, "Models of International Organization in Perpetual Peace Projects," 300–01.

"[i]n these opening words, I could not refrain from giving way to the feelings which filled my heart," yet he recovers immediately, urging, "[n]ow let us do our best to reason coolly."[43] Rousseau surveys the situation in Europe and concludes that (i) European nations are united by a loose and imperfect bond (cultural, religious, and historical), (ii) "the imperfections of this association make the state of those who belong to it worse than it would be if they formed no community at all," and (iii) that there is clearly room for improvement and that this improvement can be built on some of the existing foundations.[44] In considering the means for the realization of this project, Rousseau poses two questions: (i) whether such a federation of nations would have the desired effect of lasting peace, and (ii) whether it is in the interest of sovereigns to make the move to join such a federation.[45] Speaking from Saint-Pierre's point of view, Rousseau invokes reason and proclaims that the advantages of the *Project* are so beyond doubt, that any prince who will but consult his true interest will follow it.[46] Rousseau's numerous appeals to common sense throughout the *Abstract* reveal his admiration for Saint-Pierre's intentions, but his final sarcastic remark signals what is to come in his *Judgment*: "[i]f, in spite of all this, the project remains unrealized, that is not because it is utopian; it is because men are crazy, and because to be sane in a world of madmen is in itself a kind of madness."[47]

In the *Judgment*, Rousseau's tone is much more sober. He commends the Abbé for his "obstinacy," despite the "manifest impossibility of success" of his enterprise.[48] No doubt, many would be convinced of its merits, Rousseau continues, if only it were realizable for a day. However, in reality the apparent interests of princes and the intervention of ministers with personal agendas render peace undesirable. These difficulties and the means of overcoming them, Rousseau contends, Saint-Pierre "judged like a child."[49] Rousseau cites the failed efforts of Henry IV to form a Christian commonwealth as evidence of the impossibility of a union of European states, and concludes further that even if such a federation were possible, it would most likely be unwelcome, since "[i]t would perhaps do more harm in a moment than it would guard against for ages."[50]

---

[43] Rousseau, "Abstract and Judgment of Saint-Pierre's Project," 54.
[44] Rousseau, "Abstract and Judgment of Saint-Pierre's Project," 67.
[45] Rousseau, "Abstract and Judgment of Saint-Pierre's Project," 71.
[46] Rousseau, "Abstract and Judgment of Saint-Pierre's Project," 87–88.
[47] Rousseau, "Abstract and Judgment of Saint-Pierre's Project," 88.
[48] Rousseau, "Abstract and Judgment of Saint-Pierre's Project," 88.
[49] Rousseau, "Abstract and Judgment of Saint-Pierre's Project," 90–4.
[50] Rousseau, "Abstract and Judgment of Saint-Pierre's Project," 100.

Rousseau and many others found Saint-Pierre's project outrageous, and yet the federation that it proposes is a far cry from a world state.[51] Ambitious though he was, even Saint-Pierre recognized that there was an enormous difference between a union of European sovereign states and one that would encompass the whole world. The reasons for his choice to limit his proposal to Europe are quite telling; they reveal someone who, even in his loftiness, remains in touch with some of the realities of the international system:

In my second Draught I took in all the Kingdoms of the World; but my Friends observ'd to me, that even though in following Ages most of the Sovereigns of *Asia* and *Africa* might desire to be receiv'd into the Union, yet this Prospect would seem so remote and so full of Difficulties, that it would cast an Air of Impossibility upon the whole Project, which would disgust all the Readers, and make some believe, that tho' it were even restrain'd only to the Christian part of *Europe*, the Execution of it would be still impossible; therefore I subscribed to their Opinion, and that the more willingly, considering that the Union of *Europe* would suffice to preserve *Europe* always in Peace; and that it would be powerful enough to maintain its Frontiers and Commerce, in spight of those who should endeavour to disturb it.[52]

Throughout the *Project*, Saint-Pierre makes it clear that he is mainly concerned not just with a European union, but with a union of Christian Europe.[53] Outsiders mainly serve two functions. At worst, they provide the external threat that will motivate European sovereigns to set aside their differences and work for peace in Europe. At best, they are trading partners from whom Europe can profit.[54] The first of these functions is crucial to

---

[51] Although animated by different motivations, Voltaire's rejection of Saint-Pierre's proposal was as vehement as Rousseau's. According to Riley, "Voltaire thought the project of peace through a European super-government 'absurd,' and counted on growing enlightenment, rather than on international institutions, to end war" ("The Abbé de St. Pierre and Voltaire on Perpetual Peace in Europe," 191–92).

[52] Saint-Pierre, *A Project for Settling an Everlasting Peace in Europe*, viii–ix. Instead of a world state, Saint-Pierre sees regional unions as the means towards peace. He argues that once it has taken shape, the European union should work towards the formation of an equivalent pacific union in Asia, so "that it may have no cause to fear any *Asiatic* Sovereign, either as to its Tranquility, or its Commerce in *Asia*" (*ibid.*, 160).

[53] See, e.g., Saint-Pierre, *A Project for Settling an Everlasting Peace in Europe*, ix, 46–56, 105, 106, 157.

[54] Mastnak argues that in framing his project thus, Saint-Pierre is conforming to the irenic tradition that sees "the Muslim world as *the* enemy of Christendom and Christianity, of Europe and civilization" ("Abbé de Saint-Pierre: European Union and the Turk," 575).

the success of Saint-Pierre's proposal, because "The Nations of Europe are Enemies, they hate each other; and yet in making a Treaty of a *permanent* Society, they will all contribute to the Preservation and Felicity of each other."[55]

Saint-Pierre studies the way in which Germanic principalities came together, and offers the lessons drawn thence as reasons for the union of European states. It was the fear of their powerful neighbors that brought the German princes together, and by the same token a European union could achieve even greater security from its own surroundings: "Fear of Invasion, therefore, had no less share in the Formation of the *Germanic Union*, than it may have in the Formation of the *European Union*."[56] Just how important this *metus hostilis* is in convincing sovereigns to follow his suggestion is made clear by his assertion that "to ingage [a sovereign] to enter into the System of Peace, there is no need of any other Motive, besides [. . .] Exemption from Fear."[57] Utopian though it might have seemed, therefore, Saint-Pierre's *Project* is actually sobering in its implications for the international order. Saint-Pierre envisions a union "between sovereigns" and recognizes that negative association is the primary means by which those sovereigns will come to cede even a fraction of their sovereignty to a superior body.[58] Once formed in response to external threats, such a union will depend as much, for its common identity, on what unites its members (e.g., Christianity) as on what divides it from the outside world.[59]

---

[55] Saint-Pierre, *A Project for Settling an Everlasting Peace in Europe*, 173. Saint-Pierre claims that the formation of the European union that he proposes will be the fulfillment of the prophecy "*Salutem ex Inimicis nostris, & de manu omnium qui oderunt nos*" ("that we would be saved from our enemies and from the hand of all who hate us", Luke 2.10).

[56] Saint-Pierre, *A Project for Settling an Everlasting Peace in Europe*, 38.

[57] Saint-Pierre, *A Project for Settling an Everlasting Peace in Europe*, 59. Cf. *ibid.*, 123: "There can be no durable Union expected among Men, unless each Member is retained in it, not only by Considerations of Pleasure and Profit, which are sufficient for those that are wise and sensible; but also by some great Fear, which is necessary to retain those in it that are not so."

[58] Riley, "The Abbé de St. Pierre and Voltaire on Perpetual Peace in Europe," 189. Cf. Archibugi, "Models of International Organization in Perpetual Peace Projects," 296–98. According to Archibugi, the proposed project involves a partial surrender of external sovereignty in exchange for greater internal sovereignty, since sovereigns would be able to use the federation to protect themselves from domestic revolutions (personal communication with the author).

[59] The suggestion that such a union be based on a common belief in Christ, which Saint-Pierre and many others offer, was also anticipated by Hobbes, whose solution to his country's religious woes was that people of different denominations focus on "that main article of faith," their common belief that "Jesus is the Christ" (*Leviathan*, XXXIV § 13; cf. *ibid.*, XXXVI § 20; XLII § 13).

THE WAY WE LIVE NOW

Despite his admiration for Rousseau, Kant rejects his view of the state of nature and opts instead for Hobbes's. Thus, the natural state of men living close to one another is "one of war, which does not just consist in open hostilities, but also in the constant and enduring threat of them."[60] As in Hobbes's case, this image describes not just the hypothetical condition of human beings stripped of their social qualities, but also the condition outside the boundaries of the state.[61] For Kant, however, the term *nature* has a further meaning. It signifies the agent who has ordered things thus.[62] Through war, nature has ensured that people are driven to inhabit all regions of the world and that they enter into "more or less legal relationships" with one another.[63] The crucial role of war in these providential designs is manifest everywhere. In the remote regions of the Arctic Ocean, for example, the natives "are sufficiently occupied with their war against animals that they live in peace among themselves." "But," he continues, "it was probably nothing but war that *drove* them there."[64] As a natural means in the service of nature, "war itself requires no particular motivation, but appears to be ingrained in human nature."[65] Through this natural bellicosity, nature forces man to do what his reason dictates but what in his freedom he chooses not to. The first step requires the formation of states, wherein rational freedom is possible. Kant sees man as checked by two forces, internal discord and war. If the former fails to make man submit to public law, negative association will, because "every people finds itself neighbor to another people that threatens it, and

[60] Kant, "To Perpetual Peace," 111. Cf. *ibid.*, 110, 117, 131; "Speculative Beginning of Human History," 58; Hobbes, *On the Citizen* I.12; *Leviathan*, XIII § 8.
[61] Kant, "To Perpetual Peace," 110, 111, 116, 117, 131; *The Metaphysics of Morals* § 61, p. 487.
[62] Kant, "To Perpetual Peace," 120–21, and note . For the purposes of his argument on perpetual peace, Kant prefers the term *nature* as "less *pretentious* than a term connoting that there is a *providence* of which we can have cognitive knowledge, and on which we take flight as on Icarus's wings in order more closely to approach the secrets of some unfathomable intention" (121). Kant explains further, "[w]hen I say of nature that she *wills* that this or that happen, that does not mean that she sets it out as a duty that we do it [. . .]; rather, she does it herself, whether or not we will it [. . .]" (123). See also, "Idea for a Universal History." Kelly argues that the term *nature* refers to the external world as well as to the "full development or actualization of a thing according to its *telos*," and that "reason is the intellectual or formal creator of nature" (*Idealism, Politics and History*, 139–40; cf. 141–45).
[63] Kant, "To Perpetual Peace," 121.
[64] Kant, "To Perpetual Peace," 121. Cf. *ibid.*, 122–23.
[65] Kant, "To Perpetual Peace," 123. Cf. *ibid.*, 125; "On the Proverb: That May Be True in Theory, but Is of No Practical Use," 89.

it must form itself into a [*state*] so as to be able to prepare itself to meet this threat with *military might*."[66] The formation of states thus marks the beginning of the national system that we live in, and is the first step in the fulfillment of nature's hidden plan for mankind.

According to Kant, when viewed from up close, individual actions display nothing of the order that becomes apparent when one takes a step back and observes larger trends and patterns. The latter, however, confound the observer with the childish folly, vanity, malice, and destructiveness that they contain.[67] Faced with these unappealing alternatives, Kant wishes to find a point of view from which he can "try to discover whether there is some *natural objective* in this senseless course of human affairs from which it is possible to produce a history of creatures who proceed without a plan of their own but in conformity with some definite plan of nature's."[68] Kant thus proposes that natural capacities are to develop completely and in conformity with their end. The points of view described above lead to the conclusion that the development of these capacities will manifest itself in the species, rather than the individual, and that this will come about by means provided for by nature, namely the "**antagonism** *among them in society, as far as in the end this antagonism is the cause of law-governed order in society*."[69] This antagonism, Kant explains, is "men's *unsocial sociability*, i.e., their tendency to enter into society, combined, however, with a thoroughgoing resistance that constantly threatens to sunder this society."[70] Kant identifies a sociable and an unsociable tendency in human nature, and attributes man's progress from barbarism to culture to the conflict between them:

Man wills concord; but nature better knows what is good for the species: she wills discord. He wills to live comfortably and pleasantly; but nature wills that he should be plunged from laziness and inactive comfort into work and hardship, so that he will in turn seek by his own cleverness to pull himself up from them.[71]

From up close, then, these forces yield unpleasant results, but when they are seen in a broader context they are proof of "the design of a wise creator."[72]

---

[66] Kant, "To Perpetual Peace," 124. I have amended Humphrey's translation here to reflect Kant's use of the term *Staat* in the original (*Werke* VIII: 365).

[67] Kant, "Idea for a Universal History," 29–30.

[68] Kant, "Idea for a Universal History," 30.

[69] Kant, "Idea for a Universal History," 31.

[70] Kant, "Idea for a Universal History," 31–32.

[71] Kant, "Idea for a Universal History," 32.

[72] Kant, "Idea for a Universal History," 32. Cf. *ibid.*, 35–36.

For Kant, the full development of the capacities of mankind can only take place in a setting "in which one will find the highest possible degree of *freedom under external laws* combined with irresistible power."[73] Why would human beings choose to restrict themselves in this way? Kant's answer is Hobbesian: men's propensities "do not allow them to coexist for very long in wild freedom."[74] These propensities, then, are the ones that compel individuals to enter into civil society, and these same ones, Kant hopes, will be those that will drive nations into a federation of peoples. Reason would have led human beings to the realization that such a federation is necessary, but it is necessity itself that fulfills this purpose, "through wars, through excessive and never remitting preparation for war, through the resultant distress that every nation must, even during times of peace, feel within itself."[75] Kant sees such a federation as inevitable, and can fault others who have advanced this idea only for thinking it likely to materialize sooner rather than later.[76] Despite acknowledging that the state of nature in which individuals find themselves differs in some ways from that of states, Kant views both conditions as having the same effect, namely to force their inhabitants to wish to leave them.[77] Just as individuals were compelled to form states to escape the dangers of the state of nature, national states will have to move towards "a cosmopolitan state in which the security of nations is publicly acknowledged."[78] Kant points out, however, that organization in this next stage will not consist in a single state but in a federation of republics.[79] In this way, the constituent units will retain their

---

[73] Kant, "Idea for a Universal History," 33.

[74] Kant, "Idea for a Universal History," 33.

[75] Kant, "Idea for a Universal History," 34. Nature's means for effecting this end is "human quarrelsomeness, men's inevitable *antagonism*." Cf. "On the Proverb: That May Be True in Theory, but Is of No Practical Use," 87–89; "To Perpetual Peace," 121–23; *The Critique of Judgement* II, p. 96.

[76] Kant, "Idea for a Universal History," 34–35. Kant names Saint-Pierre and Rousseau here as advocates of this sort, but the attribution of this idea to the latter is only possible if one were to discount completely his scathing criticism of its place in Saint-Pierre's *Project*, as well as his conclusion that even if it were desirable, it would ultimately be impossible (Rousseau, "Abstract and Judgment of Saint-Pierre's Project," 88–100). Cf. Kant, "On the Proverb: That May Be True in Theory, but Is of No Practical Use," 89; Hinsley, *Power and the Pursuit of Peace*, 46–61; Riley, "Rousseau as a Theorist of National and International Federalism," 12–17.

[77] Kant, "To Perpetual Peace," 116, 137; "Idea for a Universal History," 35–36. Cf. Hinsley, *Power and the Pursuit of Peace*, 68–69; Riley, "Kant as a Theorist of Peace," 123–24.

[78] Kant, "Idea for a Universal History," 36.

[79] See Kant, "To Perpetual Peace," esp. 112–18, 124–25.

moral status and enter into an environment in which their freedom becomes meaningful.[80]

NEGATION

The proposed federation of republics marks Kant's hesitant departure from Hobbes. Kant recognizes throughout that Hobbes's description of the world is accurate, but he seeks to move beyond the state in order to solve the problems that plague it.[81] The federation of states will perform at the international level a role equivalent to the one that the state performs for individuals, but with some significant differences. For one thing, the federation will not be a state.[82] Thus, the moral status of its constitutive parts will be preserved. Equally important, however, is the fact that whereas the state performs its positive functions by waging war, the international federation will bring about peace by transcending it. Fervent though he may be in his belief that this progress will be made, Kant is nonetheless unwilling to prophecy *when* exactly this will come about.[83] Hobbes's influence endures, however, as Kant explains *how* and *why* it will. He argues that the advent of the federation is inevitable because of man's inclinations. The desire for self-preservation and for the advancement of self-interest will lead human beings to realize that therein lies the only hope for peace. The volatility of alliances and the destructiveness of war, on the one side, and the power of commerce, on the other, are nature's means of guaranteeing it perpetually.[84]

Kant refers to the proposed federation of states as the "*negative* surrogate" that replaces the "positive idea of a *world republic.*"[85] Its primary function will thus be negative: to prevent war and curb the tendency towards lawlessness.[86] Kant is so anxious to show that membership in this federation will be radically

---

[80] Kant's rationale regarding states here is the same that Hobbes offers regarding individuals, in *Leviathan* (XIII § 12).

[81] See Kersting, "Politics, Freedom, and Order," 363; Williams, *Kant's Critique of Hobbes*, 218–32.

[82] Kant, "To Perpetual Peace," 117–18.

[83] Kant, "To Perpetual Peace," 125, but cf. *The Metaphysics of Morals*: "So *perpetual peace*, the ultimate goal of the whole right of nations, is indeed an unachievable idea" (§ 61, p. 487); *ibid.*, pp. 487–92.

[84] Kant, "To Perpetual Peace," 125; cf. *ibid.*, 120. Riley identifies the difficulty involved in Kant's problematic transition from war to peace at this juncture of his argument ("Federalism in Kant's Political Philosophy," 60).

[85] Kant, "To Perpetual Peace," 117.

[86] Kant, "To Perpetual Peace," 117–18.

different from subjection to a state that he concedes that it will always be exposed to the danger that its members will break loose.[87] Kant's insistence that the autonomy of the member states will be preserved under such a federation, however, was not sufficient to convince Hegel, who saw a fatal flaw in a union of this kind:

Perpetual peace is often demanded as an ideal to which mankind should approximate. Thus, Kant proposed a league of sovereigns to settle disputes between states, and the Holy Alliance was meant to be an institution more or less of this kind. But the state is an individual, and negation is an essential component of individuality. Thus, even if a number of states join together as a family, this league, in its individuality, must generate opposition and create an enemy. Not only do peoples emerge from wars with added strength, but nations troubled by civil dissension gain internal peace as a result of wars with their external enemies.[88]

This objection is critical because it illuminates the source of a disagreement about international relations that is otherwise difficult to locate. Given that both Kant and Hegel base their systems on a view of history as progress that displays all the signs of a teleology, as well as the fact that their diagnoses of the international system in their time were quite similar and expressed in the familiar Hobbist language of the state of nature, one might expect them to agree also on the culmination of this progression in a single state.[89] However warranted such an expectation may be, however, neither sees the progress of mankind as culminating in a single state and, what is more, their views regarding the outcome of that progress diverge radically. One way of characterizing this disagreement regarding the future of the international system is in terms of the ways in which each of the two theories relates to Hobbes. Both rely heavily on Hobbist assumptions and language to describe human psychology and its effects on the international system. The difference between them is that at the point at which Kant attempts to depart from Hobbes, Hegel chooses instead to remain silent.[90] His unwillingness to render a vision of what the international order is marching towards thus becomes his loudest criticism of Kant.

[87] Kant, "To Perpetual Peace," 118.
[88] Hegel, *Elements of the Philosophy of Right* § 324, addendum. Cf. *ibid.*, §§ 333, 337; Meinecke, *Cosmopolitanism & the National State*, 199–200.
[89] On human history as progress, see Herder, *Another Philosophy of History*; Kant, "Idea for a Universal History"; Hegel, *The Philosophy of History*; Hegel, *Elements of the Philosophy of Right* §§ 341–60. Cf. Kelly, "Notes on Hegel's 'Lordship and Bondage,'" 787.
[90] Cf. Honneth, *The Struggle for Recognition*, 67.

As the passage quoted above shows, the roots of Hegel's disagreement with Kant lie in the fundamental role that he attributes to negation in the development of the individual. As stated in the *Philosophy of Right*, Hegel's view of the importance of negation for the formation and preservation of states conforms to the basic tenets of theories of negative association. Hegel's overall theory, however, stands out among those examined herein because in it the account of negative association that pertains to political groups has an explicit counterpart in the individual. This parallel follows the precedent established by Hobbes, and Hegel is well aware of this connection. He cites Hobbes's *De Cive* and *Leviathan* with approval, noting that they "contain sounder reflections on the nature of society and government than many now in circulation," and appreciates the fact that Hobbes broke with tradition and "sought to derive the bond which holds the state together, that which gives the state its power, from principles that lie within us, which we recognize as our own."[91] As proof, Hegel quotes Hobbes's claim that "[t]he origin of all society is to be found in the mutual fear of all its members" and concludes, "it is hence a phenomenon in consciousness."[92] The psychological basis of Hobbes's theory of the state, then, is the first reason for Hobbes's importance, but it is not the only one.

A second crucial point of agreement is to be found in Hobbes's account of the state of nature. At the beginning of *Elements of the Philosophy of Right*, Hegel claims that the decision between the assertions that man is by nature good or evil "depends on subjective arbitrariness."[93] This statement, however, turns out to be deceptive. In the addendum to the passage in question, Hegel states that the Christian view that man is naturally evil is "superior to the other according to which he is good." Further down, in the same work, and without naming Rousseau, Hegel criticizes depictions of the natural condition of mankind that sound as though they were extracted from the

---

[91] Hegel, *Lectures on the History of Philosophy* III, pp. 315–16. Hegel argues further, "[t]he views that he adopts are shallow and empirical, but the reasons he gives for them, and the propositions he makes respecting them, are original in character, inasmuch as they are derived from natural necessities and wants" (317). Cf. *ibid.*, 319: "in Hobbes we at least find this, that the nature and organism of the State is established on the principle of human nature, human desire, etc." In a similar vein, in *The Philosophy of History*, Hegel notes of Machiavelli's *The Prince*, "[t]his book has often been thrown aside in disgust, as replete with the maxims of the most revolting tyranny; but nothing worse can be urged against it than that the writer, having the profound consciousness of the necessity for the formation of a State, has here exhibited the principles on which alone states could be founded in the circumstances of the times" (403).

[92] Hegel, *Lectures on the History of Philosophy* III, p. 317.

[93] Hegel, *Elements of the Philosophy of Right* § 18.

Second Discourse. Portrayals of the state of nature as innocent, he argues, fail to understand the nature of spirit and the end of reason.[94] Similarly, accounts in which man's natural needs are simple and can be satisfied immediately are "mistaken."[95] In contrast with these accounts, Hobbes sees the natural condition of mankind "in its true light," and his account lacks "idle talk about a state of natural goodness."[96] Hegel sees that when Hobbes refers to man's nature, he means both "his spiritual and rational being" *and* the condition in which "man conducts himself according to his natural impulses."[97] The contradistinction between the rational and natural elements is what makes the state of nature a condition "to be cast off."[98] In Hegel's own terms, the state of nature is the condition in which the self first encounters the other, the moment at which it seeks recognition from the other but without any desire to return the favor.[99] Hegel's acceptance of the Hobbist conceptions of individual psychology and of the state of nature marks a turning point in his political philosophy.[100]

Hegel argues that self-consciousness "exists in and for itself when, and by the fact that, it so exists for another."[101] Consciousness requires the presence of another, outside the self, to know both that it is and that it is not that other consciousness. When one consciousness thus encounters another, "[t]hey *recognize* themselves as *mutually recognizing* one another."[102] In the beginning, self-consciousness arises from the exclusion of everything else outside the self. Thus, "[w]hat is 'other' for it is an unessential, negatively characterized object."[103] To develop fully, however, the self-consciousness

---

[94] Hegel, *Elements of the Philosophy of Right* § 187, addendum.

[95] Hegel, *Elements of the Philosophy of Right* § 194, addendum.

[96] Hegel, *Lectures on the History of Philosophy* III, p. 317.

[97] Hegel, *Lectures on the History of Philosophy* III, p. 318.

[98] Hegel, *Lectures on the History of Philosophy* III, p. 318.

[99] Hegel, *Phenomenology of Spirit* §§ 178–87. Taylor argues that "at a raw and undeveloped age," when men have yet to recognize themselves as universal, they "try to wrest recognition from another without reciprocating" (*Hegel*, 153); cf. *ibid.*, 155.

[100] See, e.g., Hegel, "The Philosophy of Spirit," 110–12. As Kelly points out, Hegel's account of lordship and bondage should thus be seen "from three angles that are equally valid and interpenetrable": one pertaining to the social, a second that regards "the shifting pattern of psychological domination and servitude within the individual ego," and a third that fuses the first two ("Notes on Hegel's 'Lordship and Bondage,'" 784). Honneth attributes the exceptional place of Hegel's Jena writings to "the fact that he appropriated [the] Hobbesian conceptual model of interpersonal struggle in order to realize his critical intentions" (*The Struggle for Recognition*, 10).

[101] Hegel, *Phenomenology of Spirit* § 178.

[102] Hegel, *Phenomenology of Spirit* § 184.

[103] Hegel, *Phenomenology of Spirit* § 186.

must negate its objective mode, that is, its attachment to the existence of the other. It must cease to depend on the presence and recognition of the other. This means that the initial encounter between two as yet undeveloped self-consciousnesses is a struggle of life and death. First, "each seeks the death of the other." Second, in so doing, each stakes its own life.[104] As death would terminate the development of self-consciousness, however, the self reassesses itself and the other, and posits the former as a pure self-consciousness and the latter as a "merely *immediate* consciousness, or consciousness in the form of *thinghood*."[105] In this relationship, the self is lord and the other bondsman, and the transition from mortal combat to enslavement is an easy one. Faced with the prospect of annihilation, one side submits to the rule of the other.[106] This relationship too is unsatisfactory, however, because although the other on which the self's recognition depends is alive, it is nevertheless an entity that is itself not recognized by the lord, and therefore incapable of rendering the kind of recognition that the lord requires for his self-consciousness.[107] Surprisingly, the one who benefits from the relationship is the bondsman. On the one hand, he has experienced unqualified dread in the form of the fear of death, "the absolute Lord."[108] This experience enables him to shed those aspects of his being that are particular and stable. On the other hand, in the lord the bondsman has a "*pure being-for-self*" to behold.[109] Work also contributes to the bondsman's consciousness of who he is, because of his connection to the product of his labor, a connection that does not exist for his master.[110] In beholding the product of his labor, however, the bondsman does not see only the positive manifestation of himself in it, but also the "negative significance of *fear*."[111] Juxtaposing himself as a negative vis-à-vis his master, he thus "becomes *for himself*, someone existing on his own account."[112] The attainment of self-consciousness by the bondsman thus arises from his

---

[104] Hegel, *Phenomenology of Spirit* § 187.

[105] Hegel, *Phenomenology of Spirit* § 189; cf. Taylor, *Hegel*, 152.

[106] See Taylor, *Hegel*, 154. Cf. Hobbes, *On the Citizen* I.14.

[107] Hegel, *Phenomenology of Spirit* §§ 190–92; cf. Taylor, *Hegel*, 153–54.

[108] Hegel, *Phenomenology of Spirit* § 194; cf. *ibid.*, 455; Hobbes, *The Elements of Law* I.14.6; *On the Citizen* I.7; Taylor, *Hegel*, 155.

[109] Hegel, *Phenomenology of Spirit* § 194.

[110] Hegel, *Phenomenology of Spirit* § 195.

[111] Hegel, *Phenomenology of Spirit* § 196.

[112] Hegel argues, "[i]n the lord, the being-for-self is an 'other' for the bondsman, or is only *for* him [i.e., is not his own]; in fear, the being-for-self is present in the bondsman himself; in fashioning the thing, he becomes aware that being-for-self belongs to *him*, that he himself exists essentially and actually in his own right" (*Phenomenology of Spirit* § 196).

service, but Hegel stresses that it is an absolute, deep-seated fear that makes it possible.[113]

Hegel's account of the emergence of self-consciousness in the individual shows why despite many obvious differences he agrees with Hobbes's basic approach to politics. The bond that holds us together has to be sought in the individual, and nothing short of a full account of the way in which a human being perceives himself and the world around him will suffice to explain why individuals aggregate into political associations. Hegel joins those who criticize Hobbes for arguing that the universal will, to which the individual subjects his own, is that of the ruler, but this seems to be his only serious objection.[114] More important for him is the foundation laid by Hobbes for the exploration of the origin of the state in the psychology of the individual. Hegel's theory of self-consciousness is the first step in the further development of this Hobbist starting point.

In Hegel's account, individuals come together in three successive stages: the family, civil society, and the state. The first is based on feeling.[115] Civil society intervenes between the family and the state, and marks a stage in which the individual is his own end. His association with others serves the accomplishment of his ends. Individuals pool together to provide goods and services that they cannot attain on their own. The mutual benefit that results from this arrangement, however, exposes individuals to the satisfaction of helping others, and thus paves the way for universality, which is realized in the state.[116] The division of labor brought about by civil society leads to the formation of estates characterized by their different ways of life.[117] The individual's "activity, diligence, and skill" make him a member of one of these estates, and the convergence of these in a whole brings about the state. This structure has undeniable Platonic roots, but it also shares a fundamental

---

[113] Hegel, *Phenomenology of Spirit* § 196.

[114] Hegel, *Lectures on the History of Philosophy* III, pp. 318–19. Cf. Honneth, *The Struggle for Recognition*, 10, 17.

[115] Hegel, *Elements of the Philosophy of Right* § 158.

[116] Hegel, *Elements of the Philosophy of Right* §§ 182, 255, 349. Taylor explains that because needs at this stage can multiply without end, there emerges a further and deeper division of labor, which in turn renders relations and interdependence among individuals more complex, and thus educates man to the universal (*Hegel*, 433).

[117] Hegel, *Elements of the Philosophy of Right* §§ 201–08. The three estates are (i) the substantial or agricultural (§ 203), (ii) the estate of trade and industry (§ 204), and (iii) the universal estate of civil servants (§205); cf. *ibid.*, §§ 250–51. Taylor points out that these estates "can be lined up against the three levels of *Sittlichkeit*: family, civil society, and state" (*Hegel*, 434).

conclusion with Hobbes's theory of human psychology. The world is too complex for a single individual to comprehend and manage. To navigate it, it is necessary to compartmentalize, specialize, and make use of convenient signposts.[118] The consequence of this conclusion for Hegel is that individuals cannot encompass everything, they "cannot stretch their identification so wide as to include everyone."[119] A limit of this kind is essential because the spirit is "*infinitely negative* reference *to itself*" and therefore "exclusive."[120] Kant's proposed federation is therefore unacceptable because it violates the individuality of the independence of member states vis-à-vis other states.[121] The national state thus becomes "the absolute power on *earth*."[122]

The negative relation of the state to other entities outside it manifests itself as an event from without, that is, war. Hegel argues that "this negative relation is the state's *own* highest moment," the moment in which its absolute power over everything within it "gives the nullity of such things an existence."[123] The challenge posed by war to life and property becomes the force that affirms the individuality of the members of the state through their duty to preserve it.[124] Hegel notes that this duty is not of the kind that social contract theories identify. Those who base a call to arms on the need for individual security and the preservation of private property miss the fundamental contradiction involved therein: to save his life, the individual has to offer to sacrifice it. A justification of this type mistakes the state for civil society.[125] The state, however, is more than that. It is the realm in which the individual has "objectivity, truth, and ethical life."[126] Whereas one enters into civil society for the preservation of one's own life and property, "[a] multitude of human beings can only call itself a state if it be united for the common defence of *the entirety* of its property."[127] Thus, for Hegel the litmus

---

[118] Hegel, *Elements of the Philosophy of Right* § 207. As Taylor observes, "[t]he spiritual scope of modern society is too great for one man; he cannot realize it all in his life." As a result, "men must particularize: the synthesis must come from the fact that each in his particularization senses himself as part of a larger common life" (*Hegel*, 434).

[119] Taylor, *Hegel*, 447. Taylor adds that the state "must be the object of a powerful feeling of identification," a feeling that "cannot just be stretched at will to cover the whole human race" (*ibid.*).

[120] Hegel, *Elements of the Philosophy of Right* § 321.

[121] Hegel, *Elements of the Philosophy of Right* §§ 322, 331, 333, 337.

[122] Hegel, *Elements of the Philosophy of Right* § 331.

[123] Hegel, *Elements of the Philosophy of Right* § 323.

[124] Hegel, *Elements of the Philosophy of Right* § 324.

[125] Hegel, *Elements of the Philosophy of Right* § 324. Cf. *ibid.*, § 328; "The Positivity of the Christian Religion," 165.

[126] Hegel, *Elements of the Philosophy of Right* § 258.

[127] Hegel, *The German Constitution*, 153, emphasis added.

test that determines whether a union of human beings constitutes a state is war.

War, according to Hegel, should be considered neither an absolute evil nor a contingency to be blamed on things that are not as they ought to be. Rather, it is a condition in which priorities are rearranged, and "the vanity of temporal things [...] takes on a serious significance."[128] The process by which this reassessment takes place has its origin in the way in which self-consciousness is formed by contrast to others. In this respect, Hegel's account of the effects of war displays all the main traits of other theories of negative association. His account differs only in the centrality that he accords to the notion that this opposition is *essential* to the self-consciousness of the state and its constituents. He argues,

> The ideality which makes its appearance in war in the shape of a contingent external relationship is the same as the ideality whereby the internal powers of the state are organic moments of the whole. This is apparent in various occurrences in history, as when successful wars have averted internal unrest and consolidated the internal power of the state. [...]
>
> Not only do peoples emerge from wars with added strength, but nations troubled by civil dissension gain internal peace as a result of wars with their external enemies.[129]

Kant's proposal is thus undesirable not only because the federation would jeopardize the individuality of the state, but also because war itself is necessary. Were it to materialize, such a federation would have to "generate opposition and create an enemy."[130] The presence of enemies outside the boundaries of states makes it possible for individuals to surrender their personal actuality and offer themselves to the "true, absolute, and ultimate end, the *sovereignty* of the state."[131] War, then, tests the difference between civil society and the state.[132]

Social contract theories that prize security and private property suffer from a fundamental problem. When faced with a threat to its existence, the state has to ask the contracting parties to sacrifice the very things that they

---

[128] Hegel, *Elements of the Philosophy of Right* § 324. Cf. Avineri, *Hegel's Theory of the Modern State*, 195–97; Smith, "Hegel's Views on War, the State, and International Relations," 625, 628, 631.

[129] Hegel, *Elements of the Philosophy of Right* § 324. Cf. *Phenomenology of Spirit* § 455.

[130] Hegel, *Elements of the Philosophy of Right* § 324, addendum.

[131] Hegel, *Elements of the Philosophy of Right* § 328.

[132] Smith notes, "[t]he ethical significance of war resides [...] above all in its ability to raise us above the level of mere civil association with its rootedness in material possessions," because "[i]n times of war, common values and commitments are not only preserved but enhanced" ("Hegel's Views on War, the State, and International Relations," 627). Cf. Nederman, "Sovereignty, War and the Corporation," 508.

sought to protect through the contract. Hegel's distinction between civil society and the state enables him to identify this problem, but whether the state as he describes it succeeds in solving it is quite another matter. In the end, he argues that spirit is "the power of the whole" that forms a "negative unity" out of parts by making them feel their "lack of independence, and keeping them aware that they have their life only in the whole."[133] Within the confines of this unity, the parts will still have the tendency to isolate themselves, forcing the government to resort to negative association. Hegel argues,

> In order not to let them become rooted and set in this isolation, thereby breaking up the whole and letting the [communal] spirit evaporate, government has from time to time to shake them to their core by war. By this means the government upsets their established order, and violates their right to independence, while the individuals who, absorbed in their own way of life, break loose from the whole and strive after the inviolable independence and security of the person, are made to feel in the task laid on them their lord and master, death.[134]

The crucial difference between civil society and the state lies in the fact that whereas the former is a mere aggregation of private interests, the latter unites human beings in the pursuit of a universal end.[135] By forcing the individual to attach primary importance to the state and secondary importance to his particular self-interest, external threats provide the impetus for a radical shift in identity. For Hegel, an aggregation of such individuals is a whole greater than the sum of its parts.

Just as the individual human being has to juggle multiple relationships with others, the state is also faced with a complex social environment. The realization that each state will seldom have the luxury to devote its exclusive

---

[133] Hegel, *Phenomenology of Spirit* § 455.

[134] Hegel, *Phenomenology of Spirit* § 455. In "The German Constitution," Hegel writes,

> The health of a state is generally revealed not so much in the calm of peace as in the stir of war. Peace is the state of enjoyment and activity in seclusion, when government is a prudent paternalism, making only ordinary demands on its subjects. But in war the power of the association of all with the whole is in evidence; this association has adjusted the amount which it can demand from individuals, as well as the worth of what they may do for it of their own impulse and their own heart (143–44).

[135] Hegel, *Elements of the Philosophy of Right* § 260. "In its initial stage," argues Hegel, "a nation is not a state, and the transition of a family, tribe, kinship group, mass [of people], etc. to the condition of a state constitutes the *formal* realization of the Idea in general within it" (*ibid.*, § 349). See also Avineri, *Hegel's Theory of the Modern State*, 195; Nederman, "Sovereignty, War and the Corporation," 508–09; Smith, "Hegel's Views on War, the State, and International Relations," 628.

attention to any single other brings Hegel back to Hobbes. Having set out from the same point of origin, their paths diverged when their respective visions of the state emerged. Hegel saw Hobbes's state as "a condition of absolute rule, of perfect despotism," because of the subjection of individual wills to the single will of the ruler.[136] Inwardly, Hegel's state is quite different, but with respect to international relations, the sovereign is the sole bearer of responsibility.[137] The prominent role played by sovereigns means that the relations between states will always be vulnerable to contingencies from which war can break out.[138] Because moral, religious, and other similar considerations are insufficient to bind sovereign wills, a federation of the kind proposed by Kant would be all the more at risk of dissolution, and war would remain the only means of settling disputes.[139] Moreover, Hegel argues, reasons for war are never lacking, since the determination of a state's interests and honor lie with it.[140] To make matters worse, a state need not sit back and wait to be attacked, but can act preemptively to counter an emerging threat.[141] In a disturbing conclusion with faint echoes of the Hippocratic maxim encountered earlier, Hegel argues that a state "will be all the more inclined to take offence if it possesses a strong individuality which is encouraged, as a result of a long period of internal peace, to seek and create an occasion for action abroad."[142] These grim observations do not prevent Hegel from agreeing with those, such as Botero and Saint-Pierre, who find that a stronger bond exists between European nations than among others. At best, this "family," which arises from the "universal principle of their legislation, customs, and culture," mollifies the effects of war but seems to be otherwise inadequate and unpredictable.[143]

The optimism that pervades Kant's eponymous essay is more indicative of the author's good intentions than his expectation that perpetual peace will materialize. In the more sober *Metaphysics of Morals*, Kant proclaims it

---

[136] Hegel, *Lectures on the History of Philosophy* III, 318. See also Honneth, *The Struggle for Recognition*, 10.

[137] Hegel, *Elements of the Philosophy of Right* § 329 and addendum. Nederman emphasizes the usefulness of the distinction between the "outward state" and its domestic manifestation ("Sovereignty, War and the Corporation," 504–05).

[138] Hegel, *Elements of the Philosophy of Right* §§ 324, 333. See Avineri, *Hegel's Theory of the Modern State*, 200–01.

[139] Hegel, *Elements of the Philosophy of Right* §§ 333–34. Hegel argues that the normal condition is one in which relations among states are governed by treaties or war (§ 333; cf. "The German Constitution," 208–10).

[140] Hegel, *Elements of the Philosophy of Right* § 334.

[141] Hegel, *Elements of the Philosophy of Right* § 335.

[142] Hegel, *Elements of the Philosophy of Right* § 334.

[143] Hegel, *Elements of the Philosophy of Right* § 339.

to be "indeed an unachievable idea," and settles for such political principles as would bring states together in a congress in which law rather than war would resolve disputes.[144] This union of states is Kant's attempt to respond to Hobbes's observation that the sovereign marks the boundary between the state of nature and a sphere in which commodious living is possible and freedom meaningful.[145] Despite Kant's good intentions, however, Hobbes's objection turns out to be insuperable. For his part, having set out from a starting point very similar to Hobbes's, Hegel realizes this crucial aspect of international relations and thus draws conclusions very different from Kant's.[146] For Hegel, "negation is an essential component of individuality," for human beings as well as states.[147] Through negation individuals begin their quest towards self-consciousness, a quest that culminates in the moral existence made possible by the state.

CONFLICT

The intense interest in matters pertaining to state sovereignty and international relations that drew so much attention in the eighteenth and nineteenth centuries, however, was but one side of the coin. Hegel's choice to center his philosophy on the role of a dialectic in which negation is an essential means towards identity formation also had a profound influence on the study of conflict more generally. The observation that "[e]nmity, not friendship, is by far the more characteristic condition of human beings" was by no means novel.[148] Through his systematic analysis of human relations at the individual as well as the collective level, however, Hegel provided it with a new vocabulary and made it an essential part of a system of philosophy that seems in other ways very different from it. As a result, Hobbist ideas dressed in Hegelian language became the starting point for the investigation of conflict by economists, sociologists, and psychologists. In many ways, the focus on conflict during the nineteenth century marked the foundation of

---

[144] Kant, *The Metaphysics of Morals* § 61.

[145] Hobbes, *Leviathan*, XIII § 12.

[146] This divergence occurs despite their apparent agreement on a historicist outlook with evident signs of a teleology.

[147] Hegel, *Elements of the Philosophy of Right* § 324, addendum. Kant's conception of the individual is open to the same criticism, since subjection to reason means that one is at best lord and bondsman at the same time (see Kroner, Introduction to Hegel's *Early Theological Writings*, 11).

[148] Smith, "Hegel's Views on War, the State, and International Relations," 628.

these disciplines. Many of the developments associated with their rise took place in the German-speaking world. This is not surprising given Hegel's influence, but it should be borne in mind that that world was also one in which Hobbes continued to be read. Evidence of a Hobbist influence is harder to locate, but it is present in the writings of Marx, Freud, Tönnies, and Simmel, for whom conflict, in one form or another, was a point of reference. This influence is most evident in Simmel, who, in his theory of sociology, provides the most explicit and comprehensive treatment of conflict, yet names neither Hobbes nor Hegel.[149]

In that treatment, Simmel sees the role of conflict in shaping groups as indisputable, and proposes further that it also constitutes a form of sociation.[150] This suggestion is not as paradoxical as it may seem at first, since conflict may result from dissociating tendencies, such as hatred and envy, but is "designed to resolve divergent dualisms; it is a way of achieving some kind of unity, even if it is through the annihilation of one of the conflicting parties."[151] Fraught with negative connotations, conflict nevertheless contains significant positive elements, since it entails the recognition of the parties involved and carries within it the possibility of resolution. Simmel locates conflict at the core of human existence, whether individual or social. Although one ought to be able to distinguish between relations that constitute a unit and those that counteract unity, Simmel argues that such a neat distinction is in fact artificial and flies in the face of the evidence. In fact, "every historically real situation" displays characteristics of both unity and conflict, and even the unity of the individual is the result of contradiction and conflict, which "not only precede this unity but are operative in it at every moment of its existence." There is an obvious sense in which this is true, since a group comes into being by delineating members and nonmembers, and the fluctuating dynamics within and between these define and redefine it. Hence, for Simmel, "[a]n absolutely centripetal and harmonious group, a pure 'unification,' not only is empirically unreal, it could show no real life process."[152] Simmel suggests that the positive role of conflict in the formation and preservation of groups is obscured by a misunderstanding regarding the

---

[149] There is sufficient evidence that Simmel was familiar with Hobbes's theories. See, e.g., *Gesamtausgabe*, 1: 129–30; 3: 85; 8: 187; 11: 166.

[150] Simmel, "Conflict," 13.

[151] Simmel, "Conflict," 13.

[152] Simmel, "Conflict," 15. Further down, Simmel argues that antagonism is a sociological element never absent from sociation (*ibid.*, 25).

concept of unity. While on the one hand we think of unity as "the consensus and concord of interacting individuals, as against their discords, separations, and disharmonies," on the other hand we use it to refer also to "the total group-synthesis of persons, energies, and forms," a synthesis that includes both unitary and dualistic relations.[153] Too much emphasis on the former, however, results in the disregard of the latter.

At the same time, Simmel insists that keeping this balance in mind is essential, since excessive emphasis on conflict is no more productive than its counterpart, for relations of conflict cannot produce a social structure unless aided by unifying forces.[154] "Human nature," he argues, "does not allow the individual to be tied to another by one thread alone, even though scientific analysis is not satisfied until it has determined the specific cohesive power of elementary units," and this is true not only of relations among individuals, but also within the individual himself.[155] Simmel finds evidence for this view in what he sees as broad agreement between those, such as La Rochefoucauld and Hobbes, who see a natural enmity between human beings, and those who are of the opposite opinion.[156] At the very least, natural hostility will be found where sympathy lies. It shows itself in the reflex-like reactions that reveal an instinct of opposition, such as "the quiet, often hardly known, fleeting temptation to contradict an assertion or demand, particularly a categorical one."[157] Simmel likens this tendency to the instinctual reactions of animals which, when touched, "automatically use their protective and aggressive apparatus," and concludes, "the first instinct with which the individual affirms himself is the negation of the other."[158]

Evidence of a Hobbist influence becomes apparent in Simmel's search for further proof of a natural state of hostility among human beings in actual

---

[153] Simmel, "Conflict," 17.

[154] Simmel, "Conflict," 20–21.

[155] Simmel, "Conflict," 21.

[156] Simmel, "Conflict," 28. Simmel names neither of the two, but he quotes Plautus's famous dictum "*homo homini lupus*," which Hobbes cites in *De Cive* (*On the Citizen*, Ep. Ded., § 1) alongside La Rochefoucauld's maxim, "in the misfortune of our best friends there is something which does not wholly displease us" (Simmel, "Conflict," 28; cf. La Rochefoucauld, *Maxims*, number 583, p. 117).

[157] Simmel, "Conflict," 29.

[158] Simmel, "Conflict," 29. Cf. Hegel, *Phenomenology of Spirit* § 178. That Simmel's formulation of this conclusion is strikingly reminiscent of Hegel is no accident. In "On the Metaphysics of Death," Simmel identifies the relationship between life and death as the deepest signification of the Hegelian formulation that everything demands an opposite (Simmel, "Zur Metaphysik des Todes" in *Gesamtausgabe* 12: 85–86; cf. "Lebensanschauung" in *Gesamtausgabe* 16: 308–09).

manifestations of the state of nature. He considers it "well known that [...]
the mutual relation of primitive groups is almost always one of hostility"
and cites as "decisive" the case of the American Indians, "among whom
every tribe was on principle considered in a state of war with every other
tribe with which it had not concluded an explicit peace treaty."[159] This condition is a natural consequence of the fact that in "early stages of culture,
war is almost the only form in which contact with alien groups is brought
about at all."[160] The presence of such a tendency towards hostility means
that something other than positive unifying characteristics will be necessary
if individuals are to come together and form groups. Simmel recognizes that
conflict has a crucial role to play in the preservation of existing groups, but
he moves beyond that role and considers the sequentially prior moment in
which a group comes into being. There, too, conflict can "bring persons and
groups together which have otherwise nothing to do with each other."[161]
Once again, the evidence of this dynamic lies right before our eyes: individuals come together to fight others so often that sometimes the very act
of their aggregation may appear threatening. Historical evidence of this tendency abounds, and comes from reactions to the formation of threatening
associations as well as from their cultivation. Simmel points out that the
Romans, who were masters of group dynamics, fostered a "wholly unpolit-
ical pan-Hellenism" to distract the Greek city-states from potential political
associations.[162] The variety of examples from antiquity and contemporary
life is of such an extent, argues Simmel, as to prove the point beyond dispute. There, one finds evidence of group formation through conflict from
the highest level, that of the unified state, down to federations of states and
class systems.[163]

In peace, coexistence is characterized by indifference. Active recipro-
cal significance comes through war. Simmel's description of the difference

---

[159] Simmel, "Conflict," 32.
[160] Simmel, "Conflict," 33.
[161] Simmel, "Conflict," 99. See also *ibid*., 18; Smith, *National Identity*, 27.
[162] Simmel, "Conflict," 99–100.
[163] Simmel argues, "Essentially, France owes the consciousness of its national unity only to its
fight against the English, and only the Moorish war made the Spanish regions into one
people. The next lower grade of unification is constituted by confederacies and federations
of states, with additional numerous gradations according to their cohesion and the measure
of power of their central authorities. The United States needed the War of Independence;
Switzerland the fight against Austria; the Netherlands, rebellion against Spain; the Achaean
League, the struggle against Macedonia; and the founding of the new German Empire
furnishes a parallel to all of these instances" ("Conflict," 100). Simmel's paradoxical ranking
of these associations from highest to lowest is a further sign of Hobbes's influence.

between domestic tranquility and external conflict calls to mind Machiavelli's account of the effects of foreign policy on internal order: "the same drive to expand and to act, which *within* the group requires unconditional peace for the integration of interests and for unfettered interaction, may appear to the outside as a tendency toward war."[164] Simmel notes, however, that one ought to distinguish further, "according to whether the unification for the purpose of conflict refers to attack *and* defense or to defense only."[165] The latter "is the collectivistic minimum, because even for the single group and the single individual it constitutes the least avoidable test of the drive for self-preservation."[166] The reasoning here is simple: the greater the number of individuals who congregate, the less likely will be the convergence of their interests. The bare minimum on which all can agree, however, is self-preservation, and this, at least, will serve as the basis of their union.

The purpose and consequent duration of the association is a further consideration that needs to be taken into account. The effects of negative association on groups formed for the specific purpose of dealing with a particular threat are greater than they are on groups that are preexisting and intend to continue after the resolution of the conflict in question. As an example of the former kind, Simmel cites the case of the league of Greek cities that formed in response to the Persian invasion and dissolved upon victory. Labor unions in England and the United States exemplify the latter type.[167] In general, where the desideratum is the unification of divergent elements over a long period of time, as in the preservation of a state with warring classes, a chronic danger with "an always latent but never exploding conflict" is the best remedy.[168] This was true of the Achaean League while the Persian threat was alive, but, more importantly, this seems to be what Montesquieu had in mind when he suggested that republics need someone to fear.[169]

Simmel notes that perhaps the most intriguing aspect of negative association is that it makes for strange bedfellows, as it often unites parties previously indifferent to one another and sometimes even former adversaries. Thus, "[t]he unifying power of the principle of conflict nowhere emerges more strongly than when it manages to carve a temporal or contentual area out of

---

[164] Simmel, "Conflict," 33.
[165] Simmel, "Conflict," 101.
[166] Simmel, "Conflict," 101.
[167] Simmel, "Conflict," 101–02.
[168] Simmel, "Conflict," 106.
[169] Simmel, "Conflict," 106; cf. Montesquieu, *The Spirit of the Laws*, VIII.5.

competitive or hostile relationships."[170] Given the importance of the instinct for self-preservation, Simmel concludes that "[t]he more purely negative or destructive a given enmity is, the more easily will it bring about a unification of those who ordinarily have no motive for any community."[171] On the whole, therefore, associations for conflict tend to bring about the widest possible unions, including elements that would not otherwise come together. This is so for several reasons. First, because "people engaging in peaceful actions usually limit themselves to those who are close to them in other respects as well," whereas, "war, and not only political war, often constitutes an emergency in which one cannot be choosy about friends."[172] Second, the reprioritization that takes place through negative association tends to leave preexisting interests unaffected. The temporary allies can therefore return to the status quo ante once their conflict with their common enemy has been resolved. Third, though dangerous, gains through war are quick and intensive. Fourth, the instinct for self-preservation is so intense that it suppresses other aspects of the individual's identity and therefore makes room for concessions that would otherwise not be possible. Thus, it opens the door to association with others who under different circumstances would be deemed unacceptable. Finally, notes Simmel, the outbreak of hostilities between two groups often pushes latent hostility in a third group to the breaking point, causing it to join the fight. Simmel's indebtedness to Hobbes and Hegel shines through once more, as he concludes that this was the reason why "convergent relations among *peoples* as *wholes*, especially in earlier times, existed only for purposes of war, while other relations, such as trade and commerce, hospitality, and intermarriage, only concerned *individuals*."[173]

Simmel's discussion of conflict is but one example of the development of Hobbes's ideas throughout the eighteenth and nineteenth centuries. Though he too never names Hobbes in his discussion of conflict, Freud quotes Plautus's dictum "*homo homini lupus*," which Hobbes used in the opening of *De Cive*, and wonders, "[w]ho, in the face of all his experience of life and of history, will have the courage to dispute this assertion?"[174] He therefore concludes, "[i]t is always possible to bind together a considerable number of people in love, so long as there are other people left over to receive the

---

[170] Simmel, "Conflict," 102. Cf. *ibid.*, 41, 103.
[171] Simmel, "Conflict," 103.
[172] Simmel, "Conflict," 106.
[173] Simmel, "Conflict," 106–07.
[174] Freud, *Civilization and Its Discontents*, 69; cf. *ibid.*, 81.

manifestations of their aggressiveness."[175] For Hobbes, the world is a complicated place and others are necessary signposts that can facilitate movement
within it. This realization is one of the reasons why Hobbes's choice to
begin with the psychology of the individual was appealing to Hegel.[176] The
mere presence of signposts with similar needs, however, is pregnant with
the seeds of conflict. The conflictual model that Hobbes developed from the
psychology of the individual was one of the least well-received aspects of his
thought, because the story that it tells about human nature is not a particularly encouraging one. The potency of this model, however, is evident in the
range of reactions to Hobbes's political theory, from Rousseau's vociferous
disagreement, through Kant's respectful departure, to Hegel's acceptance.[177]
As interest in the realm beyond the boundaries of the state grew into an obses-
sion, it became clear that the contrast between the state and the international
realm, delineated so succinctly by Hobbes, was of paramount importance,
not least as the test case for the role of negative association in the formation
and preservation of political groups. Rousseau's position, purportedly the
most extreme of the ones examined above, attests to this. Whereas he begins
by rejecting that part of Hobbes's state of nature that describes the lives of
individuals prior to the state, he ends by accepting the part that describes
the lives of states in the international realm.[178] The conclusion of Hegel's
political theory adds to this impression. Although he refuses to render a definite vision of the future, he is clear that the state marks the culmination of
political life because it provides the environment within which the individual
can develop. The strongest evidence of Hobbes's influence, however, can be
found in the writings of German political theorists of the late nineteenth and
early twentieth centuries, who identified him as the thinker who captured
the essence of the political.

---

[175] Freud, *Civilization and Its Discontents*, 72.

[176] Cf. Taylor, *Hegel*, 434.

[177] See also Sieyès, *What Is the Third Estate?*, 134, 137; Mazzini, "The Duties of Man," 11.

[178] In "The State of War," e.g., another work riddled with vociferous rejections of Hobbes's
views, Rousseau argues, "[m]an to man we live in the civil state and subject to laws; people
to people, each enjoys natural freedom: which at bottom makes our situation worse than if
these distinctions were unknown," and adds, "[f]or by living both in the social order and in
the state of nature, we are subject to the inconveniences of both without finding security
in either" (§ 5).

7

THE POLITICS OF ENMITY

Tell me who your enemy is, and I will tell you who you are.

– Carl Schmitt[1]

Among German Hobbists, Carl Schmitt stands out for several reasons. Schmitt identified Hobbes as a major political thinker early in his career and spent the larger part of his very long life thinking and writing about Hobbes. As a political theorist, Schmitt is best known for his definition of the political as the relationship between friends and enemies, a concept that owes much to Hobbes. Schmitt's Hobbist conception of politics in turn influenced the political theory of Hans Morgenthau, who became one of the principal theorists of international relations and the chief proponent of realism in the twentieth century. Those who know Morgenthau only through his American writings may be surprised to hear of his connection to Schmitt. Yet an account of Morgenthau's early, European, intellectual activities reveals a direct connection with Schmitt that is of the highest importance, since it explains, among other things, why Hobbes has come to be considered a key thinker by theorists of international relations.

Schmitt and Morgenthau form part of the tradition of thinkers for whom negative association is an important element of group formation and preservation. What makes them a particularly important part of that tradition, however, is their recognition of Hobbes as its outstanding representative, and their roles in the reintroduction of a Hobbist realism to the English-speaking world. Schmitt and Morgenthau's great realization, no doubt facilitated by the events of the twentieth century, was that the ultimate domain of Hobbesian self-definition through juxtaposition with outsiders was that of

---

[1] *Glossarium*, 243.

international politics. This realization, articulated most forcefully by Schmitt, was eventually accepted by Morgenthau and was brought by him to the United States, and put to use in the establishment of contemporary political science.

ENMITY

In 1889, Tönnies made a significant contribution to the advancement of the study of Hobbes by publishing, for the first time since its composition and dissemination in approximately ten manuscripts, in 1640, *The Elements of Law*, as well as the first modern critical edition of *Behemoth*, from Hobbes's manuscripts.[2] On July 11 of the previous year, the year of the 300th anniversary of Hobbes's birth, Schmitt was born in Plettenberg, in the Sauerland region of the Rhineland. Shklar points out that those who value decisionism are "those who feel that they have no place to go, [...] those who are self-conscious 'outsiders.'"[3] For much of his early life, Schmitt was an outsider, both as a Catholic in Protestant Plettenberg, and later on, despite the odds, as an unknown law student at the Friedrich-Wilhelm University in Berlin.[4] Schmitt left Berlin for Munich and eventually for Strasbourg, which at the time was a center of antipositivist thought.[5] Legal positivism had emerged in opposition to natural law theories and sought to "make the formal analysis of the meaning of legal terms in statutes the exclusive focus of jurisprudence and treat the entire body of law as if it formed a seamless system of

[2] Thomas Hobbes, *The Elements of Law Natural & Politic*, ed. Ferdinand Tönnies (London: Simpkin, Marshall, & Co., 1889); Thomas Hobbes, *Behemoth or The Long Parliament*, ed. Ferdinand Tönnies (London: Simpkin, Marshall, & Co., 1889). Hobbes's *Behemoth* was written in 1668 but was not published until unauthorized versions were printed in 1679. The first authorized publication "from the Author's true Copy" was printed in London, by W. Crooke, in 1682. With the exception of an edition printed by R. Wilks (1815), the Molesworth edition in *The English Works of Thomas Hobbes of Malmesbury* (London: J. Bohn, 1839–1845), vol. 6, was the only one available prior to the publication of Tönnies' edition; that too is a reproduction of the 1682 Crooke edition. Cf. Goldsmith, Introduction to *The Elements of Law Natural & Politic*, v–xxi; Holmes, Introduction to *Behemoth or The Long Parliament*, vii–ix.
[3] Shklar, "Decisionism," 5.
[4] According to Balakrishnan, "[a]lthough there was a Catholic majority in the region, tiny Plettenberg was an Evangelical community" (Balakrishnan, *The Enemy*, 12); cf. Bendersky, *Carl Schmitt*, 3–8. In his own words, in Berlin Schmitt felt like "an obscure young man of modest origin," neither a part of the ruling strata nor of the opposition, and so, "stood in the dark" and "remained outside" (quoted in Noack, *Carl Schmitt*, 21). Cf. Schmitt's view of Berlin in *Ex captivitate salus*, 35–36.
[5] Bendersky, *Carl Schmitt*, 9.

norms."[6] Although reasonably successful in civil law, positivism was much less so with respect to constitutional law, and thus "sought to conceal the inherently political nature" of unresolved problems in fundamental constitutional issues, such as sovereignty and the control of the budget.[7] Schmitt saw the relationship between rules and decisions and the inability of rules to provide solutions in these most pressing and extreme situations as a major weakness of positivism, and this vantage point came to shape much of his political theory.[8] Hobbes does not figure in Schmitt's very first writings, but his dissertation, which addresses the issue of the judicial decision in the context of criminal law, reveals this early concern with the importance of the decision, a theme that would eventually dominate his thought.[9] This concern no doubt owes something to the predominance of legal positivism, as well as to what he saw as the increasing romanticization of politics, a problem that he would address eventually, in *Political Romanticism*.

Perhaps surprisingly, given his subsequent political activity and persuasion, Schmitt was largely indifferent to World War I; he certainly did not display any of the youthful enthusiasm of Hans J. Morgenthau on behalf of the German cause.[10] Nevertheless, upon completion of his studies, he joined the army and ended up serving in the censorship section of the regional martial law administration, in Munich.[11] Schmitt's experience during the war was an important, formative, one, as well as one that he shared with his two favorite political thinkers, Bodin and Hobbes, whom he viewed as shaped by civil war.[12] Communist uprisings in Bavaria at the time led to civil unrest, which he experienced first hand. During one of these, revolutionaries broke into Schmitt's office and shot one of his colleagues.[13]

It is in the nature of a constitutional crisis to raise the issue of who decides, and the events that followed the institution of the Weimar Republic strengthened Schmitt's interest in the importance of the decision. In his first major political work, Schmitt attacks political romanticism, which he sees as the

[6] Balakrishnan, *The Enemy*, 13. Cf. Bendersky, *Carl Schmitt*, 9–10.
[7] Balakrishnan, *The Enemy*, 14.
[8] See Williams, "Words, Images, Enemies," 517.
[9] See Noack, *Carl Schmitt*, 32. Cf. Balakrishnan, *The Enemy*, 14–15.
[10] Balakrishnan, *The Enemy*, 16, 64. Cf. Frei, *Hans J. Morgenthau*, 15–16.
[11] Balakrishnan, *The Enemy*, 16.
[12] Schmitt, *Ex captivitate salus*, 64. Cf. *The Concept of the Political*, 52–53.
[13] Balakrishnan argues, "[s]uch experiences gelled into an abiding fear of civil wars, but also a fascination for the political and moral atmosphere they generated; this fear and fascination were to shape his whole political outlook" (Balakrishnan, *The Enemy*, 20). Cf. Bendersky, *Carl Schmitt*, 22; Müller, *A Dangerous Mind*, 19.

source of the culture of indecision that characterized the Weimar Republic. Schmitt accuses the intellectual heirs of the romantic movement of trying to avoid making a decision between two alternatives by inventing a third possibility, which they present as higher than the mundane either/or.[14] In so doing, they destroy not only the normality of a legal order but also the importance of the exceptional situation that demands a decision.[15] Furthermore, by overstressing the subjective emotion, the romantic approach favors individuality, but thereby fails to transcend the limits of subjectivity and for this reason "cannot be the foundation of a community."[16] Although primarily a critique of political romanticism, this work also contains a hint at the solution. Schmitt considers Hobbes the antithesis of romantic thought, and it would be this thinker, whom Schmitt would soon thereafter identify as "[t]he classical representative of the decisionist type," who would provide the theoretical basis for a political response.[17] In his later reminiscences, Schmitt reveals that he found more current answers to the legal and constitutional questions of his time in the writings of Hobbes and Bodin than in the commentaries on the Bismarckian and Weimar constitutions.[18]

Schmitt's admittedly curious choice of subtitle for his main work devoted to Hobbes (*Der Leviathan in der Staatslehre des Thomas Hobbes: Sinn und Fehlschlag eines politischen Symbols* [The Leviathan in the State Theory of Thomas Hobbes: Meaning and Failure of a Political Symbol, 1938]) has led some commentators to pronounce that he apparently lost his faith in the significance of Hobbes.[19] Yet despite that subtitle, Schmitt concludes that work with the following words:

To us he is thus the true teacher of a great political experience; lonely as every pioneer; misunderstood as is everyone whose political thought does not gain acceptance among his own people; unrewarded, as one who opened a gate through which others marched on; and yet in the immortal community of the great scholars of the ages, "a sole retriever of an ancient prudence." Across the centuries we reach out to him: *Non jam frustra doces, Thomas Hobbes!*[20]

[14] Schmitt, *Political Romanticism*, 115, 117.
[15] See Schmitt, *Political Romanticism*, 124–25.
[16] Schmitt, *Political Romanticism*, 161. Schmitt adds, "[t]he intoxication of sociability is not a basis of a lasting association." It is in this emphasis on subjectivity and individuality that Schmitt sees the affinity between romanticism and liberalism. On the relationship between the two, see Rosenblum, *Another Liberalism*, esp. 187–88.
[17] Schmitt, *Political Theology*, 33.
[18] Schmitt, *Ex captivitate salus*, 64.
[19] See, e.g., Balakrishnan, *The Enemy*, 209; Kahn, "Hamlet or Hecuba," 74, 80.
[20] [Thomas Hobbes, now you do not teach in vain!] Schmitt, *The Leviathan in the State Theory of Thomas Hobbes*, 86.

Nor did Schmitt ever change his mind about Hobbes.[21] In his autobiographical reflections of the years 1945 to 1947, Schmitt declares that although he
is familiar with the works, lives, and reputations of the great jurists of the *jus
publicum Europaeum*, such as Vitoria, Gentili, and Grotius, all of whom he
loves, none of these men is close to him. Instead, he states that nearest him
are two other thinkers, who have founded international law out of public
law, Jean Bodin and Thomas Hobbes: "These two names out of the age
of the confessional civil wars have become for me the names of living and
present men, the names of brothers."[22] Schmitt claims that over thirty years,
and even through the worst of times, Bodin and Hobbes "kept my thinking
awake and drove it forward, even as the Positivism of my time oppressed me,
and a blind need for security wanted to paralyze me."[23] Indeed, Schmitt's fascination with Hobbes never abated. He was foremost among the celebrants
of the 350th anniversary of Hobbes's birth, in 1938, and is likely to have been
the author of a 1952 commemorative piece marking the 300th anniversary
of the publication of *Leviathan*.[24] As late as 1965, and even though no longer
affiliated with an academic institution, Carl Schmitt published an extensive
review essay of recent works on Thomas Hobbes.[25] According to Schelsky,
Hobbes was Schmitt's teacher, and Bendersky claims that Schmitt compared
his fate with those of Machiavelli and Hobbes.[26]

Schmitt's appreciation of Hobbes is easy to understand given the effect that
Hobbes's political thought had on the formation of Schmitt's own theory. In
the closest that he ever came to explaining his view of human nature, Schmitt

---

[21] In addition to Schmitt's own claims to this effect, there is the testimony of Helmut Schelsky,
a student of Schmitt's and interlocutor on Hobbes. On Schelsky's relationship to Schmitt
around the time of the composition of "The State as Mechanism in Hobbes & Descartes"
and *The Leviathan in the State Theory of Thomas Hobbes*, see Schelsky, *Thomas Hobbes*, 5, 13;
cf. Balakrishnan, *The Enemy*, 210. Another disciple of Schmitt's, Günter Maschke, concurs.
In his obituary for Schmitt for the *Frankfurter Allgemeine Zeitung*, he portrays Schmitt as a
"Hobbes for the twentieth century" (see Müller, *A Dangerous Mind*, 154).

[22] Schmitt, *Ex captivitate salus*, 63–64. Cf. Carl Schmitt, *Glossarium*, entries for January 12,
1948, 81; February 3, 1948, 91; February 28, 1948, 107.

[23] Schmitt, *Ex captivitate salus*, 64.

[24] On the 1938 celebration, see Rumpf, *Carl Schmitt und Thomas Hobbes*, 108–09. Although
published anonymously, "Dreihundert Jahre *Leviathan*" is attributed to Schmitt by Rumpf
(113) as well as Weiler (*From Absolutism to Totalitarianism*, 62).

[25] Schmitt, "Vollendete Reformation." The essay is signed "Carl Schmitt, Plettenberg."

[26] Schelsky, "Begriff des Politischen," 324; Bendersky, *Carl Schmitt*, 287. McCormick lists
several sources that examine the relationship between Schmitt and Hobbes (*Carl Schmitt's
Critique of Liberalism*, 252, note 7). Cf. ibid., 250–53; Schwab, *The Challenge of the Exception*, 57, 114, 120–21; Weiler, *From Absolutism to Totalitarianism*, 4; Dyzenhaus, "'Now the
Machine Runs Itself,'" 2; Bendersky, "The Definite and the Dubious," 44.

argued that political theories could be tested according to their view of man as by nature of evil or good.[27] Schmitt explains that he means this distinction not in the way in which it is usually applied, that is, not in a moral or ethical sense, but rather as "the answer to the question whether man is a dangerous being or not, a risky or a harmless creature."[28] Recall that for Hobbes, man's natural desires and aversions are expressed in ways that are acceptable in infants but obnoxious in adults, and hence that it makes sense to refer to an adult who persists in displaying them in a childlike fashion as evil only if we mean that he is behaving "like a sturdy boy, or a man of childish mind."[29] Schmitt agrees, and points out that evil "may appear as corruption, weakness, cowardice, stupidity, or also as brutality, sensuality, vitality, irrationality, and so on."[30] On the basis of this interpretation of evil, Schmitt argues that "all *genuine* political theories presuppose man to be evil, i.e., by no means an unproblematic but a dangerous and dynamic being."[31] Schmitt explains what he considers to be genuine political theories in *The Concept of the Political*, a work that displays his indebtedness to Hobbes in the most striking manner. Although Hobbes lurks behind every corner in that work, there are five fundamental elements of Schmitt's theory that indicate a strong Hobbesian influence and that should be singled out: (i) a concern with the *proper* study of politics, (ii) the claim that politics (i.e., conflict) precedes the state, (iii) the role of the exception, (iv) the importance of the decision, and (v) the fundamental realism of the political.

THE PROPER STUDY OF POLITICS

Both versions of Schmitt's essay begin with a statement that has been called "curious and provocative": "The concept of the state presupposes the concept of the political."[32] Although he did not address this matter in his "Observations" on the 1932 edition of Schmitt's essay, Leo Strauss did so in a letter to

---

[27] Schmitt, *The Concept of the Political*, 58.
[28] Schmitt, *The Concept of the Political*, 58. Cf. Hobbes, *On the Citizen*, Pref., §§ 11–12.
[29] Hobbes, *On the Citizen*, Pref., § 13.
[30] Schmitt, *The Concept of the Political*, 58.
[31] Schmitt, *The Concept of the Political*, 61, emphasis added. See also *Political Romanticism*, 1, 3; *Political Theology*, 56. Cf. Hobbes, *On the Citizen*, Pref., §§ 11–12, I.2, note 2.
[32] Schmitt, "Der Begriff des Politischen" (1927), 1; *Der Begriff des Politischen* (1932), 20; *The Concept of the Political*, 19. The characterization is Balakrishnan's (*The Enemy*, 102).

Schmitt, on September 4 of the same year.[33] Strauss objected that Schmitt's opening sentence is "ambiguous" because

The *tendency* to separate (and therewith the grouping of humanity into friends and enemies) is given with human nature; it is in this sense destiny, period. But the political thus understood is not the constitutive principle of the state. Now this relationship of rank between the political and the state does not emerge sufficiently, I believe, in your text. Your statement "The concept of the state presupposes the concept of the political is ambiguous: "presupposition" can mean constitutive principle *or* condition. In the first sense the statement can hardly be maintained, as the etymology (political-*polis*) already proves.[34]

There is no record of a response from Schmitt, but Strauss's acceptance of his fundamental claim as self-evident would no doubt have pleased Schmitt, regardless of the latter's view of the etymological criticism.[35] Neither thinker cites Hobbes in this context, but it is clear that it is Hobbes's state of nature that is guiding both.[36] With Schmitt's help, Strauss had been awarded a Rockefeller fellowship and was at the time engaged in research on Hobbes that would eventually culminate in his book *The Political Philosophy of Hobbes* (1936). Moreover, Strauss's first major study of Hobbes was published in the same year as his notes on Schmitt's essay.[37] Finally, Strauss's remarks on Schmitt's essay identify Hobbes's central role in *The Concept of the Political*, and Schmitt is said to have thought highly of Strauss's analysis.[38]

Schmitt's opening statement, however, also recalls his concerns in *Political Romanticism* and *Political Theology*, and seeks to delineate a distinct sphere for the political that recognizes it as prior in a temporal – and therefore also a historical – sense, *and* primary in an ordinal as well as a sociological

---

[33] Leo Strauss, Letter to Carl Schmitt, Berlin, September 4, 1932 (in Meier, *Carl Schmitt and Leo Strauss*). Cf. Strauss, "Anmerkungen zu Carl Schmitt, Der Begriff des Politischen."

[34] Strauss, Letter to Carl Schmitt, Berlin, September 4, 1932 (in Meier, *Carl Schmitt and Leo Strauss*, 125).

[35] See Meier, *Carl Schmitt and Leo Strauss*, 129–31.

[36] This despite their often divergent interpretations of Hobbes, as well as Strauss's curious distinction between Hobbes's and Schmitt's states of nature, which is amended in the next paragraph ("Anmerkungen zu Carl Schmitt, Der Begriff des Politischen," 737).

[37] See Strauss, Letter to Carl Schmitt, Berlin, March 13, 1932 (in Meier, *Carl Schmitt and Leo Strauss*, 123); Strauss, Letter to Carl Schmitt, Berlin, July 10, 1933 (*ibid.*, 127). Cf. Strauss, "Quelques remarques sur la science politique de Hobbes"; *The Political Philosophy of Hobbes*.

[38] Günther Krauss, Schmitt's student and assistant, told Meier that Schmitt had said of Strauss's notes: "You've got to read that. [Strauss] saw through me and X-rayed me as nobody else has" (*Carl Schmitt and Leo Strauss*, xvii).

sense.[39] Schmitt's earlier works had addressed the ways in which political romanticism and liberalism had diluted politics, and which are illustrated aptly by the absence of a clear definition of the political.[40] His opening statement thus reveals his intended response on behalf of the political.[41] His task in this respect is to carve out a space for the study of the political wherein it can be studied properly and without the intrusions of other disciplines. It is only fitting that a Hobbesian endeavor should have a Hobbesian basis, and Schmitt paves the way for this undertaking by claiming that the political is prior to the state, much in the way in which Hobbes considers conflict in the state of nature prior to the foundation of the commonwealth. Indeed, in his analysis of Hobbes's political theory, Schmitt points out that fear of the state of nature is the "starting point of Hobbes's construction of the state" and proceeds to identify correctly the process through which the isolated individuals in the state of nature band together to form a commonwealth in their quest for security.[42]

Spheres of human activity are guided by fundamental distinctions that characterize them. Thus, morality is concerned with good and evil, and aesthetics with the beautiful and the ugly. Schmitt's search for a positive definition of the political leads him to conclude that "[t]he specific political distinction to which political actions and motives can be reduced is that between friend and enemy."[43] The independence of the political realm, however, comes from the fact that it cannot be defined through the use of any

[39] Schmitt's concern with the proper study of politics also calls to mind Hobbes's concern with a proper foundation for politics, as well as his statement that civil science is no older than his own book De Cive. Cf. Hobbes, The Elements of Law, Ep. Ded., xvi; On the Citizen, Ep. Ded., §§ 3–12.

[40] In Political Theology, Schmitt notes that "[n]obody seems to have taken the trouble to scrutinize the often-repeated but completely empty phraseology used to denote the highest power by the authors of the concept of sovereignty" (7–8). Towards the end of the same work, he observes "[t]oday nothing is more modern than the onslaught against the political" (65).

[41] See Schmitt, Political Romanticism, esp. 160–62. Cf. Balakrishnan, The Enemy, 105. Balakrishnan also points out that at a time when there were very few German academics working in political science, and perhaps as a result of his having attended Max Weber's lectures, Schmitt became increasingly interested in the emerging discipline, and argues that this interest culminated in "The Concept of the Political" (see Balakrishnan, The Enemy, 101).

[42] Schmitt, "The State as Mechanism in Hobbes & Descartes," 91. Schmitt adds, "[t]he terror of the state of nature drives anguished individuals together; their fear rises to an extreme; a spark of reason (ratio) flashes; and suddenly there stands in front of us a new god" (92).

[43] Schmitt, The Concept of the Political, 26. Schmitt cautions that this definition is not intended to be exhaustive, but rather a criterion, an antithesis meant to characterize distinctly political conditions, in the same way that other distinctions are characteristic of particular realms.

other criterion ("antithesis") or combination of criteria. Where its particular attributes are concerned, Schmitt claims that the distinction between friend and enemy "denotes the utmost degree of intensity of a union or separation, of an association or dissociation."[44] Thus, the enemy need not be evil or ugly, but "he is, nevertheless, the other, the stranger; and it is sufficient for his nature that he is, in a specially intense way, existentially something different and alien, so that in the extreme case conflicts with him are possible."[45] The intensity of these conflicts renders them exceptional, and thereby places them outside the realm of that which can be addressed by preestablished formal norms. It is for this very reason that they cannot be left to the normativist, but must be dealt with by the decisionist, since only "the actual participants can correctly recognize, understand, and judge the concrete situation and settle the extreme case of conflict."[46] In a phrase that could have been taken from Hobbes, Schmitt argues that only the participant is "in a position to judge whether the adversary intends to negate his opponent's way of life and therefore must be repulsed or fought in order to preserve one's own form of existence."[47] Nor is Schmitt's claim as extreme as one might think at first. The law in most cases recognizes claims of self-defense as legitimate so long as the person invoking this defense believed that his life was in danger.[48]

EXCEPTION AND DECISION

Schmitt notes that recent and contemporary linguistic usage defines the state as the political status of a territorially enclosed organized people, but finds this definition tautological and lacking a distinctly political character, which is

---

[44] Schmitt, *The Concept of the Political*, 26. Schmitt's emphasis on the degree of intensity here (26–27) is crucial for his argument but also for the history of this idea in the period under examination. Morgenthau claims that Schmitt's emphasis on intensity is one of the changes that Schmitt made in response to Morgenthau's criticisms, albeit one that he did not acknowledge (Morgenthau, "Fragment of an Intellectual Biography," 15–16). It should be noted, however, that the idea, as expressed in the 1932 edition of *The Concept of the Political*, is also present in Schmitt's first formulation, in the 1927 essay that inspired Morgenthau's thesis (Schmitt, "Der Begriff des Politischen," 4). For a more detailed analysis of the intellectual relationship between the two men, see below.
[45] Schmitt, *The Concept of the Political*, 27.
[46] Schmitt, *The Concept of the Political*, 27. Cf. *Political Theology*, 3.
[47] Schmitt, *The Concept of the Political*, 27. Cf. Hobbes, *On the Citizen*, I.9.
[48] For the sake of comparison, consider Hobbes's position, in *De Cive*: "By natural law one is oneself the judge whether the means he is to use and the action he intends to take are necessary to the preservation of his life and limbs or not" (*On the Citizen*, I.9).

that which makes a state a state.[49] Schmitt had laid the foundation for a proper definition of the state in the equally famous and enigmatic first sentence of *Political Theology*, where he argued that "[s]overeign is he who decides the exception."[50] In *The Concept of the Political*, he returns to that idea, and declares that out of all the possible conditions of a people a state is that which is the ultimate authority in the decisive case.[51] With this preliminary definition of the state as the bearer of the decisive authority, Schmitt turns his attention to the political and notes that it too seldom receives a clear definition.[52] Most of the time the word is used in a negative sense, opposed to another concept, such as economics, morality, law, or the state, but these juxtapositions do little to elucidate its meaning.[53] Schmitt finds an abundance of references to the political in juristic literature, but those are unsatisfactory in their turn because they presuppose "a stable state within whose framework they operate."[54] Such stability, moreover, is not characteristic of the conditions that Schmitt is most concerned with and which render meaningful the real definitions of the political and of the state, namely exceptional circumstances.[55]

In the context of a constitutional state, such circumstances arise most notably when there are gaps in the law.[56] German jurists had struggled to interpret the precise meaning of Article 48 of the Weimar Constitution, which dealt with emergency powers, and to determine its implications.[57] Schmitt was an active participant in this debate, and had published a number of articles on the subject that culminated in the more systematic *Political Theology* (1922). Therein, Schmitt defines the exception as a case "not codified

---

[49] Schmitt, *Der Begriff des Politischen* (1963), 20.

[50] Schmitt, *Political Theology*, 5. Cf. ibid., 33–35; *The Concept of the Political*, 38, 42–45.

[51] Schmitt, *The Concept of the Political*, 19–20.

[52] Schmitt, *The Concept of the Political*, 20.

[53] Schmitt considers negative definitions one of the consequences of romanticism (cf. *Political Romanticism*, 5–7). It is interesting in this context that Schmitt's own definition does not manage to escape reliance on the negative completely, as it is based on the opposition of friends to enemies.

[54] Schmitt, *The Concept of the Political*, 21. Cf. *The Nomos of the Earth*, 176–77.

[55] Schmitt notes, "Hobbes himself had experienced this truth [The *protego ergo obligo* is the *cogito ergo sum* of the state] in the terrible times of civil war, because then all legitimate and normative illusions with which men like to deceive themselves regarding political realities in periods of untroubled security vanish" (*The Concept of the Political*, 52).

[56] Balakrishnan explains, "[a] gap is a grey area in the Constitution, a point at which the Constitution avoids specifying how a particular conflict should be resolved, and leaves it open to interpretation, which in the absence of a norm invariably becomes political" (*The Enemy*, 46).

[57] For a translation of the relevant parts of Article 48 of the Weimar Constitution, see Balakrishnan, *The Enemy*, 31.

in the existing legal order," one that "can at best be characterized as a case of extreme peril, a danger to the existence of the state, or the like."[58] Contrary to conventional wisdom, Schmitt argues, it is decisions under such circumstances that are decisions properly speaking. It is not the norm, but the exception that defines the rule, because "the seriousness of an insight goes deeper than the clear generalizations inferred from what ordinarily repeats itself" and thus "[t]he decision on the exception is a decision in the true sense of the word."[59] The exception assumes particular significance where the identity of the political association is concerned. As Hobbes points out in the preface to *De Cive*, although it is clear that most men are not evil, a few are, but it is impossible to know who these men are. Thus, even though these men are the exception, they nevertheless define the rule by guiding the way in which a political association determines its friends and enemies and makes arrangements for its security.[60]

Schmitt notes that not every extraordinary situation is an exception, since the existing law may prescribe what is to be done. Rather, an exception is characterized by "principally unlimited authority, which means the suspension of the entire existing order," except for the identity of the institutions and offices in charge of the suspension.[61] This type of situation reveals the true relationship of the law to the state, as the former "recedes" and the latter maintains order "even if it is not of the ordinary kind."[62] This suspension of the law in extraordinary circumstances, Schmitt argues, takes place on the basis of the state's right of self-preservation.[63] From this it follows that as the authority that decides the exception, the state is also the determinant of what is normal, and therefore of what is subject to the law. In short, the sum of those decisions is a reflection of the monopoly to decide, and it is this power, rather than the power to coerce, Schmitt argues, that renders the state sovereign.[64]

If Schmitt's conception of sovereignty too is beginning to sound very much like Hobbes's, there is good reason. Even though he credits Bodin

---

[58] Schmitt, *Political Theology*, 6.

[59] Schmitt, *Political Theology*, 15, 6. Schmitt argues: "The exception is more interesting than the rule. The rule proves nothing; the exception proves everything: It confirms not only the rule but also its existence, which derives only from the exception" (*Political Theology*, 15). According to Shklar, "[t]o a historian the most interesting thing about decisions is the fact that everyone is talking about them" ("Decisionism," 3).

[60] See Hobbes, *On the Citizen*, Pref., §§ 11–12.

[61] Schmitt, *Political Theology*, 12. Cf. Bendersky, *Carl Schmitt*, 76.

[62] Schmitt, *Political Theology*, 12.

[63] Schmitt, *Political Theology*, 12.

[64] Schmitt, *Political Theology*, 13.

with the first modern theory of the state that takes account of the importance of the exception, Schmitt considers Hobbes at least as important for
his insistence that *autoritas, non veritas facit legem.*[65] In *Political Romanticism*,
Hobbes makes a reluctant debut in Schmitt's thought as the very antithesis
of the Romantics whom Schmitt criticizes for suspending decision. Already
here, Schmitt seems to be aware of what he would later term Hobbes's
"decisionism": "Lyrically and sentimentally, [the romantic feeling for life
and nature] perceives the systematic rationalism of the political philosophy
of Hobbes as particularly hostile."[66] In his subsequent study of dictatorship,
Schmitt juxtaposes Hobbes to Grotius, and argues that whereas in the latter's
theory there exists a law with a particular content prior to the state, for
Hobbes

> prior to the state and outside the state there is no law (*Recht*), and the value of
> the state lies precisely therein, in that it makes the law (*Recht*), in that it decides
> the controversy surrounding the law (*Recht*). Therefore, the contrast between right
> (*Recht*) and wrong (*Unrecht*) exists only within the state and through the state. The
> state can do no wrong (*Unrecht*) because any regulation can only thus become law
> (*Recht*), namely by being included into an instruction of the state, rather than by
> corresponding to some ideal notion of justice. Autoritas, non Veritas facit Legem.
> (Leviathan, ch. 26)[67]

It is thus not surprising that in *Political Theology*, which brings together his
concerns with sovereignty and the question *quis judicabit*, Schmitt returns
to Hobbes, a juristic thinker who was sensitive to the "specific reality of
legal life inherent in the legal form," for which "[w]hat matters [...] is
who decides."[68] For Schmitt, the decisionist's response to that question is
superior to the normativist's, because the latter "thinks in terms of imper-
sonal rules," whereas the former "implements the good law of the correctly

---

[65] Schmitt, *Political Theology*, 33. Cf. *ibid.*, 34–5; Hobbes, *Leviathan*, XXVI, esp. §§ 1–10.
According to Schmitt, Bodin is rightly hailed as the initiator of the theory of the modern state, but for the wrong reason; those who cite him usually refer to this claim that
"sovereignty is the absolute and perpetual power of a republic," but his real contribution
lies in having realized the significance of the emergency (*Political Theology*, 8). Cf. Bodin,
The Six Bookes of a Commonweale, I.x, 153–82.

[66] Schmitt, *Political Romanticism*, 56.

[67] Schmitt, *Die Diktatur*, 22. Cf. Hobbes, *Leviathan*, XXVI, esp. §§ 1–10; Schmitt, *The Crisis
of Parliamentary Democracy*, 43; *Political Theology*, 52; *Verfassungslehre*, 140. In a notebook
entry of March 5, 1948, Schmitt argues that the abolition of the difference between enemy
and criminal destroys not only the law (*Recht*) but also justice as a concrete order (*Ordo*)
(*Glossarium*, 109).

[68] Schmitt, *Political Theology*, 34; *Verfassungslehre*, 49.

recognized political situation by means of a personal decision."[69] As we shall see, this crucial distinction and his preference for decisionism mark the point of departure from which Schmitt defines the sphere of the political as that which concerns the designation of friends and enemies.[70]

REALISM

Concerned as he is with the clear definition of the concept of the political, Schmitt is at pains to avoid misconceptions. To that end, he stresses that the existential threat posed by the enemy is not meant in a metaphorical sense, but must be taken seriously as a distinct possibility.[71] Schmitt's concern here is not with highfalutin abstractions, but rather with what Machiavelli refers to as "the effectual truth": a "philosophy of concrete life" must recognize the inevitability of exceptional circumstances and must therefore not shy away from the exception, but rather be "interested in it to the highest degree."[72] In *Political Theology*, Schmitt had expressed concern for reality and an aversion to normative considerations. In *The Concept of the Political*, he repeats that he is not interested in abstractions and normative ideals, and argues that even though one might find the friend–enemy distinction barbaric or undesirable, it is nevertheless a fact of life that "nations continue to group themselves according to the friend and enemy antithesis, that the distinction still remains actual today, and that this is an ever present possibility for every people existing in the political sphere."[73] Schmitt's insistence on the possibility of conflict reveals, once again, the extent of his indebtedness to Hobbes, who likens the state of war to an inclination to foul weather and calls attention to the uncertainty involved in judging between good and evil

---

[69] Schmitt, *Political Theology*, 3. This comparison of the normativist and decisionist ways of juristic thinking takes place in the context of Schmitt's introduction to the second edition of *Political Theology* (1934). There, for reasons that have as much to do with timing as with the substance of his argument, Schmitt amends the earlier version (1922) by adding a third type of thinking that he calls "institutional" and attributes to the influence of Maurice Hauriou. The political reason for the addition seems to be that it introduced the political movement as an actor and was thereby able to account for the increasingly powerful role of the Nazi party in the aftermath of Hitler's rise to power. Schmitt expressed this new theory of state, movement, and people in a short work entitled *Staat, Bewegung, Volk*. Cf. Balakrishnan, *The Enemy*, 184–85; Schwab, *The Challenge of the Exception*, 108–13.

[70] Cf. Schwab, *The Challenge of the Exception*, 115.

[71] Compare Schmitt, *Political Theology*, 15.

[72] Schmitt, *Political Theology*, 15. Cf. Machiavelli, *The Prince*, Chapter XV, 61.

[73] Schmitt, *The Concept of the Political*, 28. Schmitt's emphatic rejection of a normative dimension of conflict per se is an important and often overlooked part of his argument.

men.[74] For Schmitt, those, like the political romantics, who are repulsed by the friend–enemy distinction may try to translate a political situation into something else, such as an economic dispute, but such attempts are misguided and "irrelevant"; to the extent that the negation of one's existence is possible, the other is the enemy and the distinction is a political one.[75]

Schmitt then points out that not every opponent or competitor is an enemy, and explains further that an enemy is "not the private adversary whom one hates," but rather that he

exists only when, at least potentially, one fighting collectivity of people confronts a similar collectivity. The enemy is solely the public enemy, because everything that has a relationship to such a collectivity of men, particularly to a whole nation, becomes public by virtue of such a relationship. The enemy is *hostis*, not *inimicus* in the broader sense; πολέμιος not ἐχθρός.[76]

The distinction between private and public here is crucial for Schmitt's theory. It is also yet another indication of his agreement with Hobbes, since the designation of enemies for both thinkers is a public matter, a determination to be made by the sovereign, to whom private individuals have surrendered their right to judge.[77] Moreover, the enemy in Schmitt's passage poses a threat to a collectivity of men, and his claim that such a relationship of enmity can never exist between two individuals seems to rest on an acceptance of a world with states as a condition from which there is no retreat.[78] Thus, private threats to one's existence within the confines of a state do not constitute a political matter, but rather one of policing and application of existing norms.[79] As Kennedy observes, Schmitt's claim that the friend–enemy

[74] Hobbes, *Leviathan*, XIII § 8; *On the Citizen*, Pref., § 12.

[75] Schmitt, *The Concept of the Political*, 28.

[76] Schmitt, *The Concept of the Political*, 28. Schmitt provides the Greek and Latin terms, as well as a series of examples, because German and other languages do not have different words to capture the difference between private and public enmity (28–29). On the Latin terms, see Cicero, *On Duties*, I.xii; Varro, *On the Latin Language*, V.3. Cf. *The Concept of the Political*, 51; Simmel, "Conflict," 39, 48–49.

[77] See, e.g., Hobbes, *Leviathan*, XXVIII § 13.

[78] For Schmitt, this is characteristic of individualism, whose "negation of the political [. . .] leads necessarily to a political practice of distrust toward all conceivable political forces and forms of state and government, but never produces on its own a positive theory of state, government, and politics" (*The Concept of the Political*, 70). This negation of real political forces paves the way for the liberal misconception that private and domestic disputes and antagonisms are political (cf. *The Concept of the Political*, 30–32, 46–47, 70).

[79] Schmitt argues "[t]he endeavor of a normal state consists above all in assuring total peace within the state and its territory" (Schmitt, *The Concept of the Political*, 46). This interpretation is also in accordance with Schmitt's emphasis in *The Concept of the Political* (30–32)

distinction is not a private matter is the "most important aspect" of his argument for a theory of the state, because of the challenge that it poses for "the existence of the political unity of the people."[80] Schmitt is keenly aware of the fact that a challenge to the unity of a people is also the means by which that unity is affirmed. Inclusion and exclusion are two sides of the same coin, and the formation of a group entails by definition the formation of another, that including all those excluded from the first.[81] After all, it is the exception that defines the rule, and no situation is more exceptional than one in which there is a challenge to the existence of a group.[82] In keeping with the teachings of Bodin, Schmitt recognizes that the "intensification of internal antagonisms has the effect of weakening the common identity vis-à-vis another state."[83] Conversely, an external threat that focuses on what domestic antagonists have in common challenges the very being of the association, and as such has to take precedence: "*If a political entity exists at all*, the right of vendettas between families or kinsfolk would have to be suspended at least temporarily during a war."[84]

These mentions of war and external threat to a collectivity of men are indicative of why Schmitt is so concerned with the enemy. It is because "to the enemy belongs the ever present possibility of combat," albeit combat understood in its existential sense and not in a watered-down version, such as competition or controversy.[85] Once again, the emphasis is on *real* danger:

The friend, enemy, and combat concepts receive their real meaning precisely because they refer to the real possibility of physical killing. War follows from enmity. War is the existential negation of the enemy. It is the most extreme consequence of enmity. It does not have to be common, normal, something ideal, or desirable. But it must

on the distinction between domestic disputes and political situations. Schmitt illustrates this point further when he contrasts a death sentence and a *hostis* declaration (*The Concept of the Political*, 47).

[80] Kennedy, "Hostis *Not* Inimicus," 101. Rumpf argues that Schmitt's conception of the enemy as public has its origin in legal thought, within which no conception of the enemy can have a private dimension (*Carl Schmitt und Thomas Hobbes*, 90).

[81] Schmitt, *The Concept of the Political*, 53.

[82] Schmitt, *Political Theology*, 6, 15; cf. *The Concept of the Political*, 35.

[83] Schmitt, *The Concept of the Political*, 32. Cf. Sallust, *The War with Jugurtha*, XLI; Bodin, *The Six Bookes of a Commonweale*, I.ix. Schmitt's remark here occurs in the context of his explanation of the differences between domestic and external antagonisms and the ways in which the latter can become political, i.e., escalate into civil war.

[84] Schmitt, *The Concept of the Political*, 47, emphasis added. Cf. McCormick, *Carl Schmitt's Critique of Liberalism*, 257.

[85] Schmitt, *The Concept of the Political*, 32–33.

nevertheless remain a real possibility for as long as the concept of the enemy remains valid.[86]

Schmitt's insistence on the reality of the threat goes hand in hand with his aversion for normativity. He cautions that attention to the reality of intense enmity does not mean a celebration of war, and certainly not an idealization of it. In short, he is not trying to replace others' ideals with war, but merely seeks to accord it its proper status *qua* "real possibility."[87] This realization is the reason why Schmitt is so fond of Machiavelli and Hobbes; they are "always aware of the concrete possibility of an enemy." It is also the reason why they are so unpopular: "Their realism can frighten men in need of security."[88] Despite its somber message, this realism captures the essence of a political community, since it sees it in its true setting and for what it really is, namely the product of negative association: "The political entity presupposes the real existence of an enemy and therefore coexistence with another political entity."[89] Schmitt sees Hobbes's focus on reality as one of the most striking features of his thought, a contribution that was eventually overshadowed by the attempts of idealists, liberals, and positivists to dilute the essence of the political.[90] In this diagnosis, as well as in his proposed remedies, Schmitt foreshadows a man who was slightly younger than he, and whose name has become synonymous with political realism in the twentieth century, Hans J. Morgenthau.

Morgenthau was born in Coburg, in 1904. During the early years of his life, he had little reason to feel ill at ease in that small German town, and Frei recounts the enthusiasm with which the ten-year-old Morgenthau saw the German troops depart for the Great War, and continued to follow their progress.[91] Unlike Schmitt, who at the time was a young man and by all accounts largely indifferent to the war, Morgenthau displayed the interest one might expect of a boy his age. Soon after the war, however, the combination of the German defeat and the ensuing economic hardship upset the peace

---

[86] Schmitt, *The Concept of the Political*, 33.

[87] Schmitt, *The Concept of the Political*, 33; cf. 48–49. Despite Schmitt's explicit statement that his observation does not constitute a celebration or endorsement of war, commentators often attribute normative intentions to him. For a corrective see Andreas Kalyvas, "Who's Afraid of Carl Schmitt?," esp. 94–95.

[88] Schmitt, *The Concept of the Political*, 65.

[89] Schmitt, *The Concept of the Political*, 53. Schmitt adds, "[a]s long as a state exists, there will thus always be in the world more than just one state." Cf. Kennedy, *Constitutional Failure*, 46.

[90] Schmitt, *Political Theology*, 34.

[91] Frei, *Hans J. Morgenthau*, 15–16.

and tranquility of Coburg and awakened Morgenthau to a new reality. As a high school student, he became the target of his schoolmates' anti-Semitic taunts, and – like Schmitt in Plettenberg before him, albeit for different reasons – he began to feel like an outsider.[92] In 1923, Morgenthau went on to university, first to study philosophy and then law. Morgenthau's foray into the study of law and politics began at a time when the fight against legal positivism was raging, and Morgenthau became actively interested in it.[93] It was during this early period that Schmitt's and Morgenthau's paths crossed.

CAT AND MOUSE

To the reader of *The Concept of the Political* and *Politics among Nations*, the similarity between some of the key theoretical elements of the two works is striking. As a result, the intellectual relationship between Schmitt and Morgenthau has not gone unnoticed.[94] Frei reports that Morgenthau's diaries between 1923 and 1930 contain a "carefully recorded list of his leisure-time reading" with numerous entries, but notes that "[o]nly a few authors [. . .] are represented by several, by three or, at most, four book titles: Niccolò Machiavelli, Arthur Schopenhauer, Jacob Burckhardt, Georg Simmel, Max Weber, Thomas Mann, and Carl Schmitt."[95] Schmitt's appearances in Morgenthau's writings tell their own, peculiar story. Morgenthau's doctoral dissertation, completed towards the end of 1928, shows the first signs of Schmitt's influence. Originally entitled "The International Judicial Function and the Concept of Politics," the thesis met with his advisors' approval, but Morgenthau's supervisor objected to the presence of the term *politics* in a doctoral thesis in law, and so the final title was changed to "The International Judicial Function: Its Nature and Limits."[96] Although the published version of the

---

[92] Frei, *Hans J. Morgenthau*, 16–22; cf. Morgenthau, "Fragment of an Intellectual Biography," 1–4. Indicative of the situation in Coburg is the fact that the Nazis won there a full eleven years before their 1933 victory in the national elections (Frei, *Hans J. Morgenthau*, 17).

[93] Schmitt had already published *Political Romanticism*, *Die Diktatur*, and *Political Theology* by this time. On Morgenthau's views towards positivism and its opponents, see Frei, *Hans J. Morgenthau*, 115–20.

[94] See, e.g., Honig, "Totalitarianism and Realism"; Pichler, "Godfathers of 'Truth'"; Scheuerman, *Carl Schmitt*, 225–51; Frei, *Hans J. Morgenthau*, 160–63; Koskenniemi, *The Gentle Civilizer of Nations*, 413–509; Wolin, "Reasons of State, States of Reason"; Bendersky, "The Definite and the Dubious"; Haslam, *No Virtue like Necessity*, 190–91; Williams, "Words, Images, Enemies."

[95] Frei, *Hans J. Morgenthau*, 108.

[96] See Morgenthau, "Fragment of an Intellectual Biography," 9; Frei, *Hans J. Morgenthau*, 39.

dissertation cites only one work by Schmitt, *Die Kernfrage des Völkerbundes*, the magnitude of Schmitt's influence on Morgenthau's thought is clear, even in the absence of any mention of the political in its revised title. Morgenthau's first work is concerned with the relationship between law and politics, and the question of the concept of the political occupies a central place in his examination, even though he does not cite Schmitt's 1927 essay.[97] "The Concept of the Political" is, however, cited in a 1933 revision of this work, wherein Morgenthau attacks Schmitt openly and offers his own account of the distinctiveness of the political. Schmitt's name then disappears altogether from Morgenthau's writings until it resurfaces much later, in "Fragment of an Intellectual Biography."[98]

Morgenthau's autobiographical essay is a mere sixteen pages, and yet he devotes almost two of these to Schmitt. Therein, Morgenthau considers it "inevitable" that he would have been influenced by Schmitt, whom he calls the German thinker with the greatest intellectual ability during the interwar years, but also notes his notorious "servility" to the Nazis and lack of principle.[99] Morgenthau remembers "The Concept of the Political" as having had "a sensational impact upon German political thinking," and reveals:

I conceived my doctor's thesis partly as a reply to that book [*sic*] although, as indicated above, the final title did not show it. But Schmitt recognized it immediately for what it was and wrote me a very complimentary letter, one of the few that I received on the publication of this, my first book. I was understandably overjoyed and asked Schmitt for an interview. I looked forward to the visit with enthusiastic anticipation.[100]

---

[97] See Morgenthau, *Die internationale Rechtspflege, ihr Wesen und ihre Grenzen*, esp. 59–72.

[98] The 1933 revision of Morgenthau's doctoral thesis and of the subsequent *Die internationale Rechtspflege, ihr Wesen und ihre Grenzen* is entitled *La notion du 'politique' et la théorie des différends internationaux*, which bears the author's name as "Morgenthan" throughout, presumably as a result of a typographical error. A fourth version can be found in *Politics among Nations*, part 6. Cf. Honig, "Totalitarianism and Realism," 286, note 13.

[99] Morgenthau, "Fragment of an Intellectual Biography," 15. In his own work, Morgenthau considers the refutation of Schmitt's concept of the political an essential prerequisite for the construction of his theory (*La notion du 'politique' et la théorie des différends internationaux*, 61), and cites Schmitt's considerable influence on public opinion (45).

[100] Morgenthau, "Fragment of an Intellectual Biography," 15. As reproduced in "Fragment of an Intellectual Biography", Morgenthau's account contains certain errors. For example, Morgenthau claims, "Schmitt had published in 1921 [*sic*] a short book [*sic*] called *The Concept of Politics* [. . .]" (*ibid.*). Schmitt's book was published in 1932 and reissued in 1933. The article on which the book was based was published in 1927. Thus, given that Morgenthau's thesis was published in 1929, in the passage quoted above, Morgenthau is confusing Schmitt's 1927 article with the eponymous book. Cf. Honig, "Totalitarianism and Realism," 297.

Morgenthau remembers the encounter as a public relations stunt on Schmitt's part, to impress Karl Bilfinger, a professor of public law who was also present, and sums it up as "a charade – cold, contrived, dishonest, and worthwhile only in revealing in capsule form the character of that brilliant, inventive scholar." Morgenthau concludes his references to Schmitt with the following bitter remark: "Yet Schmitt paid me still a further compliment. He changed the second edition [sic] of his *Concept of Politics* in the light of the new proposi- tions of my thesis without lifting the veil of anonymity from their author."[101] Morgenthau's brief account is the only source of evidence on the interac- tion between the two men. Researchers have been unable to find the letter mentioned by Morgenthau or any other correspondence between the two, although there is some evidence to back Morgenthau's claims: Schmitt's library contains two copies of Morgenthau's *Die internationale Rechtspflege, ihr Wesen und ihre Grenzen*, one of which is annotated.[102] In and of itself, the presence of these copies is perhaps not suspicious, but the publication of Morgenthau's book, in 1929, coincided with the slight revision of Schmitt's argument regarding the concept of the political, first in a short essay on Hugo Preuss, wherein Schmitt emphasizes the importance of the intensity of the political relationship far more than he had done in the 1927 version of "The Concept of the Political," then in Schmitt's 1931 work *Der Hüter der Verfassung*, and finally in the 1932 edition of *The Concept of the Political*.[103]

Morgenthau's disagreement with Schmitt's early formulation of the con- cept of the political is twofold. Despite the fact that he too is concerned

---

[101] Morgenthau, "Fragment of an Intellectual Biography," 16. Morgenthau seems to be refer- ring here to the differences between Schmitt's 1927 article and 1932 book of the same title.

[102] On the absence of any correspondence in the papers of either, see Scheuerman, *Carl Schmitt*, 230. Frei, who has carried out extensive research on the Morgenthau papers, mentions the correspondence but cites no source other than Morgenthau's "Fragment of an Intellectual Biography" (*Hans J. Morgenthau*, 40, 160). According to Laak and Villinger, Schmitt's library contained two copies of *Die internationale Rechtspflege: ihr Wesen und ihre Grenzen*, one printed in Frankfurt am Main (1929) and the other in Leipzig (1929); the second is annotated. Schmitt's library contained a third work of Morgenthau's, a copy of a part of "Théorie des différends internationaux" (Paris, 1939), presumably part of his *La notion du 'politique' et la théorie des différends internationaux* (see Laak & Villinger, *Nachlass Carl Schmitt*, 465).

[103] See Schmitt, *Hugo Preuss*, esp. note 1, on p. 26; cf. *Der Hüter der Verfassung*, 111. Cf. Frye, "Carl Schmitt's Concept of the Political", 819. Morgenthau himself tracks Schmitt's changes in *La notion du 'politique' et la théorie des différends internationaux* (35, note 2). Bendersky notes rightly that the concept of intensity was already present in the 1927 article, and that "[w]hat appears in the 1932 edition is an elaboration of that original idea" ("The Definite and the Dubious," 44).

about the intrusion of other spheres of activity and interpretation into the province of the political, he finds that Schmitt goes too far in separating the political from other domains.[104] Morgenthau's rival claim that the political is not as distinct from other spheres, as Schmitt maintains, stems from his related position according to which the political is a matter of degree, rather than an absolute quality. Morgenthau thus compares it to heat, which is not an absolute property but may be present, to a greater or lesser degree, in any object.[105] The political for Morgenthau is thus a matter of intensity.[106] It is precisely on the importance of intensity for the political that Schmitt seems to have been most influenced by Morgenthau's work. As Morgenthau and several commentators since have pointed out, intensity becomes prominent in the 1932 version of *The Concept of the Political*, and as was shown above, Schmitt came to place great emphasis on the intensity of the existential threat that the enemy poses. Morgenthau thus seems justifiably frustrated by Schmitt's refusal to cite him as the source of this important correction, but there is another side to this story.

Those who have studied the intellectual relationship between the two men have relied too heavily on Morgenthau's assessment in his autobiographical essay, which is the only direct source of information on the matter. One should not forget, however, that by the time of the composition of this essay, Schmitt had already become notorious, in Germany and beyond, for his association with the Nazis, and that Morgenthau, who had suffered considerable personal and professional difficulties in the 1930s and 1940s, and therefore had good reason to feel a grudge, would not have wanted any association with him.[107] Morgenthau, who was a Jewish intellectual and a conservative, would almost certainly not have wanted to remind his readers of his indebtedness to the ideas of a prominent Nazi sympathizer. This hypothesis is supported by the fact that while the intellectual influence of Schmitt never disappears from Morgenthau's postwar writings, explicit references to Schmitt and his works do.[108] Where Morgenthau's charge against Schmitt for having appropriated his idea regarding intensity is concerned, one should bear in mind that although Morgenthau − by his own admission − is heavily indebted to

[104] Morgenthau, *La notion du 'politique,'* 57–60.
[105] Morgenthau, *Die internationale Rechtspflege*, 69–71; cf. *La notion du 'politique,'* 34–37.
[106] Morgenthau, *Die internationale Rechtspflege*, 69–71; cf. *La notion du 'politique,'* 34–35.
[107] See Scheuerman, *Carl Schmitt*, 238 and Pichler, "The Godfathers of 'Truth,'" 192, note 36, but cf. Bendersky, "The Definite and the Dubious," 45.
[108] See esp. Morgenthau, *Scientific Man vs. Power Politics* and *Politics among Nations*.

Schmitt's essay, he never cites it in *Die internationale Rechtspflege*, nor does he acknowledge Schmitt in the sections in which he discusses the concept of the political.[109] More importantly, however, the extent of the accusation is itself suspect. Although commentators – aided, no doubt, by Schmitt's notoriety – mostly accept Morgenthau's version of events unchallenged, and despite the fact that Schmitt did increase the amount of emphasis on the importance of intensity for the concept of the political, it is nevertheless the case that the 1927 version of the essay already contains the core of that idea.[110] Schmitt explains therein that the enemy need not be morally evil, aesthetically ugly, or economically unprofitable, but that he is "in a particularly intense sense, existentially something other and foreign."[111] Where the relationship of the political to other spheres of human activity is concerned, Schmitt argues that

The political can draw its power from the most diverse areas of human life, from religious, economic, and moral antitheses. But the real friend–enemy grouping is in itself so strong and decisive that the non-political antithesis, in the moment in which this grouping begins, resets its former criteria and subjects itself to the wholly new conditions and consequences of the political.[112]

At the very least, then, the seeds for the ideas that Morgenthau accuses Schmitt of having appropriated from his thesis are present in Schmitt's conception of the political from the outset.

Morgenthau's stance, in *La notion du "politique"* vis-à-vis Schmitt's theory of the political as the distinction between friends and enemies provides an interesting entry point into Morgenthau's own theory, precisely because it captures his uneasy relationship with some of his greatest sources of inspiration, but also because it provides a key to understanding the rest of his theory, which is more familiar and was developed in his American writings. One of the main differences between the European and the American Morgenthau is that whereas in his earlier writings he is relatively silent about some of the fundamental aspects of his theory, such as his view of human nature, he is quite

---

[109] See Morgenthau, *Die internationale Rechtspflege*, § 7, 59–72. Koskenniemi lists other instances in which the roles are reversed and Morgenthau engages in the same practice that he accuses Schmitt of in his autobiographical essay (*The Gentle Civilizer of Nations*, 438).

[110] Frei (*Hans J. Morgenthau*, 160) and Koskenniemi (*The Gentle Civilizer of Nations*, 436), among others, accept Morgenthau's version of the story; the latter claims mistakenly, "this idea of politics as an *intensity* concept did not exist in the earlier edition of [Schmitt's] book" (436).

[111] Schmitt, "Der Begriff des Politischen," 4. Cf. *The Concept of the Political*, 27.

[112] Schmitt, "Der Begriff des Politischen," 10.

explicit in the later ones. There, one sees a basic agreement with Schmitt, and this signals that Morgenthau's earlier objections were more about status and appearances than about a substantive intellectual divide. Frei argues that despite the fact that his name figures only very rarely in Morgenthau's writings, Nietzsche should be considered one of the main hidden influences on Morgenthau.[113] Although there is some evidence that Nietzsche's influence on Morgenthau has been underestimated, the juxtaposition of Morgenthau's earlier and later writings makes it clear that two other thinkers who also appear only infrequently, Carl Schmitt and Thomas Hobbes, are far more important than Nietzsche for understanding Morgenthau's political theory.[114]

Morgenthau engages in a linguistic and logical examination of the concept of the political as defined by Schmitt, and concludes that the friend–enemy distinction does not correspond to equivalent central distinctions in other spheres, such as that between good and bad in the moral realm. For Morgenthau, the friend–enemy distinction is "radically different."[115] Whereas, he argues, we can say that the pious man has moral value and that the sinner does not, there is no equivalent meaningful sense in which one can claim that the enemy does not have political value. Yet, it is unclear to what extent this evaluation of the epistemological status of the friend–enemy distinction is relevant to Schmitt's concept of the political, and it is doubtful that it constitutes a fatal criticism. For example, Schmitt never claims or implies that the enemy is devoid of political value. If anything, the enemy is even more important than the friend, since it is the exception that defines sovereignty and thereby gives meaning to the actors and their struggles, and

---

[113] Frei, *Hans J. Morgenthau*, esp. 98–113. Cf. Wolin, "Reasons of State, States of Reason," 55–56.

[114] Schmitt's influence is apparent throughout Morgenthau's writings, but one should also bear in mind the personal side of the story when attempting to understand the intellectual relationship between the two. By 1933, when *The Concept of the Political* had appeared in its revised form and Schmitt was at the height of his powers, Morgenthau had begun to experience considerable difficulties. He had had to flee Germany and seek employment abroad. For him, this was a time of hardship and uncertainty. Morgenthau would no doubt have been grateful for a genuine acknowledgment from Schmitt, but he never received the kind of help that he had hoped for. Under these circumstances, it is understandable that whatever disagreements Morgenthau may have had with Schmitt on the nature of the political would have become amplified. On the Hobbesian character of Morgenthau's theory, see Algosaibi, "The Theory of International Relations," 229; Hoffmann, "The Limits of 'Realism,'" 656–58; Wight, "Review of *Dilemmas of Politics*," 199–200, as well as Morgenthau's response ("Correspondence: Dilemmas of Politics," 502) and Wight's rejoinder (*ibid.*); Haslam, *No Virtue like Necessity*, 195; Bendersky, "The Definite and the Dubious," 44.

[115] Morgenthau, *La notion du 'politique,'* 52.

as we have seen, the exception is the domain of the enemy.[116] Morgenthau objects to the fact that Schmitt attributes to the enemy a particular standing in political matters, and claims, rather, that friends and enemies are designated on the basis of their usefulness in the achievement of one's political goals. Thus, a friend is one who helps or does not impede, whereas an enemy is one who stands in one's way.[117] To the extent that Schmitt's use of the terms *friend* and *enemy* is intended to correspond to their meanings in ordinary parlance, Morgenthau's criticism may be correct. Indeed, Schmitt's emphasis on reality and his linguistic analysis of the real content of the term *enemy* seem to point in this direction.[118] Nevertheless, it is also true that Morgenthau's criticism ignores the fact that Schmitt attributes to the enemy the property of a real existential threat, which is a characteristic that does distinguish, in a fundamental sense, the one who possesses it from everyone else who does not.

After a series of twists and turns, Morgenthau retreats from his more extreme criticisms and concludes his assessment of Schmitt's concept of the political with a more modest claim. He explains that he "did not at all intend to contest the importance of the friend–enemy relationship for the determination of the content of the domain of the political."[119] Rather, he claims, he sought to establish "only that the determination of Schmitt's fundamental categories for the genre is not, scientifically, of any great value for the definition of the content of the political and its delimitation from other domains of value, and, moreover, that the distinction between friend and enemy is neither a fundamental distinction of this genre, nor one of its derivatives."[120] Morgenthau's choice to criticize Schmitt's concept for its lack of scientific value is quite interesting, since he and Schmitt eventually turned out to be on the same side on that issue as well.

---

[116] Morgenthau's argument here is also contradicted by his subsequent claim that "[m]oreover, the distinction between friend and enemy in the political realm does not have an absolute character [...] it is not given once and for all" (*La notion du 'politique,'* 59). Recall that for Schmitt the designation of the enemy occurs irrespective of moral, aesthetic, or other differences, and only at the time when another poses an existential threat. See also, Schmitt, *The Concept of the Political*, 53.

[117] See, e.g., Morgenthau, *La notion du 'politique,'* 54–55, 57–58. Morgenthau proposes that one means by "political" or "of political value" that which is of value for the realization of a political goal. As the presence of the word "political" in both the term to be defined and the definition shows, however, this conception borders on the tautological and does not contribute to an explanation of the ways in which the political is a distinct sphere of activity (*La notion du 'politique,'* 57–58).

[118] See Schmitt, *The Concept of the Political*, 28–29.

[119] Morgenthau, *La notion du 'politique,'* 60.

[120] Morgenthau, *La notion du 'politique,'* 60.

IN AMERICA

In purpose and style, Morgenthau's first major American work, *Scientific Man vs. Power Politics*, is strikingly reminiscent of Schmitt's *Political Romanticism*. Where Schmitt had traced the source of the political decline of his age to the inability of the romantics to decide, Morgenthau attacks "scientific man," the descendant and heir of the rationalists of the Enlightenment, for his overzealous devotion to the powers of reason that result in the misapplication of scientific methods to the understanding of political phenomena not amenable to such an approach.[121] Man has always been aware of the fact that the moral and intellectual history of mankind is one of "inner insecurity, of the anticipation of impending doom," but Morgenthau detects in his contemporaries a tendency to run away from their problems.[122] As a result, reality contradicts philosophy, and there is a consequent inability to seek and find solutions, leaving the age vulnerable to "being overwhelmed by the enemies from within and from without."[123] Morgenthau argues that this tendency to flee from reality stems from a contempt for power politics, but warns that the real world of politics is too complex to yield to the simple rules of science, and that the statesman is more an artist than a scientist; the statesman stands with the great realists, such as Thrasymachus and Machiavelli, whereas the idealistic rationalist is akin to Don Quixote.[124]

In sketching out the rationalist attack on the political, Morgenthau is once again reminiscent of Schmitt, in *Political Romanticism*. Morgenthau argues that these attacks began as attempts to reduce political matters into technical ones, and presumably this was when the vocabulary of other spheres of human activity began to invade the domain of the political, so that previously political disputes became economic, social, or other technical matters.[125] One of the most dangerous consequences of the ensuing confusion, for Morgenthau, is the conflation of domestic and international politics, for it assumes that all conflict is the same, thereby blinding one to the crucial

---

[121] One might find this line of attack somewhat surprising, since it is bound to also target such thinkers as Hobbes, who would otherwise seem necessary to Morgenthau's project. Indeed, Morgenthau places Hobbes within the rationalist tradition (cf. *Scientific Man vs. Power Politics*, 13), but acknowledges also that "the scientism of Machiavelli and Hobbes is [...] merely an accident without consequences, a sudden flash of lightning illuminating the dark landscape of man's hidden motives but kindling no Promethean fire for a grateful posterity" (*Scientific Man vs. Power Politics*, 169).

[122] Morgenthau, *Scientific Man vs. Power Politics*, 1.

[123] Morgenthau, *Scientific Man vs. Power Politics*, 2.

[124] Morgenthau, *Scientific Man vs. Power Politics*, 10, 35–36.

[125] See Morgenthau, *Scientific Man vs. Power Politics*, 46.

differences between disputes within the safe and generally reasonable boundaries of a liberal state and international war.[126] Morgenthau warns that the
difference is fundamental and cautions: "[n]o [...] community of rational
interests and values exists [...] on the international scene, at least not per-
manently and universally."[127] Here, too, Schmitt makes no appearance, but
one cannot help but notice the similarity between Morgenthau's distinction
and Schmitt's insistence on the public nature of the political enemy.[128]

One of Morgenthau's strongest objections to Schmitt's concept of the
political is that it does not possess a sufficiently strong differentia. If, as
Morgenthau claims, the political is a matter of degree, then what is the
particular object that gives rise to it? Morgenthau's attempts to answer that
question in a manner more satisfactory than Schmitt's culminated in a theory that emphasizes the importance of power. Although initially one might
interpret Morgenthau's choice as a significant departure from Schmitt, it
turns out that because of its proximity to Hobbes's understanding of power,
Morgenthau's theory of power politics is much closer to Schmitt's theory
than he may have wished. In *Scientific Man vs. Power Politics*, Morgenthau
offers the sketch for a theory of human psychology and motivation that
places a great deal of weight on man's relationship to others. In that short
sketch, Morgenthau makes it clear that our existence among others of our
kind renders our actions and inactions social, by definition, and whether we
like it or not. Even altruism requires a certain amount of selfishness, because
without first preserving oneself, one will simply not be around to do good
to others.[129] The means that enable us to preserve ourselves and to act or
refrain from doing so can be summed up as power, and the relationship of the
individual to power in Morgenthau's early formulation bears the impression
of Hobbes quite distinctly:

There are two reasons why the egotism of one must come into conflict with the
egotism of the other. What the one wants for himself, the other already possesses
or wants, too. Struggle and competition ensue. Finding that all his relations with his
fellow-men contain at least the germs of such conflicts of interest, man can no longer
seek the goodness of his intentions in the almost complete absence of selfishness and

[126] See, e.g., Morgenthau, *Scientific Man vs. Power Politics*, 50, 106; cf. *Politics among Nations*,
37–38, 40–43; Hobbes, *Leviathan*, VIII § 12.

[127] Morgenthau, *Scientific Man vs. Power Politics*, 107.

[128] Cf. Schmitt, *The Concept of the Political*, 28–29.

[129] Morgenthau, *Scientific Man vs. Power Politics*, 191–92. In "Über die Herkunft des Politischen
aus dem Wesen des Menschen," Morgenthau writes: "We conceive of the political as a force
that resides in each individual human being and that is of necessity directed toward another
human being" (quoted in Frei, *Hans J. Morgenthau*, 125–26).

of the concomitant harm to others but only in the limitations which conscience puts upon the drive toward evil. Man cannot hope to be good but must be content with being not too evil.

The other root of conflict and concomitant evil stems from the *animus dominandi*, the desire for power. This lust for power manifests itself as the desire to maintain the range of one's own person with regard to others, to increase it, or to demonstrate it. In whatever disguises it may appear its ultimate essence and aim is in one of these particular references of one person to others.[130]

Morgenthau notes that one should not rush therefore to confuse this desire for power with selfishness, because he sees the "typical" goals of selfishness as concerned with the basics of survival, but finds that man's *animus dominandi* is concerned with one's "position among his fellows once his survival has been secured," which is why the former has limits, whereas the latter does not.[131] Morgenthau is quick to point out, however, that in distinguishing thus, "one is already doing violence to the actual nature of that desire; for actually it is present whenever man intends to act with regard to other men."[132] The ubiquity of this desire is what makes men and their actions evil, and to the extent, then, that politics in particular is characterized by this *animus*, politics is evil.[133] For Morgenthau, the evil and corruption of politics are thus prototypical of evil and corruption in any other sphere, and it is for this reason, rather than because of the alleged existence of different moral standards, that political actions are public.[134] Given the inevitability of evil in any political decision, Morgenthau notes that the statesman is the one who must step forward and make the unpleasant decision that the indecisive – romantics in the case of Schmitt, perfectionists in the case of Morgenthau, but liberals for both – shrink away from.[135] "Political ethics," he argues, "is the endeavor to choose, since evil there must be, among several possible actions the one that is least evil."[136] This conclusion, which is further evidence of Morgenthau's agreement with Hobbes, foreshadows one of the main themes of his subsequent theory of politics.[137]

---

[130] Morgenthau, *Scientific Man vs. Power Politics*, 192.

[131] Morgenthau, *Scientific Man vs. Power Politics*, 193. Cf. Morgenthau, *Politics among Nations*, II, 31–43.

[132] Morgenthau, *Scientific Man vs. Power Politics*, 194.

[133] Morgenthau, *Scientific Man vs. Power Politics*, 194–95.

[134] This despite those, like some in the reason of state tradition, who argue that there are two ethical standards, one for private actions and another for public ones (Morgenthau, *Scientific Man vs. Power Politics*, 195–96; cf. 178–80).

[135] Cf. Söllner, "German Conservatism in America," 164.

[136] Morgenthau, *Scientific Man vs. Power Politics*, 202.

[137] See Hobbes, *On the Citizen*, Pref., § 20; *Leviathan*, XVI § 29.

Morgenthau's understanding of the centrality of the search for the lesser evil comes in his major work, *Politics among Nations*.[138] By 1948, when this work made its first appearance, Schmitt's name had disappeared completely from Morgenthau's theory, but his influence was omnipresent and strong. Morgenthau argues that the six fundamental characteristics of political realism are (1) that politics and society are governed by objective laws that have their roots in human nature; (2) that the political sphere is autonomous from other spheres and is to be understood on the basis of interest defined in terms of power; (3) that although interest is the formal concern of all politics, particular manifestations of interest will vary with circumstances; (4) that there is a fundamental difference between the demands of morality on the individual and on the state that requires a correspondingly different evaluation of political situations, and that prizes prudence, rather than the traditional ethical virtues; (5) that the moral aspirations of nations are particular and not universal; and (6) that political realism is different from other theories of politics as well as from other points of view, such as the economic, especially in its refusal to allow these points of view to infiltrate and therefore dilute the political.[139] Given Morgenthau's attack on the rationalists, in *Scientific Man vs. Power Politics*, for trying to describe the rules of politics, it might seem surprising that he is now arguing that such rules do exist and that they are universal.[140] In fact, his argument in *Politics among Nations* builds upon that earlier epistemology by emphasizing that the error lay not in the pursuit of rules but rather in ignoring the fact that these rules are based on an unchanging human nature.[141] Morgenthau claims that all methodological disputes about the study of politics stem from and boil down to a fundamental dispute regarding human nature.[142] There are two basic views of man,

---

[138] Morgenthau, *Politics among Nations*, 3–4.

[139] Morgenthau, *Politics among Nations*, 4–17.

[140] Tucker attacks Morgenthau's own brand of scientific analysis in the context of a review of *In Defense of the National Interest* (see Tucker, "Professor Morgenthau's Theory of 'Political Realism,'" esp. 215, 219). Hoffmann, on the other hand, considers this and other aspects of Morgenthau's theory useful for the development of political science, despite their shortcomings (*Janus and Minerva*, 6–7).

[141] Morgenthau, *Politics among Nations*, 3–4; cf. *Scientific Man vs. Power Politics*, 1–2.

[142] In his inaugural lecture at Geneva, Morgenthau stated, "all reflection about this reality must go back to the basis of everything pertaining to the political realm, everything related to the state, and this basis is man himself" (quoted in Frei, *Hans J. Morgenthau*, 119). Elements of Morgenthau's belief in the connection between human nature and politics are evident in all his major works to a greater or lesser extent, but it should also be pointed out that he had composed a short work entitled "Über die Herkunft des Politischen aus dem Wesen des Menschen" [On the Derivation of the Political from the Nature of Man], which was

one that sees him as perfectible and essentially good, and another that sees conflicting interests that result from the makeup of human beings and that cannot be completely reconciled, and that therefore require that one seek the lesser evil rather than an absolute good.[143] It is because, like Schmitt, he subscribes to the second of these that Morgenthau accepts the title of realist.[144] In this respect too, Schmitt and Morgenthau reveal once more their indebtedness to Hobbes, who argues that "man by nature chooseth the lesser evil."[145]

Given Morgenthau's adherence to a view of human nature that is virtually identical to those of Hobbes and Schmitt, his choice of the concept of power as the organizing principle for his theory of political realism is not surprising. Once again, although Hobbes is not mentioned in the relevant parts of *Politics among Nations*, evidence of his influence is abundant:

International politics, like all politics, is a struggle for power. Whatever the ultimate aims of international politics, power is always the immediate aim. Statesmen and peoples may ultimately seek freedom, security, prosperity, or power itself. They may define their goals in terms of a religious, philosophic, economic, or social ideal. They may hope that this ideal will materialize through its own inner force, through divine intervention, or through the natural development of human affairs. They may also try to further its realization through nonpolitical means, such as technical co-operation with other nations or international organizations. But whenever they strive to realize their goal by means of international politics, they do so by striving for power.[146]

---

never published (see Frei, *Hans J. Morgenthau*, 124–26; cf. Koskenniemi, *The Gentle Civilizer of Nations*, 448–49).

[143] Morgenthau, *Politics among Nations*, 3–4. Cf. Hoffmann, "International Relations: The Long Road to Theory," 350: "much of the international (or domestic) evil of power is rooted not in the sinfulness of man but in a context, a constellation, a situation, in which even good men are forced to act selfishly or immorally." See also Smith, *Realist Thought from Weber to Kissinger*, 1.

[144] "This theoretical concern with human nature as it actually is, and with the historic processes as they actually take place, has earned for the theory presented here the name of realism" (Morgenthau, *Politics among Nations*, 4); cf. Schmitt, *The Concept of the Political*, 58. Scheuerman argues that Morgenthau's views on this matter grew closer to Schmitt's in time: "Morgenthau's mature reflections on the authentically political character of pessimistic views of human nature parallel Schmitt's similar reflections from the 1932 *Concept of the Political*" (*Carl Schmitt*, 243). This is certainly so insofar as Morgenthau's American writings contain explicit references to the issue of human nature, whereas his European ones do not, although the absence of such references from the former does not necessarily entail a shift such as that suggested by Scheuerman.

[145] Hobbes, *Leviathan*, XIV § 29; cf. *On the Citizen*, Pref. § 20.

[146] Morgenthau, *Politics among Nations*, 31. The universality of power as the differentia of politics is evident in the fact that with respect to it, Morgenthau considers domestic and international politics alike. This passage also shows, *pace* Malcolm (*Aspects of Hobbes*, 433, 442), that Morgenthau sees power as a means, rather than an end, and that his view on this matter is fully consistent with Hobbes's.

Morgenthau's understanding of power as the means for the fulfillment of ends is all the more striking as it extends beyond physical force and contains everything that might potentially help a political actor achieve his goals. He argues that "[t]he threat of physical violence in the form of police action, imprisonment, capital punishment, or war is an intrinsic element of politics," and claims that the move from threat to actual violence signifies an abdication of political power.[147] The reason for this pronouncement is that for Morgenthau,

Political power is a psychological relation between those who exercise it and those over whom it is exercised. It gives the former control over certain actions of the latter through the influence which the former exert over the latter's minds. The influence derives from three sources: the expectation of benefits, the fear of disadvantages, the respect or love for men or institutions. It may be exerted through orders, threats, persuasion, the authority or charisma of a man or of an office, or a combination of any of these.[148]

To test the validity of his claims, Morgenthau always returns to reality, which for him is the ultimate touchstone. There, he finds that history is full of contests for power among states and an absence of any serious evidence for the existence of peoples free from the *animus dominandi*.[149] This strategy

[147] Morgenthau, *Politics among Nations*, 33.
[148] Morgenthau, *Politics among Nations*, 32–33. Cf. Morgenthau, *Science: Servant or Master?*, 31:

> As politics in the specific sense is but a special manifestation of man's longing for power over other men, so that longing is but a special manifestation of man's desire for power that expresses itself as well in non-political spheres, that is, where the object is not man but other animate or inanimate objects. Thus the scholar seeking knowledge seeks power; so does the poet who endeavors to express his thoughts and feelings in words. So do the mountain climber, the hunter, the collector of rare objects. They all seek to assert themselves as individuals against the world. It is only when they choose as their object other men that they enter the political sphere.

> Based on the fact that this conception of power is not limited to self-preservation, Frei considers it not Hobbesian, but Nietzschean (*Hans J. Morgenthau*, 127, esp. note 53). Frei's pronouncement, however, is based on a very narrow conception of power in Hobbesian theory, which as we have seen does not capture the full range of the concept for Hobbes. For a view contrary to Frei's, see Aron, *Peace and War*, 595–96. See also Hoffmann, *Janus and Minerva*, 72–73.

[149] Morgenthau, *Politics among Nations*, 37–40. As Pichler points out, Morgenthau's aim in so doing is to overcome the subjective character of interests and particular situations by focusing on power and self-preservation, which are seen by him as the objective aims of all statesmen ("The Godfathers of 'Truth,'" 192). Cf. Hobbes, *Decameron Physiologicum*: "But know you not that men from their very birth, and naturally, scramble for every thing they covet, and would have all the world, if they could, to fear and obey them" (*The English Works of Thomas Hobbes*, 7: 73). For a discussion of the difference between "power to" and "power over" and the possible link of the *animus dominandi* to innate aggression, see Wrong, *Power*, 218–27.

is part of the trend that Aron identifies in arguing that when Treitschke's concept of *Machtpolitik* crossed the Atlantic and became 'power politics,' it "underwent a spiritual mutation" and "became fact, not value."[150]

Despite the different formulations and references, Morgenthau's theory in *Scientific Man vs. Power Politics* and *Politics among Nations* never departs in substance from that laid out in his earlier European writings.[151] War remains an ever-present possibility, just as it did in *Die internationale Rechtspflege*, and given the obstacles that lie between a state and the attainment of the power necessary for the realization of its goals, the statesman will be faced with some hard choices.[152] Morgenthau himself is aware that the pressing nature and urgency of those choices is a vindication of Hobbes.[153] In a 1951 discussion of the national interest, he writes: "There is a profound and neglected truth hidden in Hobbes's extreme dictum that the state creates morality as well as law and that there is neither morality nor law outside the state."[154] Like Hobbes and Schmitt before him, Morgenthau acknowledges that the moment of the decision spurred by the presence of an external threat is constitutive not only of the state, but also of the benefits that come with a pocket of security and protection. The *de facto* ability of the sovereign to provide this security is for Morgenthau, as for Hobbes, a defining characteristic of sovereignty.[155] Explicit references to the enemy disappear from Morgenthau's theory at the same time as Schmitt's name drops from his writings. For all his objections to Schmitt's concept of the political, however, Morgenthau is unable to dispense with it completely. In a telling section of *Politics among Nations*, wherein he considers the connection between personal insecurity and social disintegration, Morgenthau lists three events that in his view weakened the social fabric of Germany and paved the way for the Nazis. As one might expect by now, all three involve the specters of external enemies.[156] Ironically, in his quest for greater precision than Schmitt's friend–enemy distinction could afford, Morgenthau has expanded the scope of potential enemies to include

---

[150] Aron, *Peace and War*, 592.

[151] Honig claims that the "realist" Morgenthau did not emerge until *Scientific Man vs. Power Politics* ("Totalitarianism and Realism," 304), but his own analysis shows that this judgment is based more on nomenclature and issues of expediency than on substance.

[152] Morgenthau, *Die internationale Rechtspflege*, 77.

[153] In a 1977 interview, Smith suggested to Morgenthau that his conception of the state as the ultimate source of morality sounded Hegelian, to which Morgenthau replied "Hegel was the furthest thing from my mind" (*Realist Thought from Weber to Kissinger*, 155 and note 34).

[154] Morgenthau, *In Defense of the National Interest*, 34.

[155] For Morgenthau, nations are sovereign when they are "the supreme law-creating and law-enforcing authorities" (*Politics among Nations*, 329). Cf. Aron, *Peace and War*, 739.

[156] Morgenthau, *Politics among Nations*, 122–26.

everyone. Too broad to be helpful, this realization is perhaps of use only in that it highlights the essence of the decision. Morgenthau's agreement with Hobbes and Schmitt has thus come full circle, when he too proclaims that the state's law-making and law-enforcing ability, that is, its ability to decide and back up that decision, is what makes it sovereign.

It is hard to exaggerate the effect of Hans Morgenthau on political science and international relations. Commentators and intellectual opponents alike agree that he is one of the principal theorists of international relations in the twentieth century. Stanley Hoffmann has called him the founder of the discipline and Reinhold Niebuhr "the most brilliant and authoritative political realist."[157] Similarly, realism remains one of the dominant approaches to international relations, even for its critics.[158] There is even greater consensus, however, where the lineage of this school of thought is concerned. Invariably, histories of realist thought in international relations point to Thucydides, Machiavelli, and Hobbes as principal representatives of the genre. To some extent, the reasons for these associations are clear enough, as both Thucydides and Machiavelli are greatly concerned with a state's external relations.

Although it is relatively clear why realists would wish to count him as one of their own, however, the case for Hobbes as a theorist of international relations is less clear; beyond a handful of admittedly famous lines on the subject, he remains silent. The foregoing history of the idea of negative association reveals that there are good reasons for according Hobbes a principal place among realists and international relations theorists, because through his image of the state of nature he brought the distant battle front into the minds of men. Both Schmitt and Morgenthau were products of an intellectual culture in which Hobbes was a political thinker of the highest order, and in that long history of Hobbist influence, their contributions stand out as particularly important to an understanding of the transition from early modern theories of international politics to the contemporary fascination

---

[157] Hoffmann, *Janus and Minerva*, 6; Niebuhr is quoted in Smith, *Realist Thought from Weber to Kissinger*, 134. Cf. Wight, "Review of *Dilemmas of Politics*," 199; Hoffmann, "Raymond Aron and the Theory of International Relations," 13; Tucker, "Professor Morgenthau's Theory of 'Political Realism,'" 214; Söllner, "German Conservatism in America," 163, 168; Honig, "Totalitarianism and Realism," 283–84; Smith, *Realist Thought from Weber to Kissinger*, 134; Wolin, "Reasons of State, States of Reason," 51; Koskenniemi, *The Gentle Civilizer of Nations*, 446, 465; Haslam, *No Virtue like Necessity*, 190.

[158] Legro and Moravcsik, e.g., claim that "[r]ealism remains the primary or alternative theory in virtually every major book and article addressing world politics, particularly in security affairs" ("Is Anybody Still a Realist?," 5).

with the international realm and its consequences for state sovereignty. The rise and prominence of political realism in the English-speaking world owes much to the influence that Schmitt's early writings had on the revival of a dormant Hobbist realism and the bequeathing of it to Morgenthau, who in turn, through his unexpected emigration to the United States, introduced it into the country that not only witnessed the revival of political science and the establishment of international relations as an academic discipline, but also became the driving force of international politics in the twentieth century.

EPILOGUE

When viewed side by side, the episodes of negative association examined earlier constitute a history that is striking on two counts. First, because it consists of waves of actions and reactions: those exemplified by the Sallustian reaction to Thucydides, Gentillet's reaction to Machiavelli, and Rousseau's reaction to Hobbes, respectively. Although in some ways each wave is different from the ones that follow, they are also very similar. The first part of each wave is marked by a detached, provocative, and ultimately disturbing account of the workings of negative association. This is evident not only in the proclamations that accompany the actions but also, and most importantly, in the furor that characterizes the reactions. Second, the history of negative association is striking because despite the fact that it consists of a series of actions and reactions, it displays a remarkable degree of continuity and agreement. This agreement can be seen on two levels. The first of these concerns the events that gave rise to each wave of action. The Peloponnesian War, the woes of Florence, and the English Civil War make for very different settings, and yet the means by which political associations are formed in each show the same fundamental elements of collective action at work. The second level, however, is even more surprising because it concerns the reactions. After all, Hobbes's agreement with Thucydides is to be expected. What is unexpected, however, is the degree to which those who react to each wave – because they disagree fundamentally about the very premises of each argument, be they about human nature or God – are also forced to make room in their reactions for the undeniable role of negative association. From Sallust's measured regret to Rousseau's fiery indignation, these reactions are understandable because they convey the frustration that can result only from a hard look at the human condition.

The waves that make up the history of negative association through fear contain a further similarity. Each thinks its circumstances unprecedented. In an obvious but uninteresting sense, they are correct. More important, however, is the way in which they are mistaken. Human beings cannot resist the tendency to think that they are special. Even though he writes for all time, Thucydides considers the Peloponnesian War the greatest that ever was. Machiavelli declared his intention to go where no one had gone before, and Hobbes proclaimed his *De Cive* the foundation of political science. Kant, along with many of his contemporaries, saw a grand plan in which each successive stage of mankind was one step closer to the ultimate purpose than the next, and Hegel divided history into moments of which his own was the highest. This tendency continues unabated. In the twentieth century, World War I was dubbed the "Great War" and the "War to End All Wars," but not long thereafter it was followed by an even greater war, which in turn gave way to the Cold War. Upon cessation of the hostilities that never were, came the declaration of "The End of History," only to be followed by the "War on Terror." It is worth remembering, however, that everywhere and at all times, peoples are "chosen," rulers and nations "ordained by God," epochs evidence of "progress," and circumstances special. We are fond of thinking that what we are experiencing has never been encountered before, that the world has never seen the likes of this or that. At each moment, things no doubt seem tremendous and unprecedented, yet, as Kant observes, none of this is surprising when it comes to a species so taken with its own superiority.

The events that followed the collapse of the Soviet Union confirm the lessons learned from the tradition of negative association. In an opinion piece published in 2003, the prime minister of Belgium called for the formation of a "true European defense" and explained the European disapproval of the United States' foreign policy in the following terms:

As long as we Europeans feel threatened, the use of war and weapons can more or less be justified. However, without this sentiment, a transatlantic gulf has opened up. I fear this rift will only grow. As long as Soviet divisions could reach the Rhine in 48 hours, we obviously had a blood brotherhood with our cousins overseas. But now that the cold war is over, we can express more freely our differences of opinion.[1]

Just as the presence of Carthage alone could not account for Roman unity, by itself the Soviet threat could not explain transatlantic convergence. Nevertheless, in each case the presence of an external threat provided a focal point that rendered the situation intelligible and manageable. The brief duration of "The End of History" and the speed with which it gave way to the "Clash of Civilizations" and the "War on Terror" are testaments to the need for such

---

[1] Verhofstadt, "Europe Has to Become a Force in NATO."

a focal point. It is necessary to note, however, that identifying this need is not the same thing as endorsing it or reveling in it.

MONTAIGNE'S PARADOX

In his reflections on fear, Montaigne had declared, "The only thing I fear is fear itself." This deeply paradoxical statement offers cause for reflection on three counts. As many commentators observed readily, the declaration of a "War on Terror" was one of the responses to the gap left by the collapse of the Soviet Union. The vagueness of this new enemy has certain obvious advantages. For one, it is open ended with respect to content and duration. This flexibility, however, is no panacea. How one fills the blanks makes a big difference, and not every choice is as good as every other. Moreover, the indefinite perpetuation of such a struggle is bound to render it anodyne. Machiavelli had observed that it was necessary to take the state back to its beginnings, but only every so often.

Montaigne's paradox has bearing on a related issue as well. The response to the terrorist attacks on the United States, in 2001, displayed many of the characteristics of negative association through fear. Partisan bickering was set aside, priorities were rearranged. Issues that had dominated the political scene until the day before were forgotten. People expressed their shock and horror. Many commentators noted that the attacks were unprecedented and marked a new era for mankind. Many others, siding with Montaigne, whether they knew it or not, decried the deterioration into a "politics of fear" and urged that we move beyond it. Much ink continues to be spilled on either side of this divide, but it is important to remember that this type of reaction and counterreaction is part and parcel of traumatic events. On everyone's behalf, some will scream the loudest and then others will tell them to be quiet. In the end, however, the balance will be restored.

THE HEAT AND THE LIGHT

Because we tend to associate fear with its undesirable consequences, we usually classify it as an emotion, but this classification is fundamentally flawed. Fear partakes of reason as much as of the passions, which is why it provides a unique point of entry into human motivation. Those who protest fear-mongering, and the celebration and manipulation of fear, continue to employ the categories of reason and emotion. Fearmongers appeal to the passions, they argue, and the remedy is to restore our faith in reason. Montaigne's paradoxical statement about fear is cryptic enough that it seems to contain an element of this position, but it is unclear how much. Among those who sought to establish the universal reign of reason, however, there is no such ambiguity. The passions represent everything that is base in human beings. They are the source of our problems, and reason is the solution. As Walzer cautions, however, replacing the heat of passion with the light of reason is simply not possible.[2] The most rudimentary analysis of human behavior shows that the two operate side by side. This is especially true in politics, which is conflictual by nature. Walzer notes,

the dichotomies that set passionate intensity against some sort of interested or principled rationality, heat against light, are so pervasive in political thinking that perhaps it is enough to say simply that they are useless, that they correspond to nothing at all in the actual experience of political engagement.[3]

By making this observation regarding human conduct central to his political thought, Machiavelli paved the way for Hobbes, who seized it, made it explicit, and used it to construct his political science.[4]

In considering *metus hostilis* as a psychological explanation and political maxim it becomes clear that there are deeper reasons for its widespread appeal. On a very basic level, we use entities outside ourselves as signposts to help us navigate a complex world. The usefulness of outside entities in this task is manifold. It is perhaps clearest when our survival and security are in danger. The demands of survival, let alone commodious living, are too high for any individual or small group. As others threaten us or aid us in the achievement of our goals, we classify them as enemies and friends, and thereby render our universe manageable. Beyond survival, however, others serve as points of reference and thereby contribute to our understanding of the world that surrounds us. The properties and positive attributes of things are not always readily apparent, and grasping them is not an easy task. In some cases, it may be impossible. Contrasting one thing to another provides us with information that may not be available to us otherwise. Where our personal identity is concerned, self-discovery is a never-ending process, and juxtaposition with and contradistinction from others tell us something about ourselves. We learn something about who we are by finding out who we are not. In its most benign form, this is the contrast that Harrington, Hume, and Deutsch have in mind when they speak of the effects of travel to foreign

---

[2] Walzer, *Politics and Passion*, 117.
[3] Walzer, *Politics and Passion*, 130. Cf. ibid., 117–19, 126, 128.
[4] See Wolin, *Hobbes and the Epic Tradition of Political Theory*, 29–30; cf. Robin, *Fear*, 28.

places.[5] Nozick takes one step further, when he argues that it is through comparison with others that people acquire their sense of self-esteem.[6]

Whether one accepts the minimal version – that others are mostly relevant to self-definition when security is at stake – or the larger claim – that others are essential to self-definition – the implications for politics are enormous. Although in his account of perception Hobbes subscribes to the latter, his political theory is constructed so as to stand even on the former, lesser assumption. He recognizes that the essential corollary to the individual's right to self-preservation is that he be the judge of the threat and of the means necessary to counter it. This right, which in the state of nature is the source of conflict, is what individuals cede to the sovereign when they form a commonwealth. In the hands of the sovereign, this right, which Schmitt calls the right to decide the exception, becomes the hallmark of sovereignty and the defining characteristic, in times of crisis, of the state. The most frequent manifestation of this right is the act of declaring war – and thereby identifying one's enemies – but there are other examples of its importance. As Hobbes points out in *Leviathan*, sovereigns create pockets of order in a dangerous world. Inside those pockets, individuals are given the collective freedom not only to live but also to pursue all those activities that are unattainable through individual freedom alone.[7] These activities, whatever they may be, form the identity of a commonwealth and its members. The commonwealth's borders are therefore more than mere demarcations of its territory and sovereignty. They are also signals and guarantors of its identity. External challenges to the commonwealth thus test its identity by testing its borders.

The exceptional circumstances associated with such challenges raise anew the question of the commonwealth's identity, often in troubling ways. How threatened do we feel, and how far are we willing to go to keep the enemy at bay? The first reaction to an external challenge is usually contradistinction from the source of the challenge, the enemy. This immediate response, however, is often followed by distinct, yet related, reactions, such as extreme vilification of the enemy. The depth and profundity of the challenge may

---

[5] Harrington argues, "No man can be a Politician, except he be first an Historian or a Traveller; for except he can see what Must be, what May be, he is no Politician: Now if he have no knowledge in story, he cannot tell what hath been; and if he hath not been a Traveller, he cannot tell what is: but he that neither knoweth what hath been, nor what is, can never tell what must be or what may be" (*The Common-Wealth of Oceana*, 226). Cf. Hume, *A Treatise of Human Nature*, 3.2.1 § 12; Deutsch, *Nationalism and Its Alternatives*, 15.

[6] Nozick argues, "[p]eople generally judge themselves by how they fall along the most important dimensions in which they differ from others" (*Anarchy, State, and Utopia*, 243).

[7] Hobbes, *Leviathan*, XIII § 12.

also lead to scapegoating, xenophobia, and excessive emergency powers. The extent, frequency, and troubling nature of these effects are sad confirmations of the role that outsiders play in supplementing even the strongest and most positive of collective identities. Most troubling of all, however, is the realization that no political group is immune to them.

BIBLIOGRAPHY

A Complete Collection of State Trials and Proceedings for High Treason and Other Crimes and Misdemeanors from the Earliest Period to the Year 1783, with Notes and Other Illustrations. 21 volumes. London: T. C. Hansard for Longman, Hurst, Rees, Orme, and Brown, [etc.], 1816.

Acton, John Emmerich Dahlberg, Lord. *Introduction to Il Principe* by Niccolò Machiavelli. Edited by L. Arthur Burd. Oxford: The Clarendon Press, 1891.

Ahrensdorf, Peter J. "The Fear of Death and the Longing for Immortality: Hobbes and Thucydides on Human Nature and the Problem of Anarchy." *American Political Science Review* 94, no. 3 (2000): 579–93.

Algosaibi, Ghazi A. R. "The Theory of International Relations: Hans J. Morgenthau and His Critics." *Background* 8, no. 4 (1965): 221–56.

Allen, Don Cameron. "An Unmentioned Elizabethan Opponent of Machiavelli." *Italica* 14, no. 3 (1937): 90–92.

Althusser, Louis. *Machiavelli and Us.* Translated by Gregory Elliott. Edited by François Matheron. London: Verso, 1999.

Anglo, Sydney. *Machiavelli – The First Century: Studies in Enthusiasm, Hostility, and Irrelevance.* Oxford: Oxford University Press, 2005.

―――. "'Le plus gentil esprit qui soit apparu au monde depuis les derniers siecles': The Popularity of Machiavelli in Sixteenth-Century France." In *Renaissance Reflections: Essays in Honor of C. A. Mayer,* edited by Pauline M. Smith and Trevor Peach, 195–212. Paris: Honoré Champion Éditeur, 2002.

Archibugi, Daniele. "Models of International Organization in Perpetual Peace Projects." *Review of International Studies* 18, no. 4 (1992): 295–317.

Aristotle. *Ethica Nicomachea.* Edited by John Bywater. Oxford: The Clarendon Press, 1991.

―――. *Nicomachean Ethics.* Translated by David Ross. Oxford: Oxford University Press, 1998.

―――. *Politica.* Edited by W. D. Ross. Oxford: The Clarendon Press, 1990.

―――. *Politics Books I and II.* Translated by Trevor J. Saunders. Oxford: The Clarendon Press, 1995.

Armitage, David. "Empire and Liberty: A Republican Dilemma." In *Republicanism: A Shared European Heritage*, 2 vols., edited by Martin van Gelderen and Quentin Skinner, 2: 29–46. Cambridge: Cambridge University Press, 2002.

——. Introduction to *The Free Sea* by Hugo Grotius. Translated by Richard Hakluyt. Indianapolis: Liberty Fund, 2004.

Aron, Raymond. *Main Currents in Sociological Thought I: Montesquieu, Comte, Marx, Tocqueville; the Sociologists and the Revolution of 1848*. Garden City, N.Y.: Anchor Books, 1968.

——. *Peace and War: A Theory of International Relations*. Translated by Richard Howard and Annette Baker Fox. Garden City, N.Y.: Doubleday & Company, Inc., 1966.

Augustine of Hippo, Saint. *Concerning the City of God against the Pagans*. Translated by Henry Bettenson. Harmondsworth: Penguin, 1984.

Avineri, Shlomo. *Hegel's Theory of the Modern State*. Cambridge: Cambridge University Press, 1972.

Bailey, Cyril. *Lucretius*. Vol. 35, *Proceedings of the British Academy*. London: Geoffrey Cumberlege, 1949.

Bakos, Adrianna. "'*Qui nescit dissimulare, nescit regnare*': Louis XI and Raison d'état during the Reign of Louis XIII." *Journal of the History of Ideas* 52, no. 3 (1991): 399–416.

Balakrishnan, Gopal. *The Enemy: An Intellectual Portrait of Carl Schmitt*. London: Verso, 2000.

Baudrillart, Henri. *Bodin et son temps: tableau des théories politiques et des idées économiques au 16ème siècle*. Aalen: Scientia Verlag, 1964.

Beame, Edmond M. "The Use and Abuse of Machiavelli: The Sixteenth-Century French Adaptation." *Journal of the History of Ideas* 43, no. 1 (1982): 33–54.

Bellen, Heinz. *Metus Gallicus, metus Punicus: zum Furchtmotiv in der römischen Republik*. Mainz: Akademie der Wissenschaften und der Literatur, 1985.

Bendersky, Joseph W. *Carl Schmitt: Theorist for the Reich*. Princeton, N.J.: Princeton University Press, 1983.

——. "The Definite and the Dubious: Carl Schmitt's Influence on Conservative Political and Legal Theory in the U.S." *Telos*, no. 122 (2002): 33–47.

Benhabib, Seyla. "Citizens, Residents, and Aliens in a Changing World: Political Membership in the Global Era." In *The Postnational Self: Belonging and Identity*, edited by Ulf Hedetoft and Mette Hjort, 85–119. Minneapolis, Minn.: University of Minnesota Press, 2002.

——. *The Rights of Others: Aliens, Residents, and Citizens*. Cambridge: Cambridge University Press, 2004.

Berlin, Isaiah. *Against the Current: Essays in the History of Ideas*. Edited by Henry Hardy. New York: The Viking Press, 1980.

Bireley, Robert. *The Counter-Reformation Prince: Anti-Machiavellism or Catholic Statecraft in Early Modern Europe*. Chapel Hill: The University of North Carolina Press, 1990.

Blackburne, Richard. *Thomæ Hobbes Angli Malmesburiensis philosophi vita*. London: William Cooke, 1681.

Bock, Gisela. "Civil Discord in Machiavelli's *Istorie Fiorentine*." In *Machiavelli and Republicanism*, edited by Gisela Bock, Quentin Skinner, and Maurizio Viroli, 181–201. Cambridge: Cambridge University Press, 1990.

Bodin, Jean. *Method for the Easy Comprehension of History*. Translated by Beatrice Reynolds. New York: Columbia University Press, 1945.

—————. *The Six Bookes of a Commonweale*. Translated by Richard Knolles. London: [Printed by Adam Islip] for G. Bishop, 1606.

—————. *The Six Bookes of a Commonweale*. Translated by Richard Knolles. Edited by Kenneth Douglas McRae. Cambridge, Mass.: Harvard University Press, 1962.

—————. *Les six livres de la république*. Paris: Jacques du Puys, 1583.

Bolotin, David. "Thucydides." In *History of Political Philosophy*, edited by Leo Strauss and Joseph Cropsey, 7–32. Chicago: The University of Chicago Press, 1987.

Bonamente, G. "Il metus Punicus e la decadenza di Roma in Sallustio, Agostino ed Orosio." *Giornale Italiano di Filologia* 27 (1975): 137–69.

Botero, Giovanni. *The Cause of the Greatnesse of Cities, etc.* London: Henry Seile, 1635.

—————. *The Reason of State*. Translated by P. J. Waley and D. P. Waley. London: Routledge & Kegan Paul, 1956.

—————. *Relations, of the Most Famovs Kingdoms and Common-Weales throvgh the World. Discoursing of Their Scituations, Manners, Customes, Strengthes, and Pollicies, etc.* London: John Jaggard, 1608.

Bowen, Willis H. "Sixteenth Century French Translations of Machiavelli." *Italica* 27, no. 4 (1950): 313–20.

Bowle, John. *Hobbes and His Critics: A Study in Seventeenth Century Constitutionalism*. New York: Barnes & Noble, Inc., 1969.

Bradley, A. C. "Aristotle's Conception of the State." In *A Companion to Aristotle's Politics*, edited by David Keyt and Fred D. Miller, Jr., 13–56. Oxford: Blackwell, 1991.

Brewer, Marilyn B., and Rupert J. Brown. "Intergroup Relations." In *The Handbook of Social Psychology*, 2 vols., edited by Daniel T. Gilbert, Susan T. Fiske, and Gardner Lindzey, 2: 554–94. Boston: The McGraw-Hill Companies, Inc., 1998.

Breyer, Stephen. *Breaking the Vicious Circle: Toward Effective Risk Regulation*. Cambridge, Mass.: Harvard University Press, 1993.

Brown, Clifford W., Jr. "Thucydides, Hobbes, and the Derivation of Anarchy." *History of Political Thought* 8, no. 1 (1987): 33–62.

Bruell, Christopher. "Thucydides' View of Athenian Imperialism." *American Political Science Review* 68, no. 1 (1974): 11–17.

Bunge, Frederica M. *Indonesia: A Country Study*. Vol. 4. Washington, D.C.: Government Printing Office, 1982.

Burke, Peter. "A Survey of the Popularity of Ancient Historians, 1450–1700." *History and Theory* 5, no. 2 (1966): 135–52.

—————. "Tacitism, Scepticism, and Reason of State." In *The Cambridge History of Political Thought 1450–1700*, edited by J. H. Burns with the assistance of Mark Goldie, 479–98. Cambridge: Cambridge University Press, 1991.

Cardascia, G. "Machiavel et Jean Bodin." *Bibliothèque d'humanisme et renaissance* III (1943): 129–67.

Cartledge, Paul. *The Greeks: A Portrait of Self & Others*. 2nd edition. Oxford: Oxford University Press, 2002.

Cary, M. and H. H. Scullard. *A History of Rome down to the Reign of Constantine*. 3rd ed. New York: St. Martin's Press, 1975.

Chabod, Federico. *Scritti sul Rinascimento.* Turin: Giulio Einaudi Editore, 1967.

Chappell, Vere, ed. *Hobbes and Bramhall on Liberty and Necessity.* Cambridge: Cambridge University Press, 1999.

Chauviré, Roger. *Jean Bodin, auteur de la "République."* Paris: Librairie Ancienne Honoré Champion, 1914.

Christensen, Thomas J. *Useful Adversaries: Grand Strategy, Domestic Mobilization, and Sino-American Conflict, 1947–1958.* Princeton, N.J.: Princeton University Press, 1996.

Churchill, Winston S. *Triumph and Tragedy.* Vol. 6, *The Second World War.* Boston: Houghton Mifflin Company, 1953.

Cicero, Marcus Tullius. *De re publica, De legibus.* Translated by Clinton Walker Keyes. Vol. 16, Cicero. Loeb Classical Library. Cambridge, Mass.: Harvard University Press, 1988.

————. *On Duties.* Translated by Walter Miller. Vol. 21, Cicero. Loeb Classical Library. Cambridge, Mass.: Harvard University Press, [1913] 1997.

Clarendon, Edward Hyde, Earl of. *A Brief View and Survey of the Dangerous and Pernicious Errors to Church and State, in Mr. Hobbes's Book Entitled Leviathan.* Oxford: Printed at the Theater, 1676.

Clark, Michael T. "Realism Ancient and Modern: Thucydides and International Relations." *PS: Political Science and Politics* 26, no. 3 (1993): 491–94.

Coleman, Janet. "Machiavelli's *Via Moderna*: Medieval and Renaissance Attitudes to History." In *Niccolò Machiavelli's The Prince: New Interdisciplinary Essays,* edited by Martin Coyle, 40–64. Manchester: Manchester University Press, 1995.

Colish, Marcia L. "Machiavelli's *Art of War*: A Reconsideration." *Renaissance Quarterly* 51, no. 4 (1998): 1151–68.

Commynes, Philippe de. *The Memoirs of Philippe de Commynes.* Translated by Isabelle Cazeaux. Edited by Samuel Kinser. 2 vols. Columbia: University of South Carolina Press, 1969.

Coser, Lewis A. *The Functions of Social Conflict.* New York: The Free Press, 1956.

Cumberland, Richard. *A Treatise of the Laws of Nature.* Translated by John Maxwell. Edited by Jon Parkin. Indianapolis: Liberty Fund, 2005.

Dahrendorf, Ralf. *Class and Class Conflict in Industrial Society.* Stanford, Calif.: Stanford University Press, 1959.

————. "The New Germanies: Restoration, Revolution, Reconstruction." *Encounter* 22, no. 4 (1964): 50–58.

D'Andrea, Antonio. "The Political and Ideological Context of Innocent Gentillet's *Anti-Machiavel.*" *Renaissance Quarterly* 23, no. 4 (1970): 397–411.

De Grazia, Sebastian. *Machiavelli in Hell.* New York: Vintage Press, 1994.

Della Casa, Giovanni. *Rime et prose di M. Giovanni Della Casa. Con le confessioni, priuilegij di tutti i prencipi.* Venice: Niccolò Bevilacqua, 1558.

De Luca, Luigi. *Stato e chiesa nel pensiero politico di G. Botero.* Rome: R. Danesi Editore, 1946.

Delumeau, Jean. *Sin and Fear: The Emergence of a Western Guilt Culture, 13th–18th Centuries.* Translated by Eric Nicholson. New York: St. Martin's Press, 1990.

De Mattei, Rodolfo. *Dal premachiavellismo all'antimachiavellismo.* Florence: G. C. Sansoni Editore, 1969.

Derathé, Robert. *Jean-Jacques Rousseau et la science politique de son temps*. 2nd edition. Paris: J. Vrin, 1995.

Deutsch, Karl W. *Nationalism and Its Alternatives*. New York: Alfred A. Knopf, 1969.

Diderot, Denis. "Droit naturel." In *Oeuvres complètes de Diderot*, edited by Jules Assézat. Vol. 14, 296–301. Paris: Garnier Frères, 1876.

Diodorus of Sicily. *Library of History*. Translated by Francis R. Walton. 12 vols. Loeb Classical Library. Cambridge, Mass.: Harvard University Press, 1933–1967.

Donnelly, Jack. *Realism and International Relations*. Cambridge: Cambridge University Press, 2000.

Doyle, Michael W. *Ways of War and Peace: Realism, Liberalism, and Socialism*. New York: W. W. Norton & Company, Inc., 1997.

Dyzenhaus, David. "'Now the Machine Runs Itself': Carl Schmitt on Hobbes and Kelsen." *Cardozo Law Review* 16, no. 1 (1994): 1–19.

[Eachard, John]. *Mr. Hobbs's State of Nature Considered, in a Dialogue between Philautus and Timothy*. London: E. T. and R. H. for Nath. Brooke, 1672.

Earl, Donald C. *The Political Thought of Sallust*. Cambridge: Cambridge University Press, 1961.

Ehrenreich, Barbara. *Blood Rites: Origins and History of the Passions of War*. New York: Metropolitan Books, 1997.

Evrigenis, Demetrios I. *Committee of Inquiry into the Rise of Fascism and Racism in Europe: Report on the Findings of the Inquiry*. Brussels: European Parliament, 1985.

Evrigenis, Ioannis D. "Hobbes's Thucydides." *Journal of Military Ethics* 5, no. 4 (2006): 303–16.

————. "The Psychology of Politics: The City-Soul Analogy in Plato's Republic." *History of Political Thought* 23, no. 4 (2002): 590–610.

Ferguson, Adam. *An Essay on the History of Civil Society*. Edited by Fania Oz-Salzberger. Cambridge: Cambridge University Press, 1995.

Feuerbach, D. Paul Johann Anselm. *Anti-Hobbes, Oder über die Grenzen der höchsten Gewalt und das Zwangsrecht der Bürger gegen den Oberherrn*. Erfurt: Henningssche Buchhandlung, 1798.

Fichte, Johann Gottlieb. *Addresses to the German Nation*. Translated by R. F. Jones and G. H. Turnbull. Chicago: The Open Court Publishing Company, 1922.

Figgis, John Neville. *Political Thought from Gerson to Grotius: 1414–1625*. New York: Harper Torchbooks, 1960.

Finley, Moses I. *The Use and Abuse of History*. London: The Hogarth Press, 1986.

Fischer, Markus. "Machiavelli's Rapacious Republicanism." In *Machiavelli's Liberal Republican Legacy*, edited by Paul A. Rahe, xxxi–lxii. Cambridge: Cambridge University Press, 2006.

Fontana, Benedetto. "Sallust and the Politics of Machiavelli." *History of Political Thought* 24, no. 1 (2003): 86–108.

Forde, Steven. "International Realism and the Science of Politics: Thucydides, Machiavelli, and Neorealism." *International Studies Quarterly* 39, no. 2 (1995): 141–60.

Forsyth, Murray. "Thomas Hobbes and the External Relations of States." *British Journal of International Studies* 5, no. 3 (1979): 196–209.

Franklin, Julian H. *Jean Bodin and the Rise of Absolutist Theory*. Cambridge: Cambridge University Press, 1973.

Frei, Christoph. *Hans J. Morgenthau: An Intellectual Biography*. Baton Rouge: Louisiana State University Press, 2001.

Freud, Sigmund. *Civilization and Its Discontents*. Translated by James Strachey. New York: W. W. Norton & Company, Inc., 1989.

Fried, Morton H. "The State, the Chicken, and the Egg; or, What Came First?" In *Origins of the State: The Anthropology of Political Evolution*, edited by Ronald Cohen and Elman R. Service, 35–47. Philadelphia: Institute for the Study of Human Issues, 1978.

Friedrich, Carl J. *Constitutional Reason of State: The Survival of the Constitutional Order*. Providence, R.I.: Brown University Press, 1957.

Frye, Charles E. "Carl Schmitt's Concept of the Political." *The Journal of Politics* 28, no. 4 (1966): 818–30.

Garosci, Aldo. *Jean Bodin: Politica e diritto nel Rinascimento francese*. Milan: A. Corticelli, 1934.

Garst, Daniel. "Thucydides and Neorealism." *International Studies Quarterly* 33, no. 1 (1989): 3–27.

Gellner, Ernest. *Nationalism*. New York: New York University Press, 1997.

———. *Nations and Nationalism*. Ithaca: Cornell University Press, 1983.

[Gentillet, Innocent]. *A Discourse upon the Meanes of Well Governing and Maintaining in Good Peace, a Kingdome, or Other Principalitie. Divided into Three Parts, Namely, the Counsell, the Religion, and the Policie, which a Prince Ought to Hold and Follow. Against Nicholas Machiavell the Florentine*. Translated by Simon Patrick. London: Adam Islip, 1602.

Gentillet, Innocent. *Discours contre Machiavel: A New Edition of the Original Text with Selected Variant Readings, Introduction, and Notes*. Edited by Antonio D'Andrea and Pamela D. Stewart. Florence: Casalini Libri, 1974.

———. *Discours sur les moyens de bien gouverner et maintenir en bonne paix un royaume ou autre principauté. Divisez en trois parties: asavoir, du conseil, de la religion & police que doit tenir un prince. Contre Nicolas Machiavel florentin [Anti-Machiavel]*. Edited by C. Edward Rathé. Geneva: Librairie Droz, 1968.

Germino, Dante. "Machiavelli's Thoughts on the Psyche and Society." In *The Political Calculus: Essays on Machiavelli's Philosophy*, edited by Anthony J. Parel, 59–82. Toronto: The University of Toronto Press, 1972.

Gert, Bernard. "Hobbes and Psychological Egoism." *Journal of the History of Ideas* 28, no. 4 (1967): 503–20.

———. "Hobbes, Mechanism, and Egoism." *The Philosophical Quarterly* 15, no. 61 (1965): 341–49.

Gilbert, Felix. "The Concept of Nationalism in Machiavelli's *Prince*." *Studies in the Renaissance* 1 (1954): 38–48.

———. *Machiavelli and Guicciardini: Politics and History in Sixteenth Century Florence*. Princeton, N.J.: Princeton University Press, 1965.

———. "Machiavellism." In *Dictionary of the History of Ideas: Studies of Selected Pivotal Ideas*, 5 vols, edited by Philip P. Wiener, 3: 116–26. New York: Charles Scribner's Sons, 1973.

Gilpin, Robert. "The Richness of the Tradition of Political Realism." In *Neorealism and Its Critics*, edited by Robert O. Keohane, 301–21. New York: Columbia University Press, 1986.

Gökalp, Ziya. *The Principles of Turkism*. Translated by Robert Devereux. Leyden: E. J. Brill, 1968.

———. *Turkish Nationalism and Western Civilization: Selected Essays*. Translated by Niyazi Berkes. New York: Columbia University Press, 1959.

Goldsmith, M. M. Introduction to *The Elements of Law Natural & Politic, by Thomas Hobbes*. Edited by Ferdinand Tönnies. 2nd edition. London: Frank Cass, & Co., 1969.

Gomme, Arnold W. *A Historical Commentary on Thucydides*. 4 vols. Oxford: The Clarendon Press, 1945–70.

Gooch, George Peabody. *Hobbes*. Vol. 25, *Proceedings of the British Academy*. London: Humphrey Milford, Amen House, 1939.

Gordon, M. D. "The Collection of Ship-Money in the Reign of Charles I." *Transactions of the Royal Historical Society, 3rd series* 4 (1910): 141–62.

Graham, William. *English Political Philosophy from Hobbes to Maine*. London: E. Arnold, 1899.

Grene, David. *Greek Political Theory: The Image of Man in Thucydides and Plato*. Chicago: The University of Chicago Press, 1967.

Guicciardini, Francesco. *Considerations of the Discourses of Niccolò Machiavelli*. In *The Sweetness of Power: Machiavelli's Discourses & Guicciardini's Considerations*. Translated by James B. Atkinson and David Sices. DeKalb: Northern Illinois University Press, 2002.

———. *Dialogue on the Government of Florence*. Translated and edited by Alison Brown. Cambridge: Cambridge University Press, 1994.

———. *Opere*, 2 vols. Edited by Roberto Palmarocchi. Milan: Rizzoli, 1941.

Hale, J. R. "Sixteenth-Century Explanations of War and Violence." *Past and Present* 51 (1971): 3–26.

Hall, Edith. *Inventing the Barbarian: Greek Self-Definition through Tragedy*. Oxford: The Clarendon Press, 1989.

Hamilton, Alexander, James Madison, and John Jay. *The Federalist Papers*. Edited by Clinton Rossiter with an introduction and notes by Charles R. Kessler. New York: Signet, 2003.

Hardin, Russell. *Collective Action*. Baltimore: The Johns Hopkins University Press for Resources for the Future, 1982.

———. *One for All: The Logic of Group Conflict*. Princeton, N.J.: Princeton University Press, 1995.

Hariot, Thomas. *A Briefe and True Report of the New Found Land of Virginia, of the Commodities and of the Nature and Manners of the Naturall Inhabitants, Etc.* Frankfurt am Main: J. Wechel, 1590.

Harrington, James. *The Common-Wealth of Oceana*. London: Printed by J. Streater for Livewell Chapman, [etc.], 1656.

Haslam, Jonathan. *No Virtue like Necessity: Realist Thought in International Relations since Machiavelli*. New Haven, Conn.: Yale University Press, 2002.

Hegel, Georg Wilhelm Friedrich. *Elements of the Philosophy of Right*. Translated by H. B. Nisbet. Edited by Allen W. Wood. Cambridge: Cambridge University Press, 1991.

————. "The German Constitution." In *Political Writings*, edited by T. M. Knox, 143–242. Oxford: The Clarendon Press, 1964.

————. *Lectures on the History of Philosophy*. Translated by E. S. Haldane and Frances H. Simpson. 3 vols. Reprint. Lincoln: University of Nebraska Press, 1995.

————. *Phenomenology of Spirit*. Translated by A. V. Miller. Oxford: Oxford University Press, 1977.

————. *The Philosophy of History*. Translated by J. Sibree. New York: Dover Publications, Inc., 1956.

————. "The Philosophy of Spirit." In *Hegel and the Human Spirit: A Translation of the Jena Lectures on the Philosophy of Spirit (1805–6) with Commentary*, edited by Leo Rauch. Detroit: Wayne State University Press, 1983.

————. "The Positivity of the Christian Religion." In *Early Theological Writings*, edited by T. M. Knox, 67–181. Philadelphia: University of Pennsylvania Press, 1971.

Heinz, Wolff-Rüdiger. *Die Furcht als politisches Phänomen bei Tacitus*. Amsterdam: Verlag B. R. Grüner, 1975.

Herder, Johann Gottfried. *Another Philosophy of History for the Education of Mankind: One among Many Contributions of the Century*. In *Another Philosophy of History and Selected Political Writings*, translated & edited by Ioannis D. Evrigenis and Daniel Pellerin, 1–97. Indianapolis: Hackett Publishing Company, 2004.

Herodotus. *Historiae*. 2 vols. Edited by K. Hude. 3rd edition. Oxford: The Clarendon Press, 1927.

————. *The History*. Translated by David Grene. Chicago: The University of Chicago Press, 1987.

Herzl, Theodor. *The Jewish State: An Attempt at a Modern Solution to the Jewish Question*. Translated by Sylvie D'Avigdor. London: Rita Searl, 1946.

Hinsley, F. H. *Power and the Pursuit of Peace: Theory and Practice in the History of the Relations between States*. Cambridge: Cambridge University Press, 1963.

Hippocrates. *Decorum*. Translated by W. H. S. Jones. Vol. 2, Hippocrates. Loeb Classical Library. Cambridge, Mass.: Harvard University Press, 1967.

Hirschman, Albert O. *The Passions and the Interests: Political Arguments for Capitalism before Its Triumph*. Twentieth anniversary edition. Princeton, N.J.: Princeton University Press, 1997.

Hobbes, Thomas. *Behemoth or the Long Parliament*. Edited by Ferdinand Tönnies. London: Simpkin, Marshall, & Co., 1889.

————. *Behemoth or the Long Parliament*. Edited by Ferdinand Tönnies, with a new introduction by Stephen Holmes. Chicago: The University of Chicago Press, 1990.

————. *A Briefe of the Art of Rhetorique*. London: Tho. Cotes for Andrew Crooke, 1657.

————. *The Correspondence of Thomas Hobbes*. Edited by Noel Malcolm. 2 vols. Oxford: The Clarendon Press, 1994.

————. *De Cive, the English Version, Entitled in the First Edition Philosophicall Rudiments of Government and Society*. Oxford: The Clarendon Press, 1983.

————. *De Cive, the Latin Version, Entitled in the First Edition Elementorum Philosophiæ Sectio Tertia de Cive and in Later Editions Elementa Philosophica de Cive*. Oxford: The Clarendon Press, 1983.

———. *A Dialogue between a Philosopher and a Student of the Common Laws of England.* Edited by Joseph Cropsey, Chicago: The University of Chicago Press, 1997.

———. *The Elements of Law Natural and Politic.* Edited by Ferdinand Tönnies. London: Simpkin, Marshall, & Co., 1889.

———. *The Elements of Law Natural and Politic.* 2nd edition. Edited by Ferdinand Tönnies, with an Introduction by M. M. Goldsmith. London: Frank Cass, 1969.

———. *The Elements of Law, Natural and Politic: Part I, Human Nature, Part II, De Corpore Politico; with Three Lives.* Edited by J. C. A. Gaskin. Oxford: Oxford University Press, 1994.

———. *The English Works of Thomas Hobbes of Malmesbury.* Edited by Sir William Molesworth, 11 vols. London: John Bohn, 1839–45.

———. *Leviathan, or the Matter, Forme & Power of a Common-Wealth Ecclesiasticall and Civill.* London: Andrew Crooke, 1651.

———. *Leviathan: With Selected Variants from the Latin Edition of 1668.* Edited by Edwin Curley. Indianapolis: Hackett Publishing Company, 1994.

———. *Man and Citizen.* Translated by Charles T. Wood, T. S. K. Scott-Craig, and Bernard Gert. Indianapolis: Hackett Publishing Company, 1991.

———. "Of Liberty and Necessity." In *Hobbes and Bramhall on Liberty and Necessity,* edited by Vere Chappell, 15–42. Cambridge: Cambridge University Press, 1999.

———. "Of the Life and History of Thucydides." In *The Peloponnesian War,* by Thucydides, edited by David Grene, 569–86. Chicago: The University of Chicago Press, 1989.

———. *On the Citizen.* Edited by Richard Tuck and Michael Silverthorne. Cambridge: Cambridge University Press, 1998.

———. *Thomae Hobbesii Malmesburiensis vita.* London: n.p., 1679.

———. *Thomas White's De Mundo Examined.* Translated by Harold Whitmore Jones. London: Bradford University Press in association with Crosby Lockwood Staples, 1976.

Hobsbawm, Eric. "Introduction: Inventing Traditions." In *The Invention of Tradition,* edited by Eric Hobsbawm and Terence Ranger, 1–14. Cambridge: Cambridge University Press, 1997.

Hoffmann, Stanley. "International Relations: The Long Road to Theory." *World Politics* 11, no. 3 (1959): 346–77.

———. *Janus and Minerva: Essays in the Theory and Practice of International Politics.* Boulder, Colo.: Westview Press, 1987.

———. "Nationalism and World Order." In *Nationalism and Internationalism in the Post-Cold War Era,* edited by Kjell Goldmann, Ulf Hannerz, and Charles Westin, 195–215. London: Routledge, 2000.

———. "Notes on the Limits of 'Realism.'" *Social Research* 48, no. 4 (1981): 653–59.

———. "Raymond Aron and the Theory of International Relations." *International Studies Quarterly* 29, no. 1 (1985): 13–27.

Holmes, Stephen. Introduction to *Behemoth or the Long Parliament* by Thomas Hobbes, edited by Ferdinand Tönnies. Chicago: The University of Chicago Press, 1990.

Homer. *Homer's Odysses.* Translated by Thomas Hobbes. London: J. C. for W. Crook, 1675.

Honig, Jan Willem. "Totalitarianism and Realism: Hans Morgenthau's German Years." In *Roots of Realism*, edited by Benjamin Frankel, 283–313. London: Frank Cass, 1996.

Honneth, Axel. *The Struggle for Recognition: The Moral Grammar of Social Conflicts.* Translated by Joel Anderson. Cambridge: Polity Press, 1995.

Höpfl, Harro. "Orthodoxy and Reason of State." *History of Political Thought* 23, no. 2 (2002): 211–37.

Hornblower, Simon. *A Commentary on Thucydides.* 2 vols. Oxford: The Clarendon Press, 1991.

Hörnqvist, Mikael. *Machiavelli and Empire.* Cambridge: Cambridge University Press, 2004.

Horrocks, John Wesley. "Machiavelli in Tudor Political Opinion and Discussion." D. Litt. thesis, University of London, 1908.

Hume, David. "Of Political Society." Vol. 4, *The Philosophical Works of David Hume.* Edinburgh: Printed for A. Black, W. Tait, and C. Tait, 1826.

——. *A Treatise of Human Nature.* Edited by David Fate Norton and Mary J. Norton. Oxford: Oxford University Press, 2001.

Inglehart, Ronald, Mansoor Moaddel, and Mark Tessler. "Xenophobia and In-Group Solidarity in Iraq: A Natural Experiment on the Impact of Insecurity." *Perspectives on Politics* 4, no. 3 (September 2006): 495–505.

Huppert, George. *The Idea of Perfect History: Historical Erudition and Historical Philosophy in Renaissance France.* Urbana: University of Illinois Press, 1970.

Jacoby, Felix. *Die Fragmente der griechischen Historiker.* 3 vols. Berlin: Weidmann, 1923–1958.

Johnson Bagby, Laurie. "The Use and Abuse of Thucydides in International Relations." *International Organization* 48, no. 1 (1994): 131–53.

Johnson, James Turner. *Ideology, Reason, and the Limitation of War.* Princeton, N.J.: Princeton University Press, 1975.

Kagan, Donald. *The Outbreak of the Peloponnesian War.* Ithaca: Cornell University Press, 1989.

Kahn, Victoria. "Hamlet or Hecuba: Carl Schmitt's Decision." *Representations* 83 (2003): 67–96.

——. *Machiavellian Rhetoric: From the Counter-Reformation to Milton.* Princeton, N.J.: Princeton University Press, 1994.

——. "Reading Machiavelli: Innocent Gentillet's Discourse on Method." *Political Theory* 22, no. 4 (1994): 539–60.

——. "Reduction and the Praise of Disunion in Machiavelli's *Discourses.*" *Journal of Medieval and Renaissance Studies* 18, no. 1 (1988): 1–19.

Kalyvas, Andreas. "Who's Afraid of Carl Schmitt?" *Philosophy & Social Criticism* 25, no. 5 (1999): 87–125.

Kalyvas, Stathis N. "The Ontology of 'Political Violence': Action and Identity in Civil Wars." *Perspectives on Politics* 1, no. 3 (2003): 475–94.

Kant, Immanuel. *The Critique of Judgement.* Translated by James Creed Meredith. Oxford: Oxford University Press, 1952.

_____. "Idea for a Universal History with a Cosmopolitan Intent." In *Perpetual Peace and Other Essays*, edited by Ted Humphrey, 29–40. Indianapolis: Hackett Publishing Company, 1983.

_____. "The Metaphysics of Morals." In *Practical Philosophy*, edited by Mary J. Gregor, 353–603. Cambridge: Cambridge University Press, 1996.

_____. "On the Proverb: That May Be True in Theory, but Is of No Practical Use." In *Perpetual Peace and Other Essays*, edited by Ted Humphrey, 61–92. Indianapolis: Hackett Publishing Company, 1983.

_____. "Speculative Beginning of Human History." In *Perpetual Peace and Other Essays*, edited by Ted Humphrey, 49–60. Indianapolis: Hackett Publishing Company, 1983.

_____. "To Perpetual Peace: A Philosophical Sketch." In *Perpetual Peace and Other Essays*, edited by Ted Humphrey, 106–43. Indianapolis: Hackett Publishing Company, 1983.

_____. *Werke*. 9 vols. Berlin: Walter de Gruyter & Co., 1968.

Kavka, Gregory S. "Hobbes's War of All against All." *Ethics* 93, no. 2 (1983): 291–310.

Keir, David Lindsay. "The Case of Ship-Money." *The Law Quarterly Review* 52, no. 208 (1936): 546–74.

Kelley, Donald R. "Murd'rous Machiavel in France: A Post Mortem." *Political Science Quarterly* 85, no. 4 (1970): 545–59.

Kelly, George Armstrong. *Idealism, Politics and History: Sources of Hegelian Thought*. Cambridge: Cambridge University Press, 1969.

_____. "Notes on Hegel's 'Lordship and Bondage.'" *The Review of Metaphysics* 19, no. 4 (1966): 780–802.

Kennedy, Ellen. *Constitutional Failure: Carl Schmitt in Weimar*. Durham, N.C.: Duke University Press, 2004.

_____. "Hostis Not Inimicus: Toward a Theory of the Public in the Work of Carl Schmitt." In *Law as Politics: Carl Schmitt's Critique of Liberalism*, edited by David Dyzenhaus, 92–108. Durham, N.C.: Duke University Press, 1998.

Keohane, Nannerl O. *Philosophy and the State in France: From the Renaissance to the Enlightenment*. Princeton, N.J.: Princeton University Press, 1980.

Keohane, Robert O. "Theory of World Politics: Structural Realism and Beyond." In *Political Science: The State of the Discipline*, edited by Ada Finifter, 503–40. Washington, D.C.: American Political Science Association, 1983.

Kersting, Wolfgang. "Politics, Freedom, and Order: Kant's Political Philosophy." In *The Cambridge Companion to Kant*, edited by Paul Guyer, 342–66. Cambridge: Cambridge University Press, 1992.

Kidd, Ian Gray. "Posidonius." In *Oxford Classical Dictionary*, edited by Simon Hornblower and Antony Spawforth, 1231–33. Oxford: Oxford University Press, 1996.

Kishlansky, Mark A. *A Monarchy Transformed: Britain 1603–1714*. The Penguin History of Britain. London: Penguin Books, 1997.

Klosko, George, and Daryl Rice. "Thucydides and Hobbes's State of Nature." *History of Political Thought* VI, no. 3 (1985): 405–09.

Kluxen, Kurt. *Politik und menschliche Existenz bei Machiavelli*. Stuttgart: W. Kohlhammer Verlag, 1967.

Kneppe, Alfred. *Metus temporum: Zur Bedeutung von Angst in Politik und Gesellschaft der römischen Kaiserzeit des 1. und 2. Jhdts. n. Chr.* Stuttgart: Franz Steiner Verlag, 1994.

Kokaz, Nancy. "Moderating Power: A Thucydidean Perspective." *Review of International Studies* 27 (2001): 27–49.

Koskenniemi, Martti. *The Gentle Civilizer of Nations: The Rise and Fall of International Law 1870–1960.* Cambridge: Cambridge University Press, 2001.

Kroner, Richard. Introduction to *Early Theological Writings* by Georg Wilhelm Friedrich Hegel. Translated by T. M. Knox and Richard Kroner. Philadelphia: University of Pennsylvania Press, 1971.

Laak, Dirk van and Ingeborg Villinger, eds. *Nachlass Carl Schmitt: Verzeichnis des Bestandes im Nordhein-Westfälischen Hauptstaatsarchiv.* Siegeburg: Respublica Verlag, 1993.

La Rochefoucauld, François Duc de. *Maxims.* Translated by Leonard Tancock. Harmondsworth: Penguin, 1959.

Lawson, George. "An Examination of the Political Part of Mr. Hobbs His Leviathan." In *Leviathan: Contemporary Responses to the Political Theory of Thomas Hobbes*, edited by G. A. J. Rogers, 15–114. Bristol: Thoemmes Press, 1657.

LeDoux, Joseph. *The Emotional Brain: The Mysterious Underpinnings of Emotional Life.* New York: Simon & Schuster, 1996.

Legro, Jeffrey W. and Andrew Moravcsik. "Is Anybody Still a Realist?" *International Security* 24, no. 2 (1999): 5–55.

Leibniz, Gottfried Wilhelm. *The Political Writings of Leibniz.* Translated by Patrick Riley. Cambridge: Cambridge University Press, 1972.

Leijenhorst, Cees. *The Mechanisation of Aristotelianism: The Late Aristotelian Setting of Thomas Hobbes' Natural Philosophy.* Leiden: Brill, 2002.

Levene, D. S. "Pity, Fear and the Historical Audience: Tacitus on the Fall of Vitellius." In *The Passions in Roman Thought and Literature*, edited by Susanna Morton Braund and Christopher Gill, 128–49. Cambridge: Cambridge University Press, 1997.

Levy, Jack S. "The Diversionary Theory of War: A Critique." In *Handbook of War Studies*, edited by Manus I. Midlarsky, 259–88. Ann Arbor: The University of Michigan Press, 1996.

Liddell, H. G. *An Intermediate Greek–English Lexicon Founded upon the Seventh Edition of Liddell and Scott's Greek–English Lexicon.* Oxford: The Clarendon Press, 1997.

Lipsius, Justus. *Politica: Six Books of Politics or Political Instruction.* Translated by Jan Waszink. Assen: van Gorcum, 2004.

Livy [Titus Livius]. *Ab urbe condita.* Translated by B. O. Foster et al. Vols. 1–4 of Livy. Loeb Classical Library. Cambridge, Mass.: Harvard University Press, 1919–1959.

Locke, John. *Two Treatises of Government.* Edited by Peter Laslett. Cambridge: Cambridge University Press, 1997.

Lucretius [Carus, Titus]. *On the Nature of Things.* Translated by W. H. D. Rouse. Revised by Martin F. Smith. Loeb Classical Library. Cambridge, Mass.: Harvard University Press, 1975.

Lynch, Christopher. Introduction to *Art of War* by Niccolò Machiavelli. Translated by Christopher Lynch. Chicago: The University of Chicago Press, 2003.

Machiavelli, Niccolò. *The Art of War.* A revised edition of the Ellis Farneworth translation with an introduction by Neal Wood. New York: Da Capo Press, 1965.

———. *Art of War*. Translated by Christopher Lynch. Chicago: The University of Chicago Press, 2003.

———. *Discourses on Livy*. Translated by Harvey C. Mansfield and Nathan Tarcov. Chicago: The University of Chicago Press, 1996.

———. *Florentine Histories*. Translated by Harvey C. Mansfield and Laura F. Banfield. Princeton, N.J.: Princeton University Press, 1988.

———. *Mandragola*. Translated by Mera J. Flaumenhaft. Prospect Heights, Ill.: Waveland Press, 1981.

———. *Opere*. Edited by Corrado Vivanti. 3 vols. Torino: Einaudi-Gallimard, 1997–2005.

———. *The Prince*. Translated by Harvey C. Mansfield. 2nd edition. Chicago: The University of Chicago Press, 1998.

Maitland, Frederic William. *A Historical Sketch of Liberty and Equality as Ideals of English Political Philosophy: From the Time of Hobbes to the Time of Coleridge*. Cambridge: Macmillan & Co., 1875.

Malcolm, Noel. *Aspects of Hobbes*. Oxford: The Clarendon Press, 2002.

———. "Hobbes and Spinoza." In *The Cambridge History of Political Thought, 1450–1700*, edited by J. H. Burns and Mark Goldie, 530–57. Cambridge: Cambridge University Press, 1991.

———. "Hobbes, Sandys, and the Virginia Company." *Historical Journal* 24, no. 2 (1981): 297–321.

Mandeville, Bernard. *The Fable of the Bees; or, Private Vices, Publick Benefits*. 2 vols. Indianapolis: Liberty Fund, 1988.

Mannoni, Pierre. *La peur*. Paris: Presses Universitaires de France, 1995.

Mansfield, Harvey C. "Hobbes and the Science of Indirect Government." *American Political Science Review* 65, no. 1 (1971): 97–110.

———. *Machiavelli's New Modes and Orders: A Study of the Discourses on Livy*. Chicago: The University of Chicago Press, 2001.

———. *Machiavelli's Virtue*. Chicago: The University of Chicago Press, 1998.

———. "On the Impersonality of the Modern State: A Comment on Machiavelli's Use of *Stato*." *American Political Science Review* 77, no. 4 (1983): 849–57.

Mardin, Sherif. "The Ottoman Empire." In *After Empire: Multiethnic Societies and Nation-Building; the Soviet Union and the Russian, Ottoman, and Habsburg Empires*, edited by Karen Barkey and Mark von Hagen, 115–28. Boulder, Colo.: Westview Press, 1997.

Mariana, Juan de. *The King and the Education of the King*. Translated by George Albert Moore. Chevy Chase, Md.: The Country Dollar Press, 1948.

Martinich, Aloysius P. *Hobbes: A Biography*. Cambridge: Cambridge University Press, 1999.

Mastnak, Tomaz. "Abbé de Saint-Pierre: European Union and the Turk." *History of Political Thought* 19, no. 4 (1998): 570–98.

May, Rollo. *The Meaning of Anxiety*. New York: The Ronald Press Company, 1950.

Mazzini, Giuseppe. "The Duties of Man." In *The Duties of Man and Other Essays*, edited by Thomas Okey, 7–122. London: J. M. Dent & Sons, Ltd., 1910.

McCormick, John P. *Carl Schmitt's Critique of Liberalism: Against Politics as Technology*. Cambridge: Cambridge University Press, 1997.

McGushin, Patrick. *C. Sallustius Crispus, Bellum Catilinae, a Commentary.* Vol. 45, *Mnemosyne.* Leiden: J. Brill, 1977.

McNeilly, F. S. "Egoism in Hobbes." *Philosophical Quarterly* 16, no. 64 (1966): 193–206.

Meier, Heinrich. *Carl Schmitt and Leo Strauss: The Hidden Dialogue.* Translated by Harvey J. Lomax. Chicago: The University of Chicago Press, 1995.

Meinecke, Friedrich. *Cosmopolitanism & the National State.* Translated by Robert B. Kimber. Princeton, N.J.: Princeton University Press, 1970.

————. *Machiavellism: The Doctrine of Raison d' État and Its Place in Modern History.* Translated by Douglas Scott. New York: Praeger, 1965.

Meyer, Edward. *Machiavelli and the Elizabethan Drama.* Weimar: Verlag von Emil Felber, 1897.

Milton, John. *The History of Britain, That Part Especially Now Call'd England.* London: Printed by J. M. for James Allestry, 1670.

Mintz, Samuel I. *The Hunting of Leviathan: Seventeenth-Century Reactions to the Materialism and Moral Philosophy of Thomas Hobbes.* Cambridge: Cambridge University Press, 1970.

Montaigne, Michel de. *The Complete Essays of Montaigne.* Translated by Donald M. Frame. Stanford, Calif.: Stanford University Press, 1958.

Montesquieu, Charles-Louis de Secondat, baron de la Brède et de. *The Spirit of the Laws.* Translated by Anne Cohler, Basia Miller, and Harold Stone. Cambridge: Cambridge University Press, 1989.

Morgenthau, Hans J. "Correspondence: Dilemmas of Politics." *International Affairs* 35, no. 4 (1959): 502.

————. "Fragment of an Intellectual Biography: 1904–1932." In *Truth and Tragedy: A Tribute to Hans J. Morgenthau,* edited by Kenneth Thompson and Robert J. Myers with the assistance of Robert Osgood and Tang Tsou, 1–17. New Brunswick, N.J.: Transaction Books, 1984.

————. *In Defense of the National Interest: A Critical Examination of American Foreign Policy.* New York: Alfred A. Knopf, 1951.

————. *Die internationale Rechtspflege, ihr Wesen und ihre Grenzen.* Vol. 12, *Frankfurter Abhandlungen zum Kriegsverhütungsrecht.* Leipzig: Universitätsverlag von Robert Noske, 1929.

————. *La notion du "politique" et la théorie des différends internationaux.* Paris: Librairie du Recueil Sirey, 1933.

————. *Politics among Nations: The Struggle for Power and Peace.* 6th edition. New York: McGraw-Hill, Inc., 1985.

————. *Science: Servant or Master?* New York: American Library, distributed by W. W. Norton & Co., Inc., 1972.

————. *Scientific Man vs. Power Politics.* Chicago: The University of Chicago Press, 1974.

Mowrer, O. H. "A Stimulus–Response Analysis of Anxiety and Its Role as a Reinforcing Agent." *Psychological Review* 46, no. 6 (1939): 553–65.

Müller, Jan-Werner. *A Dangerous Mind: Carl Schmitt in Post-War European Thought.* New Haven, Conn.: Yale University Press, 2003.

Nederman, Cary J. "Machiavelli and Moral Character: Principality, Republic and the Moral Psychology of Virtù." *History of Political Thought* 21, no. 3 (2000): 349–64.

———. "Sovereignty, War and the Corporation: Hegel on the Medieval Foundations of the Modern State." *The Journal of Politics* 49, no. 2 (1987): 500–20.

Noack, Paul. *Carl Schmitt: Eine Biographie.* Frankfurt am Main: Propyläen, 1993.

Nozick, Robert. *Anarchy, State, and Utopia.* New York: Basic Books, 1974.

Oakeshott, Michael. Letter to John Watkins, May 24, 1963. *Political Theory* 29, no. 6 (2001): 834–36.

Öhman, Arne. "Fear and Anxiety: Evolutionary, Cognitive, and Clinical Perspectives." In *Handbook of Emotions,* edited by Michael Lewis and Jeannette M. Haviland-Jones, 573–93. New York: The Guilford Press, 2000.

Olson, Mancur. *The Logic of Collective Action: Public Goods and the Theory of Groups.* Cambridge, Mass.: Harvard University Press, 1965.

Oppenheimer, Franz. *The State: Its History and Development Viewed Sociologically.* Translated by John M. Gitterman. Indianapolis: The Bobbs–Merrill Company Publishers, 1914.

Orwin, Clifford. *The Humanity of Thucydides.* Princeton, N.J.: Princeton University Press, 1994.

———. "Justifying Empire: The Speech of the Athenians at Sparta and the Problem of Justice in Thucydides." *The Journal of Politics* 48, no. 1 (1986): 72–85.

Osmond, Patricia J. "Sallust and Machiavelli: From Civic Humanism to Political Prudence." *Journal of Medieval and Renaissance Studies* 23, no. 3 (1993): 407–38.

Panella, Antonio. *Gli antimachiavellici.* Florence: G. C. Sansoni Editore, 1943.

Parel, Anthony J. *The Machiavellian Cosmos.* New Haven, Conn.: Yale University Press, 1992.

[Parker, Henry]. *The Case of Shipmony Briefly Discoursed, According to the Grounds of Law, Policie, and Conscience.* London: n.p., 1640.

Paul, G. M. *A Historical Commentary on Sallust's Bellum Jugurthinum.* Liverpool: Francis Cairns, 1984.

Petersen, Roger D. *Understanding Ethnic Violence: Fear, Hatred, and Resentment in Twentieth-Century Eastern Europe.* Cambridge: Cambridge University Press, 2002.

Pichler, Hans-Karl. "The Godfathers of 'Truth': Max Weber and Carl Schmitt in Morgenthau's Theory of Power Politics." *Review of International Studies* 24, no. 3 (1998): 185–200.

Pittman, Thane S. "Motivation." In *The Handbook of Social Psychology,* edited by Daniel T. Gilbert, Susan T. Fiske, and Gardner Lindzey. 2 vols. Vol. 1, 549–90. Boston: The McGraw-Hill Companies, Inc., 1998.

Plato. *The Laws of Plato.* Translated by Thomas L. Pangle. Chicago: The University of Chicago Press, 1980.

———. *Republic.* Translated by Allan Bloom. New York: Basic Books, 1991.

———. *Statesman.* Translated by Harold N. Fowler. Vol. 8, Plato. Loeb Classical Library. Cambridge, Mass.: Harvard University Press, 1990.

Plutarch. "How to Profit by One's Enemies." Translated by Frank Cole Babbitt. Vol. 2, *Moralia.* Loeb Classical Library. Cambridge, Mass.: Harvard University Press, 2002.

———. "Marcus Cato". Translated by Bernadotte Perrin. Vol. 2, *Lives.* Loeb Classical Library. Cambridge, Mass.: Harvard University Press, 1948.

Pocock, John G. A. *The Machiavellian Moment: Florentine Political Thought and the Atlantic Republican Tradition.* Princeton, N.J.: Princeton University Press, 1975.

Polsby, Nelson W. *Congress and the Presidency*. 3rd ed. Englewood Cliffs, N.J.: Prentice–Hall, Inc., 1976.

Polybius. *The Histories*. Translated by W. R. Paton. 6 vols. Loeb Classical Library. Cambridge, Mass.: Harvard University Press, 1922–1927.

Posidonius. *Poseidonios: Die Fragmente I: Texte*. Edited by Willy Theiler. Berlin: Walter de Gruyter, 1982.

_____. *Poseidonios: Die Fragmente II: Erläuterungen*. Edited by Willy Theiler. Berlin: Walter de Gruyter, 1982.

_____. *Posidonius I. The Fragments*. Edited by L. Edelstein and Ian Gray Kidd. Cambridge: Cambridge University Press, 1972.

Post, Gaines. *Studies in Medieval Legal Thought: Public Law and the State, 1100–1322*. Princeton, N.J.: Princeton University Press, 1964.

Price, Jonathan J. *Thucydides and Internal War*. Cambridge: Cambridge University Press, 2001.

Project for the New American Century. 2000. Rebuilding America's Defenses: Strategy, Forces and Resources for a New Century. http://www.newamericancentury.org/RebuildingAmericasDefenses.pdf. Accessed April 2005.

Quintilian. *Institutio oratoria*. Translated by H. E. Butler. 4 vols. Loeb Classical Library. Cambridge, Mass.: Harvard University Press, 1920–1922.

Rachman, Stanley J. *Fear and Courage*. 2nd edition. New York: W. H. Freeman & Company, 1990.

_____. *The Meanings of Fear*. Harmondsworth: Penguin, 1974.

Rahe, Paul A. *Republics Ancient & Modern*. 3 vols. Chapel Hill: The University of North Carolina Press, 1994.

_____. "Thucydides' Critique of Realpolitik." *Security Studies* 5 (1995/1996): 105–41.

Rathé, C. Edward. "Innocent Gentillet and the First 'Anti-Machiavel.'" *Bibliothèque d'humanisme et Renaissance* 27 (1965): 186–225.

Rebhorn, Wayne A. *Foxes and Lions: Machiavelli's Confidence Men*. Ithaca: Cornell University Press, 1988.

Riley, Patrick. "The Abbé de St. Pierre and Voltaire on Perpetual Peace in Europe." *World Affairs* 137, no. 3 (1974–1975): 186–94.

_____. "Federalism in Kant's Political Philosophy." *Publius* 9, no. 4 (1979): 43–64.

_____. "Kant as a Theorist of Peace through International Federalism." *World Affairs* 136, no. 2 (1973): 121–31.

_____. "Rousseau as a Theorist of National and International Federalism." *Publius* 3, no. 1 (1973): 5–17.

Robertson, George Croom. *Hobbes*. Edinburgh: W. Blackwood, 1886.

_____. "Leibniz and Hobbes." *Mind* 13, no. 50 (1888): 312–14.

_____. "*The Quarterly Review* on Hobbes." *Mind* 12, no. 47 (1887): 480–84.

_____. "Review of Thomas Hobbes, *The Elements of Law, Natural and Politic; Behemoth or the Long Parliament*, ed. Ferdinand Tönnies." *Mind* 14, no. 55 (1889): 429–33.

Robin, E. Corey. "Fear: Biography of an Idea." Ph.D. Dissertation, Yale University, 1999.

_____. *Fear: The History of a Political Idea*. Oxford: Oxford University Press, 2004.

_____. "Why Do Opposites Attract? Fear and Freedom in the Modern Political Imagination." In *Fear Itself: Enemies Real & Imagined in American Culture*, edited by Nancy Lusignan Schultz, 3–22. West Lafayette, Ind.: Purdue University Press, 1999.

Rogers, G. A. J. "Hobbes's Hidden Influence." In *Perspectives on Thomas Hobbes*, edited by G. A. J. Rogers and Alan Ryan, 189–205. Oxford: The Clarendon Press, 1988.

————. Introduction to *Perspectives on Thomas Hobbes*, edited by G. A. J. Rogers and Alan Ryan, 1–10. Oxford: The Clarendon Press, 1988.

————, ed. *Leviathan: Contemporary Responses to the Political Theory of Thomas Hobbes*. Bristol: Thoemmes Press, 1995.

Romilly, Jacqueline de. *La Crainte et l'angoisse dans le théâtre d'Eschyle*. Paris: Les Belles Lettres, 1958.

————. *Thucydides and Athenian Imperialism*. Translated by Philip Thody. Salem, N.H.: Ayer Company Publishers, Inc., 1988.

Rosenblum, Nancy L. *Another Liberalism: Romanticism and the Reconstruction of Liberal Thought*. Cambridge, Mass.: Harvard University Press, 1987.

————. *Bentham's Theory of the Modern State*. Cambridge, Mass.: Harvard University Press, 1978.

Rousseau, Jean-Jacques. "Abstract and Judgment of Saint-Pierre's Project for Perpetual Peace." In *Rousseau on International Relations*, edited by Stanley Hoffmann and David P. Fidler, 53–100. Oxford: The Clarendon Press, 1991.

————. *Correspondence générale de J.-J. Rousseau*. Edited by Théophile Dufour. 20 vols. Paris: Librairie Armand Colin, 1924–34.

————. *Discourse on the Origin and Foundations of Inequality among Men*. In *The Discourses and Other Early Political Writings*, translated by Victor Gourevitch, 111–222. Cambridge: Cambridge University Press, 1997.

————. *Émile*. Translated by Allan Bloom. New York: Basic Books, 1979.

————. "Geneva Manuscript." In *On the Social Contract with Geneva Manuscript and Political Economy*, edited by Roger D. Masters, 157–202. New York: St. Martin's Press, 1978.

————. *Of the Social Contract*. In *The Social Contract and Other Later Political Writings*, translated by Victor Gourevitch, 39–152. Cambridge: Cambridge University Press, 1997.

————. "The State of War." In *The Social Contract and Other Later Political Writings*, edited by Victor Gourevitch, 162–76. Cambridge: Cambridge University Press, 1997.

Rumpf, Helmut. *Carl Schmitt und Thomas Hobbes: Ideelle Beziehungen und aktuelle Bedeutung. Mit einer Abhandlung über die Frühschriften Carl Schmitts*. Berlin: Duncker & Humblot, 1972.

Russett, Bruce. *Controlling the Sword: The Democratic Governance of National Security*. Cambridge, Mass.: Harvard University Press, 1990.

Saint-Pierre, Charles Irenée Castel, Abbé de. *A Project for Settling an Everlasting Peace in Europe*. London: Printed for J. Watts, 1714.

————. *Projet pour rendre la paix perpétuelle en Europe*. Paris: Fayard, 1986.

Sallust [Caius Sallustius Crispus]. *The Histories*. 2 vols. Translated by Patrick McGushin. Oxford: The Clarendon Press, 1992.

————. *The War with Catiline*. In *Sallust*, translated by J. C. Rolfe. Loeb Classical Library. Cambridge, Mass.: Harvard University Press, 1921.

———. *The War with Jugurtha*. In *Sallust*, translated by J. C. Rolfe. Loeb Classical Library. Cambridge, Mass.: Harvard University Press, 1921.

Salmon, J. H. M. *Renaissance and Revolt: Essays in the Intellectual and Social History of Early Modern France*. Cambridge: Cambridge University Press, 1987.

Salt, S. P. "Sir Simonds D'Ewes and the Levying of Ship Money, 1635–1640." *The Historical Journal* 37, no. 2 (1994): 253–87.

Sanger, David E. "Russia, China, and the U.S.; in Terror, at Last a Common Enemy for the Big Three." *The New York Times*, October 28, 2001, 1.

Sasso, Gennaro. *Machiavelli e gli antichi e altri saggi*. Vol. I. Milan: Riccardo Ricciardi Editore, 1987.

Scanlon, Thomas Francis. *The Influence of Thucydides on Sallust*. Heidelberg: Carl Winter Universitätsverlag, 1980.

Schellhase, Kenneth C. *Tacitus in Renaissance Political Thought*. Chicago: The University of Chicago Press, 1976.

Schelsky, Helmut. "Der 'Begriff des Politischen' und die politische Erfahrung der Gegenwart." *Der Staat* 22, no. 3 (1983): 321–45.

———. *Thomas Hobbes: Eine Politische Lehre*. Berlin: Duncker & Humblot, 1981.

Scheuerman, William E. *Carl Schmitt: The End of Law*. Lanham, Md.: Rowman & Littlefield Publishers, Inc., 1999.

Schlatter, Richard. "Thomas Hobbes and Thucydides." *Journal of the History of Ideas* 6, no. 3 (1945): 350–62.

Schmitt, Carl. "Der Begriff des Politischen." *Archiv für Sozialwissenschaft und Sozialpolitik* 58 (1927): 1–33.

———. *Der Begriff des Politischen*. Berlin: Duncker & Humblot, 1963.

———. *The Concept of the Political*. Translated by George Schwab. Chicago: The University of Chicago Press, 1996.

———. *The Crisis of Parliamentary Democracy*. Translated by Ellen Kennedy. Cambridge, Mass.: The MIT Press, 1988.

———. *Die Diktatur, Von den Anfängen des modernen Souveränitätsgedankens bis zum proletarischen Klassenkampf*. Munich: Duncker & Humblot, 1921.

———. *Ex captivitate salus: Erfahrungen der Zeit 1945/47*. Cologne: Greven Verlag, 1950.

———. *Glossarium: Aufzeichnungen der Jahre 1947–1951*. Berlin: Duncker & Humblot, 1991.

———. *Hugo Preuss: Sein Staatsbegriff und seine Stellung in der deutschen Staatslehre*. Vol. 72, *Recht und Staat in Geschichte und Gegenwart*. Tübingen: Verlag von J. C. B. Mohr, 1930.

———. *Der Hüter der Verfassung*. 2nd edition. Berlin: Duncker & Humblot, 1969.

———. *Die Kernfrage des Völkerbundes*. Berlin: F. Dümmler, 1926.

———. *The Leviathan in the State Theory of Thomas Hobbes: Meaning and Failure of a Political Symbol*. Translated by George Schwab and Erna Hilfstein. Westport, Conn.: Greenwood Press, 1996.

———. *The Nomos of the Earth in the International Law of the jus publicum Europaeum*. Translated by G. L. Ulmen. New York: Telos Press, Ltd., 2003.

———. *Political Romanticism*. Translated by Guy Oakes. Cambridge, Mass.: The MIT Press, 1986.

———. *Political Theology: Four Chapters on the Concept of Sovereignty*. Translated by George Schwab. Cambridge, Mass.: The MIT Press, 1985.

————. *Politische Theologie: Vier Kapitel zur Lehre von der Souveränität.* Munich: Duncker & Humblot, 1922.

————. "Der Staat als Mechanismus bei Hobbes und Descartes." *Archiv für Rechts- und Sozialphilosophie* 30, no. 4 (1937): 158–68.

————. *Staat, Bewegung, Volk: Die Dreigliederung der politischen Einheit.* Hamburg: Hanseatische Verlagsanstalt, 1933.

————. "The State as Mechanism in Hobbes & Descartes." In *The Leviathan in the State Theory of Thomas Hobbes: Meaning & Failure of a Political Symbol,* translated by George Schwab and Erna Hilfstein, 91–103. Westport, Conn.: Greenwood Press, 1996.

————. *Verfassungslehre.* Munich: Duncker & Humblot, 1928.

————. "Die vollendete Reformation: Bemerkungen und Hinweise zu neuen Leviathan-Interpretationen." *Der Staat* 4, no. 1 (1965): 51–69.

Schwab, George. *The Challenge of the Exception: An Introduction to the Political Ideas of Carl Schmitt between 1921 and 1936.* 2nd edition. Westport, Conn.: Greenwood Press, 1989.

Service, Elman R. *Origins of the State and Civilization: The Process of Cultural Evolution.* New York: W. W. Norton & Company, Inc., 1975.

Shakespeare, William. *The Second Part of King Henry IV.* In *The Annotated Shakespeare,* edited by A. L. Rowse, 1210–77. New York: Greenwich House, 1988.

Shklar, Judith N. "Decisionism." In *Rational Decision,* edited by Carl J. Friedrich, 3–17. New York: Atherton Press, 1964.

————. "The Liberalism of Fear." In *Liberalism and the Moral Life,* edited by Nancy L. Rosenblum, 21–38. Cambridge, Mass.: Harvard University Press, 1989.

————. *Ordinary Vices.* Cambridge, Mass.: The Belknap Press of Harvard University Press, 1984.

Sieyès, Emmanuel Joseph. *What Is the Third Estate?* In *Political Writings,* edited by Michael Sonenscher, 92–162. Indianapolis: Hackett Publishing Company, 2003.

Simmel, Georg. "Conflict." In *Conflict & the Web of Group Affiliations,* translated by Kurt H. Wolff and Reinhard Bendix. New York: The Free Press, 1964.

————. *Gesamtausgabe.* 24 vols. Edited by Otthein Rammstedt. Frankfurt am Main: Suhrkamp, 1989-.

Skinner, Q. R. D. "Ambroggio Lorenzetti: The Artist as Political Philosopher." *Proceedings of the British Academy,* no. 72 (1986): 1–56.

————. *The Foundations of Modern Political Thought.* 2 vols. Cambridge: Cambridge University Press, 1978.

————. *Machiavelli.* New York: Hill and Wang, 1981.

————. "Machiavelli's *Discorsi* and the Pre-Humanist Origins of Republican Ideas." In *Machiavelli and Republicanism,* edited by Gisela Bock, Q. R. D. Skinner, and Maurizio Viroli, 121–41. Cambridge: Cambridge University Press, 1990.

————. *Reason and Rhetoric in the Philosophy of Hobbes.* Cambridge: Cambridge University Press, 1996.

————. "Thomas Hobbes's Antiliberal Theory of Liberty." In *Liberalism without Illusions: Essays on Liberal Theory and the Political Vision of Judith N. Shklar,* edited by Bernard Yack, 149–69. Chicago: The University of Chicago Press, 1996.

————. *Visions of Politics.* 3 vols. Cambridge: Cambridge University Press, 2002.

Slomp, Gabriella. "Hobbes, Thucydides and the Three Greatest Things." *History of Political Thought* 11, no. 4 (1990): 565–86.

Smith, Anthony D. *National Identity.* Reno: University of Nevada Press, 1991.

Smith, Craig S. "Europe's Jews Seek Solace on the Right." *The New York Times,* February 20, 2005, 3.

Smith, Michael Joseph. *Realist Thought from Weber to Kissinger.* Baton Rouge: Louisiana State University Press, 1986.

Smith, Steven B. "Hegel's Views on War, the State, and International Relations." *American Political Science Review* 77, no. 3 (1983): 624–32.

Söllner, Alfons. "German Conservatism in America: Morgenthau's Political Realism." *Telos* 72 (1987): 161–72.

Spackman, Barbara. "Machiavelli and Maxims." *Yale French Studies* 77 (1990): 137– 55.

Stein, Arthur A. "Conflict and Cohesion: A Review of the Literature." *Journal of Conflict Resolution* 20, no. 1 (1976): 143–72.

Stephen, Leslie. *Hobbes.* London: Macmillan & Co., 1904.

Stewart, Pamela D. *Innocent Gentillet e la sua polemica antimachiavellica.* Florence: La Nuova Italia Editrice, 1969.

Strauss, Leo. "Anmerkungen zu Carl Schmitt, Der Begriff des Politischen." *Archiv für Sozialwissenschaft und Sozialpolitik* 67 (1932): 732–49.

_____. *The City and Man.* Chicago: The University of Chicago Press, 1978.

_____. *Natural Right and History.* Chicago: The University of Chicago Press, 1953.

_____. "Quelques remarques sur la science politique de Hobbes." *Recherches Philosophiques* 2 (1933): 609–22.

_____. *The Political Philosophy of Hobbes: Its Basis and Its Genesis.* Translated by Elsa M. Sinclair. Chicago: The University of Chicago Press, 1984.

_____. *Thoughts on Machiavelli.* Chicago: The University of Chicago Press, 1958.

Sullivan, Vickie B. *Machiavelli, Hobbes, & the Formation of a Liberal Republicanism in England.* Cambridge: Cambridge University Press, 2004.

Sumner, William Graham. "War." In *Essays of William Graham Sumner,* edited by Albert Galloway Keller and Maurice R. Davie, vol. 1, 136–73. New Haven, Conn.: Yale University Press, 1934.

Tacitus, Cornelius. *The Annals of Imperial Rome.* Translated by Michael Grant. Harmondsworth: Penguin, 1956.

Tarlton, Charles D. "Rehabilitating Hobbes: Obligation, Anti-Fascism and the Myth of a 'Taylor Thesis.'" *History of Political Thought* 19, no. 3 (1998): 407–38.

Taylor, A. E. *Thomas Hobbes.* London: Archibald Constable & Co., 1908.

Taylor, Charles. *Hegel.* Cambridge: Cambridge University Press, 1975.

Thucydides. *The Peloponnesian War.* Translated by Thomas Hobbes. Edited by David Grene. Chicago: The University of Chicago Press, 1989.

Tocqueville, Alexis de. *Democracy in America.* Translated by Harvey C. Mansfield and Delba Winthrop. Chicago: The University of Chicago Press, 2000.

Tönnies, Ferdinand. *Hobbes: Leben und Lehre.* Stuttgart: Friedrich Frommanns Verlag, 1896.

Treitschke, Heinrich von. *Politics.* 2 vols. Edited by Hans Kohn. New York: The Macmillan Company, 1916.

Tricaud, François. "Hobbes's Conception of the State of Nature from 1640 to 1651: Evolution and Ambiguities." In *Perspectives on Thomas Hobbes*, edited by G. A. J. Rogers and Alan Ryan, 107–23. Oxford: The Clarendon Press, 1988.

Tuck, Richard. "Grotius and Selden." In *The Cambridge History of Political Thought, 1450–1700*, edited by J. H. Burns and Mark Goldie, 499–529. Cambridge: Cambridge University Press, 1991.

———. *Hobbes*. Oxford: Oxford University Press, 1989.

———. "Hobbes and Tacitus." In *Hobbes and History*, edited by G. A. J. Rogers and Tom Sorell, 99–110. London: Routledge, 2000.

———. "Optics and Sceptics: The Philosophical Foundations of Hobbes's Political Thought." In *Conscience and Casuistry in Early Modern Europe*, edited by Edmund Leites, 234–63. Cambridge: Cambridge University Press, 1988.

———. *Philosophy and Government, 1572–1651*. Cambridge: Cambridge University Press, 1993.

———. *The Rights of War and Peace: Political Thought and the International Order from Grotius to Kant*. Oxford: Oxford University Press, 1999.

———. "The Utopianism of *Leviathan*." In *Leviathan after 350 Years*, edited by Tom Sorell and Luc Foisneau, 125–38. Oxford: The Clarendon Press, 2004.

Tucker, Robert W. "Professor Morgenthau's Theory of 'Political Realism.'" *American Political Science Review* 46, no. 1 (1952): 214–24.

Van Creveld, Martin. *The Rise and Decline of the State*. Cambridge: Cambridge University Press, 1999.

Varro, Marcus Terentius. *On the Latin Language*. Translated by Roland G. Kent. 2 vols. Loeb Classical Library. Cambridge, Mass.: Harvard University Press, 1938.

Velleius Paterculus. *Compendium of Roman History*. Edited by Frederick W. Shipley. Loeb Classical Library. Cambridge, Mass.: Harvard University Press, 1924.

Verdon, Michel. "On the Laws of Physical and Human Nature: Hobbes' Physical and Social Cosmologies." *Journal of the History of Ideas* 43, no. 4 (1982): 653–63.

Verhofstadt, Guy. "Europe Has to Become a Force in NATO." *Financial Times*, February 21, 2003, 17.

Vico, Giambattista. *The New Science*. Translated by Thomas Goddard Bergin & Max Harold Fisch. Garden City, N.Y.: Doubleday & Company, Inc., 1961.

Villari, Pasquale. *The Life and Times of Niccolò Machiavelli*. 2 vols. Translated by Linda Villari. New York: Charles Scribner's Sons, 1929.

Virgil. *Aeneid*. Translated by Henry Rushton Fairclough. Revised by G. P. Goold. 2 vols. Loeb Classical Library. Cambridge, Mass.: Harvard University Press, 1999.

Viroli, Maurizio. *From Politics to Reason of State: The Acquisition and Transformation of the Language of Politics 1250–1600*. Cambridge: Cambridge University Press, 1992.

Walt, Stephen M. *The Origins of Alliances*. Ithaca, New York: Cornell University Press, 1987.

Waltz, Kenneth. *Theory of International Politics*. Reading, Mass.: Addison-Wesley, 1979.

Walzer, Michael. *Politics and Passion: Toward a More Egalitarian Liberalism*. New Haven, Conn.: Yale University Press, 2004.

———. *The Revolution of the Saints: A Study in the Origins of Radical Politics*. New York: Atheneum, 1968.

————. *Spheres of Justice: A Defense of Pluralism and Equality.* New York: Basic Books, 1983.

Waszink, Jan. Introduction to *Politica: Six Books of Politics or Political Instruction* by Justus Lipsius. Edited by Jan Waszink, 1–213. Assen: van Gorcum, 2004.

Weiler, Gershon. *From Absolutism to Totalitarianism: Carl Schmitt on Thomas Hobbes.* Durango, Colo.: Hollowbrook Publishing, 1994.

Weissberger, L. Arnold. "Machiavelli and Tudor England." *Political Science Quarterly* 42, no. 4 (1927): 589–607.

Whitfield, John Humphreys. *Machiavelli.* New York: Russell & Russell, 1965.

Wight, Martin. "Correspondence: Dilemmas of Politics." *International Affairs* 35, no. 4 (1959): 502.

————. "Review of *Dilemmas of Politics*, by Hans J. Morgenthau." *International Affairs* 35, no. 2 (1959): 199–200.

Williams, Howard. *Kant's Critique of Hobbes: Sovereignty and Cosmopolitanism.* Cardiff: University of Wales Press, 2003.

Williams, Michael C. "Words, Images, Enemies: Securitization and International Politics." *International Studies Quarterly* 47 (2003): 511–31.

Wolin, Richard. "Reasons of State, States of Reason." *The New Republic*, June 4, 2001, 51–58.

Wolin, Sheldon. *Hobbes and the Epic Tradition of Political Theory.* Los Angeles: William Andrews Clark Memorial Library, University of California, Los Angeles, 1970.

————. *Politics and Vision: Continuity and Innovation in Western Political Thought.* Expanded edition. Princeton, N.J.: Princeton University Press, 2004.

Wood, Neal. Introduction to *The Art of War* by Niccolò Machiavelli. Translated by Ellis Farneworth. New York: Da Capo Press, 1965.

————. "Machiavelli's Concept of Virtù Reconsidered." *Political Studies* 15, no. 2 (1967): 159–72.

————. "Machiavelli's Humanism of Action." In *The Political Calculus: Essays on Machiavelli's Philosophy*, edited by Anthony J. Parel, 33–57. Toronto: The University of Toronto Press, 1972.

————. "Sallust's Theorem: A Comment on 'Fear' in Western Political Thought." *History of Political Thought* 16, no. 2 (1995): 174–89.

Worden, Blair. "English Republicanism." In *The Cambridge History of Political Thought, 1450–1700*, edited by J. H. Burns with the assistance of Mark Goldie, 443–75. Cambridge: Cambridge University Press, 1991.

Wrong, Dennis H. *Power: Its Forms, Bases, and Uses.* New Brunswick, N.J.: Transaction Publishers, 1995.

————. *The Problem of Order: What Unites and Divides Society.* Cambridge, Mass.: Harvard University Press, 1994.

Xenophon. *Oeconomicus.* Translated by E. C. Marchant. Vol. 4, *Xenophon.* Loeb Classical Library. Cambridge, Mass.: Harvard University Press, 2002.

Zainu'ddin, Ailsa Gwennyth. *A Short History of Indonesia.* North Melbourne: Cassell Australia, 1968.

INDEX

INDEX

state of nature (*cont.*)
  Hobbes on, 10n40, 71, 93, 98, 111–19,
    120, 121, 122, 123, 124, 125, 126–28,
    129, 130, 133, 156, 169, 169n36, 170,
    193
  Kant on, 143, 156
  Rousseau on, 134–38, 162n178
  Schmitt on, 169n36, 175–76
  Simmel on, 158–59
  Strauss, Leo, 27n20, 28n24, 28n25, 50n7,
    52n10, 71n92, 98n21, 98n22, 99n26,
    107n60, 130n160, 132n6, 168–69,
    169n33, 169n36, 169n37
  Sullivan, Vickie B., 68n83, 70n91
  Sumner, William Graham, 1n2

Tacitism, 79n30, 79n31, 86, 94–95
Tacitus. *See* Cornelius Tacitus
Taylor, A.E., 132n8
Taylor, Charles, 149n99, 150n105, 150n106,
    150n107, 150n108, 151n116, 151n117,
    152, 152n118, 152n119, 162n176
Terentius Varro, Marcus, 176n76
Thrasymachus, 186
Thucydides, 3n6, 4, 6n20, 15, 15n61, 24–32,
    25n11, 26n16, 28n25, 34, 39–40, 43,
    44, 45, 46, 46n101, 47, 70, 92,
    104n46, 108n62, 112n82, 114n93,
    193, 195, 196
  and Hobbes, 26n13, 26n15, 26n19,
    104n46, 108n62, 112n82, 114n93,
    195
  and Sallust, 39–40, 45
  on negative association, 26–32, 40, 43
  on psychology, 31–32
  on *stasis*, 31, 39, 39n77
  on the "truest cause" of the
    Peloponnesian War, 26–30
  on the political economy of fear, 30–32
Tiberius Iulius Caesar Augustus, 86,
    94n3
Titus Lucretius Carus, 112

Tocqueville, Alexis de, 20n82
Tönnies, Ferdinand, 132n6, 157, 164,
    164n2
Treitschke, Heinrich von, 11n46, 192
Tricaud, François, 105n50, 112n81,
    117n102
Tuck, Richard, 94–95, 95n4, 96, 96n10,
    96n11, 97n13, 97n14, 97n15, 98n21,
    98n22, 100n30, 106n55, 119n111,
    120n113, 120n115, 123n125
Tullius Cicero, Marcus, 37, 55n24, 176n76

Varro. *See* Terentius Varro, Marcus
Velleius Paterculus, 39, 42
Vico, Giambattista, 4n12
Virgil [Publius Vergilius Maro], 36n62, 57,
    57n32
Virginia Company, 117n105
Voltaire, François-Marie Arouet de, 139,
    141n51

Walt, Stephen M., 15, 15n60
Waltz, Kenneth, 15n58, 25n8
Walzer, Michael, 2n4, 75n13, 117n101, 198,
    198n3
War on Terror, 19, 196, 197
Warrender, Howard, 111n78
Waszink, Jan, 82n41, 94n3
Weimar Republic, 165–66, 172
Wolin, Sheldon S., 5, 91, 99n26, 130n160,
    198n4
Wood, Neal, 16n66, 19, 19n76, 23–24,
    36n62, 41n82, 43n92, 44, 44n96,
    45n98, 51n7, 52n10, 53n11, 66n74,
    67n79, 68n85, 69n85, 70n91, 74n8,
    75n11, 93n98
  "Sallust's Theorem", 16n66, 19, 23–24,
    72, 93n98
  on Sallust's influence, 43n92, 44

xenophobia, 16–21, 200
Xenophon, 47n103